BRINGING UP BABY

BRINGING UP BABY

The Psychoanalytic Infant Comes of Age

Dianna T. Kenny

KARNAC

First published in 2013 by
Karnac Books Ltd
118 Finchley Road, London NW3 5HT

British Library Cataloguing in Publication Data

A C.I.P. for this book is available from the British Library

ISBN 978 1 78049 043 4

Edited, designed and produced by The Studio Publishing Services Ltd
www.publishingservicesuk.co.uk
e-mail: studio@publishingservicesuk.co.uk

Printed in Great Britain

www.karnacbooks.com

CONTENTS

ACKNOWLEDGEMENTS

Dr Toni Schofield, Associate Professor of Sociology in the Discipline of Behavioural and Social Sciences in Health, Faculty of Health Sciences, the University of Sydney, whose sociological imagination assisted in the naming of this book, and whose friendship I have valued during the crumbling of the sandstone around my monastic cubicle wherein I penned this volume.

Dr Peter Wilson, Professor of Classics at The University of Sydney, who not only assisted with the text, translation, and referencing of the quotes by Plato and Aristotle used in this book, but who is raising twin infants while keeping the Classics alive during a challenging time for genuine scholarship in Australian universities.

Dr Timothy Keogh, a practising psychoanalyst, valued friend, and worthy model of the well-analysed man, made insightful comments on psychoanalytic theory that provided added perspective during the writing of this book.

Dr Diana Wong, who has taught this wordsmith not only that the beginning is the most important part of the work, but also that the work is not just about the words!

My daughter, Giselle, was magician-like in the speed and efficiency with which she assisted me to organise hundreds of journal articles into a coherent reference list.

Rod Tweedy, from Karnac, sent supportive emails to the lone scribbler in her turret and provided careful editorial assistance. Thanks also to Catherine Harwood of Karnac, and to The Studio's production team, who efficiently supported the project to publication.

Dianna Kenny, PhD, MA (School Counselling), BA (Hons), Dip Ed, ATCL, MAPsS, MAPA, is a Professor of Psychology at the University of Sydney, Australia, with discipline specialisations in developmental and educational psychology and developmental psychopathology. For the past twenty-five years, she has lectured undergraduate, postgraduate, and clinical doctorate students in psychology and the health sciences, and published widely in these and related disciplines. Dianna is a member of the Australian and American Psychological Societies. She serves as research and education officer on the national executive and the psychoanalytically informed interest group of the Australian Psychological Society. She has devoted most of her professional career, in various roles, including teacher, school counsellor, specialist counsellor for emotionally disturbed children, marriage and family therapist, child and adolescent psychologist, and academic researcher to the understanding, care, welfare, education of, and advocacy for children. In 2002, Dianna established a foundation in Nepal to improve the education, health, and welfare of Nepalese children living in poverty.

FOREWORD

Studying and understanding infancy has always been a major challenge. Daniel Stern (1985), in his book, *The Interpersonal World of the Infant*, expresses this concern thus:

> Since we can never crawl inside an infant's mind, it may seem pointless to imagine what an infant might experience. Yet that is at the heart of what we really want and need to know. What we imagine infant experience to be like shapes our notions of who the infant is. These notions make up our working hypotheses about infancy. (p. 4)

Professor Kenny has taken on an immense and daunting task—to attempt, through multiple kaleidoscopic lenses, to articulate infant experience. She states at the beginning of Chapter One that the two central constructs in her text are "infancy and psychoanalysis". Yet this remarkable book offers so much more than that, covering as it does the major theories and ideas from the past century or more that have informed our thinking and behaviour concerning infants: how they should be known, understood, and cared for so that they set off on the best possible trajectory for the rest of their lives. The intention is to promote high quality care for infants by setting out, for inspection and debate, the diverse views, sometimes influential despite the lack of quality evidence, in this vast and controversial field. Parents know only too well what strong emotions issues related to infant care elicit and how everyone around them, including total strangers, will forcefully offer advice and instructions. Many readers of this book will, just as I did, want to argue about some of the author's contentions, but will then pause and re-examine their own views and identify implicit cherished, yet anachronistic, beliefs that are no longer supported by the evidence.

A book that encourages and nourishes informed discussion at all levels of society is welcome, but rarely found. I was particularly pleased that this text is not aimed at an academic readership alone, but is clearly accessible to interested readers in the community and all relevant professions. It provides information and guidance about bringing up babies to all those who have infants, study infants, teach about infancy, make policy with respect to infant welfare, or who work medically or therapeutically with parents.

The author demonstrates not only an impressive intellectual capacity and excellent communication skills, but a breadth and depth of knowledge about infant development that she pours into this volume. There are few, if any, texts to my knowledge that have so eruditely spanned and integrated the psychological, psychoanalytic, psychiatric, and developmental neuroscience literatures to bring us such a rich and varied, but always coherent, perspective on infant development. The comprehensiveness of the treatment and the erudition in the argumentation will ensure an enduring and useful life for this volume.

A flexible, creative, sustainable society has to be based on—and will, indeed, be measurable by— the way it ensures that children are provided with a physically and psychosocially healthy environment in which to develop both before and after birth. The foundation for lifelong health and well-being is laid down very early, with our experiences at those stages being indelibly inscribed into our bodies and brains. In the past decade or two, much has been researched and written on this topic.

I believe that this text will promote lively discussion and debate on this critical theme—what an infant is and what the optimal environment should provide—and will, thus, enhance our knowledge and competence in the field. This can only be a good thing for infants and their many care-givers.

Professor Bryanne Barnett AM[1]
School of Psychiatry, University of New South Wales
Perinatal and Infant Psychiatrist, St John of God Health Care, NSW
Karitane Early Parenting Services
Australia

Note

1. Professor Barnett was appointed, in 1999, to the first Chair in Perinatal and Infant Psychiatry in Australia.

Για

τους γονείς μου
Ιωάννα και Χριστόδουλος Κατελάρης
που ήταν εκεί στην αρχή

Οὐκοῦν οἶσθ' ὅτι ἀρχὴ παντὸς ἔργου μέγιστον, ἄλλως τε δὴ καὶ νέῳ καὶ ἁπαλῷ ὁτῳοῦν; μάλιστα γὰρ δὴ τότε πλάττεται, καὶ ἐνδύεται τύπος ὃν ἄν τις βούληται ἐνσημήνασθαι ἑκάστῳ.

(Πλάτων)

To my parents,
Ioanna and Christodoulos Katelaris,
who were there in the beginning

Do you not know, then, that the beginning in every task is the chief thing, especially for any creature that is young and tender? For it is then that it is best moulded and takes the impression that one wishes to stamp upon it. (Plato[1])

Note

1. Plato *Republic* Book 2, 377a,b.
   Translation: *Plato in Twelve Volumes*, Vols. 5 & 6, translated by Paul Shorey, Cambridge, MA: Harvard University Press, 1969.

PREFACE

Come away, O human child!
To the waters and the wild
With a faery, hand in hand,
For the world's more full of weeping than you can understand.

(W. B. Yeats, 1889)[1]

In ageing societies and in an era in which our life expectancy is extending with every generation, we must take care not to neglect the beginning, human infancy, which, as Plato reminds us, is the most important part of the work. Freud (1900a) agreed: "The deepest and eternal nature of man . . . lies in those impulses of the mind which have their roots in . . . childhood . . ." (p. 247). The poets William Wordsworth and Gerard Manley Hopkins both expressed similar sentiments: "The child is father to the man!" Such insights anticipated the last hundred years of research in developmental psychology.

A review of the welfare of children by the United Nations Children's Fund (2007)[2] contained the following statement:

> The true measure of a nation's standing is how well it attends to its children—their health and safety, their material security, their

education and socialization, and their sense of being loved, valued, and included in the families and societies into which they are born. (p. 1)

Infants and children around the world have always faced critical challenges to their well-being. The assaults of war, poverty, exploitation, social and cultural dislocation, discrimination, and abandonment have featured in every historical period reaching back into antiquity. Children from affluent homes and societies are not exempt from threats to their development. Marital discord, separation and divorce, insufficient quality time with busy professional parents, impingements in the form of unrealistic expectations and pressure to succeed, and "hothousing" are some of the issues that result in chronic misattunements between care-givers and children that impair attachment quality and long-term emotional health.

The United Nations High Commissioner for Human Rights[3] considers play an essential component of optimal child development to the extent that the opportunity for free play has been declared a human right. The insight that drove this declaration represents an enormous improvement in the understanding of what children need compared with the views of previous generations. However, we have not yet realised this ideal. Children who have grown up amid war, never knowing peace; children indoctrinated with hateful fundamentalism; children exploited as child labourers and child soldiers; children sold into the sex trade; children whose physical growth is stunted by malnutrition and whose emotional development is marred by physical, emotional, or sexual abuse or neglect have no time for play; indeed, they never learn to play.

It is difficult to measure the quality of children's emotional and social environments (i.e., relationships) on a large scale. However, certain questions have proved sensitive to the assessment of this dimension. For example, The United Kingdom's National Family and Parenting Institute[4] has conducted surveys that included questions such as:

- My parent/s are always there for me when I need them (76%)[5]
- My parent/s make me feel loved and cared for (65%)
- I can talk to my parent/s about any problem I may have (56%).

These figures are remarkable for their concordance with research in attachment theory that shows that, on average, in western cultures such as the USA, about 65% people are securely attached (van IJzen-doorn & Sagi, 1999) (see Chapter Four of this volume). Economic security does not guarantee emotional health.

One of the principal motivations for writing this book was to provide a wide-ranging, evidence-based, yet nuanced portrait of the infant and young child on which intelligent discussion can occur about what constitutes a minimally acceptable environment in which infants can develop and reach their full potential as self-actualised, autonomous adults.

The breadth of theoretical scholarship in the field of infant and child development is vast; accordingly, difficult decisions had to be made with respect to the selection of exemplars from available theories and exponents of those theories. I hope that I have selected wisely to satisfy my aims: first, of even-handed representation of the major theories and thinkers, and second, to support the demonstration of historical progression of scholarship and its convergences and divergences in the field of infant and child psychology.

One of the most interesting observations I have made while researching the life histories of some of the main contributors to theories of child development discussed in this book, including Freud, Klein, Winnicott, and Bowlby, is the degree to which these exponents' own developmental experiences have influenced their theorising about infant and child development, thus providing support for Plato's contention that the beginning is indeed the most important, influential, and enduring part of the work!

Notes

1. W. B. Yeats (1889). The stolen child. In: *The Wanderings of Oisin, and Other Poems*. London: Kegan Paul.
2. UNICEF (2007). *Child Poverty in Perspective: An Overview of Child Well-being in Rich Countries*. Innocenti Report Card 7, UNICEF Innocenti Research Centre, Florence.
3. Office of the United Nations High Commissioner for Human Rights. Convention on the Rights of the Child 20 November 1989. Available at: www.unicef.org.
4. Pedace, L. (2008). *Child Well-being in England, Scotland and Wales*. UK: National Family and Parenting Institute.
5. Percentage responding "yes".

CHAPTER ONE

Psychoanalysis and infancy: a historical and theoretical overview

The two central constructs of this book—infancy and psycho-analysis—are both rich in imagery and allusion. Discourses around these constructs are powerful; both are so much a part of our everyday lexicon that their meanings are taken for granted. However, although pervasive, they remain elusive. In order to truly understand them it is necessary to deconstruct these concepts and find their core. This is no easy matter. Heisenberg (1958) reminds us that even "natural science does not simply describe and explain nature; it is part of the interplay between nature and ourselves; it describes nature as exposed to our method of questioning" (p. 5). Similarly, Gadamer (1975), in *Truth and Method*, argues that we are embedded in a historically conditioned set of prejudices enshrined in culture, which constitute pre-formed understandings that organise our subjective experience. Nietzsche expressed a similar, although more pessimistic view, since he concludes that truth is an illusion:

> What then is truth? A mobile army of metaphors, metonyms, and anthropomorphisms—in short, a sum of human relations, which have been enhanced, transposed, and embellished poetically and rhetori-cally, and which after long use seem firm, canonical and obligatory to

a people: truths are illusions about which one has forgotten that this is what they are; metaphors which are worn out and without sensuous power; coins that have lost their pictures and now matter only as metal, no longer as coins. (Nietzsche, 1870, in Breazeale, 1979, pp. 46–47)

If one has a view that scientific development is possible, Nietzsche's position is untenable. We can, however, use as our starting point for scientific investigation Gadamer's proposition that truth is obscured by conditioning, but can be accessed via careful methodologies. We must, therefore, be mindful that constructs like psychoanalysis and infancy have been shaped not only by our method of questioning, but also by powerful cultural, social, political, and economic forces, pre-formed understandings or biases of which we are hardly aware. Both constructs have undergone significant modification over time in response to their changing ecologies, to research and development in each field, and in the cross-fertilisation between the two fields.

This book is an exploration of the changing constructions of infancy and psychoanalysis viewed through multiple theoretical lenses over time. In recent history, psychoanalytic conceptualisations of infancy have been influential, indeed dominant, and have permeated all subsequent theories of infant development and, by extension, child-rearing practices and the practice of psychotherapy. Much of this book is, therefore, about psychoanalytic theory as it reflects on conceptions of infancy and the post-psychoanalytic infant as informed by post-classical psychoanalytic theory, ethology, and attachment theory, and the cognitive and neurosciences. We begin with a brief overview of the concept of infancy through history.

The infant in history

"We have evolved to be born as a human being who will, with a very high probability, very early attempt and succeed in becoming a person" (Tomkins, 1978, p. 215).

There is no part of the human lifespan more intriguing than infancy. The human infant is unique among mammalian and primate species because human infants are born very immature and remain so for the longest period of any species. Infancy is simultaneously a period of helplessness and a time of rapid growth and development. In the first year, the brain doubles in volume, reaching 60% of its final adult size (Bogin, 1999). Importantly, it is a time during which infants can only communicate indirectly, that is, non-verbally (the word "infant" is derived from the Latin, *infans*, meaning speechless, inarticulate, new born, childish, foolish), thereby requiring care-givers and scientists to infer their nature, capacities, physical needs, and emotional states. Such situations are ripe for the activation of the imagination, particularly the psychoanalytic imagination, as we shall see in the coming chapters.

In the 1960s, the physical anthropologist, Michael Konner (2010), made systematic ethological observations of mother–infant interactions in the !Kung San, a primitive tribe of hunter-gatherers in Botswana, in order to better understand the evolutionary unfolding of the human species. He was particularly interested in human childhood, since it differs in significant ways from other mammalian and primate species. For example, the prolonged dependency of human infants promotes the development of social behaviour, pair bonding, and family groupings, as well as brain and behavioural development that extends over a greater proportion of the lifespan compared with other primates. Konner argued that these long, protected childhoods provide extended opportunities for play through which cognitive, social, behavioural, and motor skills develop. Humans' upright bipedal locomotion also conferred significant advantages over their evolutionary predecessors—human hands became skilled instruments and instrument makers. Superior adaptability and flexibility are other unique features of human evolution that promote survival in diverse environments. Although Konner focused on behavioural and cultural "universals" across ethnic groups, the development of cultural specifics, including different child-rearing practices, have also had profound effects on child development throughout history.

Child rearing practices are measured against society's success in developing characteristics and behaviours considered consistent and acceptable to prevailing social norms. In medieval times, children were regarded as adults as soon as they could walk and talk (Barrington, 2004). This view of children meant that they were expected to behave, work, dress, and think like adults. Children's behaviour was, therefore, judged according to mature adult standards, and childish deviations, such as bedwetting, were the subject of harsh physical punishment. Children from the poorer classes took their places along-side adults in the workforce, with some children being sent to work in mines and factories as soon as they could perform any useful, menial task (Orme, 2003).

Contrary to popular belief, children from the poorer classes were not alone in being subjected to what we would today characterise as child abuse. In his psycho-history on childhood in seventeenth-century France, Hunt (1970) applied Erikson's (1980a) developmental stage theory to assess the quality of parenting at this time and place in history. Hunt was appalled by what he discovered: children were subjected to all manner of brutalities that included starvation and tight binding in swaddling clothes as infants, whippings, and admin-istration of enemas during toddlerhood to "break the child's will", sexual abuse for the amusement of courtiers in the kings' courts, and abandonment. Accounts derived from the detailed diaries of Louis XIII's paediatrician describe the terrifying nightmares experienced by the young Dauphin in response to his daily morning whippings. Similarly, Hunt details the callous abuse of young boys as sexual objects and presents eye-witness accounts of their terrified, uncontrol-lable shaking. Hunt speculates on the connection between these modes of child rearing and adult personality and behaviour, a connec-tion with which this book will be centrally concerned, although it was beyond the scope of Hunt's project to provide a detailed argument.

Social, economic, and political conditions through the ages have exerted significant impacts on maternal behaviour, often overriding powerful maternal biologically-based nurturing and attachment behaviours. Indeed, "[h]uman mothers have been known to aban-don children, sell them, foster them, give them to the church as oblates, drown them, strangle them, even eat them . . ." (Hrdy, 1999, pp. 41–42). Even in current times, we have witnessed with horror as widespread female infanticide became an unexpected consequence of the one child policy in China.

Wet nursing (i.e., the practice of breastfeeding another woman's infant) was a prominent feature of child-rearing throughout European history, peaking in the late eighteenth century. It was thought to have originated in ancient Ur and Egypt, and was mostly practised by the wealthier classes. There are records from the second century AD that indicate that wet nursing was a widespread commercial enterprise, although servants and slaves were also required to wet nurse their mistresses' babies as part of their duties. In times of famine, poverty-stricken women would abandon their own children in foundling homes and wet nurse other infants for pay as a means of survival. This practice was widespread in late Czarist Russia and elsewhere (Konner, 2010). Boswell (1988) traced the history of foundling homes in Europe from antiquity to the Renaissance, and concluded that parents either sold their children or abandoned them in foundling homes to save them from death by starvation or infection. Boswell concluded, quoting the fourth century saint, St Basil of Caesarea, that parents were engaged in a "struggle between the desperation of hunger and the bonds of parenthood . . . [parents] are conquered by necessity and inexorable need . . . After a thousand tears [the father] comes to sell a beloved child" (pp. 165–166). Hunt (1970) also described mothers who found child-rearing unrewarding, giving their children over to the care of wet nurses, not because of poverty, hunger, or homelessness, but because they did not feel inclined to care for their own infants. Fathers supported their wives in this practice because they wanted no rivals for their wives' attention. Further, breastfed infants were thought to drain the mothers' life-blood and were characterised as "devouring serpents".

Child-rearing practices at the turn of the twentieth century continued to emphasise the need for firm control of the child, beginning from birth. Rigid schedules for feeding, toilet training, play, and socialisation, accompanied by strict disciplinary practices, often including harsh physical punishment (Grogan-Kaylor & Otis, 2007) have finally given way in recent times to a much more relaxed view of "good" parenting that is underpinned by the view that children should be permitted to self-regulate and encouraged in self-exploration and self-expression. Harsh disciplinary practices and authoritarian parenting are now discouraged in favour of more authoritative parenting and flexible limit setting (Simons & Conger, 2007).

Medieval Europe relied on both children and the aged to contribute to the workforce, and, hence, both groups were integral to the social fabric (Rahikainen, 2004). In modern western society, neither children nor the aged are members of the labour force, so the relative value of these life stages cannot be measured in economic terms. In affluent cultures, economic prosperity permits us to take a more humane, indulgent, and responsible attitude towards our more dependent members. Children are seen as an investment in the country's future and the elderly as deserving reward for their contribution to their country's economic growth. However, in cultures such as the Ik of Uganda, who are fighting for the survival of their tribe, the adult members are cruel and neglectful of both their young and aged, viewing both groups as expendable burdens. Only those children who can fend for themselves and who do not constitute a drain on limited tribal resources survive to adulthood. The infirm elderly are not fed and are left to die (Darkwa & Mazibuko, 2002; Hartley, Ojwang, Baguwemu, Ddamulira, & Chavuta, 2005; Witter, 2004).

Situating infancy within a lifespan development perspective

Developmental psychology is the study of how people develop and change throughout the lifespan, beginning at conception and ending in death. Development is a lifelong process and significant change can occur at any time. Most people experience common transitional events called rites of passage (Thomson et al., 2002) that are determined by the cultures in which they grow up. In western culture, commencing and finishing school and entering and retiring from the workforce are examples of traditional rites of passage that shape our lives.

To make the study of human development more manageable, developmental researchers investigate its various components separately for each life stage (Richter, 2006; Street, 2007). One way that developmental psychologists categorise the various stages of the life cycle is presented in Table 1.

Age as a criterion of development assumes greater or lesser importance at different stages of the lifespan. You will notice that the age bands for each life stage are narrow in the early part of life, increase between young adulthood and middle age, and narrow again toward the end of the lifespan. The differences reflect the different rates at which people change over the lifespan. For example, the changes in the physical, cognitive, and psychosocial development between one and two years of age are greater than those between seven and eight years of age, which are in turn greater than those between twenty-five and twenty-six years of age.

Table 1. Stages in the human lifespan and associated chronological ages.

Life stage	Approximate chronological ages
1. Prenatal period	Conception to birth (nine months)
2. Infancy	Birth to 2 years
3. Toddlerhood	2–3 years
4. Early childhood	3–5 years
5. Middle and late childhood	6–9 years and 9–12 years
6. Adolescence	13–19 years
7. Young adulthood	20–30 years
8. Middle adulthood	30–60 years
9. Late adulthood	60–75 year
10. Old age	75+ years

Psychoanalytic definitions of development and life stages

Early psychoanalytic theory offers fewer stages, with wider age groups (e.g., infancy (years 0–3), early childhood (years 3–6), latency (years 6–12), adolescence (years 12–18), and adulthood) (Moore & Fine, 1990b)). Because we are concerned in this book with psychoanalytic theories of development, the term "infancy" will denote that part of the lifespan between birth and five years of age, consistent with current psychoanalytic usage (Tuckett & Levinson, 2010). The early years of development represent an intense growth period during which children develop in overlapping "stages". Because there is considerable developmental variation among young children, I wanted to avoid being too prescriptive with respect to age and stage in order to convey the essentially organic unfolding of development over a more extended time frame in the early part of the lifespan.

Different psychoanalytic theories offer differing, but not necessarily incompatible, definitions of development. As with mainstream developmental theories (e.g., Piaget's stage theory of cognitive development—see Chapter Five), most of the early psychoanalytic theories subscribed to stage or phase theories of development, assuming that there is a predictable, sequential progression in the developmental process. Perhaps the best known psychoanalytic developmental stage theory is Freud's (1905d) psychosexual stage theory that will be discussed in Chapter Two. In his later work (e.g., Freud, 1940a[1938]),

Freud questioned the concept of stages, recognising that development might not be linear and that overlap between stages was the rule rather than the exception. With the advent of object relations theory, definitions of development changed to account for processes related to psychosocial (rather than psychosexual) development. Melanie Klein's conceptualisation represented a transitional view that included both psychosexual stages and the development of object relations. In her model, psychological development proceeded along six trajectories: (i) physiological maturation; (ii) phases of the libido; (iii) the reality principle; (iv) development of object-relations; (v) development of the ego; and (vi) the sequence of anxiety-situations (see Chapter Three) (Hinshelwood, 1991; Tyson & Tyson, 1999). Other examples of psychoanalytic models of development include Spitz's indicators and organisers, Anna Freud's developmental lines (see Chapter Three), Mahler's stages in the separation–individuation process (see Chapter Four), and Daniel Stern's (1985, 1994, 1995) interpersonal theory of self development (see Chapter Four).

In more recent psychoanalytic scholarship, the concept of stage theories has been softened and replaced with more process-orientated theories such as those proposed by Beebe and colleagues (see Chapter Four). Demos (2008) has called for a more integrated approach to defining development from a psychoanalytic perspective that incorporates advances in our knowledge from other disciplines such as developmental psychology, non-linear system theory, affect theory, and neuroscience. Below is a psychoanalytic definition of development that recognises the importance of both biological and environmental factors and the continuity of developmental unfolding while retaining the structuralist concepts of early Freudian theorising.

> [Development is a]n ongoing process in which the psychic structures and functions determining the human personality gradually evolve from the experiences of a biologically maturing individual in interaction with his or her environment. Such interaction involves genetically determined maturational sequences and inherent potentialities, environmental influences, and personal experiences. In psychoanalytic usage the term is applied specifically to those growth processes directly dependent on interaction with the environment and through which the major psychic structures (id, ego, and superego) form.

Maturation refers to physical and psychic growth related to the inherent genetic potential and largely independent of external factors. This distinction has become less clear, however, with recognition that environmental interaction plays a role in both maturation and development. (Moore & Fine, 1990a, p. 395)

While calling for a more integrated definition of infancy and development, the excerpt below also admonishes that the psychoanalytic perspective still has much to offer a scientific definition and that the neglect or abandonment of the unique insights offered by psychoanalytic theory will impoverish our understanding of human development.

The metaphorical "baby" of psychoanalytic theory which stands for "the past" will probably have to be abandoned and replaced by more appropriate neuropsychologically informed notions consistent with what we now understand about the development of the central nervous system. Yet a unique advantage of the psychoanalytic model over neuropsychoanalytic-based developmental views is its vision of development as a series of compromise formations. Both unconscious and conscious representations of the self are helpfully viewed as the product of competing environmental pressures and intrapsychic processes in an effort to regulate positive and negative affect. These compromises may have involved defensive distortion of mental representations; where the competing pressures have occurred particularly early or intensely, wholesale distortion or disabling of some of the mental processes which generate representations may also have occurred, leading to far more pervasive and extensive abnormalities of development. (Rubinstein, 1997)

The collective psychoanalytic imagination has contributed an impressive set of metaphors with which to begin our task of understanding human development and psychopathology. However, continued reliance on creative and metaphorical concepts in psychoanalytic theorising that are not grounded in rigorous observational research are problematised because the discipline now has a firm basis on which to argue its case that "early experience is formative and that symptoms can be understood as the re-emergence of early, prototypically infantile modes of thinking and feeling" (Skelton, 2006).

Developmental domains

Developmental research is subdivided into domains (areas of study), with each domain investigating a particular aspect of development. The broad subdivisions are physical (e.g., gene–environment interactions, sensation, motor skills, nutrition, accidents, and diseases); cognitive (i.e., mental processes such as perception, imagination, memory, language development); and psychosocial development (i.e., intra- and interpersonal processes such as personality, social and emotional development). Although we study these domains separately in order to more clearly present their developmental progression, they are interdependent. For example, children develop language when there is sufficient physiological maturation of the organs and muscles needed to produce speech, and cognitive development that allows the child to understand and use symbols, which occurs in a psychosocial setting that provides sufficient support and stimulation for learning and which determines the language that will be learnt. This book's primary focus is psychosocial; it examines how the infant forms relationships with significant others, and how these relationships contribute to his developing sense of self. However, cognition is central to the formation of self-concept; memory, language, perception, and imagination all interact with the infant's intra- and interpersonal experiences in the unfolding of these formative processes.

The preceding brief discussion has highlighted the impact that historical, cultural, and economic factors exert on the manner in which different stages in the life cycle are characterised. We will now examine some important ongoing theoretical issues and controversies that enliven the study of human development and ways in which they may be resolved.

Nature–nurture controversy

"Thus all the actions of men must necessarily be referred to seven causes: chance, nature, compulsion, habit, reason, anger, and desire" (Aristotle[1]).

Although most developmentalists today would agree that both nature (the inborn, genetically determined characteristics and capacities of an individual) and nurture (the environmental conditions under which a child is reared, incorporating his life experiences and the influences of parents, school, neighbourhood, and culture) are important determinants of human behaviour (McLafferty, 2006), many still argue about the relative importance of these two factors. This is known as the nature–nurture controversy or debate. This debate is inherent in many issues in lifespan psychology and has profound implications in applied settings. At one extreme is the modern Vygotskian approach that argues that human mental life is a cultural product. A number of important anthropologists (e.g., Margaret Mead, Claude Lévi-Strauss, Franz Boas) have supported this position (Konner, 2010). Similarly, early experimental behavioural scientists such as Skinner (1938, 1953) also took an extreme nurture stance in arguing that all behaviour can be learnt. These positions are no longer sustainable. Both maturation and learning interact with individual differences and environmental contingencies to determine development. We will revisit this issue in our discussion of psychoanalytic theories, which also grapple with the relative contribution of intrapsychic (i.e., nature) and interpersonal (i.e., nurture) forces in shaping the human personality. Bowlby's attachment theory (1958, 1973, 1980, 1981) is an ethologically based psychoanalytic theory that recognised the roles of both evolution and genetics and the social and ecological milieu at every stage of development (Bretherton, 1994a) (see Chapter Four). In human infants, for example, behaviours like crying, smiling, cooing, and walking emerge without learning. While maturation makes a larger contribution to the acquisition of some behaviours, such as learning to walk, learning makes a more significant contribution to others, for example, learning to swim (Zelazo & Weiss, 2006). However, cultural differences in child-rearing practices result in more precocious walking and motor skill development in, for example, Ugandan and indigenous infants compared with children from English-speaking backgrounds (Keller, Yovsi, & Voelker, 2002).

Early interactionists (e.g., Esther Thelen, Robert Siegler) recognised the complex interrelationships between nature and nurture, but were unable to make precise causal attributions about these relationships. The advent of developmental behaviour genetics allowed these nature–nurture interactions to be understood more precisely. This discipline demonstrated how genes select environments (that is, people gravitate to activities for which they have a genetic advantage).

Because identical twins share the same genetic makeup, research on identical twins reared together and apart allowed the relative effects of genes and environment to be assessed (Scarr, 1995, 1996, 1997, 1998; Scarr & Weinberg, 1990). Developmental social neuroscientists have shown that some aspects of brain development are under genetic control, while other neural processes (e.g., fear conditioning) are profoundly affected by adverse environments (Johnson, 2010; Johnson & Gilmore, 2000; Lewis & Carmody, 2008; Lipina & Colombo, 2009; Music, 2011; Panzer, 2008). Even at the cellular level, it can be very difficult to determine the relative contributions of nature and nurture. For example, the genetically programmed function of cells in the brain will fail to develop in the absence of appropriate stimulation. In the case of visual cells, absence of light results in the development of fewer nerve connections in the visual cortex of the brain. During the earliest developmental stages, embryonic cells genetically programmed to become neurons or brain cells can be removed and placed in another region, where they will be transformed into cells appropriate to that bodily region. Hence, a cell destined to become a neuron might be transformed into a cell that will line the intestines. These phenomena indicate the importance of environment even at the cellular level of development (Jaenisch & Bird, 2003).

The human brain develops uniformly despite the vastly different environments encountered by people around the world. This fact, together with the complexity of the human brain, the precision of its neural connections, and the rapidity and organisation of brain development all suggest a genetic programme (de-Graaf-Peters & Hadders-Algra, 2006). However, the complexity and organisation of the developing brain are dependent on environmental stimulation. Dramatic differences in the brains of animals reared in deprived and enriched environments are observable at the cellular level, with enriched animals demonstrating a greater number of cells and a greater complexity of connections (or synapses) between cells (Kolb & Whishaw, 1998). Recent evidence suggests that the brain's synaptic organisation can be altered by the external environment throughout the lifespan, not just during the prenatal (before birth) and perinatal (post birth) periods, as once thought (Colicos & Syed, 2006).

Many behavioural traits are highly species-specific (i.e., genetically determined) but many can be modified by the environment within the limits of that prescribed by their genetic programme (Lorenz, 1965).

Genes and environment combine co-operatively to determine human development, but genetic makeup drives the organism's response to the environment (Kim-Cohen et al., 2006). Appropriate environmental stimulation and learning opportunities must be provided, but the way individuals respond to these is determined by their genetic potential; that is, individuals selectively attend to aspects of their environments that resonate with their genes. If a good enough environment is available to the infant, with increasing age, autonomy, and skill differentiation, the child will select from that environment experiences and opportunities that are self-enhancing. Individuals self-select environments that match their genotypes (genetic makeup), and the degree to which experiences resemble each other is a function of genetic similarities between individuals (Scarr, 1992). The field of developmental neuroscience explores the complex ways in which biology impacts on human behavioural development and relationships using brain imaging technologies that are clarifying the neurological basis of attachment, the role of myelination in language development, the processes of synaptogenesis and pruning in skill specialisation in adolescence and the role of mirror neurons in imitation, social learning, and empathy. We return to some of these topics in the last chapter.

Continuity–discontinuity debate

The question regarding whether human development occurs so smoothly and gradually as to make the division of the lifespan into stages inappropriate, or whether there are discernible stages in the lifespan that are distinctly different from each other, is an important and fundamental question for developmental psychology. An infant is very different from a child and an adolescent is different from an adult. The problem for a discontinuous perspective of development is to define those points at which the infant becomes a child or the adolescent an adult.

Stage-based theories

Staged-based theories are predicated on the view that development is discontinuous and that there are definable points or ages in the lifespan during which a person is qualitatively different from a previous age or stage in development. In stage-based theories, ages are grouped together to define a particular stage of development. These stages are then analysed from a particular theoretical perspective, depending upon the developmental domain under study and the part of the life-span being investigated. The theories of Sigmund Freud and Jean Piaget, both stage-based theories, will be discussed more fully in later chapters, along with a number of post-Freudian, stage-based, psycho-analytically orientated theories of development (e.g., Margaret Mahler, Heinz Kohut, Daniel Stern).

Stage-based theories share a reliance on chronological age as the index level of accomplishment of a particular developmental task, but here their commonality ends. The "stages" that each of the different theories propose differ in the explanation as to their cause, timing, and specificity. For example, Gesell (1940) proposed universal biologically determined stages in the physical and motor components of develop-ment, such as the creeping, crawling, and walking sequence and stages of language acquisition, which are highly specific behaviours. On the other hand, the theories of Frieze (Frieze, Parsons, Johnson, Ruble, & Zellman, 1978) and Levinson (1978) focus on developmental patterns that are culturally determined, follow a more flexible social, rather than biological, clock, and are less specific in the types of behav-iours studied, for example, male and female sex roles, rather than discrete behaviours such as walking and talking.

Stages are theoretical notions rather than objective realities that are useful in organising specific observations into a coherent conceptual framework. They are descriptive rather than explanatory. Individuals accomplish developmental tasks and progress through developmental stages at different chronological ages. Many factors influence the timing of an individual's development and the ages at which develop-mental milestones are reached. These factors include genetic potential, quality of the physical and psychosocial environment, and the complexity of the developmental process. It is easier to define the age limits around the appearance and cessation of reflexive behaviours in infants than it is to predict the age at which children reach particular stages of cognitive or moral development.

Even though an individual might have reached a particular "stage" of development, this does not mean that s/he will behave accordingly all the time or in every domain. A major problem exists for socio-cultural theories in that cultural bias and, hence, value judgements influence the definition of those stages that are thought necessary for human development. For example, because most adults marry, should marriage be defined as an indicator that a certain stage of adult development has been reached? Freud (1930a), Erikson (1980b), Levinson (1978), and Havighurst (1972) all include marriage as an indicator of the attainment of mature genital sexuality and the capacity for intimacy. A recent longitudinal study has found support for Erikson's theory by showing that generativity, an advanced developmental stage, was associated with successful marriage in men (Westermeyer, 2004). However, stage theories have not addressed issues related to alternative or minority lifestyles. How, for example, would psychosocial stage theories assess those who are homosexual or who remain single? How do never-married people compare developmentally with those 30–40% of married people who eventually divorce? Divorce, although experienced by a significant minority of adults, does not constitute a stage in any of the available theories of adult development. Recent psychosocial theories have recognised that early theories were problematically constructed on Anglo-Celtic, heterosexual populations and have become increasingly inclusive of minority groups (Chickering & Reisser, 1993).

The life cycles of some insects and butterflies can be readily identified as a series of discontinuous stages. The human life cycle does not undergo such sudden transformations from one level of functioning to another. Often, cognitive and behavioural structures of preceding stages are incorporated into subsequent ones, making the actual transition points, if they exist, difficult to identify. Notwithstanding, there are four behaviours in infancy that mark critical social transitions. These are mutual gaze interactions with primary care-givers, the appearance of the social smile at about six weeks of age, increased response to contingently responsive stimuli at about three months of age that includes stimuli provided by an attuned care-giver, and responsiveness to facial expressions at about four months of age as a result of emergent right hemisphere specialisation for the processing of emotion and social communication (Flom, Lee, & Muir, 2007; Rigato, Menon, Johnson, Faraguna, & Farroni, 2011). Mutual gaze and social smiling can have a profound impact on parent–infant relationships, with some mothers reporting the emergence of these behaviours as marking the beginning of their relationships with their infants and their feelings of love for them (Messinger & Fogel, 2007; Reddy, 1993).

Ecological theories

Ecological theories propose that age-related changes are not automatic; rather, they occur within the context of experience and as a result of learning and socialisation processes to which the individual is exposed. This continuous view of human development underpins the human ecology model (Bronfenbrenner, 1979), cybernetic or systems theories based on family structures (Hoffman, 1981), the learning theories based on behaviourism—classical (Watson, 1928) and operant conditioning (Skinner, 1953), social learning theory (Bandura, 1977)—and information-processing theories (Chen & Hancock, 2011).

While environmental influences are important and powerful contributors to development, ecological theories adopt a somewhat passive view of the learner and underestimate the degree to which the individual can create, as well as react to, his environment (Siegler, 2005). In the past, children were viewed as products of their child-rearing experiences. Now, research focuses on the ways in which children and parents mutually influence each other's behaviour (Pinquart & Silbereisen, 2004). Infants and children are not merely passive recipients of external events, but show some capacity to control and regulate their own development (Rodriguez et al., 2005). Beatrice Beebe and her colleagues, discussed in detail in later chapters, demonstrated how even very young infants are co-constructors of their relationships and learning experiences.

In attempting to arrive at a synthesis of stage-based and ecological perspectives, Goldhaber (1986) concluded:

> Both age-related developmental processes and social structure influence all aspects of human development across the lifespan. The process is multi-determined, interdependent and cumulative. It involves the successive products of a biological organism maturing within a sociohistorical context. (p. 34)

An evolving field that investigates the mutual interaction of genes and environment is developmental cognitive neuroscience. Research in this area has not only demonstrated how genetics can affect an individual's learning experience, but it has also shown how learning experiences affect genetic expression. The physical environment can determine which genes will be activated and how the activation will be expressed (Munakata, Casey, & Diamond, 2004). Consequently, enriched environments are widely used to accelerate or enhance early development in areas such as music (Gruhn, 2002) and sport. We will return to the insights of developmental neuroscience in Chapter Six.

Stability and change

Lifespan developmental psychology emerged as a discipline less than seventy years ago and one of its major tasks has been to integrate research findings from the age-specific disciplines of infant study, child and adolescent psychology, and ageing. A longitudinal perspective on human development allows researchers to investigate the relationships between early experiences and later outcomes, an issue with which we are centrally concerned in this book. Lifespan developmental psychology explores questions that are also of vital interest to psychoanalytical theories. For example:

- Are our personalities and intellectual capacities fixed at some point in childhood or are we capable of change throughout our lifespan?
- To what extent can the effects of early experiences of loss, divorce, parental death, separation, deprivation, or abuse be ameliorated in later life through psychotherapy or reparative experiences?
- To what extent can adult outcomes be predicted from infancy?

Underlying these questions is the stability *vs.* change controversy; that is, the question as to whether adult characteristics are fixed and irreversible at some early stage in the lifespan. A key proponent of such a view was Freud (1940a[1938]), who believed that development was complete once an individual had reached adulthood. Subsequently, research has shown that people are capable of change throughout the lifespan and that the significance of infancy and childhood might have been overstated (Tisserand et al., 2004). This is not to say that events in early childhood are not significant; rather, events at other life stages might be equally important. It is also apparent that some human characteristics show greater stability across the lifespan

than others; for example, temperaments—biologically based personality traits—can be identified even in very young infants. Some may
endure over a lifetime (Nelson, 1994) (see Chapter Six for a further
discussion). Chess and Thomas (1996) identified nine dimensions of
infant temperament as follows: (i) activity: child's physical energy and
activity levels; (ii) regularity/rhythmicity: predictability in a child's
biological functions, such as their sleep–wake cycle, hunger, and
bowel movements; (iii) approach/withdrawal: child's response to
novelty, new people, or environments; (iv) adaptability: response to
change over time, ease of settling into new routines; (v) intensity:
emotional intensity of responding; (vi) mood: child's general tendency
towards positive or negative affect; (vii) distractibility: child's level of
attentional control; (viii) persistence: degree to which a child can
maintain task focus, even when frustrated; (ix) sensitivity: degree to
which the child is disturbed by changes in the environment, which is
also called the sensory threshold or threshold of responsiveness.

Behavioural inhibition (i.e., shyness/timidity) is a personality trait
that shows considerable stability over the lifespan. Although biologically based, behavioural inhibition is also affected by environmental
conditions, in particular, the level of interparental conflict (Pauli-Pott
& Beckmann, 2007) and maternal depression (Field, 2002; Jones, Field,
& Almeida, 2009). It places the infant at high risk for later psychological difficulties, such as depression, anxiety, fears, and phobias (Perez-
Edgar et al., 2010). Behaviourally inhibited infants show greater
reactivity to novel stimuli, greater inhibition in novel environments,
and greater risk for later development of social withdrawal and social
anxiety (Fox & Reeb-Sutherland, 2010). They also have recognisable
differences in heart rate variability, higher circulating cortisol (Gunnar,
Kryzer, Van Ryzin, & Phillips, 2011; Tarullo, Mliner, & Gunnar, 2011;
Tops & Boksem, 2011) and norepinephrine (stress hormones), and
lower limbic arousal thresholds (Gunnar, Kryzer, Van Ryzin, &
Phillips, 2011; Kagan & Snidman, 2004; Kagan, Snidman, Kahn, &
Towsley, 2007; Tarullo, Mliner, & Gunnar, 2011; Tops & Boksem, 2011).
Similarly, aggression shows a considerable degree of stability over the
lifespan, with childhood levels of aggression reliably predicting juve-
nile delinquency and other externalising disorders during adolescence
(Bierman, Bruschi, Domitrovich, Fang, & Miller-Johnson, 2004;
Campbell, Spieker, Burchinal, & Poe, 2006; Hay, 2005; Huesmann,
Eron, & Dubow, 2002). Of course, even with genetically determined

stable characteristics, such as behavioural inhibition and aggression, there are significant environmental contributors that interact with these genes. For example, first-born children are significantly less likely to be behaviourally inhibited compared with later born children (Kagan, 2004).

The question of stability *vs.* change, which is embedded in the Jesuit aphorism, "Give me a child until he is seven, and I will show you the man", motivated film-maker Michael Apted to produce his celebrated longitudinal documentary, the 7 *Up* series. The first instalment, released in 1964, features interviews with fourteen British seven-year-olds from diverse social backgrounds about their hopes, fears, and plans for the future. Apted captured their developmental progress by re-interviewing them at seven-year intervals for the next forty years. The lives of the children are remarkable both for the continuities (e.g., the child interested in astronomy grows up to become a professor of physics) and discontinuities (e.g., a seemingly happy, well-adjusted child succumbs to chronic mental illness beginning in young adulthood).

Baltes (1987) proposed a theoretical framework for lifespan psychology that contributes to an integration of these opposing dichotomies. He argued that an individual's potential depends on age (lifespan stage), genetic endowment (plasticity), the prevailing historical, cultural, and economic conditions in which development unfolds (historical embeddedness), and the context in which the individual develops (contextualism). Take, for example, disorders such as attention deficit hyperactivity disorder (ADHD). Most diagnoses of this condition occur in the school or home environments (contextualism) of children living in modern developed countries who have access to sophisticated diagnostics and medical treatments (historical embeddedness), in which children are expected and socialised to perform particular behaviours, including attending to adults such as parents and teachers, sitting still and quietly when requested, and co-operating with peers. It is difficult to know whether children living in primitive hunter-gatherer societies would have received this diagnosis at the same frequencies as modern, urban children, but it would certainly be true that fewer hunter-gatherer children would be adversely affected by the condition. Notwithstanding, ADHD also shows high heritability (genetic component) (Miller, Gelfand, & Hinshaw, 2011). Kagan (2004) has derived a similar set of interwoven factors that determine the infant's developmental trajectory. He identified temperament, parental behaviours, parental values, identifications, social class, birth order, school failure or success, and historical era as predictors of developmental outcome.

Debates in psychoanalytic theory

Psychoanalytic theory was besieged with similar debates as those found in lifespan developmental psychology. Theoretical schisms arose early around the primacy that Freud assigned to sexuality. Post-Freudian scholarship shifted emphasis from sexual (intrapsychic) to social (interpersonal) causes of psychopathology, in the same way that developmental psychology oscillated between genes and environment as determinants of behaviour. The interpersonal focus in psychoanalysis appeared in the 1920s, in the theories of Harry Stack Sullivan, who worked with people with schizophrenia. Akin to Baltes' construct of contextualism, Sullivan argued that personality unfolds in the interpersonal domain (context), in the recurrent interactions between self and others (Sullivan, 1953, 1964). Unlike Freud, who focused his attention on the individual's intrapsychic conflictual wishes and fantasies, Sullivan stressed that human behaviour could only be understood within an "organism-environment complex" and that the innate physiological and emotional needs of the infant could only be satisfied in an interpersonal context, in the first instance, by his mother. Thus, in therapy, Sullivan sought explanations for psychopathology in a detailed analysis of the interactions between the patient and his significant others. Sullivan argued that infants developed "personifications" that represented the infant's experience of self and significant others, to which the infant attaches either a positive ("good") or negative ("bad") valence depending on experiences of relative satisfaction or dissatisfaction.

Both Freud and Sullivan assigned a central role to anxiety in the aetiology of psychopathology and in shaping key interpersonal relationships. Infantile anxiety, generated by an anxious or neglectful mother, constitutes the first form of differentiation in Sullivan's theory—that is, between anxious ("bad mother") and non-anxious ("good mother") states. These states eventually become associated with aspects of the self, the "good me" and the "bad me". A third state, "not me", is a dissociated state that originates in feelings of intense anxiety in the care-giver that have been provoked by the infant. The "self-system"—that part of the person that one recognises as "me" or "my personality"—arises mostly from awareness of the "good me" from which "not me" is excluded. Part of the self-system is devoted to the implementation of "security operations" (Freud called them defences) that keep intolerable anxiety at bay. One of Sullivan's most significant contributions was his understanding of the devastating effect that an attack via ridicule, mockery, misattunement, or other invalidating response on the "tender emotions", that is, feelings of love and gratitude or the expression of highly valued thoughts or memories, has on development. Repeated failure of validating experiences of these tender emotions from care-givers results in a chronic sense of personal devaluation, dysphoria, emptiness, and worthlessness. Future exposure or expression of these feelings risks the experience of shame, which is felt with devastation (Sullivan, 1953).

Another change that occurred was a shift in focus from pathological development to normal development, a change that mirrored the struggle in developmental psychology to identify both human universals and individual differences and to identify the relative contributions of genes and environment to the commonalities and differences between people. While Freud was primarily concerned with psychopathology and its origins, Hartmann and Anna Freud brought an interest in the processes underlying normal development to centre stage, including the role of the environment in shaping personality (Hartmann, 1939). Hartmann argued that humans, like all living organisms, were designed to survive in their environments—not just physically, but psychologically. Consistent with his views about the human capacity for adaptation, Hartmann believed that the infant was born ready, with "conflict-free ego capacities", to interact with an "average expectable" environment. He further argued that the psychological defences that arose in response to conflict could become adaptive in the service of socialisation, through a process of neutralisation of their sexual and aggressive origins.

Hartmann's work was foundational for a generation of developmental ego psychologists like René Spitz (1945), whose study of children who failed to thrive in foundling homes during and after the Second World War left no one in doubt about the crucial role that the care-giving environment plays in both physical and emotional development. Spitz was responsible for critical new conceptualisations of the role of the mother in development, the reciprocal influence of the mother–infant dyad, and stranger anxiety, all concepts derived from detailed observations, interviews, and longitudinal follow-up of mother–infant dyads (Spitz, 1945, 1950a,b, 1951). Other developmental ego psychologists who had an impact on the development of psychoanalysis and our understanding of infant and child development were Margaret Mahler (see Chapter Four) and Edith Jacobson. Jacobson (1964), in her book, *The Self and the Object World*, reworked Freud's concepts of inwardly directed sexual and aggressive drives to include the importance of environmental influences, in particular, early relationships, and the importance of interactions between biology and experience in shaping development. One of the most influential thinkers to emerge from ego psychology was Heinz Kohut (1913–1981). His work departs in significant ways from his predecessors, in particular, with respect to his conceptualisation of human experience, not in terms of forbidden wishes, conflict, and guilt, but in terms of self-experience, isolation and alienation from oneself and others that give rise to a sense of meaninglessness and an absence of inner vitality or *joie de vivre*.

Perhaps the greatest difference between classical psychoanalysis and the more interpersonal approaches of self psychology and attachment-related psychotherapies is the belief, derived from infant research, in the centrality of the causative and curative power of attunement/empathy in healthy development and its absence in psychopathology. Kohut (1984) believed that optimal empathic failures, that is, those failures of empathy in the parent/analyst that can be successfully managed by the child/patient contribute to the development and consolidation of self-capacity, which entails the ability to tolerate the reintegration of previously rejected or split-off parts of the self. This process constitutes structural change in psychoanalysis, which is argued to have strong parallels with the development of psychic structure in the infant (Beebe, 2005; Beebe & Lachmann, 1988), but more of this later.

The increasing importance assigned to the mutual influence of the analyst–analysand dyad as the locus of therapeutic action became known as the intersubjective field (Atwood & Stolorow, 1984). The importance of interactive mutual influence patterns in psychological development has been recognised by a number of key researchers, and it appears in many forms; for example, in Vygotsky's concept of the "intermental" (Vygotsky, Hanfmann, & Vakar, 1962), in Fairbairn's (1946) "innate interpersonal relatedness", Sullivan's (1953) interpersonal field as discussed above, and in the accounts of both self psychologists (Kohut, 1971, 1977, 1984) and intersubjective psychoanalysts (Stolorow, 2005). All question some of Freud's basic tenets (e.g., the primacy of the aggressive and sexual impulses). Both the new wave of psychoanalysts and existential phenomenologists (e.g., Heidegger, Sartre, and Merleau-Ponty) argue that we are embedded (and only exist) within our social/relational context. There is no being; only a "being-in-the-world" (Heidegger, 1962); there is no baby, only a "nursing couple" (Winnicott, 1965a, p. 138). Interactive mutual influence has its origins in patterns of interaction that have been observed and documented within the mother–infant dyad (Beebe, 2006; Beebe & Jaffe, 2008). None the less, current research confirms that there is indeed a baby, who is born with sufficient competencies to be a contributing partner to the mother–baby couple, a topic to which we will return in due course.

The term "relational" was first used by Greenberg and Mitchell (1983) to separate the new psychoanalytic thinking from classical drive theory and to integrate two major theoretical traditions—the British object relations theories and American interpersonal psychoanalysis. The emphasis in the latter was focused on current interactions between analyst and analysand, rather than on intrapsychic structure, while object relations theory's emphasis on the internal world of objects resulted in the neglect of actual relationships beyond the earliest primary relationships between mother/care-giver and infant.

There has been much heated, but often little enlightened, debate between relational–constructivist and classical–structural analytic schools; see, for example, Hoffman (2007) and Mitchell (1995), who are both critical of the poor quality of the arguments mounted against relational approaches. Rangell (2006) deplored the proliferation of theories and the consequent fragmentation of theorising in the field. He argued that many post-Freudian theories suffered from either one of two fallacies, the first of which was *pars pro toto* (substituting a part of the theory and treating it as a whole). He includes in this group Carl Jung (focus on mysticism and spirituality), Alfred Adler (focus on aggression and power), and Otto Rank (focus on infancy and the birth process). On Jung's position with regard to archetypes, Freud had this to say:

> I fully agree with Jung in recognizing the existence of this phylogenetic heritage; but I regard it as a methodological error to seize on a phylogenetic explanation before the ontogenetic possibilities have been exhausted. I cannot see any reason for obstinately disputing the importance of infantile prehistory while at the same time freely acknowledging the importance of ancestral prehistory. (Freud, 1918b, p. 97)

Freud described his erstwhile protégés' (Jung and Adler) contributions to psychoanalysis as "twisted re-interpretations" of his own theories (Freud, 1918b, p. 7).

The second fallacy involves setting up false dichotomies and polarising camps along those lines. Rangell cites the very public dispute between Otto Fenichel and Franz Alexander with respect to the proper analytic attitude. Fenichel advocated adherence to the neutral analytic stance requiring the analyst to give insights via interpretations while Alexander asserted that the curative factor in therapy was the corrective emotional experience, in which the analyst provided what had been missing in the analysand's early life. A careful reading of Freud's case studies show that such a division is a false dichotomy—the analytic attitude was intended from the outset to be both insight producing and emotionally corrective. Although Freud had not yet fully formulated his analytic attitude in his early cases, it is implicit in the notes he recorded, for example, during his treatment of Frau Emmy von N:

> ... my influence has already begun to affect her; she grows quieter and clearer in the head, and even without questioning under hypnosis [I] can discover the cause of her ill-humour on that day. Nor is her conversation ... so aimless as would appear. On the contrary, it contains a fairly complete reproduction of the memories and new impressions which have affected her since our last talk, and it often leads on, in a quite unexpected way, to pathogenic reminiscences of which she unburdens herself without being asked to. It is as though she had adopted my procedure and was making use of our conversation, apparently unconstrained and guided by chance, as a supplement to her hypnosis. (Freud, 1895d, p. 56)

The field abounds with "straw man" fallacies. Stolorow (2006) argued that attempts to dichotomise human experience as subjective (internal) or objective (external), or intrapsychic or interpersonal, are misguided and constrain genuine understanding of experience. He argued that the initial danger situation that signals anxiety—helplessness in the face of overwhelming affect—is an internal experience. When the infant learns that an external object, such as a parent or other care-giver, can alleviate his distress, the danger situation becomes one of fear of the loss of the love object or fear of the loss of love from the love object, which are interpersonal experiences. When the love object is internalised, that is, a mental representation of the care-giver is constructed "in mind" as primarily nurturing or punishing, available or unavailable, predictable or unpredictable, the experience once again becomes internal. Mitchell (1993), a relational psychoanalyst, likewise argues that all personal motives have a long relational history.

> The very capacity to have experiences necessarily develops in and requires an interpersonal matrix . . . there is no experience that is not interpersonally mediated. The meanings generated by the self are all interactive products (p.125) . . . If the self is always embedded in relational contexts, either actual or internal, then all important motives have appeared and taken on life and form in the presence and through the reactions of significant others. (p. 134)

Sources of evidence for the psychoanalytic theory of infancy

Stern (1985) identifies two major sources of evidence about infants on which psychoanalytic theory rests—the observed infant and the clinical infant. The observed infant has been constructed from precise observations and recordings of those observations in controlled conditions in scientific settings; the clinical infant has been constructed, or, rather, co-constructed retrospectively in clinical, mostly psychoanalytic settings with mostly adult patients. Until the advent of ingenious and precise ways of understanding infants, adult inferences about the subjective experience of infants that were fashioned into narratives or life stories or psychoanalytic theories provided most of the "evidence" related to the subjective experiences of infants. Stern argued that this latter method resulted in distortions of the "reality" of the lived experience of infants and gave rise to two serious conceptual fallacies regarding infant development. The first is the tendency to adultomorphise infants and to ascribe to them capacities that developmental neuroscience has subsequently demonstrated do not exist at the age/stage of development asserted by many psycho-analytic theories. The second fallacy is the tendency to re-create infancy from the histories of adult psychoanalytic patients and to pathologise early states of normal development based on adult psy-choanalytic material. Some writers (e.g.Wolff, 1996) argue that infant research is not relevant to psychoanalysis because the data of psycho-analysis is language, a capacity that has not yet been acquired by the infant. This is a specious argument, because research has shown that infants develop knowledge about themselves, their world, and their relationships non-verbally, non-symbolically and implicitly, and that this knowledge forms the basis of their object relationships, which later become accessible in the transference (Lecours, 2007; Talberg, Cuoto, De Lourdes, & O'Donnell, 1988; Talvitie & Ihanus, 2002). Transference is understood to be the "process of actualisation of unconscious wishes . . . *infantile prototypes re-emerge and are experienced with a strong sensation of immediacy* . . . testifying to the proximity of the unconscious conflict" (Laplanche & Pontalis, 1973, p. 455, my italics).

While transference phenomena are important sources of evidence, this source must now be combined with the vast literature that has emerged on infant development in a wide diversity of areas, includ-ing infant observation, ethology, behavioural genetics, attachment, cognitive development, and developmental neuroscience, areas to be covered in the proceeding pages.

In this chapter, we have focused a wide lens on the subject of the infant self, situating the developing person in biological, historical, social, and theoretical frameworks. In the next chapter, we will review the theorising that resulted in the conceptualisation of Freud's psycho-analytic infant.

Note

1. Aristotle *Rhetoric* Book 1, 10 (1369a):
    ὥστε πάντα ὅσα πράττουσιν ἀνάγκη πράττειν δι' αἰτίας ἑπτὰ διὰ τύχην διάφυσιν διὰβίαν δι' ἔθοξ διαλογιόν διὰθυμόν δι' ἐπιθυμίαν. Translation: Aristotle in 23 Volumes, Vol. 22, J. H. Freese (Trans.). Aristotle. Cambridge: Harvard University Press; William Heinemann, 1926.

CHAPTER TWO

Freud's theory of infant sexuality

"There are no indications of reality in the unconscious, so that one cannot distinguish between truth and fiction that has been cathected with affect"

(Strachey, 1966, p. 264)

To fully understand the origins of Freud's conception of infancy, it is necessary to understand the role played by sexuality and affect in Freud's psychoanalytic theory, specifically Freud's theory of infant sexuality and the Oedipus complex. Freud's conception of sexuality can be found in the opening paragraph of his *Three Essays on the Theory of Sexuality* (Freud, 1905d).

The fact of the existence of sexual needs in human beings and animals is expressed in biology by the assumption of a "sexual instinct", on the analogy of the instinct of nutrition, that is, of hunger. Everyday language possesses no counterpart to the word "hunger", but science makes use of the word "libido" for that purpose. (p. 135)

Sexuality was a topic of great importance to Freud, and he became convinced of the central role that sexuality played in human development.

He was equally concerned about the avoidance of the topic by other theorists.

> It is noticeable that writers who concern themselves with explaining the characteristics and reactions of the adult . . . ascribed much more influence to heredity—than to the other primeval period, which falls within the lifetime of the individual himself—that is, to childhood . . . [which is] easier to understand and could claim to be considered before that of heredity . . . [O]ne occasionally comes across remarks upon precocious sexual activity in small children—upon erections, masturbation and even activities resembling coitus. But these are always quoted only as exceptional events, as oddities or as horrifying instances of precocious depravity. . . . [N]ot a single author has clearly recognized the regular existence of a sexual instinct in childhood; and in the writings that have become so numerous on the development of children, the chapter on 'Sexual Development' is as a rule omitted. (Freud, 1905d, p. 173)

Freud's first theoretical model, the affect-trauma model, proposed that the symptoms of hysterical patients had hidden psychological meaning related to major emotional traumata that the patient had repressed. Pierre Janet, who was a pupil of Jean-Martin Charcot at the same time as Freud, drew the same conclusion—that hysteria was caused by trauma so difficult to assimilate that the patient entered an altered state of consciousness to cope with it. Janet called this state "dissociation" (Liotti, 1999). Freud was later to name it "repression". The struggle for expression of this trauma resulted in the presenting symptoms that constituted a symbolic expression of the "strangulated affect" related to the trauma. Freud believed that the processes of abreaction and catharsis (initially achieved under hypnosis) related to this trauma would resolve the patient's symptoms and cure them of their hysteria.

The affect-trauma model was co-extensive with Freud's seduction theory, because Freud initially believed that a significant proportion of the traumas reported by his patients related to child sexual abuse. This was the short-lived "seduction theory" (1893–1897).

> I . . . put forward the thesis that at the bottom of every case of hysteria there are one or more occurrences of premature sexual experience, occurrences which belong to the earliest years of childhood but which

can be reproduced through the work of psycho-analysis in spite of the intervening decades. I believe that this is an important finding, the discovery of a caput Nili in neuropathology. (Freud, 1896b, p. 203)

In his first cases of hysteria, (actual) sexual trauma was frequently recalled in patients' accounts of their illnesses.

Doubts about the genuineness of the infantile sexual scenes can, however, be deprived of their force here and now by more than one argument. In the first place, the behaviour of patients while they are reproducing these infantile experiences is in every respect incompatible with the assumption that the scenes are anything else than a reality which is being felt with distress and reproduced with the greatest reluctance. Before they come for analysis the patients know nothing about these scenes. They are indignant as a rule if we warn them that such scenes are going to emerge. Only the strongest compulsion of the treatment can induce them to embark on a reproduction of them. While they are recalling these infantile experiences to consciousness, they suffer under the most violent sensations, of which they are ashamed and which they try to conceal; and, even after they have gone through them once more in such a convincing manner, they still attempt to withhold belief from them, by emphasizing the fact that, unlike what happens in the case of other forgotten material, they have no feeling of remembering the scenes. (Freud, 1896b, p. 204)

Freud soon came to doubt that actual sexual trauma had occurred in the majority of cases and that instead, sexual fantasies related to the instinctual drives, for example, incestuous wishes involving the parents, were the traumatising elements (Freud (with Breuer), 1895d). With further clinical experience, Freud came to believe that some of these reports were of sexual fantasies related to unconscious wishes that arose from biological drives and that the presenting psychopathology was a failed attempt to master these sexual drives, about which patients felt ashamed and guilty. By 1905, Freud had modified his views on the frequency of the actual occurrence of sexual abuse in his patients.

. . . great and lasting importance attaches at this period to the accidental external contingencies. In the foreground we find the effects of seduction, which treats a child as a sexual object prematurely and teaches him, in highly emotional circumstances, how to obtain satisfaction from his genital zones, a satisfaction which he is then usually obliged to repeat again and again by masturbation. An influence of this kind may originate either from adults or from other children. I cannot admit that in my paper on "The Aetiology of Hysteria" ... I exaggerated the frequency or importance of that influence, though I did not then know that persons who remain normal may have had the same experiences in their childhood, and though I consequently overrated the importance of seduction in comparison with the factors of sexual constitution and development. Obviously seduction is not required in order to arouse a child's sexual life; that can also come about spontaneously from internal causes. (Freud, 1905d, p. 190)

The seduction theory was based on the idea that children before puberty were not developed sexually and therefore could not be sexually aroused. Freud abandoned his seduction theory in 1897, consequent upon his "discovery" of the Oedipus complex in his self-analysis. Freud concluded from this discovery that sexual impulses operate in very young, normally developing children in the absence of outside stimulation and did not make their first appearance during puberty, as previously supposed. His revised theory of sexuality refers not only to the various kinds of sexual activity or sexual self-exploration displayed by young children, but also to a process that begins from birth and the experience of sucking at the mother's breast. Most children, do, in fact, engage in some sexually orientated behaviour during childhood, usually some form of self-stimulatory behaviour such as masturbation or exploration of sexual organs. This behaviour forms part of a normal, developmental process in which children explore their bodies and discover how they respond to their touch (Kellogg, 2009; Mallants & Casteels, 2008). Freud argued that the stimulation brought about by micturition in the glans of boys and the clitoris in girls "gives an early start to sexual excitation" because "the pleasurable feeling which this part of the body is capable of producing should be noticed by children even during their earliest infancy, and should give rise to a need for its repetition" (Freud, 1905d, p. 188). These experiences, which form the basis of a "normal" sexual life, have their origins in early infantile masturbation, which Freud divided into three phases: early infancy, "the brief efflorescence of sexual activity in the fourth year of life" (Freud, 1905d, p. 189), and pubertal masturbation.

> Small children whose attention has once been drawn – as a rule by
> masturbation – to their own genitals usually take the further step
> without help from outside and develop a lively interest in the genitals
> of their playmates. (Freud, 1905d, p. 192)

Freud argued that the early "sexual" scene was not repressed at the
time it occurred. After puberty, however, a new event triggers a
memory of the earlier incident, and because the person is now sexually mature and understands the purport of the earlier experience,
feels traumatised by it and retrospectively represses the memory of it.
Freud called this process "deferred action" (Freud, 1898a). His concept
of "screen memory" is similar. Freud described the paradox in which
a childhood memory remains vivid, although the importance of the
content or meaning of the memory is not understood until a later
experience or recollection triggers the screen memory and associations
related to its pathogenic content (Freud, 1899a). These two concepts
have significant implications with respect to the nature of childhood
memories, which Freud believed could not be accepted unchallenged.
Rather, re-triggered memories represented an interpretation of the
original memory, and the experience it represents, made at a later
time, is not the actual memory as it had originally arisen.

Freud did not abandon the belief that some children had suffered
actual sexual trauma and that any subsequent psychopathology that
followed could not be explained by fantasy alone. He also recognised
the severe and lasting effects that "seduction" can have on a child's
development.

> ... [T]he effects of seduction, which treats a child as a sexual object
> prematurely and teaches him, in highly emotional circumstances, how
> to obtain satisfaction from his genital zones, a satisfaction which he is
> then usually obliged to repeat again and again by masturbation ...
> under the influence of seduction children can become polymor-
> phously perverse, and can be led into all possible kinds of sexual irreg-
> ularities. (Freud, 1905d, p. 190)

Freud changed his view about the prevalence of sexual abuse of
children after further clinical experience and as a result of his own
self-analysis. This realisation represented a critical turning point in
Freud's conceptualisation of the psychoanalytic project, because the
abandonment of the seduction theory in its original form resulted in

the birth of the concept of "psychic reality", as opposed to actual or objective reality (Rosegrant, 2010). However, as Dervin (1988) observes: "As [psychic reality] became the subjective terrain of a new science, its conquest would be continually coloured by the explorer's own subjectivity" (p. 79). Psychoanalysis became a science of the imagination of which Freud's theory of infantile sexuality was a product. However, the issue of actual *vs.* fantasised sexual encounters in childhood continued to be controversial, such that Bernstein (1989) concluded:

> [W]e can no longer imagine that incest in childhood is either rare, or always to be analysed as if it were a fantasy. Indeed, Freud was aware of this even as he withdrew his original postulate that actual seduction was the keystone on the arch of the understanding of hysterical symptoms. (p. 207)

Indeed, Freud remained committed to the belief that "seduction" could be both real and fantasised. For example, he stated in his *Introductory Lectures*: "Phantasies of being seduced are of particular interest because so often they are not phantasies but real memories" (Freud, 1916–1917, p. 370). In his analysis of the "Wolf man", Freud (1918b) was careful to provide corroborating evidence of this patient's actual childhood sexual experience.

> . . . his seduction by his sister was certainly not a phantasy. Its credibility was increased by some information which had never been forgotten and which dated from a later part of his life, when he was grown up. A cousin who was more than ten years his elder told him in a conversation about his sister that he very well remembered what a forward and sensual little thing she had been: once, when she was a child of four or five, she had sat on his lap and opened his trousers to take hold of his penis. (p. 21)

Throughout his professional life, Freud believed that the seduction of children was "common enough" (Freud, 1931b, p. 232). The point of change in his theorising post seduction theory was that he no longer believed that actual seduction was a necessary and sufficient condition for the development of hysterical neuroses; rather, Freud concluded, it was the nature of the memories of particular events and the degree to which they became charged with unmanageable affect that resulted in neurotic illnesses.

Freud's psychosexual theory of development

". . . love [is] one of the foundations of civilisation" (Freud, 1930a, p. 101).

Freud's understanding of infant sexuality is based on three assumptions: it (i) originates in the erogenous zones; (ii) arises in the course of satisfaction of bodily needs; (iii) is auto-erotic. Each erogenous[1] zone interacts in a particular way with the outside world in order to satisfy fundamental needs in the child. Because the activities associated with these zones are pleasurable, the infant will repeat actions associated with these pleasurable activities in the absence of the need to satisfy a bodily demand. At those times, the actions of the infant become auto-erotic. Sexual development, according to Freud's psychosexual theory of development, unfolds in a series of predicable stages until mature genital sexuality is reached during adolescence. These five stages—oral, anal, phallic, latency, and genital, each of which is associated with a particular erogenous zone—are outlined in Table 2. A summary of the achievements of each stage is provided, together with the possible consequences to personality development if a problem or fixation occurred during that stage. Freud defined a fixation as a developmental arrest at one of the psychosexual stages, due, paradoxically, to either insufficient or excessive gratification at the fixated psychosexual stage (Freud, 1905d).

Freud elaborates his views on the importance of sexuality in normal development in his *Three Essays on the Theory of Sexuality* (Freud, 1905d). The major conclusions of these essays, for our purposes,[2] were that (i) sexual impulses were present in infancy and did not first emerge during puberty as previously believed; (ii) the repressed drives of hysterical and neurotic individuals were sexual in nature. Another very important concept—infantile amnesia—was also canvassed. Freud was intrigued with the phenomenon from the outset:

> . . . we take the fact of infantile amnesia – the loss . . . of the memories of the first years of our life – much too easily; and we fail to look upon it as a strange riddle. We forget how high are the intellectual achievements and how complicated the emotional impulses of which a child of . . . four years is capable, and we ought to be positively astonished that the memory of later years has as a rule preserved so little of these mental processes, especially as we have every reason to suppose that

Table 2.   Freud's psychosexual stages of development.[3]

Age	Stage	Characteristics	Outcome	Personality development
0–1 year	Oral "cannibalistic pregenital sexual organisation" (p. 198).	The mouth is the focus of pleasure and gratification. Feeding at mother's breast and oral exploration of the world are the primary activities. "Sexual activity has not yet been separated from the ingestion of food" (p. 198). Thumb-sucking prototypical expression of infant sexuality.	Ego begins to develop. Rudimentary concept of reality emerges. Distinction between self and other.	Harsh or abrupt weaning or over-indulgence by prolongation of breastfeeding results in oral fixation (cessation of the developmental process at oral stage) resulting in either ⇨oral–sadistic personality, tries to take what he needs from others by force; becomes a predatory exploitative character; or ⇨ oral-receptive personality, who expects to be fed; is passive and dependent.
1–3 years	Anal(-sadistic) "the impulse of cruelty arises from the instinct for mastery" (p. 193).	Shift in focus of pleasurable sensation to the anus. Primary activities are voiding and toilet training. ". . . opposition between two currents . . . active (mastery) and passive sexual)" (p. 198).	Beginning of socialisation process in which developing ego must learn to control and regulate impulses. Child is angry at these restrictions.	Harsh or over-indulgent toilet training may result in anal fixation and the development of the anal–retentive personality, which is orderly, parsimonious, obstinate and actualistic, or the anal-expulsive personality, who repetitively acts out his anger and rebellion.

(*continued*)

[Handwritten margin notes: "Fear loss of object" beside the oral row; "Fear loss Love object + Seperation anxiety" beside the anal row.]

Table 2.   *(continued)*.

Age	Stage	Characteristics	Outcome	Personality development
3–5 years	Phallic "[this phase] knows only one kind of genital: the male one" (p. 199).	The genital region is the focus of pleasure. Boys masturbate and girls become envious because they do not have a penis. "[this] phase presents a sexual object and . . . convergence of the sexual impulses upon that object" (p. 199).	Emergence of superego. Development of Oedipus complex in boys, who experience sexual feelings for their mothers and see their fathers as rivals whom they fear will castrate them (castration anxiety).	Resolution of Oedipus complex results in identification with father and adoption of male sex role. Failure to resolve Oedipus complex results in guilt, depression, and a sense of failure.
6–11 years	Latency ". . . sexual aims [of infant object choice] have become mitigated and . . . now represent . . . the "affectionate current' of sexual life" (p. 200).	Sexual needs and bodily focus are subordinated to intellectual tasks. "Latency children learn to feel for other people who help them in their helplessness and satisfy their needs for a love which is [akin to] . . . their their relation as sucklings to their nursing mother" (p. 222).	Regulation of repressed impulses from from Oedipal period. Turning away from sexual aims to cultural pursuits.	Fascination with rules and establishment of order in their lives. Sublimation of Oedipal wishes and establish-ment of adult personality.
12–18 years	Genital "Establishment of primacy in the service of reproduction is the last phase through which the organisation of sexuality passes" (p.199).	Upsurge of sexual feelings focused on the genitals. "The object-choice of the pubertal period is obliged to dispense with the objects of childhood and to start afresh as a 'sensual' current" (p. 200).	Rebelliousness against parents. Intense peer relationships.	The emergence of intimate love relationships and capacity for meaningful work, characteristics that define the mature adult.

these same forgotten childhood achievements have not, as might be thought, slipped away without leaving their mark on the subject's development, but have exercised a determining influence for the whole of his later life. (Freud, 1901b, p. 46)

Freud later concluded that the amnesia of infancy and of his hysterical patients (hysterical amnesia) were due to repression of sexual activity during infancy and that these repressed feelings find expression through feelings of disgust, modesty, and moral standards (Kahane, 1992).

I am . . . inclined to relate normal infantile amnesia to . . . infantile sexual activity. Psycho-analytic investigation enables us to make what has been forgotten conscious and thus do away with a compulsion that arises from the unconscious psychical material. (Freud, 1905d, p. 189)

This work caused a storm of protest, and in the second edition, published in 1909, Freud stated in the preface that "The author is under no illusion as to the deficiencies and obscurities of this little work" (p. 130); in the third edition, published in 1914, he commented:

I have now been watching for more than ten years the effects produced by this work and the reception accorded to it; and I take the opportunity offered by the publication of its third edition to preface it with a few remarks intended to prevent misunderstandings and expectations that cannot be fulfilled [p. 130] . . . my aim has been to discover how far psychological investigation can throw light upon the biology of the sexual life of man. (p. 131)

In the preface to the fourth edition, published in 1920, Freud sums up the status of psychoanalysis in general and of his theory of sexuality in particular as follows:

Now that the flood-waters of war have subsided . . . interest in psycho-analytic research remains unimpaired in the world at large. But the different parts of the theory have not all had the same history. The purely psychological theses and findings of psycho-analysis on the unconscious, repression, conflict as a cause of illness, the advantage accruing from illness, the mechanisms of the formation of symptoms, etc., have come to enjoy increasing recognition and have won notice even from those who are in general opposed to our views. That part of the theory, however, which lies on the frontiers of biology and the foundations of which are contained in this little work is still faced with undiminished contradiction. It has even led some who for a time took a very active interest in psycho-analysis to abandon it and to adopt fresh views which were intended to restrict once more the part played by the factor of sexuality in normal and pathological mental life. (p. 133)

Freud also defends himself against the many spurious arguments mounted against his theory, for example: "People have gone so far in their search for high-sounding catch words as to talk of the "pan-sexualism" of psycho-analysis and to raise the senseless charge against it of explaining "everything" by sex" (p. 134). Towards the end of his life, Freud partially retracted his libidinal development theory, recognising that behaviour does not fit neatly into prescribed stages, that stages might overlap, and behaviour thought to be characteristic of one stage might also appear in other stages. There is also some recognition that infant development is influenced by other factors, such as relationship.

The Oedipus complex and the case of Little Hans

"The most interesting information comes from children, for they tell all they know and then stop" (Mark Twain).

Details of Freud's biography might be instructive to our understanding of the development of Freud's theory of infant sexuality, in particular, the Oedipus complex. When Freud's father, Jacob, was forty years old, he married the third of his three wives, Amalia Nathanson, who was twenty years of age. Freud had two half-brothers from Jacob's first marriage who were about the same age as Amalia. This apparently confused the young Sigmund, who imagined himself the son of Amalia and one of his half-brothers, believing his father to be too old to occupy that role (Quinodoz, 2005). The eldest of eight children, Sigmund was clearly his mother's favourite and he grew up believing, as she did, that he was destined for greatness. Although Freud did not specifically identify his childhood as comprised of a series of traumatic losses, in fact, it was just that. When he was two years old, his mother, pregnant with her second child, was mourning the loss of her brother, Julius, who died at the age of twenty from tuberculosis. She named her second son Julius in honour of her dead brother, but he, too, succumbed to illness and died in infancy. At about the same time, Freud lost his nanny, his father lost his business, and his family was forced to relocate from Freiberg to Vienna. Amalia subsequently gave birth to six more children before Sigmund reached his tenth birthday (Marrone & Cortina, 2003).

Perhaps these developmental experiences influenced how Freud understood the dynamics of what he later called the Oedipus complex through his own self-analysis, which included the analysis of his dreams. Through this process, he became aware of feelings of love for his mother and jealousy towards his father, which, unfortunately, led him to conclude that this phenomenon was a universal of childhood (Quinodoz, 2005). The fully developed theory was presented in *The Ego and the Id* (Freud, 1923b), in which both forms of the complex, for boys and girls, were articulated. For boys, the desire was to replace the father in his relationship with his mother; for girls, there is the desire to take over the mother's role with respect to her relationship with her father. Subsequent Freud scholarship has offered possible explanations as to why Freud erroneously conflated two separate motivational systems—the affectional drives of the attachment system and erotic feelings from the sexual system—in his theory of the Oedipus complex, an error that was subsequently corrected by Ferenczi (1933), who called Freud's confusion a "conflation of tongues". Bowlby explicitly separated the two motivational systems in his attachment theory account (1940, 1958); while Marrone and Cortina (2003) dubbed it a "cover story" (p. 11) designed to protect Freud from re-experiencing the traumatic losses of his early childhood. By sexualising attachment longing, Freud could remain defended against his intense feelings of dependence and vulnerability in relation to an increasingly unavailable mother. Freud (1920g) perhaps acknowledged the longing for the lost mother in his observation of his eighteen-month-old grandson playing the "cotton reel" game, in which the child continually threw the reel away and retrieved it. Freud believed that the reel represented the mother; the child used the game to cope with the loss of her and to master her absence. This grandson, W. Ernest Freud, became an infant psychoanalyst who argued that maternal skin-to-skin contact was essential for babies in neonatal intensive care units (W. E. Freud, 1981; von Lupke, 2003).

The discipline of infant observation is usually attributed to Esther Bick and Melanie Klein, but Freud himself was keenly interested in infant/child observation and recommended that his students engage in the dedicated observation of infants as a rich source of information on human development and for further theorising psychoanalysis (Freud, 1918b, 1920g). The case of little Hans provided an important opportunity to assess the value of early child observations, before it was developed into a rigorous scientific method, as a way of collecting data for theoretical formulation. Because early observations did not have the methodological safeguards that have developed since Freud's day, this observational data is a useful study in teleology. Freud had already formulated his theory of infant sexuality and he was looking for confirmation of this theory from case material. His excitement at purportedly having his theories confirmed occurs throughout this long case study. For example, Freud writes, "Surely there must be a possibility of observing in children at first hand and in all the freshness of life the sexual impulses and wishes which we dig out so laboriously in adults from among their own debris . . ." (Freud, 1909b, p. 6).

A criticism of Freud's later theorising, which is not evident in the early studies on hysteria, was that he paid inadequate attention to actual events in the lives of his patients and focused primarily on their "psychic reality" (Ross, 2007). The case of "little Hans" is notable in this regard. This is a pivotal work; the remainder of the chapter will be devoted to its analysis.

Hans was a five-year-old boy whom Freud treated indirectly. Hans' father was in the role of therapist and he corresponded with Freud seeking advice and direction about his son's phobia—a fear that a horse would bite him in the street that made him reluctant to leave his home (Freud, 1909b). Hans' father was a Freud devotee who attended Freud's Wednesday evening seminars at his home and who engaged in a period of child observation of his son at Freud's behest until the appearance of a psychological problem, at which point the observation became therapy. Mr Graf alerted Freud to the problem of the development of his son's "nervous disorder" thus:

> No doubt the ground was prepared by sexual over-excitation due to his mother's tenderness; but I am not able to specify the actual exciting cause. He is afraid a horse will bite him in the street, and this fear

seems somehow to be connected with his having been frightened by a large penis. (Freud, 1909b, p. 22)

The earliest account of the onset of Hans' condition was as follows:

> Hans (aged four and three-quarters) woke up one morning in tears. Asked why he was crying, he said to his mother: "When I was asleep I thought you were gone and I had no Mummy to coax with (i.e., caress)". An anxiety dream, therefore . . . (p. 23)

Mr Graf reported daytime incidences in which Hans spoke about his anxiety: "Suppose I was to have no Mummy, or suppose you were to go away . . ." On one occasion, he was out with his nurse and began to cry and asked to be taken home because he wanted to be with his mother. The following day, his mother took him out and it was during this outing to the zoo that Hans confided to his mother that he was afraid that a horse would bite him.

Freud interpreted this early material to indicate that Hans had both anxiety and a phobia. The anxiety centred on what Freud thought was increased affection for his mother, which Hans had repressed. "Hans' anxiety, which thus corresponded to a repressed erotic longing, was, like every infantile anxiety, without an object to begin with: it was still anxiety and not yet fear" (Freud, 1909b, p. 25). Freud expressed puzzlement in several places through his long exposition of this case about the relationship between Hans' two conditions. For example, during the only face-to-face consultation that Freud had with Hans, he recalled: "We were . . . forced to confess that the connections between the horses he was afraid of and the affectionate feelings towards his mother which had been revealed were by no means abundant" (p. 41); later he stated, ". . . it seemed to be merely by chance that horses had become his bugbear" (p. 120).

Freud, who referred to the boy, Hans, as "small Oedipus", understood his symptoms in terms of his recently formulated theory of infant sexuality. The symptom, refusal to leave his home for fear that he might be knocked over or bitten by a horse, was interpreted by Freud as a compromise formation.

> . . . all that the repressed instincts got from the neurosis was the honour of providing pretexts for the appearance of the anxiety in consciousness. But however clear may have been the victory in Hans's

phobia of the forces that were opposed to sexuality, nevertheless, since such an illness is in its very nature a compromise, this cannot have been all that the repressed instincts obtained. After all, Hans' phobia of horses was an obstacle to his going into the street, and could serve as a means of allowing him to stay at home with his beloved mother. (Freud, 1909b, p. 139)

According to Freud, Hans displaced his unconscious anxiety about being punished by castration, presumably by his father, for his forbidden incestuous desires towards his mother. Freud believed that Hans was experiencing an Oedipal conflict that he could not resolve—hating his beloved father, whom he perceived as his rival for his mother. Freud argued that the aggressive impulses and death wishes Hans entertained towards his father were so anxiety laden that they were repressed into his unconscious; his castration anxiety was displaced on to the horse/father, thus allowing him to feel and express only his loving feelings towards his father, although there is evidence of his ambivalent feelings, for example,

> his father recollected that Hans had quite unexpectedly butted his head into his stomach . . . he now recognised it as an expression of the little boy's hostile disposition towards him, and perhaps also as a manifestation of a need for getting punished for it. Later on the boy repeated his reaction towards his father in a clearer and more complete manner, by first hitting his father on the hand and then affectionately kissing the same hand. (p. 42)

Freud at first argued that (forbidden) libidinous impulses are repressed and transformed into anxiety, but later rejected this explanation in favour of the view that anxiety signals repression. In Hans' case, his castration anxiety resulted in repression of his libidinous impulses towards his parents. Freud argued that the essentials of the Oedipus complex are the same in both normal and pathological development; that is, Oedipal anxiety differs only in quantity, not quality in normal and pathological manifestations. Those for whom castration anxiety, incestuous libidinal or aggressive impulses feel intolerable will develop symptoms such as the phobia developed by little Hans. Freud later argued that the structure of this infantile neurosis was also reflected in adult Oedipal anxieties (see, for example, *Inhibitions, Symptoms and Anxiety* (Freud, 1926d)), in which he reconsiders the case of little Hans in light of a new concept, superego, which had not been developed in his original theorising about the Oedipus complex.

Essentially, Freud saw evidence of all the elements of his Oedipus complex in Hans' behaviour—his heightened interest in "widdlers", his attempts to seduce his mother into stroking his penis as his mother was powdering round it (after his bath) and taking care not to touch it,

Hans:	Why don't you put your finger there?
Mother:	Because that'd be piggish.
Hans:	What's that? Piggish? Why?
Mother:	Because it's not proper.
Hans (laughing):	But it's great fun. (p. 19)

his desire to sleep with his mother, his masturbation fantasy of seeing his mother naked, his need to "coax" with his mother, his talk of marrying his mother and becoming a father, are all consistent with Freud's theory.

However, that Hans should develop a fear of castration is not surprising in view of his mother's threat to ". . . send for Dr A. to cut off [his] widdler [penis] . . ." when she ". . . found him with his hand on his penis" (p. 7). Freud actually identified this experience as the beginning of Hans' castration complex (p. 8). However, contrary to the theory, it was his mother, not his father, who threatened Hans with castration. There is scant evidence that Hans feared his father; rather, he sought protection from his father from a menacing and threatening mother. Further, Freud believed that the child's incestuous desire for his mother originated intrapsychically. However, Hans' father was astute enough to discern that Hans' mother's sexual "over-excitation," which amounted to maternal seduction, played a significant role in stimulating Hans' sexual curiosity (Fromm & Narváez, 1968). Hans's mother liked to take Hans into her bed; she also allowed him to follow her into the bathroom and witness her undressing. His mother responds with jealousy when Hans expresses a wish to sleep with his friend, Mariedl.

Hans:	Oh, then I'll just go downstairs and sleep with Mariedl.
Mother:	You really want to go away from Mummy and sleep downstairs?
Hans:	Oh, I'll come up again in the morning to have breakfast and do number one.

Mother: Well, if you really want to go away from Daddy and
             Mummy, then take your coat and knickers – and good-
             bye!"

We have yet to understand how these desires become transformed
and expressed through a phobia of horses, in particular, a fear that a
horse will fall down or bite him in the street. Freud linked the fear of
horses to a displaced fear of his father and the fear of being bitten with
the fear of castration (punishment) for his forbidden wishes and
impulses towards his parents. However, a conversation between Hans
and his father suggests that Hans associates horses more with his
mother than his father and perhaps shows displaced aggression
towards a horse that properly belongs to his mother.

Father: You took it [the horse] out of the stables?
Hans: I took it out because I wanted to whip it.
Father: Which would you really like to beat? Mummy, Hanna or
             me?
Hans: Mummy.
Father: Why?
Hans: I should just like to beat her.

An alternative explanation is that horses figured prominently in
this little boy's experience, both on the farm at Gmunden, where he
witnessed his little friend, Fritzl, being injured while playing at being
a horse, and in Vienna, where horse and cart were, at that time, the
principal means of transport. Hans had actually witnessed a horse
falling in the street and flailing with its hooves. He also played at
horses with his father. Freud thus offered a third possibility—that
Hans' fear of horses was, in fact, his fear of his own impulses.

Father: We went out in front of the house. He was in very
                      good spirits and was prancing about all the time
                      like a horse . . .
Hans (promptly):   . . . I'm a young horse.
Father: During the period when his anxiety was at its
                      height, and he was frightened at seeing horses
                      frisking, he asked me why they did it; and to reas-
                      sure him I said: "Those are young horses, you see,
                      and they frisk about like little boys. You frisk about
                      too, and you're a little boy." Since then, whenever

he has seen horses frisking, he has said: "That's
right; those are young horses!" (p. 58)

In *Beyond the Pleasure Principle*, Freud defined a phobia as a flight
from the satisfaction of one's instincts or impulses (Freud, 1920g). If
the Oedipus complex is universal, as Freud claimed, we must wonder
why we do not all develop phobias in response to it. The obvious
answer is that we all have fears, but most do not develop into phobias.
Those that do develop might not have a single explanation and could
be multiply determined. Psychodynamic theories hold to the principles of psychic determinism: that is, there is a lawful regularity in
mental life and that all behaviour has one or more causes; and multiple determination, denoting that the same (unconscious) motive can
result in diverse behaviours and that a given behaviour might be a
function of multiple motives (Malan, 1979; Malan & Osimo, 1992). In
the following alternative accounts of Little Hans, we will experiment
with these notions of psychic determinism and multiple determination; you can judge with what success these alternative explanations
illuminate the dynamics of Little Hans' symptoms.

An attachment theory account

". . . we are never so defenceless against suffering as when we love,
never so helplessly unhappy as when we have lost our loved object or
its love" (Freud, 1930a, p. 82).

The case of little Hans has been re-analysed within a number of
different theoretical paradigms (Chused, 2007), including attachment
theory (see Chapter Four). Bowlby (1973) concluded that Hans was
experiencing fears of abandonment from a mother who regularly
threatened to leave him, and was thus experiencing an anxious
ambivalent attachment to an unreliable attachment figure rather than
fear of castration from his purported sexual rival, his father. Although
Freud observed and commented upon Hans' mother's threats in the
case material, and Hans' frequent references to fears of maternal abandonment (e.g., "When I was asleep I thought you were gone and I had
no Mummy to caress me"; and "Suppose I was to have no Mummy"
(Freud, 1909b, p. 23), he was determined to use the case of little Hans
to provide support for his theory of infant sexuality. Therefore, he
quarantined material such as his mother's abandoning and threaten-

ing behaviour because it was less relevant to his theory of the Oedipus complex (Juri, 2003). When he noted such material, Freud interpreted it in terms of his theory. Such anxieties were due to increased affection for his mother and his desire to seduce her, which, he argued, produced anxiety that "corresponded to a repressed erotic longing" (p. 25). Freud concluded, with respect to Hans' phobic symptoms, that "in the street he missed his mother, whom he could not caress with, and that he did not want to be away from her" (p. 25). Freud has clearly identified separation anxiety in this little boy but has sexualised it, as demonstrated by the following interpretation: "[Hans] was overwhelmed by an intensification of his libido – for its object was his mother, and its aim may perhaps have been to sleep with her" (p. 26). Such was Freud's commitment to his theory that he later observed, in his *Three Essays on Sexuality* (in a footnote added in 1910), that

> [this case] . . . has taught us much that is new for which we have not been prepared by psycho-analysis: for instance, the fact that sexual symbolism – the representation of what is sexual by non-sexual objects and relations – extends back into the first years of possession of the power of speech. (Freud, 1905d, p. 193)

Other psychoanalytic writers have argued that pre-Oedipal issues and attachment theory account for the case material and fantasies and argue that Hans' proximity seeking with his mother is not sexual but originates in non-sexual attachment motivation (Midgley, 2006). A number of factors predispose Hans to an insecure–ambivalent attachment to his mother. She appears to have had a preoccupied state of mind with respect to attachment. She was unpredictable in her emotional availability and responsiveness to her young son. At times, she was punitive and withholding: she threatened to leave him if he misbehaved (Freud, 1909b, p. 45), to send him away forever (p. 17), to have his penis cut off by Dr A if he touched it (p. 7), and to beat him with a carpet beater (p. 81). At other times, she was overly solicitous, over-stimulating, and over-involved, and frequently took him into her bed when he expressed fears of abandonment or upset over his horse phobia (p. 23). Her direct threats of abandonment and castration must have been amplified as he witnessed his mother's mistreatment of his baby sister, Hanna, whom she beat frequently. There is evidence of a basic lack of trust in his mother, for example, "I am afraid of her letting go of my head and going [into the bath]" (p. 67), fuelled by her unpredictable responding and availability to him.

Wakefield (2007) re-analysed the giraffe fantasy in terms of an attachment-based sibling rivalry account. Hans' phantasy about a big giraffe and a crumpled giraffe, which, in Hans' words, comprised the following,

> In the night there was a big giraffe in the room and a crumpled one; and the big one called out because I took the crumpled one away from it. Then it stopped calling out; and then I sat on top of the crumpled one. (Freud, 1909b, p. 37)

was interpreted by Hans' father and Freud in Oedipal terms, as follows:

> . . . the solution of this matrimonial scene transposed into giraffe life is this: he was seized in the night with a longing for his mother, for her caresses, for her genital organ, and came into our bedroom for that reason . . .[to which Freud added]: . . . The 'sitting down on top of' was probably Hans' representation of taking possession. But the whole thing was a phantasy of defiance connected with his satisfaction at the triumph over his father's resistance. (Freud, 1909b, p. 39)

However, the morning after reporting this phantasy to his father, Hans identified the crumpled giraffe, not as his mother, but as his baby sister, Hanna. Wakefield (2007) understood Hans' phantasy in terms of the sibling rivalry attachment triangle relating to the reduction in Hans' access to his mother as care-giver once Hanna, who was Hans' rival, was born, as opposed to the Oedipal triangle, in which Hans' father was perceived to be the rival. There are numerous references throughout this case history to Hans' rivalry with, and jealousy of, his new sister (Freud, 1909b). He was able to articulate this very clearly (". . . I don't want a baby sister!" (p. 11), and elsewhere expresses murderous intent towards her, for example, "I thought to myself Hanna was on the balcony and fell down off it" (p. 68), and "I'd rather [Hanna] weren't alive" (p. 72)). Freud was also well aware that Hans' father served as a more secure attachment figure than his mother (whom he knew well because he had treated her), but interpreted this as part of an ambivalent hostility–tenderness conflict on the part of Hans, who purportedly both loved and feared his father. His mother's worrying behaviour towards her children is glossed over in the account, although there is sufficient evidence to indicate that she is psychologically disturbed and emotionally dysregulated. Her frequent beatings of her infant daughter and her threats of castration and abandonment of her son are clear throughout the account. However, she was at times able to fulfil a maternal function for Hans, when Hans is overcome with separation anxiety (e.g., wanting to sleep in his parents' bedroom; having nightmares in which his mother had abandoned him; crying when away from his mother; wanting to "coax" with her; and not tolerating any separation from her, as the following excerpt shows.

> On January 7th he went to the Stadtpark with his nurse maid as usual. In the street he began to cry and asked to be taken home, saying that he wanted to "coax" with his Mummy. At home he was asked why he had refused to go any farther and had cried, but he would not say. Till the evening he was cheerful, as usual. But in the evening he grew visibly frightened; he cried and could not be separated from his mother, and wanted to "coax" with her again. Then he grew cheerful again, and slept well. (Freud, 1909b, p. 24)

Attachment theory states that infants and children can develop different types of attachment to each parent and, indeed, to other caregivers. In the case of little Hans, we see evidence of an anxious ambivalent attachment to his mother. Ambivalently attached children remain preoccupied with their mothers' whereabouts, even when the mother is present, while mothers of ambivalent infants are unpredictable in their availability, insensitive to their children's emotional signals, and discouraging of their growing autonomy. Consistent with his angry ambivalence towards his mother, Hans confesses to his father that he "should just like to beat Mummy" (Freud, 1909b, p. 81).

Hans had a healthier, more secure attachment to his father, who shows himself to be more emotionally available, predictable, attuned, and supportive of his young son. Hans perceives in his father a secure base. "When I'm not with you I'm frightened; when I'm not in bed with you, then I'm frightened. When I'm not frightened any more I shan't come any more" (Freud, 1909b, p. 43). Hans emphatically distinguishes between his parents during one of his father's attempts to gain evidence for his Oedipal theory. "Why did you tell me I'm fond of Mummy and that's why I'm frightened when I am fond of you?"

(p. 44). Notwithstanding, it would no doubt have been of concern to Hans, although it remained unstated, that his father minimised or denied his wife's regular abuse of their infant daughter. When Hans comments that he cannot stand Hanna's screaming, his father replies, "Why, she doesn't scream at all", to which Hans replies, "When Mummy whacks her on her bare bottom, then she screams" (p. 72).

The conclusions of each theory are vastly different. In Freud's paradigm, Hans would wish that his father, his sexual rival, would leave (or die) so that he could have his mother to himself. In Bowlby's separation anxiety paradigm, the opposite is true. Hans would be afraid that his father would abandon him and that he would be left alone with an abandoning mother. What is Little Hans' verdict on these two hypotheses?

Hans: When you are away, I am afraid that you are not coming home.
Father: And have I ever threatened you that I shan't come home?
Hans: Not you, but Mummy. Mummy has told me she won't come back. (Freud, 1909b, p. 45)

A learning theory account

An alternative or adjunctive case can be made for a learning theory explanation, at least of the horse phobia. At one point in his "treatment", Little Hans told his father the following story and later had a conversation with his father about his fears. Hans was visiting family friends outside Vienna, during which time a young friend, Lizzi, had to leave and a cart with a white horse came to take her to the station. Lizzi's father warned her not to put her finger close to the white horse for fear of being bitten. Hans' father responded ". . . it isn't a horse you mean, but a widdler,[4] that one mustn't put one's hand to", to which Hans sensibly replies, "But a widdler doesn't bite" (p. 29). A few days later, father and son had the following conversation:

Hans: . . . I'm most afraid of furniture-vans.
Father: Why?
Hans: I think when furniture-horses are dragging a heavy van they'll fall down.
Father: So you're not afraid with a small cart?

Hans:	No. I'm not afraid with a small cart or with a post-office van. I'm most afraid too when a bus comes along.
Father:	Why? Because it's so big?
Hans:	No. Because once a horse in a bus fell down.
Father:	When?
Hans:	Once when I went out with Mummy . . .
Father:	What did you think when the horse fell down?
Hans:	*Now it'll always be like this. All horses in buses'll fall down.*
Father:	In all buses?
Hans:	Yes. And in furniture-vans too. Not often in furniture-vans.
Father:	You had your nonsense[5] already at that time?
Hans:	No. *I only got it then. When the horse in the bus fell down, it gave me such a fright, really! That was when I got the nonsense.*
Father:	But the nonsense was that you thought a horse would bite you. And now you say you were afraid a horse would fall down.
Hans:	Fall down and bite.
Father:	Why did it give you such a fright?
Hans:	Because the horse went like this with its feet. (He lay down on the ground and showed me how it kicked about.) It gave me a fright because it made a row with its feet. (p. 50, my italics)

Here are two experiences in this little boy's life that could, in learning theory terms, be considered to have been aversive conditioning experiences (Dadds, Davey, & Field, 2001; Field, 2006; Gao, Raine, Venables, Dawson, & Mednick, 2010). There is also evidence of generalisation of the feared stimulus (Taylor, 1956) when he expressed his fear of a furniture van going past. When questioned, he replied that he was afraid because the furniture van looked like a bus, the original feared stimulus (Freud, 1909b, p. 53).

Freud actually acknowledges the temporal contiguity of the events described and the onset of Hans' phobia in his statement: "We have learned the immediate precipitating cause after which the phobia broke out . . . the boy saw a big heavy horse fall down" (p. 51). Freud then goes on: "Hans at that moment perceived a wish that his father might fall down in the same way – and be dead. His serious expression as he was telling the story no doubt referred to this unconscious meaning" (1909b, p. 52). This interpretation exceeds the available data and is a logical error; the boy's serious expression could denote many things—the topic under discussion was of great import and distressed him. There is no evidence in the account or in the conversation between father and son that is suggestive of the meaning ascribed to it by Freud. Later in the report, Freud (1909b) himself admits,

> It is true that during the analysis *Hans had to be told many things that he could not say himself, that he had to be presented with thoughts which he had so far shown no signs of possessing*, and that his attention had to be turned in the direction from which his father was expecting something to come. This detracts from the evidential value of the analysis; but the procedure is the same in every case. For a psycho-analysis is not an impartial scientific investigation, but a therapeutic measure (p. 104, my italics)

An entry in the case study notes an improvement after Hans' visit with Freud, in which he was "enlightened" with respect to sexual matters.

> While formerly he could never be induced to go out of the street door for very long, and always ran back into the house with every sign of fright if horses came along, this time he stayed in front of the street-door for an hour – even while carts were driving past, which happens fairly often in our street. Every now and then he ran into the house when he saw a cart approaching in the distance, but he turned round at once as though he were changing his mind. In any case there is only a trace of the anxiety left, and the progress since his enlightenment is unmistakable. (1909b, p. 43)

However, an alternative and perhaps more plausible explanation for Hans' improvement is his (self-) application of two of the key principles of behavioural therapy—successive approximations leading to desensitisation and exposure to the feared stimulus in a graded hierarchy. In the evening, he said, "We get as far as the street-door now, so we'll go into the Stadtpark too" (p. 43). Hans subsequently engaged in pretend play in which he was a horse that repeatedly falls down, thereby attempting to gain mastery over his fear of horses, and later he "pranced about like a horse, declaring himself to be a 'young horse'" (p. 58).

In subsequent conversations that must have seemed rather tedious to Hans, he became impatient with his father and says, "Oh! Do let me alone!" (p. 57). Father's questioning techniques were very direct and Hans had almost no opportunity to talk about topics that interested him. Many of their conversations focused on penises (widdlers), urine (widdle), and faeces (lumpf), not necessarily because Hans was intrinsically interested but because his father constantly and relentlessly brought him back to these topics (see, for example, the conversations on pp. 62–64). Freud admonished Hans' father ". . . for asking too many questions", and for pressing the enquiry along his own lines instead of allowing the little boy to express his thoughts. For this reason, "the analysis began to be obscure and uncertain" (p. 64). It is, therefore, difficult to know what we can learn from this case other than how an observation can be biased by theoretical preconceptions and how not to conduct a child psychoanalysis! Despite the fact that Freud calls Hans his "little Oedipus" (p. 97), the following conversation, showing minimal corroborative evidence of an Oedipus complex, took place between Hans and his father (pp. 88–89):

Father: Are you fond of Daddy?
Hans: Oh yes.
Father: Or perhaps not.

Hans was playing with a little toy horse. At that moment the horse fell down, and Hans shouted out: The horse has fallen down! Look what a row it's making!

Father: You're a little vexed with Daddy because Mummy is fond of him.
Hans: No.
Father: Then why do you always cry whenever Mummy gives me a kiss? It's because you're jealous.
Hans: Jealous, yes.
Father: You'd like to be Daddy yourself.
Hans: Oh yes.
Father: What would you like to do if you were Daddy?
Hans: And you were Hans? I'd like to take you to Lainz every Sunday – no, every week-day too. If I were Daddy I'd be ever so nice and good.
Father: But what would you like to do with Mummy?
Hans: Take her to Lainz, too.
Father: And what besides?
Hans: Nothing.

The most detailed behaviourist critique of the case was presented by Wolpe and Rachman (1960). However, the same criticism can be levelled at their account as they level against the psychoanalytic account. The first is selective attention to data that confirms one theory and disconfirms the other; the second is an unwillingness to concede that one theoretical orientation might be insufficient to account for all the data. For example, the early behaviourists necessarily limited their data by their rejection of the subjective; they discounted introspection and disavowed the unconscious. They were, therefore, blind to the nature of evidence that supports the existence of unconscious psychological states. The crude demand for "confirmation by direct observation" (Wolpe & Rachman, 1960, p. 219) is "as misplaced as a demand to be shown electrons" (Neu, 2000, p. 213). The behaviourist interpretation of the nature of the phobia is based on the principle of stimulus generalisation. This is plausible; so is Freud's concept of displacement. The behaviourist argument rests on the objective similarity of the phenomena that have been generalised while the psychoanalytic argument rests on the perceived similarity or association, whether conscious or not.

A major problem for the behaviourist account is the failure to acknowledge the preceding generalised anxiety that was evident in this little boy before the onset of the specific horse phobia. Freud was right in identifying two conditions in little Hans almost from the outset of therapy.

> . . . at the beginning of his illness there was as yet no phobia whatever present, whether of streets or of walking or even of horses. If there had been, his evening states would be inexplicable; for who bothers at bed time about streets and walking? (Freud, 1909b, p. 25)

The phobia of horses is perhaps explained best by learning theory and his abandonment anxiety, which clearly preceded his specific phobia of horses, is accounted for most heuristically by an attachment theory account. The case material lends itself to multiple possible explanations, and no doubt there are others that I have not addressed.

A retrospective historical account

We could perhaps be satisfied with these analyses and leave it at that, but further information that came to light many years after this observation/treatment has cast the whole case in a completely new light.

This account demonstrates the importance of Erikson's injunction to contextualise the child's symptomatic behaviours in his social world. Interviews with Hans' father (Max) and Hans himself (Herbert) with Kurt Eissler in 1952, fifty years after these events were recorded, revealed a home dominated by the severe psychopathology of Hans' mother (Olga). Mrs Graf, who was depressed, socially phobic, and agoraphobic, regularly mistreated her husband and her daughter (Hanna), beginning in her infancy. She physically abused Hanna on a daily basis (Ross, 2007). Max Graf described his wife in a late interview, when he was in his seventies, as hysterical, focused on herself, antisocial, inhibited, withdrawn, depressive, jealous, rivalrous, and neglectful of their daughter.

Hanna subsequently committed suicide as an adult, as did two of Olga's brothers (her sister also attempted suicide) and Herbert's wife (Ross, 2007). This information casts a very different light on some of the conversations between Hans and his father, which reveal the extent of the physical abuse of Hanna and Hans' anger with his mother. Here are two fragments: the first is a conversation about Hanna screaming while having her bath because her mother is beating her, the second expresses Hans' impotent rage with his mother.

Father: Are you fond of Hanna?
Hans: Oh yes, very fond.
Father: Would you rather that Hanna weren't alive or that she were?
Hans: I'd rather she weren't alive.
Father: Why?
Hans: At any rate she wouldn't scream so, and I can't bear her screaming.
Father: Why, you scream yourself.
Hans: But Hanna screams too.
Father: Why can't you bear it?
Hans: Because she screams so loud.
Father: Why, she doesn't scream at all.
Hans: When she's whacked on her bare bottom, then she screams.
Father: And you don't like that?
Hans: No. Because she makes such a row with her screaming! (p. 72).

. . .

Father: Would you like to beat the horses as Mummy beats Hanna? You would like that, too.

Hans:	It doesn't do the horses any harm when they're beaten . . .
Father:	Which would you really like to beat? Mummy, Hanna or me?
Hans:	(without hesitation) Mummy . . . I should just like to hit her . . . with a carpet beater. (His mother often threatens to beat him with the carpet-beater.) (p. 81)

There are a number of very disturbing features in these conversations that bring into sharp focus the role of insecure attachment, trauma, and abuse as factors in Hans' psychological difficulties as a child and later as an adult. Hans' mother was seductive, sadistic, and explosive towards her young son. Today, we would probably diagnose her with borderline pathology. Her husband had hinted at this in his opening statement to Freud about his son's condition, in which he hypothesised a possible explanation to lie in the "sexual over-excitation due to his mother's tenderness". He also confided to Freud that he believed his wife was ". . . responsible for the outbreak of the child's neurosis, on account of her excessive display of affection for him and her too frequent readiness to take him into her bed" (p. 28). It is also of concern that his father did not actively intervene to prevent his wife's abuse of their children, particularly his daughter. In fact, he openly denied to Hans that Hanna screamed.

Max told Eissler that he eventually became estranged from Freud because of his rigid and dogmatic stance. While acknowledging the genius of his mentor, Max also described Freud's "Moses complex" and his inability to accept alternative points of view.[6] This trait is a core symptom of the narcissistic personality, one which Freud displayed with a great many people in his life, as we shall see in the coming chapters. Eissler interviewed a reluctant Herbert seven years later. He told Eissler that his mother's analysis with Freud was not at all helpful to her and Freud's advice to her to have children was disastrous, as later events were to show. In a note to Eissler, Olga stated that "Freud had wreaked havoc on us" and refused an interview for fear that her traumatic experiences of those times would be revived (Ross, 2007, p. 784). Herbert's parents divorced when he was sixteen years old, and it was at this point that he discovered his father's notes about his "treatment" for his neurosis. Herbert reported no memory of the purported infantile neurosis, whether because of infantile amnesia or as a result of traumatic dissociation. Although Herbert had a very successful career as the stage manager of the Metropolitan Opera in New York, and later as director of the Grand Theatre in Geneva, he also said that he suffered as an adult and underwent an unsuccessful psychoanalysis. He resented the publication of his childhood case material and the revelation of his identity. He married a very disturbed, alcoholic woman who, like his sister and two uncles, committed suicide.

With the addition of this historical account of the Graf family, Hans' symptoms can now be understood as a form of communication of the traumatic abuse to which he was witness and of which he was recipient. Freud came to the view early that it was the patient's "psychic reality" rather than historical accuracy that formed the proper subject matter of psychoanalysis (Arlow, 1985, 1996). This was a major point of difference between Freud and Erikson, who emphasised the importance of "historical actuality" in case formulation (Erikson, 1968). The case of Little Hans provides a strong argument for the need of an accurate historical and social context, particularly for children. As noted by Winnicott (1966), ". . . psychoanalysis can be said to be a prolonged process of history taking" (p. 76).

Sadly, despite the mounting evidence, Freud adhered rigidly to his original theoretical perspective, interpreting comments about Hans wanting to beat his mother as the "primal scene such that Hans's wish to beat Mummy derives solely from the inherent violence of his (sexual) desire for her" (Ross, 2007, p. 792).

Freud concludes, "The picture of a child's sexual life presented in this observation of little Hans agrees very well with the account I gave of it (basing my views upon psycho-analytic examinations of adults) in my *Three Essays*" (p. 101). However, before embarking on his analysis of the case, Freud (1909b), somewhat prophetically, predicted the objections that this paper would call forth. Objections of the same kind were later directed at Freud himself.

> According to . . . [an] uncompromising objection, an analysis of a child conducted by his father, who went to work instilled with my theoretical views and infected with my prejudices, must be entirely devoid of any objective worth. A child . . . is necessarily highly suggestible, and in regard to no one, perhaps, more than to his own father; he will allow anything to be forced upon him, out of gratitude to his father for taking so much notice of him; none of his assertions can

have any evidential value, and everything he produces in the way of associations, phantasies, and dreams will naturally take the direction into which they are being urged by every possible means. (p. 102).

From sexual and instinct theories to a theory of object relations

"A child's demands for love are immoderate; they make exclusive claims and tolerate no sharing" (Freud, 1933a, p. 123).

Although Freud's sexual and instinct theories attracted dissent and controversy that continues today, he radically changed our perceptions of childhood from a time of benign innocence to one that involved a gradual, staged struggle to master and integrate biological and social strivings.

> One feature of the popular view of the sexual instinct is that it is absent in childhood and only awakens in the period of life described as puberty. This, however, is not merely a simple error but one that has had grave consequences, for it is mainly to this idea that we owe our present ignorance of the fundamental conditions of sexual life. A thorough study of the sexual manifestations of childhood would probably reveal the essential characters of the sexual instinct and would show us the course of its development and the way in which it is put together from various sources. (Freud, 1905d, p. 173)

Freud believed that adult psychopathology and the content of dreams, jokes, and slips of the tongue all have their origins in unresolved sexual conflicts arising in childhood (Freud, 1900a, 1901b, 1905d). However, with the advent of his structural model, more attention was paid to the influence of the social environment, the role of the ego, and the child's struggle to reconcile his wishes and internal realities with moral injunctions, both internalised and externally imposed, and other aspects of external reality (Frank, 1999).

In the third of his three essays on sexuality, "The transformations of puberty", Freud discusses the emergence of the sexual object:

> With the arrival of puberty, changes set in which are destined to give infantile sexual life its final, normal shape. The sexual instinct has hitherto been predominantly auto-erotic; it now finds a sexual object. Its

activity has hitherto been derived from a number of separate instincts and erotogenic zones, which, independently of one another, have pursued a certain sort of pleasure as their sole sexual aim. Now, however, a new sexual aim appears, and all the component instincts combine to attain it, while the erotogenic zones become subordinated to the primacy of the genital zone. (Freud, 1905d, p. 207)

Freud subsequently focused greater attention on the role of affects—love and hate—in object relations and their importance in development. In "The dynamics of transference", the concept of ambivalence between love and hate appeared (Freud, 1912b). For mature sexuality to be attained, the incestuous love-objects of infancy had to be relinquished, although later object choices might closely resemble the parents.

As Freud's theorising progressed, most notably in "Mourning and melancholia" (Freud, 1917e) and *The Ego and the Id* (Freud, 1923b), he moved beyond sexual and instinct theories to the idea of object relations. It was in "Mourning and melancholia" that Freud outlined the major tenets of his revised theory of mind, which presaged object relations theory. In this remarkable paper, Freud elaborates his evolving theory by comparing the psychic activity of mourning and melancholia, which today we call depression, or, more correctly, major depression (American Psychiatric Association, 2000). Freud defined mourning as a person's reaction to the loss of a loved other, or ". . . of some abstraction which has taken the place of one, such as one's country, liberty, an ideal . . ." (p. 243). He regarded mourning as a natural process that did not require medical "interference". The task of mourning, which happens naturally over time, involves the withdrawal of libido from its attachment to the lost object, thus freeing the ego to find new objects in which to invest its libido. In melancholia, the love object has not died, but has been lost as an object of love. The major distinguishing feature between the two conditions is the "disturbance in self-regard" (p. 244) in melancholia that appears largely absent in mourning. "In mourning it is the world which has become poor and empty (as a result of the loss of the loved object); in melancholia it is the ego itself" (p. 246). Through observing the melancholic process, Freud illuminated ego functioning in which

> . . . one part of the ego sets itself against the other, judges it critically, and . . . takes it as its object . . . The critical agency of the ego which

became split off, the 'conscience' was . . . along with the censorship of
consciousness and reality-testing, among the major institutions of the
ego. (p. 247)

The recognition of the ego's capacity to create defences was taken up
by Anna Freud in *The Ego and the Mechanisms of Defence* (1936a), a work
that influenced subsequent theorising and the development of ego
psychology (Hartmann, 1939).

However, Freud observed that the fierce self-accusations of the
melancholic were not applicable to the afflicted person, but were
directed against a loved object and then subsequently re-directed to
the patient's own ego. Hence, an initial state of revolt against a loved
person who has disappointed them passes over "into the crushed state
of melancholia" (Freud, 1917e, p. 248). Unlike in mourning, the libido
freed from this shattered relationship "was not displaced on to
another object; it was withdrawn into the ego". From there, it

> served to establish an *identification* of the ego with the abandoned
> object. Thus the shadow of the object fell upon the ego, and the latter
> could henceforth be judged by a special agency, as though it were an
> object, the forsaken object. In this way an object-loss was transformed
> into an ego-loss and the conflict between the ego and the loved person
> into a cleavage between the critical activity of the ego and the ego as
> altered by identification. (Freud, 1917e, p. 249)

This is a critical passage in the new theorising, because it represents the ego as a psychic structure with both conscious and unconscious components that can be split. Each part can operate independently, generating its own thoughts and feelings, and is capable of
entering into unconscious relationships with other parts of the ego.
This understanding of the structure and function of the ego foreshad-
ows the notion of multiple and sometimes disconnected "self-states",
which are characteristics of some forms of psychopathology, including
borderline personality disorder (Bateman & Fonagy, 2004). Ogden
(2002) identified multiple "subject-object, I–me pairings" (p. 769) in
which the subject (I) attacks the object (me), thereby depleting the ego.
Ogden noted the unfolding of an object relations perspective in
Freud's psychoanalysis: ". . . the interdependence of two unconscious
aspects of object loss in melancholia . . . the melancholic's tie to the
object . . . and the alteration of the self in response to the loss of the
object" (Ogden, 2002, p. 769).

Freud's psychoanalytic infant

"In infants, apart from the respiratory action of screaming, affects only produce and find expression in uncoordinated contractions of the muscles . . ." (Breuer, 1893, p. 204).

The stereotypical portrayal of Freud's infant is the quintessential Oedipal infant who is from birth beset by aggressive and sexual instincts, drives, fantasies, and wishes on the one hand and helplessness in the face of these forces on the other. Freud believed that this helplessness was not contingent upon outside environmental factors such as good parenting. The infant, he argued, was essentially helpless in the face of his own instincts, whose purpose was to restore the original state of being before external pressures, such as the need to adapt to a socialised, collective existence, forced the abandonment of such primal pleasures (Van Haute & Geyskens, 2007). The Freudian infant enters into relationships with the outside world, in particular his mother, because of his helplessness. His fear of loss of the mother is the fear that his bodily needs will not be met. Hence, attachment was conceived as an instinct secondary to the instinct for survival. Subsequent research has shown this to be an untenable proposition and we will return to it in our critique on Freud and again in the chapter on attachment. We should note that towards the end of his life, Freud came to appreciate the strength of the infant's affectional tie to its mother, but did not offer an explanation about how this tie developed. In his last works, Freud (1940a[1938]) had grasped that the infant's attachment to his mother represented something much more powerful than need gratification. He described the infant–mother relationship as ". . . the first and strongest love-object and as the prototype of all later love relations – for both sexes" (p. 188).

A careful reading of Freud reveals a more nuanced conceptualisation of the infant than is commonly presented, which incorporated, to some extent, the influence of the environment and object relations, as we discovered in the previous section. Many of Freud's statements contain the kernels of some of the major post-Freudian schools of thought. In this passage below, Freud demonstrates awareness of the infant's need for care from its mother in order to attain an ideal state of being (however fleetingly).

> It will be rightly objected that an organisation which was a slave to the pleasure principle and neglected the reality of the external world

could not maintain itself alive for the shortest time, so that it could not have come into existence at all. The employment of a fiction like this is, however, justified when one considers that the infant – provided one includes with it the care it receives from its mother – does almost realise a psychical system of this kind. (Freud, 1911b, p. 219)

Again, in a later paper in which Freud discusses the origins of the fear of death, he likened this anxiety to ". . . the first great anxiety-state of birth and the infantile anxiety of longing – *the anxiety due to separation from the protecting mother*" (Freud, 1923b, p. 58, my italics). It was this original feeling of utter helplessness in infancy, during which the child was flooded with unimaginable psychic pain, that Freud proposed was re-triggered in later traumatic neuroses (Freud, 1926d). This notion of the primitive infantile catastrophe can be found in many subsequent authors: for example, Klein (1927, 1929; Klein, Heimann, Isaacs, & Riviere, 1952), Fairbairn (1944, 1946), and Winnicott (1974). Winnicott (1974) describes the "original experience of primitive agony" and the "unthinkable state of affairs that underlies the defensive organisation" (p. 40). Bion (1962) refers to this state as "nameless dread" (p. 96). Freud believed that this original trauma remains with us throughout life and is the basis of the compulsion to repeat. Stolorow (2008) has reinterpreted these concepts from a Heideggerian intersubjective/existentialist position that characterises this state as an existential dilemma. He argues that trauma is both contextually embedded and existential (an *a priori* given).

> On one hand, emotional experience is inseparable from the contexts of attunement and malattunement in which it is felt, and painful emotional experiences become enduringly traumatic in the absence of an intersubjective context within which they can be held and integrated. On the other hand, emotional trauma is built into the basic constitution of human existence. In virtue of our finitude and the finitude of our important connections with others, the possibility of emotional trauma constantly impends and is ever present. (p. 120)

According to Freud, the infant suffers another major trauma in addition to the original trauma described above—the (parental) prohibition of anal pleasure, which reappears in consciousness in the form of disgust and shame. Freud (1920g) argued that all neurotic unpleasure has its origins in repressed infantile experiences of (sexual) pleasure; that is, "all neurotic unpleasure is of that kind of pleasure that cannot be felt as such" (p. 11). According to Freud, this "organic" repression of infantile sexual pleasure is responsible for infantile amnesia, a process that cannot be undone. Freud attributes this process to the child's upbringing, beginning with toilet training, which "make[s] the excreta worthless, disgusting, abhorrent and abominable", thus reversing the positive value the infant initially ascribes to his anal products in order to "[pave] the way to civiliza-tion" (Freud, 1930a, p. 99). Freud believed that the superego com-menced its development on the back of parental prohibitions with respect to the infant's anal eroticism. During this process, the child learns that there is a disjunction between what is "good" and what is pleasurable, a lesson that must be learnt if one is to survive in society. This process of suppression of anal eroticism forms the basis of moral masochism, "a condition imposed on sexual excitation . . . which is recognized in classical psychoanalysis as a sense of guilt which is mostly unconscious" (Freud, 1924c, p. 161). Although anal eroticism received a lot of attention in Freud's writing before 1920, his subsequent work is more focused on aggression, masochism, and guilt, which were initially yoked to anal eroticism as its products, but which were subsequently dealt with independently. Taken together, these two early traumas of infancy create, according to Freud, an unbridgeable gap, a disjunction of consciousness between infancy and adulthood; thus, infantile amnesia, unpleasure, and, hence, neurosis are the central defining characteristics of human expe-rience.

It is puzzling that Freud asserts the important role that parental authority exerts on the child with respect to the suppression of his sexual pleasure, yet he had almost nothing to say about the influence of the overall quality of parenting or the parent–child dyad (see the discussion of little Hans above). None the less, he reported in some detail on the life and character of the parents of his patients and of the relationship between parent and child. These descriptions contain a subtext about parental influences on the development of psycho-pathology in children, which is rarely explicitly articulated. Below, for example, are two excerpts on patients' parents and family back-ground—Frau Emmy von N (1895d, pp. 48–105) and the "Wolf man" (1918b). We will begin with Emmy, where the focus is on family history, modelling of pathological behaviours, experience of trauma, and the heritability of psychopathology.

> [Frau Emmy von N] was one of fourteen children, of which she herself was the thirteenth. Only four of them survive. She was brought up carefully, but under strict discipline by an over-energetic and severe mother [p. 49] . . . She told me that her mother had herself been in an asylum for some time . . . She continued her list of terrifying memories. One, at fifteen, of how she found her mother, who had had a stroke, lying on the floor (her mother lived for another four years); again, at nineteen, how she came home one day and found her mother dead, with a distorted face [p. 55] . . . how she had been so ill after her mother's death and had gone to a health resort [p. 59] . . . Her elder daughter (i.e., Frau Emmy's sister) had already followed her mother in developing neck-cramps and mild hysterical states . . . Her mother, who had handed the girl over to the doctors with her usual mixture of docility and mistrust, was overcome by the most violent self-reproaches after the unfortunate outcome of the treatment [p. 77] . . . [Frau Emmy] exhibited unbridled ambitions which were out of all proportion to the poverty of her gifts, and she became disobedient and even violent towards her mother. I still enjoyed her mother's confidence and was sent for to give my opinion on the girl's condition . . . *In her mother's family . . . there was no lack of a neuropathic heredity . . .* (p. 83, my italics)

Below is Freud's report on the parents of the "Wolf man":

> His parents had been married young, and were still leading a happy married life, upon which their ill-health was soon to throw the first shadows. His mother began to suffer from abdominal disorders, and his father from his first attacks of depression, which led to his absence from home. Naturally the patient only came to understand his father's illness very much later on, but he was aware of his mother's weak health even in his early childhood. As a consequence of it she had relatively little to do with the children. One day, certainly before his fourth year, while his mother was seeing off the doctor to the station and he himself was walking beside her, holding her hand, he overheard her lamenting her condition. *Her words made a deep impression upon him, and later on he applied them to himself.* (Freud, 1918b, p. 13, my italics)

In the last statement, Freud is perhaps intimating identificatory, projective, and introjective processes that form such an important part of post-Freudian theorising, but Freud himself did not elaborate further on this notation.

Freud had a sophisticated understanding of unconscious memory and the way in which preverbal experiences occurring in infancy, particularly of a sexual nature, can form the basis for the development of serious psychopathology, a position that is commonly held today, although with a de-emphasis on the sexual aspect of preverbal experience (Green, Crenshaw, & Kolos, 2010). Freud argued that:

> . . . a precocious sexual experience . . . can become the source of a persistent psychical abnormality like hysteria . . . because the subject is in his infancy . . . the precocious sexual excitation produces little or no effect at the time; but its psychical trace is preserved. Later, . . . at puberty . . . this unconscious psychical trace is awakened . . . the memory will display a power which was completely lacking from the event itself. *The memory will operate as though it were a contemporary event* . . . [thus] the effect of a *memory* surpass[es] that of an actual event . . . *this inverse relation between the psychical effect of the memory and of the event* contains the reason for *the memory remaining unconscious* (p. 378) . . . And since infantile experiences with a sexual content could after all only exert a psychical effect through their *memory-traces*, would not this view be a welcome amplification of the finding of psycho-analysis which tells us that *hysterical symptoms can only arise with the co-operation of memories*? (Freud, 1896a, p. 153, my italics)

Freud's infant was, to a large extent, born of the psychoanalytic process with adult patients. His infant is, thus, a clinical phenomenon; hence the focus on conflictual processes that result in repression and which subsequently become the focus of (classical) analysis in adults. Freud was more concerned with abnormal development and the risk of developing psychopathology, that is, fixating at each stage of psychosexual development—the earlier the stage, the more serious the psychopathology. The infant, or, more properly, the infant's "id", was understood to be "the locus classicus of the savage, the tyrant, the religious fanatic, the addict, the fetishist, the polymorphous perverse lover, and the diehard warrior" (Dervin, 1988, p. 82). Freud believed that normality was revealed through a study of pathological variants, not from the study of normality *per se*. Later conceptualisations of infancy, for example, those of Winnicott (1971) and Bowlby (1973), held that normality was the baseline state which could be derailed by external trauma. They challenged the primacy of the trauma hypothesis and privileged normality as the primary state of the human organism.

Freud's Oedipal infant had to wait for other "parents" to acknowledge all its attributes—gender, cognitive capacity, psychosocial experiences (object relations), and social and historical embeddedness, and to recognise the fundamental importance of the mother, object relations, and attachment quality in determining the infant's developmental trajectory.

Critiquing Freud

There have been many more volumes written to critique Freud than all of his large output many times over, from a range of perspectives—psychoanalytic, psychological, philosophical, cultural, literary, postmodern, feminist, and scientific. This field of criticism is vast and beyond the scope of this book. In this short space, I must content myself with a summary of some of the key factors that have troubled subsequent scholarship about Freud's body of work. Mitchell (2004) summarises the underlying theoretical positions in which early psychoanalytic theory was steeped and contrasts these with current thinking.

> The great nature-versus-nurture, biology-versus-culture dialectic shaped Freud's ways of understanding all fundamental psychoanalytic problems—the unconscious, sexuality, aggression, fantasy, conflict . . . For us, these polarities have been deconstructed, rethought in more complex terms. We have come to appreciate the ways in which nature and nurture, as well as biology and culture, continually interpenetrate and mutually shape each other, so that traditional psychoanalytic problems are increasingly reframed in terms of conflictual mental states and organisations, projective–introjective cycles of intrapsychic and interpersonal processes, and conflictual attachments and identifications with different . . . external and internal objects (pp. 538–539).

The remainder of this section will necessarily focus on Freud's conceptualisation of infancy and his methods of data collection. First, we will briefly consider Freud's developmental theory—his concept of infancy, psychosexual stages of development, and the Oedipus complex. We will conclude with a discussion of Freud's research methods and a summary of his enduring contributions.

Freud's developmental theory

Freud has often been criticised for focusing primarily on the intraspsychic aspects of infant development, and neglecting the importance of the dyadic relationship between infant and mother, and social experiences generally. Freud's affect–trauma model appears more consistent in some respects with current psychoanalytic theorising than his later theorising, which gave primacy to the instincts and the "structures of the mind" that tended to encumber, rather than clarify, our understanding of the infant's developing sense of self (Stern, 1985).

In his first paper, reporting on his first patients, Freud (with Breuer, 1895d) realised that a historical reconstruction of the first appearance of the symptom was necessary to effect its remission. He speaks of "provoking causes", implying recognition of some form of environmental impingement in the development of psychopathology, although the task of elucidating these provoking causes, and incorporating them into theory and therapeutic methods, was inherited by Freud's successors.

> . . . *external events determine the pathology of hysteria to an extent far greater than is known and recognized* . . . The disproportion between the many years' duration of the hysterical symptom and the single occurrence which provoked it is what we are accustomed invariably to find in traumatic neuroses. Quite frequently it is some event in childhood that sets up a more or less severe symptom which persists during the years that follow [p. 4] . . . In the case of common hysteria it not infrequently happens that, instead of a single, major trauma, we find a number of partial traumas forming a *group* of provoking causes (p. 6).

This passage also shows an early understanding of later notions of large "T" trauma and cumulative small "t" trauma (see, for example, Wallin, 2007), concepts in the attachment and self psychology literatures that highlight the central importance of failures in parental empathy (Brandchaft, 2007; Burlingham, 1967) and parental misattunement (Beebe, 2000) in the aetiology of psychological disorders. Freud (with Breuer, 1895d) also discovered early that "[t]he psychical process which originally took place must be repeated as vividly as possible; it must be brought back to its *status nascendi* and then given verbal utterance" (p. 6).

It was only a small step from understanding that symptoms must be traced back to their origins (*status nascendi*) and the realisation that adult psychopathology arises 'in a developmental process occurring during infancy and childhood.

> At first sight it seems extraordinary that events experienced so long ago should continue to operate so intensely – that their recollection should not be liable to the wearing away process to which, after all, we see all our memories succumb. (p. 8)

There is consensus in the current psychoanalytic literature regarding these views (Beebe, Knoblauch, et al., 2005; Blomfield, 1987; Bond, 2010; Bornstein, 2005). In these respects, Freud was ahead of his time; close reading of his work frequently uncovers the kernel of many such significant theoretical developments that have subsequently received empirical support and been incorporated into therapeutic modalities.

However, there are five major concerns with Freud's developmental theory: it is (i) adultomorphic; (ii) retrospective; (iii) clinically derived; (iv) pathomorphic; and (v) stage-based. Freud's psychoanalytic infant is a retrospective co-construction of analysts and (mostly adult) patients via enactments and interpretations comprising life stories, memories, and theory driven hypothesising by the analyst that undergoes many iterations and "narrative smoothing" (Spence, 1986, p. 62) in order to enhance its consistency and coherence. The psychoanalytic infant is assumed to be a in a state of trauma from birth, and, hence, embodies suffering humanity from its first breath. From this shaky beginning, the infant must negotiate the perils of each of the psychosexual stages of development, and resolve the Oedipus complex before it can strive for healthy genital sexuality. Current thinking about development takes a lifespan perspective, which states that humans can develop and change throughout life and are not completely captive to their early life experiences, as suggested by Freud's notion of fixation at particular psychosexual stages of development. Issues related to trust, autonomy, maturity, and the capacity for intimacy are now understood to be recursive and responsive to environmental challenges; they are no longer viewed as immutable if errors occur at age-specific periods of development (Carr & O'Reilly, 2007; Khaleque, 2003). None the less, early life remains critical, and while some improvements in the consequences of faulty early development can be made with psychotherapy and favourable environmental experiences, there are still some doubts about whether the early traumas can be completely overcome. See, for example, Fairbairn's assessment:

> The basic pattern of personality once fixed in early childhood can't be altered. Emotion can be drained out of the old patterns by new experience, but water can always flow again in the old dried up water courses. (In Guntrip, 1975, p. 145)

Stern (1985) argued that many of the fears and conflicts that Freud ascribed to early infancy were misapplied to this period of development because the infant is only capable of experiencing a (subjective) reality that is undistorted by defences, simply because the mental apparatus of the infant is insufficiently developed to be able to construct defensive operations. Similarly, infants cannot have wish-fulfilling, defensive, or hostile fantasies because the capacity for symbolisation does not appear until the second half of the second year of life. Psychoanalytic concepts might, therefore, be more properly applied to a later, post-infancy stage, when language and the capacity for mental representation develop. This argument necessarily implies a very different conception of infancy to that proposed by classical Freudian psychoanalytic theory. These criticisms also apply to the many variants of classical psychoanalytic theory of infancy, beginning with Freud and Melanie Klein, as we shall see in Chapter Three.

Freud's, and, indeed, the prevailing view of attachment in the early twentieth century as an instinct secondary to the instinct for survival cannot be sustained. Harlow (1958) challenged this view:

> The position commonly held by psychologists and sociologists is quite clear: The basic motives are . . . the primary drives—particularly hunger, thirst, elimination, pain, and sex—and all other motives, including love or affection, are derived or secondary drives. The mother is associated with the reduction of the primary drives—particularly hunger, thirst, and pain—and through learning, affection or love is derived . . . this is an inadequate mechanism to account for the persistence of the infant maternal ties . . . almost any external stimulus can become a secondary reinforcer if properly associated with tissue-

need reduction, but the fact remains that . . . such derived drives suffer relatively rapid experimental extinction. Contrariwise, human affection does not extinguish when the mother ceases to have intimate association with the drives in question. Instead, the affectional ties to the mother show a lifelong, unrelenting persistence and, even more surprising, widely expanding generality. (p. 460)

Evidence from animal studies has demonstrated the existence of attachment in primates, and in animals that are physically dependent on their mothers for a much shorter period of time than human infants (Harlow, 1958). Most studies (Harlow & Zimmerman, 1959, 1996) confirmed the primary importance of contact comfort or clinging over feeding as the source of bonding and attachment in both animals and humans, arguing that the principal function of nursing is to ensure frequent, close body contact between infant and mother (Baysinger, Plubell, & Harlow, 1973; Harlow, 1978; Harlow & Zimmermann, 1996; Ruppenthal, Arling, Harlow, Sackett, & Suomi, 1976). Further, children who have endured maternal physical or emotional abuse or neglect still show strong attachment to their mothers (A. Freud, 1951). Bowlby (1958) proposed that attachment to the mother was the expression and integration of the five instinctual drives with which an infant is born—sucking, clinging, following, crying, and smiling (see Chapter Four). The major points of departure with Freud are twofold: the first is that Freud viewed these five instincts as auto-erotic and did not appreciate until close to the end of his life the strength or importance of the infant's "tie to the mother"; second, Freud viewed the people who feed, care for, and protect the infant as the first sexual objects (Freud, 1905d). By describing psychosexual stages and points of fixation, with which specific psychopathologies are associated, Freud reduced psychological problems to the sexual motivational system. Subsequent scholarship (e.g., Fairbairn, Winnicott, and Bowlby) removed the sexual system from the attachment system, giving primacy to the infant's emotional tie to his/her mother. Today, few would disagree that the sexual was excessively privileged in Freud's theory (Bonomi, 1997; Lichtenstein, 1970). Further, there has been no empirical confirmation that fixations at certain points of development in Freud's psychosexual stage theory predict particular forms of psychopathology.

Stolorow and Atwood (1978) have mounted an intriguing argument that Freud's theorising is, in fact, a product of his own early experiences, and that these generally unconscious influences constrain the generalisability of his theorising.

> ... the structure of the theorist's subjective experiential world is inevitably imported into his metapsychological conceptions and hypotheses regarding human nature, limiting their generality and lending them a coloration expressive of his personal existence as an individual. By systematically interpreting ... various theories as psychological products, embedded in the theorist's life history and personal phenomenology, we hope to deepen our understanding of these limiting subjective factors and lay the foundation for the construction of a more general and inclusive theoretical system. (p. 217)

They subsequently embarked on a detailed analysis of the life and work of Sigmund Freud with the aim of identifying the experiences in Freud's life that were (defensively) absent from his self-analysis and that might have influenced his theory of psychosexual development, which arose in the absence of strong corroborating evidence from his clinical observations and practice. In brief, Stolorow and Atwood (1978) argued that much of Freud's psychology was directed towards defensively preserving his idealised image of his mother and protecting this image from his intense, unconscious rage at his mother's betrayal of him by her repeated production of additional children. Freud split off, repressed, and displaced his omnipotently destructive rage and disappointment in his mother, in order that he would not experience these emotions towards her and thereby risk losing her. In this formulation of the Oedipus complex, these hostile feelings were displaced on to the father. Freud repeated this dynamic with his wife, Martha, and his idealised mentor, Wilhelm Fleiss. In his psychosexual stage theory, Freud transposes the source of badness from his object representation (idealised mother) into the child, who internalises the blame in order to absolve the mother. The "enemy" thus becomes the child's own aggressive and sexual instincts. The good and bad parts of the mother are defensively kept separate, as were Freud's idealising and hostile impulses towards his love object. Freud was later to conclude that "Aggressiveness ... forms the basis of every relation of affection and love among people ..." (Freud, 1930a, p. 113).

Freud's theory says little about the role of mothering in overall development, focusing instead on the mother as the infant's first sexual object. He also said little about the normally developing infant or the physical, cognitive, or social/cultural aspects of development, or how these developmental processes are mutually influential. Flickers of these aspects were all present in the early case histories: see, for example, the descriptions of Anna O and Frau Emmy Von N, who were understood to be, to some extent, psychological products of a social and cultural era in which intelligent women were repressed and unfulfilled. A consideration of gender differences were also nascent in these cases studies, but the overt recognition of gender as a significant developmental factor received scant attention until Horney's (1924) paper, "On the genesis of the castration complex in women", sparked a major controversy in psychoanalytic thinking about the feminine (Bornstein et al., 2008; Fliegel, 1973). Freud (1925j) responded in the following year with his own paper, "Some psychological consequences of the anatomical distinction between the sexes", in which he confesses his "bafflement" with the nature of Oedipal development in girls. This "bafflement" has been the subject of a raging debate that is unabated to the present, and which was heightened by the advent of feminism (see, for example, Rohde-Dachser, 1992; Rosen & Zickler, 1996; Sayers, 1989).

Freud's data collection methods and sources of evidence

The psychoanalytic theories formulated by Freud and his followers, and indeed by the majority of subsequent psychoanalytic writers, were, to a great extent, derived by inference from the reconstruction of the early lives of analysands during psychoanalysis (Aleksandrowicz, 2010), a method called the clinical case study. This method is a highly attractive, yet somewhat dangerous and seductive endeavour, which is vulnerable to a range of methodological errors that necessarily render the conclusions drawn from such methods untestable and, therefore, unfalsifiable. Freud also gathered data from his self-analysis—through a process of introspection and reflection, a process that also suffers insurmountable methodological dilemmas.

Let us examine an illustrative case. Ilona Weiss, to whom Freud assigned the pseudonym Elisabeth von R, in *Studies on Hysteria* (1895d, pp. 135–181) was described by Freud as his first full-length analysis. Freud had been summoned to see her because of inexplicable pains in her legs that prevented her from walking. These pains arose during the time in which she was nursing her much-loved father, who was dying from heart disease. Two years after his death, the pains had become so bad that she was unable to walk and virtually retreated into invalidism. During this time, both of her older sisters married, the second sister to a man much admired by Ilona. This sister died during her second pregnancy, also from heart disease. Ilona had been unable to reach her sister to offer comfort and care prior to her death. It was during this time that Freud was approached for a consultation. Freud became convinced that this young woman's condition was closely associated with a number of "erotic ideas" that he uncovered during free association, the first entailing attendance at a ball from which a young man escorted her home, whereupon her euphoria was interrupted by the realisation of her father's worsening state of health. The second related to her erotic feelings towards her dead sister's husband; Ilona confessed to the momentary thought that since her sister was now dead, her husband was free to remarry (her). So horrified was this young aristocratic woman at these thoughts that she had suppressed (repressed) them and attached the affect belonging to these thoughts to intensifying her physical pain. Freud then became actively involved with Ilona's family, attempting to negotiate a situation whereby she and her brother-in-law could marry. At this point, Freud terminated the analysis. However, his suggestion regarding the marriage was met with strong opposition by Ilona's mother and Ilona's pains returned. Several months later, Freud learnt that Ilona had recovered sufficiently to attend and dance at balls and in fact had entered into a happy marriage with a man of her own choosing. In a conversation with her daughter many years later, Ilona described Freud as "just a young, bearded nerve specialist that they sent me to" who tried to "persuade me that I was in love with my brother-in-law, but that wasn't really so." Such are the quandaries arising from case histories. Who is to be believed—the analyst who had painstakingly uncovered what he believed to be the dynamic basis for this young woman's psychosomatic symptoms, but who, *a priori*, believed that they were associated with repressed erotic material, or the analysand herself, who might well have been motivated to "gild the lily" for both herself and her daughter in retelling these painful events from her past (Appignanesi & Forrester, 1993)?

Today, we can readily recognise many flaws in Freud's methods. His data are generally based on the retrospective self-reports of a highly selected and biased sample, mostly Viennese women, in a situation where clinician influence on their retrospection would have been profound. One of the primary sources of data in this method is the psychoanalytic interpretation. The question regarding how interpretations might be verified as correct has arisen in much post-Freudian scholarship (Frosh, 2003). Grünbaum (1982a,b) has offered a thoughtful critique on the subject. He argues that both analyst and patient interchanges are contaminated and unverifiable—contaminated because the material emerges within the context of a highly charged transference relationship and unverifiable because no data that could corroborate or disconfirm psychoanalytic productions are admitted into the analytic setting. Thus, he argues, it is not possible to discern what is genuinely "within" the patient and what is co-constructed between the analytic dyad in the analytic process. Others argue that objective truth claims are not relevant to the psychoanalytic process: what is important is the analytic relationship and the patient's response to interpretation—it is a "successful" interpretation if it deepens the relationship or produces new material that can be worked with to achieve greater self-understanding (Kernberg, 1994). More recently, some analysts prefer to use the word "intervention" rather than "interpretation", because the former term does not carry the presumption that the analyst is the one who knows, but, rather, one who participates in the analytic dialogue (Menninger & Holtzman, 1973), thereby entrusting the interpretation to the patient.

The critical truth in psychoanalysis is narrative truth, a process akin to meaning-making in close readings of literary texts, which leads the patient to a "form of linguistically mediated self-knowledge which gives him or her more control over experience" (Frosh, 2003, p. 81). Of course, a process of induction into a particular "narrative" truth is part of this enterprise. Different narratives will emanate from different theories, as we saw in the different theoretical readings of the case of little Hans. Patients might just as well be inducted into a cultural or religious narrative as a psychoanalytic narrative, if such systems are ego syntonic, in order to achieve a similar outcome—self-acceptance, self-knowledge, belonging, authenticity. Freud, who had no time for religion, observed that for a large number of people, the Virgin Mary had more persuasive power than a belief in the unconscious! Khan (1981) argues that psychotherapy has, to a large extent, replaced religion because of cultural shifts in the societal role of religion:

It is my inference from what I know of the history of religions, especially the three monotheistic ones that it is precisely this need in the
human individual for his or her psychic pain to be witnessed silently
and unobtrusively by the other that led to the creation of the omni-
presence of God in human lives. Over the past two centuries and
more, with the increasing disappearance of God as the witnessing
other from man's privacy with himself, the experience of psychic pain
has changed from tolerated and accepted suffering to its pathological
substitutes, and the need has rapidly increased for psycho-therapeutic
interventions to alleviate these pathological masochistic states. (p. 414)

Some of Freud's (and Breuer's) cases were recorded months or
years after the therapy had ended. Many were selectively reported,
omitting material that was problematic or difficult to explain, inconsistent with theory, or that pointed to a less than successful outcome.
Freud himself recognised that his case studies often read more like
novels than scientific expositions and, while the material is
compelling, the use of literary language such as metaphors sometimes
obfuscated rather than illuminated his underlying theory. It is
inevitable that over the course of a very long and productive intellectual life, one's ideas will change and evolve, and Freud was no exception in this regard. As a result, some of his terminology became
ambiguous, because he did not always make explicit how a particular
word or concept had developed in his thinking. One example discussed earlier is his use of the word "affect". The term "fixation" is
also problematic. In its original incarnation, the term referred to an
idée fixe, or pathological idea, to which the patient was strongly
attached; it reappeared as the term "fixation" to denote a developmental arrest at one of the psychosexual stages, following which its
use broadened to include a persistent or obsessive attachment to parts
of the self or its objects (Alpert, 1959), as a process in primal repression (Kris, 1987), and then as a fixation to the neurotic illness itself
(now defined as "secondary gain") (Katz, 1963).

We shall now return to the case of little Hans and the Oedipus
complex to show how problematic data collection can result in faulty
theorising. As we discovered in our analysis of this case, Freud "mas-
saged" the data to confirm his strongly held theories, in this case, the
Oedipus complex. The theory of the Oedipus complex is problematic for the reasons outlined by Stolorow and Atwood (1978). The
idea came to Freud as part of his self-analysis. He made the error of

generalising this "gripping" episode of imaginative introspection to a "universal event". Bergmann (2010) rightly points out that if everyone recognises in himself "a budding Oedipus", as Freud claimed, why had no one prior to Freud identified the phenomenon in the intervening 2,300 years since the play was written? One wonders the direction that psychoanalysis might have taken had Freud not read and been fascinated by Sophocles' play. Many other writers have criticised the Oedipus complex, describing it as "extreme, ethnocentric, patriarchal, misogynist, and a misreading of the original myth" (Frosh, 2003, p. 62), which highlights the father's fear of his son usurping him and not, as in Freud's interpretation, the son's fear of castration by his father. Why then, given its tenuous origins, does the Oedipus myth retain such a strong cultural resonance? Current interpretations are varied. Lachmann (2010) offers an attachment-based explanation, that "the long dependency and relative helplessness of the human infant promotes an intense attachment and longing for the mother, as well as constant desire for her love and closeness, which can threaten the separation process" (p. 557). Others offer a sociological explanation—the Oedipus allegory is concerned with the taming and socially appropriate channelling of excessive desire:

> it is the painful rite of passage of a wild desire into a socialized desire and the acceptance—which is just as painful—that our desires can never be completely satisfied . . . [the Oedipal] crisis is a devastating allegory of combat between impetuous forces of individual desire and the forces of the civilization that opposes them. (Nasio, Pettigrew, & Raffoul, 2010, p. 130)

Still others argue that the study of sexuality has taken too great a precedence over the study of love, both within and outside the therapeutic relationship (Lobb, 2009). The following is a neat summing up of the current debate over the Oedipus complex:

> Sigmund Freud's King Oedipus is still alive and well . . . He has undergone multiple transmogrifications . . . He has been analogized, metaphorized, and split into bits of conscience, guilt, fear, omnipotence, power, powerlessness, fate, helplessness, dominance, submission, archaic chaos, and rage. Our gradual attempts of incorporation and integration into the psychoanalytic field of the varying theoretical pluralities that have developed over the last century have been

accountable for the changing faces of Oedipus. *Most reformulations have vigorously deemphasized the defining raw biological male sexuality that was so important to the Freudian drive/conflict theory.* (Balsam, 2010, p. 511, my italics)

There are others (e.g., Widlocher, 2001) who "wonder whether the story of the Oedipus complex is . . . to be seen as a myth and not a social structure, more a model than the object of a refutable theory" (p. 1). The weight of current opinion is that the Oedipus complex as framed by Freud as the "universal unconscious fantasy" can no longer be sustained (Lachmann, 2010).

Freud's legacy

Freud's psychoanalytic developmental theory formed the basis of all subsequent developmental theories. This is a boundless legacy. However, it was a first pass at a very complex enterprise and subsequent iterations and the advent of neuroscience have resulted in major new advances in the field in the seventy years since Freud's death. We will discuss these in the coming chapters.

Some of Freud's eminent contemporaries recognised the enormity of Freud's contribution. G. Stanley Hall, President of the American Psychological Association, gave this assessment of Freud's contribution to knowledge in the Preface to Freud's (1920) *General Introduction to Psychoanalysis*:

Few, especially in this country, realise that while Freudian themes have rarely found a place on the programs of the American Psychological Association, they have attracted great and growing attention and found frequent elaboration by students of literature, history, biography, sociology, morals and aesthetics, anthropology, education, and religion. They have given the world a new conception of both infancy and adolescence, and shed much new light upon characterology; given us a new and clearer view of sleep, dreams, reveries, and revealed hitherto unknown mental mechanisms common to normal and pathological states and processes, showing that the law of causation extends to the most incoherent acts and even . . . insanity; gone far to clear up the terra incognita of hysteria; taught us to recognize morbid symptoms, often neurotic and psychotic in their germ;

revealed the operations of the primitive mind so overlaid and repressed that we had almost lost sight of them; fashioned and used the key of symbolism to unlock many mysticisms of the past; and in addition to all this, affected thousands of cures, established a new prophylaxis, and suggested new tests for character, disposition, and ability, in all combining the practical and theoretic to a degree salutary as it is rare. (Hall, 1920, pp. vi–vii)

Hall also offers an explanation as to why Freud and his theories received so little traction in America.

The impartial student of Sigmund Freud need not agree with all his conclusions, and indeed . . . may be unable to make sex so all-dominating a factor in the psychic life of the past and present as Freud deems it to be, to recognize the fact that he is the most original and creative mind in psychology of our generation. Despite the frightful handicap of the odium sexicum, far more formidable today than the odium theologicum, involving as it has done for him lack of academic recognition and even more or less social ostracism . . . (p. ix)

While it is easy to criticise the work of our predecessors, it is important to balance critique with a recognition of the profound and enduring contributions made by Freud's psychoanalytic theory that are not only still current, but that have received empirical confirmation from health, cognitive, and social psychology, and neuroscience (Debiec, Diaz-Mataix, Bush, Doyere, & Ledoux, 2010; LeDoux, 1998). A brief example will demonstrate this. One of the most enduring and pervasive contributions of psychoanalytic theory is the concept of the unconscious and the proposition that complex mental activity has a profound impact on our behaviour and psychological well-being that occurs outside our conscious awareness. Health researchers have often observed that self-report measures are unreliable in assessing psychological well-being or predicting health outcomes. Such measures are unable to differentiate those who are genuinely psychologically healthy from those who maintain "a facade or illusion of mental health based on denial and self-deception", and that "clinically derived assessment procedures that assess implicit psychological processes may have advantages over self-report mental health measures" (Cousineau & Shedler, 2006, p. 427). These researchers used the Early Memory Index (EMI), an implicit measure of mental health/distress and compared its capacity to predict health outcomes against a range of standard self-report measures that assessed mental health, perceived stress, life events, and mood. The EMI showed stronger associations with health service utilisation and illness onset than any of the more standard self-report measures. One of the key reasons that standard self-report measures are limited in this way is that the relevant psychological processes might be implicit, that is, they are not available to awareness and, thus, cannot be directly reported upon. A great many cognitive and affective processes, including memory, cognition, emotion, motivation, and attitudes such as racism and homophobia can be implicit (Wilson, Lindsey, & Schooler, 2000). We will return to the concept of implicit processes in the final chapter.

Another Freudian concept that has found its way into every modern theory of psychoanalysis and child development is the importance of the relationship between the mother and her infant (and between the analyst and the analysand that is mutative in therapy), which provides the basis for secure attachment in infancy and beyond, a subject to be discussed in detail in Chapter Four.

In the next chapter, we will explore how other creative minds made use of Freud's insights to progress or obfuscate our understanding of our (infant) selves: enter the child psychoanalysts.

Notes

1. The term "erogenous" has the equivalent meaning to "sexual" in Freud's theory of infant sexuality.
2. These essays cover a range of other issues including, for example, the infantile origins of the sexual perversions and the component instincts of the sexual drive.
3. These were introduced in the 1915 edition.
4. "Widdler" is the idiosyncratic word used in Hans' family to denote the penis.
5. "Nonsense" was the word used to describe Hans' fear of being bitten by a horse and of going out into the street.
6. Freud's personality flaws, including his compulsive need for fame and his Messianic thinking, are in Webster, R. (1995). *Why Freud Was Wrong: Sin, Science and Psychoanalysis*. New York: Basic Books.

CHAPTER THREE

The infant of the child
psychoanalysts

"The unconscious is not Viennese, even in children"

(Geissman & Geissman, 1998, p. 3)

As psychoanalysis evolved in both theory and practice, so, too,
did the understanding of the importance of early experiences
in shaping the adult personality. In this chapter we will investigate how this understanding became one of the principle underlying
tenets of psychoanalytic theory and practice. We will also explore the
evolution of child psychoanalysis, its key proponents, and their contributions to our understanding of infancy and subsequent human
development. Even more so than the history of adult psychoanalysis,
many competing schools of thought arose; one could almost call them
factions, such was the antipathy that erupted between the various
groups. Indeed, several social and cultural dimensions to the evolution of child psychoanalysis added to the heat of the many debates.
Among these were the issues of the place of women in society (many
child analysts were female) and the fact that, at the time of its early
development, those wishing to become psychoanalysts were required
to be medical practitioners. This was not the case for child psycho-

analysts, which might account for the fact that most of the early child analysts were women.

The beginnings of child psychoanalysis can be dated to two events: the publication, in 1905, of Freud's *Three Essays on the Theory of Sexuality*, which stimulated interest in the sexuality of young children among members of the Psychoanalytic Society of Vienna,[1] although there were lively discussions about infants and children among Freud's circle dating back to 1902, and the analysis of little Hans, the first child psychoanalytic patient,[2] in 1909 (Geissman & Geissman, 1998). As early as 1905, Freud had become convinced that "... the sexuality of neurotics has remained in, or been brought back to an infantile state. Thus our interest turns to the sexual life of children ..." (Freud, 1905d, p. 172).

Freud had undertaken an indirect observational study (via Hans' father) of Hans between the ages of three and five years, and this resulted in his 1907(c) paper, "The sexual enlightenment of children". We know from this account that Hans masturbated and that his mother had threatened to have a doctor cut off his penis if he did not desist. It was only after the appearance of Hans' fear of being bitten by a horse in the street did psychoanalytic observation become psychoanalytic treatment. Hans' father worked with his son daily over a period of five months, at which point the little boy was declared cured. Despite the fact that the case can be analysed from different perspectives, as discussed in Chapter Two, Freud used it as evidence of his theory of infant sexuality, in addition to its contribution to the understanding of phobias and the mental life of children in general. However, Freud stated that he had not really learnt anything new from the case of the Little Hans, such were the similarities between infantile and adult neuroses. In his later reflections on the history of psychoanalysis, he commented,

> ... my statements about infantile sexuality were founded ... on the findings of analysis in adults which led back into the past. I had no opportunity of direct observations on children. It was therefore a very great triumph when it became possible years later to confirm almost all my inferences by direct observation and the analysis of very young children ... (Freud, 1914d, p. 18)

While there developed a keen interest in the unconscious and psychoanalytical treatment in both Vienna and Zurich in the early

1900s, in a group that included Evgen Bleuler and Carl Jung, differences of opinion emerged between Freud and the Swiss group with respect to Freud's theory of infantile sexuality. These included the classification of childhood hysteria and traumatic neuroses as separate conditions, the argument that child hysteria and adult hysteria were different conditions requiring different formulations, and the contention that children under eight years of age could not be analysed because they were not thought to be capable of maintaining a train of thought so necessary in psychoanalysis. Jung was more interested in child analysis than Freud, and trained a number of women to undertake child analysis cases that he later presented at conferences. He believed that women's "natural psychological intuition" was better suited to the task of child analysis. As early as 1911, Jung was venturing into the territory of the collective unconscious. In a letter to Freud, Jung stated that he had been

> . . . forced to conclude that the so-called 'early memories of childhood' are not individual memories at all, but phylogenetic ones. I mean the very early memories like birth . . . I think that we shall find that infinitely more things than we now suppose are phylogenetic memories. (In Geissman & Geissman, 1998, p. 31)

After a long period of lively correspondence that revealed the growing schisms in their theorising, Freud and Jung ended their friendship and communication in 1913.

Although considered unacceptable today, many of the early psychoanalysts, including Freud, Carl Jung, Karl Abraham, and Melanie Klein observed and analysed their own children. Freud had also encouraged the father of Little Hans to undertake the psychoanalysis of his son. This practice was placed under the microscope, when, in 1924, Hermine von Hug-Hellmuth, a psychoanalyst and Freud devotee who, ironically, disagreed with the practice of analysing one's own children, was murdered by her nephew. She had not treated her eighteen-year-old nephew, Rolf, who was a very troubled young man, no doubt because of the unreliability of his care-givers after the death of his mother from tuberculosis when he was nine years old. He had, however, received some psychoanalytic treatment to address his "delinquent" nature. The case received a great deal of coverage in the press, which gave the opponents of psychoanalysis an opportunity to expose its shortcomings. William Stern, a vocal critic, argued that the manifestations of sexual behaviour in the patients of psychoanalysts were indicative of a psychological disorder and did not form part of the normal development of children (Stern & Barwell, 1924). Indeed, many of the points of disagreement of Freud's dissenters related to the proper place of sexuality in the lives of children. For example, Alfred Adler argued that social, not sexual factors were formative in the life of a child. He advocated the establishment of educational institutions for deprived children as a way of giving them compensatory experiences that might deter them from a life of crime (Adler, 1925, 1929).

Considerable debate arose in the period up to the First World War as to what the most helpful approach to childhood neuroses might be. Several possibilities were canvassed, including psychoanalytic treatment, psychoanalytic education, or sex education in the schools as possible means to prevent childhood neuroses (Pfister, 1913). Freud was of the opinion that sex education should be left to the schools. Abraham argued that trauma could not be prevented by education and that the critical element in a healthy infancy and childhood was a mother's love (Geissman & Geissman, 1998). The question of the role of psychological/psychoanalytic/sex education pervades the history of psychoanalysis, and became a frequent point of discussion and debate with respect to the role of the child analyst and of education in child psychoanalysis. It was argued that child analysts should serve not only as therapists, but also as models and teachers (von Hug-Hellmuth, 1920, 1921), a point also made by Anna Freud in relation to adult psychoanalysis (A. Freud, 1936b).

Freud (1918b) remained ambivalent about the psychoanalysis of children:

> An analysis which is conducted upon a neurotic child itself must, as a matter of course, appear to be more trustworthy, but it cannot be very rich in material; too many words and thoughts have to be lent to the child, and even so the deepest strata may turn out to be impenetrable to consciousness. An analysis of a childhood disorder through the medium of recollection in an intellectually mature adult is free from these limitations; but it necessitates our taking into account the distortion and refurbishing to which a person's own past is subjected when it is looked back upon from a later period. The first alternative perhaps gives the more convincing results; the second is by far the more instructive. (p. 8)

Two of the most influential early theorists with respect to the development of infant and child psychology were Anna Freud and Melanie Klein, so we will examine their respective theories and contributions in some detail in the next section.

Anna Freud

In the period from 1920 to 1945, Anna Freud in Vienna and Melanie Klein in Berlin established their respective "schools" of child psychoanalysis. Anna Freud remained concerned throughout her life about the practice of psychoanalysis with children; not so Melanie Klein. These two women thus became the focus of polarised schools of thought which culminated in a major confrontation in London in 1938, but more of this later.

Although Anna Freud and Melanie Klein are generally credited with the development of child psychoanalysis, it was Hermine von Hug-Hellmuth who laid the groundwork for its practice. Many of the techniques that are now central to child analysis, including the role of play as symbolic action, the tasks of the child therapist, and the concept of the therapeutic alliance, later elaborated by Anna Freud, are all explicated in von Hug-Hellmuth's (1921) paper, "On the technique of child analysis". Importantly, von Hug-Hellmuth presages the notion that the therapy needs to provide what was later called a secure base (Bowlby, 1958) and a safe container (Bion, 1959, 1963; Ogden, 2007) for the child. She stated "Intuition and patience are the foundations which must be laid right from the first contact with the young patient, so that trust is housed between solid foundations and a solid roof" (von Hug-Hellmuth, 1921, p. 287).

Anna Freud is an interesting figure in the history of psychoanalysis, and of child analysis in particular. She was the youngest of Freud's six children and one of three daughters. By all accounts, she had a somewhat unhappy childhood. As the youngest, she experienced exclusion from, and rivalry with, her older siblings; she had a particularly conflicted relationship with her sister, Sophie, that some argue might have influenced her later rivalry with Melanie Klein (Geissmann & Geissmann, 1998). Freud was a conservative father who viewed marriage, not higher education, as the proper role for women, so the young Anna was not particularly encouraged in her education and was not permitted to go to university despite her formidable intellect. She could speak several languages and had such a mastery of English she was able to translate some of her father's works from the original German. She never married, possibly owing to her father's possessiveness, his disapproval of her suitors, and his reliance on his youngest daughter as he aged.

Anna's lifelong interest in psychoanalysis as an educational tool originated from her training and experience as a primary school teacher. She taught for five years before ill health (tuberculosis) forced her resignation from her teaching position. She commenced her analysis with her father around this time (1918–1922) and became a member of the Vienna Psychoanalytic Society in 1922, at the age of twenty-seven. Anna became a lifelong advocate for child psychoanalysis and lay analysis and lobbied the International Psychoanalytic Association for recognition of lay analysts (i.e., analysts without a medical degree), which did not eventuate until 1970.

Anna Freud's work

Anna Freud made a unique contribution to psychoanalytic theory with her focus on normality and to child psychoanalysis with her emphasis on prevention. In much of her writing, she emphasised the dual role of the child analyst as both analyst and educator, stating that the second role was necessary because of the child's undeveloped superego (A. Freud, 1929). She wanted to train parents and teachers in the analytic method in order to prevent their detrimental influences on children's development. Anna believed that by enlightening parents and teachers with a psychoanalytic education, thereby changing child rearing practices and attitudes, many adult mental disorders could be prevented (A. Freud, 1968). Anna was disappointed in this aim, and discussed in her later work that psychoanalytic education had not become the preventive tool that she had hoped and that prevention of neurosis was probably not possible by this means. None the less, Anna Freud retained the view that parenting and education exerted profound influences on children throughout life (A. Freud, 1965), a view that would meet with universal agreement today (Lorber & Egeland, 2009; Masur, 2009; Model, 1994).

In *The Ego and Mechanisms of Defence*[3] (A. Freud, 1936a), Anna Freud explored the ways in which the ego adapted to the demands and pressures both from within and from the outside world, and the way in which ego defences supported that adaptation. She identified three circumstances under which ego defences operate: anxiety related to the superego, anxiety related to the outside world, and anxiety related to the strength of the instincts. Further, Anna Freud identified and named the defence, "identification with the aggressor":

> By impersonating the aggressor, assuming his attributes or imitating his aggression, the child transforms himself from the person threatened to the person making the threat . . . In identifying "identification with the aggressor" we see a by no means uncommon stage in normal development of the superego . . . the moment of criticism is internalized, the offence is externalized. [T]his . . . mechanism . . . is supplemented by another defensive measure, namely, projection of guilt. (p. 128)

This defence has elements in common with Klein's concept of projective identification. The concepts differ in that identification with the aggressor is a defence used to cope with feelings of fear and helplessness, while projective identification encompasses the whole range of emotions, both positive and negative. Anna Freud (Sandler & A. Freud, 1983) emphasised the importance of understanding this defence in analysis.

> The analysis of identification with the aggressor enables us to distinguish in the transference anxiety-attacks from outbursts of aggression. The analysis of the aggression based on the identification with what is supposed to be the analyst's criticism can only reduce the aggression when the fear of punishment and of the superego has been reduced. Abreaction of the aggression will have no effect on it. (p. 250)

Anna Freud also introduced the concept of secondary aggression, which she defined as aggression that arises from intense frustration from the environment, as opposed to the aggression arising from instinctual pressures, which Hartmann later incorporated into his own theory of aggression. In her paper, "The infantile neurosis: genetic and dynamic considerations", Anna Freud argued that psychoanalysis was, first and foremost, addressed to the formation of adult disturbance and the infantile neuroses only became relevant when it was realised that childhood experiences were the forerunners to adult neuroses: ". . . there is no adult neurosis, whether conversion hysteria, phobia, or obsessional neurosis, which does not have a neurosis in infantile life as its forerunner" (A. Freud, 1971, p. 80).

Citing the cases of Little Hans (Freud, 1909b) and the Wolf man (Freud, 1918b), Anna Freud noted that

> . . . both the adult and infantile disorder shared the same motivation by conflict, the same construction, the employment of the same mechanisms, and that their symptoms represented identical attempts at conflict solution, inadequate as the latter may be if viewed from the aspect of reality adaptation . . . what I am describing here . . . is the well known formula which covers the formation of neurosis in general: conflict, followed by regression; regressive aims arousing anxiety; anxiety warded off by means of defense; conflict solution via compromise; symptom formation. (A. Freud, 1971, p. 80)

Anna Freud argued that infantile neurosis was much more common and more "normal" in infancy than adult neuroses were in adulthood, and that many infantile neuroses spontaneously remitted once the relative calm of the latency period had been reached. According to her, it depended on the experiences of adult life as to whether childhood conflicts would be reactivated and whether such reactivation would trigger a new neurosis.

Anna Freud speculated that the origins of early difficulties with physical functions like breathing, feeding, elimination, sleeping, and skin sensitivity, for which no organic cause could be found, conditions we would today call psychosomatic, arose as a result of tension between

> inborn modes of functioning and the mother's handling of these potentialities, . . . by a kind of emotional infection emanating from her, i.e., from the infant's response to her moods, her anxieties, her preferences, and her avoidances. (A. Freud, 1971, p. 83)

Anna is here referring to the concepts of maternal (mis)attunement (Rayner, 1991) and impingement (Beebe, 2000; Winnicott, 1986a), concepts that would later take centre stage in the developmental psychology literature. She argued that physical sensations in the infant and very young child were experienced affectively and that affective states could be experienced in the body, a situation she felt was normal for infants, but which became pathological ". . . after new pathways for discharge via thought, speech and action have been opened up" (A. Freud, 1971, p. 83). She further argued that these experiences of pleasure–unpleasure, pain, and frustration formed the bedrock of the developing personality. Many current psychoanalytic writers would concur that during infancy, emotional experience is embodied and that "a developed emotional experience consists of a somatic–symbolic integration" (Stolorow, 2005, p. 101). Satisfaction of these bodily needs and ease of bodily tensions make object attachments possible, and these, in turn, form the basis of later object relationships: ". . . a mother's failure to comfort her infant adequately may have lasting results for the individual's later general ability or inability to cope with even normal amounts of unpleasure, pain or anxiety" (A. Freud, 1971, p. 83).

Anna Freud understood the mother–infant relationship to be mutually and reciprocally influential in shaping the child's later personality functioning and his/her attitudes towards the world.

> It is an old psychoanalytic assumption that the experience of being well loved in infancy creates for all later life a feeling of security and self-confidence [now called] basic trust, self-regard and self-esteem . . . these characteristics will be decisive against . . . depression and phobic mechanisms . . . The constancy and strength of early object ties . . . facilitates internalizations and identifications, and these in turn enrich the personality on the one hand and prepare the ground for conflict between the inner agencies, i.e., for neurosis, on the other hand. (A. Freud, 1971, p. 84)

This included the recognition of the importance of a secure attachment to the psychosocial development of infants and children.

> Children are known to thrive in socially and financially unstable situations if they are firmly attached to their parents, and to come to grief under the best social conditions when such emotional security is missing. (A. Freud, 1972, p. 253)

Recent research on attachment (Baker, 2001; Beebe et al., 2010; Blatt, 2008; Diamond, 2004) and the nature and impact of the mother–infant relationship is consistent with this view (Beebe, Rustin, Sorter, & Knoblauch, 2003; Lachmann & Beebe, 1992; Seligman, 2008;

Winnicott, 1960). Equally, Anna Freud (1969) understood the dire consequences that maternal separation could have for the developing child. Below is her comment on the James (a social worker in Anna Freud's nurseries) and Joyce Robertson (1948) film: *John, aged 17 months: Nine Days in a Residential Nursery*:

> The nine days are emphasized with justification. We can never be reminded sufficiently that such a period of time, short by adult standards, may be long enough for a child under two to shatter his existing personality, to disrupt the ongoing course of development, and to do long lasting harm to his normality . . . in the prevailing standards of knowledge it tends to be overlooked that even toddlers, and quite especially *toddlers, do not live by bread alone. Their needs for nourishment, cleanliness, comfort, and security are inextricably bound up with the feelings that tie them to their mothers, who carry out the function of ministering simultaneously to both sides of their natures, the material as well as the libidinal requirements.* Only while this happens will the child be sufficiently at peace for internal growth and for increasing interest in and adaptation to the external world. (p. 139, my italics)

It is interesting that this comment seems to put to rest the notion of attachment as a secondary drive. However, the issue of whether the child's tie to its mother or the pleasure principle was primary remained a source of controversy between the classical Freudians and the attachment theorists, with Anna Freud arguing that the rift between the two schools of thought was based on a theoretical misunderstanding.

> We agree with Dr. Bowlby that the infant's attachment to the mother is the result of primary biological urges and ensures survival. But although the search for gratification is a tendency inherent in all drive activity . . . the pleasure principle as such is not a drive representation at all, neither a primary nor a secondary one . . . it is conceived as a principle which governs all mental activity in the immature and insufficiently structured personality. Since it embraces all mental processes, the tie to the mother is governed by it as well. But to assume a struggle for priority . . . between mother attachment and pleasure principle as if they were mental phenomena of the same order does not . . . apply. . . . Dr. Bowlby's . . . conception of a biological tie resulting in certain patterns of behavior when activated by nursing care is paralleled . . . by the conception of an inborn readiness to cathect with

libido a person who provides pleasurable experiences . . . this latter
theory is no more nor less than the classical psychoanalytic assumption of a first "anaclitic" relationship to the mother, i.e., a phase in
which the pleasurable sensations derived from the gratification of
major needs are instrumental in determining which person in the
external world is selected for libidinal cathexis. Moreover, in both
theories, in Dr. Bowlby's as well as in the classical one, the mother is
not chosen for attachment by virtue of her having given birth to the
infant but by virtue of her ministering to the infant's needs. (A. Freud,
1960, p. 55)

Anna Freud was dissatisfied with the continued exclusive focus on
libidinal and intellectual development, viewing the unfolding personality as more complex than the narrow view provided by these foci. In
Normality and Pathology in Childhood (1936b), she elaborates her theory
of developmental lines, which proceed according to the combined
influences of innate characteristics such as the drives and ego–superego development and environmental factors. One line, relating to
feeding, proceeds from suckling at the breast to weaning, self-feeding,
and, eventually, to adult eating habits. Another line commences with
infant play and exploration of its own and mother's body, and then
progresses to the use of transitional objects, child play, and, finally,
adult work. Other lines include the progression from dependency to
autonomy and mature adult object relationships. These lines, or
behavioural clusters, formed "a complex interlocking of psychic units
reflecting id, ego, and superego components as well as adaptive,
dynamic, and genetic influences" (Moore & Fine, 1990b).

According to this schematic, the developmental lines, beginning as
constitutional potential, are expected to progress synchronously.
When the lines do not develop at the same rate, it became apparent
that developmental arrests or derailments had occurred that needed
to be addressed. In Anna's conceptual framework, regression is
viewed as normative and adaptive, that is, as a process whereby the
child returns to a period of development in which mastery was not
achieved, in order to attain the needed element from the primary
maternal relationship (A. Freud, 1963). Anna, thus, viewed psychopathology as abnormal development, a disruption in the continuity
and cumulative progression of the tasks of childhood. In so doing, she
gave due regard to the roles of both nature (maturation) and nurture
(environmental influences) in this developmental process. The task of

the child analyst was to restore the child to the particular phase-appropriate developmental line affected by the developmental perturbation, as well as to understand the meaning of problematic behaviour in its appropriate developmental and environmental context (Skelton, 2006). To achieve her therapeutic goals, Anna Freud advocated play therapy in child analysis as a process that could represent unconscious conflicts symbolically, promote development through exploration, and support creativity. She conceptualised the analytic setting as a place that satisfied the search for different types of objects—old, new, real, and externalised (A. Freud, 1965). This differentiation of objects provided a more nuanced view of the transference in child analysis and suggested different forms of therapeutic action related to the type of object sought.

Anna Freud (1972), like her father, expressed concerns about the interminability of analysis for some psychological disorders particularly those occurring in the very early years of development.

> Whenever the child analyst transcends the area of the infantile neurosis or of the neurotic conflicts preceding it, he finds himself in the area of the "basic faults" (Balint, 1968)—the arrests, the irregularities of development, i.e., the non-neurotic childhood disorders—where his analytic efforts may well become interminable . . . (p. 19)

Anna Freud's infant

Anna remained her father's daughter, as is evident in this description of the nature of children:

> . . . there are divisions within the childish personality . . . and, consequently, constant clashes among the aims of the pleasure-seeking sexual drive, the reasonable, reality-oriented ego, and the moral trends which are closely tied to the parents' wishes and instructions. In this turmoil of conflicting forces, the child's intellect was assigned the very different aspect of being merely one of the combatants, constantly threatened with being overwhelmed or at least interfered with by the urgency of feelings, wishes, and anxieties. (A. Freud, 1982, p. 260)

Inspection of some of her developmental lines also indicates an adherence to the classical Freudian position; for example, the developmental trajectory from infantile dependence to adult object relationships proceeds, according to Anna Freud, as follows: (i) biological unity between mother and infant; (ii) the part-object anaclitic relationship; (iii) object constancy; (iv) the ambivalent, pre-Oedipal, anal–sadistic stage; (v) object centred phallic oedipal phase; (vi) the post-Oedipal latency period; (vii) preadolescent regression to ambivalence, part-object, and need fulfilling attitude; and (viii) the adolescent struggle that leads to genital supremacy. None the less, Anna was interested in understanding object loss from an object relations perspective, as clearly seen in James Robertson's film, *A Two-Year-Old Goes to Hospital*, even using concepts like projective identification, proposed by her arch rival, Melanie Klein (A. Freud, 1953). Loss was a particularly painful topic, as the observations for her work, in large part, derived from children placed in nurseries during the Second World War (Young-Bruehl, 2004).

Critiquing Anna Freud

> Ms. Freud was both a conserver and an innovator, often a very difficult straddle. Sometimes these traits have been interpreted as reflecting ambivalence to her father, at other times as an extraordinary feature of her personality. (Abrams, 2001, p. 105)

Abrams (2001) identified four key areas of innovation in the work of Anna Freud. These were: (i) formulation of new diagnostic and therapeutic possibilities; (ii) introduction of the concept of developmental discontinuities; (iii) consideration of continuities in development, which we would today call constitutional or heritable factors, such as temperament, capacity for self-regulation, intellectual and social deficits, skills and talents, and (iv) attempts to differentiate and integrate different sources of data, including that derived from both child and adult analyses, infant and parent–infant observations, and observations of different subpopulations of children (e.g., institutionalised, orphaned, evacuee), integrating these observations into her theorising and with available knowledge on infant and child development. Anna Freud identified different goals of treatment for children compared with adults, arguing that the focus needed to be maintained on the restoration of normal development and a resynchronisation of the developmental lines rather than on intrapsychic conflicts (A. Freud, 1972). She also developed an assessment tool to identify the developmental profile of prospective child patients in order to determine the focus for treatment. Her goal was to ensure that child analysts had a sound knowledge of normal developmental processes in order to recognise developmental discontinuities and address them appropriately in analysis. However, the uptake was poor because it was too theoretically complex and very complicated to administer (Abrams, 2001). Edgcumbe (2000) sums up Anna Freud's analytic technique:

> Anna Freud eventually arrived at the position of distinguishing not between analytic and non-analytic work, but between the primary analytic tasks: interpretation of resistance and transference, and the subsidiary techniques, classed as developmental help. Deficit illnesses require more developmental help before and alongside interpretation. (p. 161)

Edgcumbe (2000) viewed Anna's main contributions to be her developmental focus, and her distinction between two forms of psychopathology, the first based in developmental deficits and delays and the other in conflict, for each of which she derived different therapeutic approaches. For a range of complex reasons, including the highly abstract concepts used in her theorising, and the co-extensive appearance of other developmental theories (e.g., those of Mahler, Erikson, and Piaget), her developmental lines theory and its therapeutic translation had a limited uptake during her lifetime and appear to have been marginalised since, although Mahon (2001) reported an analysis of a prepubertal boy that enlisted Anna Freud's developmental lines to inform his analytic approach. He is more generous than some commentators in asserting that

> Anna Freud spent a lifetime studying "what passes through the minds" of children and adults, forever alert to the mysterious complexities of pathology but equally alert to the mysterious complexities of normality. For Anna Freud, normality was to be defined not in the negative, as the absence of pathology, but as an organic developmental complexity whose components would not reveal themselves unless subjected to subtle and intense psychoanalytic scrutiny. (Mahon, 2001, p. 77)

Anna Freud's book, *Normality and Pathology in Childhood* (1936b), remained grounded in Sigmund Freud's theory of the instinctual drives, which, even at the time of writing, was out of step with the new directions that infant study and psychoanalysis was taking and, thus, appears conservative, if not reactionary (Young-Bruehl, 2004). Notwithstanding, Young-Bruehl (2004) asserts that ". . . her work has reached every institution concerned with the welfare of children" (p. 196).

Melanie Klein

Melanie Klein was a complex and controversial figure in the history of psychoanalysis. A brief biography of her extraordinarily tragic life might provide a basis for understanding some of her subsequent theorising. Born in Vienna in 1882, the youngest of four children of Jewish parents, Klein witnessed the death from tuberculosis of her sister, Sidonie, at age nine, when she was five years old. In 1902, at the age of twenty, she lost both her elder brother and her father. She entered an unhappy marriage with an engineer a year later, and subsequently had three children. During this period in her life, she was often depressed and suffered from a range of psychosomatic complaints, which took her away from her children as she sought cures for these ailments. Her biographer and former analysand, psychoanalyst Hanna Segal (1979), speculates that there were multiple causes for Klein's chronic depression. These included the experience of the death of three family members in early life, an unhappy marriage, which ultimately ended in divorce, life-long regret that she did not take up the opportunity to study medicine, and her removal from a culturally vibrant Vienna, her birthplace, to follow her husband's work into small provincial towns around Europe. Segal wrote,

> I think that she certainly went into analysis for depression. She was a very depressed woman and I suspect that she must have been rather hysterical because of all the symptoms but she attached so much importance to what she called the epistemophilic instinct – what we now call 'K' from Bion.[4] She was just passionate about discovering human nature . . . hence her interest in literature. She originally wanted to study medicine and she didn't because of falling in love rather unfortunately and marrying an extremely unsatisfactory man.[5]

Klein commenced psychoanalysis with Sándor Ferenczi at the age of thirty-two, following the death of her mother. He recognised her gifts and encouraged her to become a child analyst. She subsequently underwent an analysis with Karl Abraham, which was abruptly terminated by his sudden death a few months later. Klein admired Abraham, who was a strong supporter of play techniques, as she was to become, and felt his loss deeply. In 1934, her twenty-six-year-old son, Hans, was killed in a mountain-climbing accident, and, some time later, she became estranged from her daughter, Melitta, who broke off all contact with her mother. Such was the rift, Melitta did not attend her mother's funeral. Some have claimed that Melitta felt persecuted by her mother's work, which had "[given] life to such monstrous babies, with such sadistic impulses towards the mother's body . . ." (Geissman & Geissman, 1998, pp. 116–117), but perhaps Melitta's hatred of her mother originated in feelings of abandonment during her childhood when her mother was, for long periods of time, either depressed or absent.

Melanie Klein's work

". . . object-relations are at the centre of emotional life" (Klein, 1952b, p. 436).

Klein was primarily interested in psychological development in the first two years of life. By analysing children, she wanted to access, via the transference, the infant within the child in order to reach material that had been obscured by infantile amnesia and, thereby, to establish a relationship with the child's unconscious (Klein, 1952b). Klein diverged from Freud with respect to the contents of the infant's mind. In Freud's theory, phantasies arose in puberty, not at the beginning of life, as in Klein's theory (1928). Since early sexual instincts find auto-erotic satisfaction, they do not need an object outside of the infant's own body. Freud later modified his view, stating that objects become important during the second and third years, that is, during the Oedipal stage (Freud, 1917e, 1923b); phantasies also arise at this time. For Klein, the internal world comprises "primitive imagos", defined as the visceral, kinaesthetic, and emotional experiencing of internal, phantasied parental figures, in part, whole, or in combination (the parental couple), that constitute the earliest objects, which appear from birth. These phantasies are the psychic representation of the instincts—"the affective interpretations of bodily sensations" (Isaacs, 1948, p. 88)—and are necessarily preverbal and pre-visual; they are not Freud's hallucinatory wish fulfilments. Because the infant is unable to separate sensation, perception, and meaning, unpleasurable bodily sensations, such as hunger, are experienced as an attack. The phantasy is the affective "interpretation" of the corporeal experience as either pleasurable (good) or unpleasurable (bad) (Riviere, 1936).

These earliest phantasies are first corporeal, that is, they are felt in the body; they then become visual, and, finally, are able to be verbalised. Phantasies are the stuff from which the ego defences of introjection and projection arise. For Klein, the child's inner world is built upon the introjection of a good and a bad (persecuting and attacking) breast and not on chronologically continuous memories or images of reality. The quality of these first objects is a product both of the infant's perception of its mother and of its projection of its own feelings into the mother. Thus, these internal objects do not necessarily represent "real" external objects because they have been transformed by the process of introjection (King & Steiner, 1991). Through the process of symbolisation, the internal world of phantasy becomes linked to the external world and eventually to reality testing (Klein, 1930). The infant moves from "symbolic equation", in which the object is omnipotently controlled, to a position in which the object is relinquished, mourned, and then symbolised. The new introjected internal objects become available to the ego and assist, through processes of identification and assimilation, in the child's negotiation with external reality. This concept appears in subsequent literature by different names. For example, Fonagy and Target (1996) refer to "psychic equivalence" as an early mental state in which the infant equates the content of his mind with external reality. This can be experienced as distressing, because the projection of phantasy on to the outside world appears real.

Klein adhered to Freud's theory of the erogenous zones, but with some key differences. The first is that while both she and Freud agreed that the erogenous locations were sources of pleasure for the infant, Klein did not connect this pleasure with sexuality. Klein was more concerned with the physical activities associated with each of these zones. For example, the oral zone is concerned with the taking in and spitting out of food; the activities in the alimentary canal and the gastrointestinal tract are associated with bodily sensations of pleasure or unpleasure. Klein also rejected Freud's stages of auto-eroticism, in which the object is the infant's own body, and primary narcissism, during which the infant takes itself as its object. This is because Klein did not view the erogenous zones of the body as primarily a source of (sexual) pleasure, like Freud, but as a source of meaning, as mechanisms of first contact with the outside world. It is through the erogenous zones that aggression is directed outward and at which sites the infant experiences the psychic equivalent of pleasure–unpleasure, that is, pleasurable and painful corporeal sensations. Klein's theory revolves, not around sexuality, but around the defences against the experiencing of anxiety and aggression and their working through. For Klein, the Oedipal drama occurs much earlier than stated by Freud, as does the development of superego, which begins to develop from birth before the Oedipal complex appears. However, Klein's Oedipus complex is not a Freudian sexual drama, but a drama related to the loss of the object, the realisation that the object is not one's exclusive property, and the rivalry with another object, the father. It is through this experience that the infant masters his primitive anxiety as he learns to relate to whole objects.

Melanie Klein believed that object relations, the relationship between the mother, or the mother's breast, and the infant, exist from birth and that auto-eroticism and primary narcissism arise in response to frustration and accompanying phantasies about the infant's internal and external objects (Heimann, 1952; Segal, 1979).

> The primal processes of projection and introjection, being inextricably linked with the infant's emotions and anxieties, initiate object-relations; by projecting, i.e., deflecting libido and aggression on to the mother's breast, the basis for object-relations is established; by introjecting the object, first of all the breast, relations to internal objects come into being. My use of the term 'object-relations' is based on my contention that the infant has from the beginning of post-natal life a relation to the mother. . . which is imbued with the fundamental elements of an object-relation, i.e., love, hatred, phantasies, anxieties, and defences. (Klein, 1952b, pp. 432–433)

Klein is, thus, regarded as one of the founders of object relations theory, although her focus on the experience of self-and-other, which is the primary concern of object relations theorists, took a secondary position to her interest in libidinal development (Stern, 1985). In

Klein's 1946 paper, "Notes on some schizoid mechanisms", she summarises her views on early infant development.

> In early infancy anxieties characteristic of psychosis arise which drive the ego to develop specific defence-mechanisms . . . The psychotic anxieties, mechanisms and ego-defences of infancy have a profound influence on development in all its aspects, including the development of the ego, superego and *object-relations* . . . *[which] exist from the beginning of life, the first object being the mother's breast* which to the child becomes split into a good (gratifying) and bad (frustrating) breast; this splitting results in a severance of love and hate . . . the relation to the first object implies its introjection and projection, and thus from the beginning object-relations are moulded by an interaction between introjection and projection, between internal and external objects and situations. These processes participate in the building up of the ego and superego and prepare the ground for the onset of the Oedipus complex in the second half of the first year. (p. 99, my italics)

The death instinct and the defences against it

The death instinct plays a much more central role in Kleinian theory than it did for Freud. One may speculate that since death figured so prominently in Melanie Klein's life, death and the death instinct came to occupy such a prominent position in her theorising. Klein understood anxiety to be related to the activities of the death instinct and that the fear of death, that is, the fear of being destroyed, is the most fundamental anxiety (Van Haute & Geyskens, 2007). The personality is formed essentially by the way in which the individual's ego deals with anxiety and aggression and defends itself against the death instinct, which Klein understood to be a "biological metaphor that refers to the traumatic core of the unconscious and of subjectivity" (Van Haute & Geyskens, 2007, p. 40). The notion of a death instinct is, in fact, superfluous, and obfuscates rather than clarifies Klein's theory. The death instinct can be understood to denote the infant's experience of a terrifying helplessness in the face of his aggression and dependence related to the satisfaction of his basic needs. Klein (1946) argued that the death instinct (helplessness and rage) created fears of disintegration and annihilation that are defended against by their projection into the object, but are then reintrojected and experienced as persecutory.

I hold that anxiety arises from the operation of the death instinct within the organism, is felt as fear of annihilation (death) and takes the form of fear of persecution. The fear of the destructive impulse seems to attach itself at once to an object—or rather it is experienced as the fear of an uncontrollable overpowering object. Other important sources of primary anxiety are the trauma of birth (separation anxiety) and frustration of bodily needs; and these experiences too are from the beginning felt as being caused by objects. Even if these objects are felt to be external, they become through introjection internal persecutors and thus reinforce the fear of the destructive impulse within . . . If we try to visualize in concrete form the primary anxiety, the fear of annihilation, we must remember the helplessness of the infant in face of internal and external dangers. I suggest that the primary danger-situation arising from the activity of the death instinct within is felt by him as an overwhelming attack, as persecution. (p. 100)

Klein further argued that the fear of death, that is, the fear of being destroyed, is present from birth. A mental representation of death is neither possible nor required, since Klein argued that death is felt directly in the body in the same way that the breast is initially experienced as either pleasurable or unpleasurable. However, Klein (1948a) argued that the work of the death and life instincts must be considered together.

The activity of the death instinct deflected outwards, as well as its working within, cannot be considered apart from the simultaneous activity of the life instinct. Side by side with the deflection of the death instinct outwards, the life instinct—by means of the libido—attaches itself to the external object, the gratifying (good) breast, which becomes the external representative of the life instinct. The introjection of this good object reinforces the power of the life instinct within. The good internalized breast, which is felt to be the source of life, forms a vital part of the ego and its preservation becomes an imperative need. (p. 117)

Klein (1945) further asserted that:

From the very beginning of life, libido is fused with aggressiveness . . . [and] is at every stage vitally affected by anxiety derived from aggressiveness. Anxiety, guilt and depressive feelings . . . drive the libido forward to new sources of gratification. (p. 27)

Klein's view of the death instinct and its relationship to libido remained similar to that of Freud (1923b):[6]

> The dangerous death instincts are dealt with in the individual in various ways: in part they are rendered harmless by being fused with erotic components, in part they are diverted towards the external world in the form of aggression, while to a large extent they undoubtedly continue their internal work unhindered. (p. 54)

The developing ego splits the object (breast) into idealised and persecutory components. The ideal breast provides the foundation for the development of an ego ideal; the bad, persecuting breast underpins a punitive superego. The ego itself splits into libidinal and destructive parts. The libidinal part introjects the ideal part-object to protect it against internal and external persecutory objects, which are then attacked through oral-sadism by the destructive part of the ego. In explicating this process, Klein described a new defence mechanism—projective identification—that arose to protect the primitive ego. Riviere (1952) provides this definition: "[projective identification] represents the phantasy of forcing the self in part or as a whole into the inside of the object in order to obtain possession and control of it, whether in love or in hate" (p. 33).

Porder (1987) offers perhaps a more accessible definition: ". . . projective identification is a behavioral reenactment in which the patient unconsciously 'identifies with the aggressor,' a parent, while the analyst experiences the feeling of the child being acted upon" (p. 450).

Arising originally between mother and baby, this omnipotent infant phantasy was conceptualised by Klein as a defence capable of serving multiple functions, including the expulsion of a part of the self and possessing, controlling, or emptying the object. Both good and bad parts of the self can be projected into the object. The endangered good part might be projected in order that it finds shelter in a protective and/or idealised object. However, the ego is impoverished by such a manoeuvre. Klein viewed projective identification as a form of communication between a "psychotic personality" and others, including the analyst, and understanding of this process made it possible, according to Klein, to define and work with the psychotic transference (Müller, 2004). However, the term is still not well understood and is often misused in both analytic and lay contexts (Goretti, 2007). While Freud's use of the word "identification" denoted a process whereby we take in or internalise characteristics of a valued or feared other, projective identification is a process whereby we project parts of ourselves into the other, who might not be a willing recipient. Hence, the process of projective identification can be conceptualised as a process of coercive colonisation of the internal world of the other with parts of our own world. In time, the colonised person takes on the wishes and values of the person colonising them, and they come to feel the projections as ego syntonic, as if they had arisen from within (Najeeb, 2011). The relationship could become defined by this projective process, which Bion (1962) considers to be a powerful form of primitive communication. More recently, projective identification has been defined more broadly as a bi-personal field (Baranger & Baranger, 2008) in which ". . . multiple kinds of communication (verbal, postural, behavioural) in different modes (literal, abstract, symbolic) at many levels (historical, contemporary, conscious, unconscious) through different sense modalities (auditory, visual, tactile, olfactory) . . ." (Najeeb, 2011, p. 5) simultaneously take place bi-directionally in an interplay of projective and introjective identifications and counter-identifications.

The paranoid–schizoid and depressive positions

Klein introduced two other new concepts that have had a major impact on psychoanalytic thinking: the paranoid–schizoid position and the depressive position. Klein chose the word "position" in preference to stage or phase to indicate "a configuration of object relations, anxieties and defences that persist throughout life" (Segal, 1964, p. ix). Although the paranoid–schizoid position appears earlier in development, Klein expounded the depressive position first, in 1935; it was not until 1946 that she proposed the paranoid–schizoid position. However, we will discuss them in developmental rather than historical sequence.[7] Segal (1964) observed that these two "positions" were subdivisions of Freud's oral stage of development, the first occupying the first three to four months of life, with the second following approximately in the second half of the first year. Klein (1975) outlines her conceptualisation of the paranoid–schizoid position thus:

There are ... primal activities of the ego which ... derive from the imperative need to deal with the struggle between life and death instincts. One of these functions is gradual integration which stems from the life instinct and expresses itself in the capacity for love. The opposite tendency of the ego to split itself and its objects occurs ... because it constitutes a defence against the primordial anxiety ... and is therefore a means of preserving the ego. I ... attribute ... importance to ... splitting: the division of the breast into a good and a bad object ... [which is] an expression of the innate conflict between love and hate and of the ensuing anxieties. ... Concurrently with the greedy and devouring internalization of the object—first of all the breast—the ego in varying degrees fragments itself and its objects, and in this way achieves a dispersal of the destructive impulses and of internal persecutory anxieties. This process ... is one of the defences during the paranoid–schizoid position, which... normally extends over the first three or four months of life. ... Whenever anxiety arises, it is mainly of a paranoid nature and the defences against it ... are predominantly schizoid ... During the first few months [the infant] ... keeps the good object apart from the bad one and thus ... preserves it—which also means that the security of the ego is enhanced ... the capacity for love gives impetus both to integrating tendencies and to a successful primal splitting between the loved and hated object [the earliest internalized persecutory object—the retaliating, devouring, and poisonous breast]. ... Excessive envy, an expression of destructive impulses, interferes with the primal split between the good and bad breast, and the building up of a good object cannot sufficiently be achieved ... In normal development, these schizoid and paranoid trends (the paranoid–schizoid position) are ... overcome during the period which is characterized by the depressive position, and integration develops successfully. (p. 191)

Unlike Freud, Klein believed that the ego was present from birth, but was undeveloped and lived in a world of part objects that were not integrated. Thus, the infant experiences the "good" and "bad" breasts as unconnected, as two separate objects that have no necessary connection. Indeed, Klein argues that, because of their very different characteristics, the infant works hard to keep these part objects separate by using one of the most primitive defence mechanisms—splitting. The defence of splitting allows the infant to idealise and identify with the good breast and to disavow the bad breast, and, with it, its feelings of frustration and rage at the deprivations it experiences.

Thus, Klein named this process paranoid. In the first few months of life, Klein's infant suffers from the anxiety of persecution and destruction at the "hands" of the bad breast. Because of the need for splitting, the world of the infant and the infant's ego is experienced as fragmented, that is, schizoid.

Klein (1935) introduced her concept of the depressive position in "A contribution to the psychogenesis of manic–depressive states". She proposed that this developmental advance occurred at about the age of six months, when the infant had achieved the capacity to perceive his mother as a whole person, with both good and bad parts, rather than as part-objects (good and bad breasts). When this occurs, the infant's anxiety transforms from persecutory fears about the destruction of the self into anxiety about the damage it might inflict on the mother on whom it is totally dependent, and guilt about its aggressive feelings. The infant can now identify with, and introject, the mother as a good internal object, thereby securing protection from internal and external persecutory objects.

> . . . when the child's belief and trust in his capacity to love, in his reparative powers and in the integration and security of his good inner world increases . . . manic omnipotence decreases and the obsessional nature of impulses towards reparation diminishes, which means in general that the infantile neurosis has passed. (Klein, 1940, p. 135)

However, the infant can attack his mother in fits of rage when frustrated, and at those times will experience a sense of loss, sadness, and guilt for his attacks and the need for reparation. However, the ego now has sufficient strength to mobilise its resources and love to restore the damaged object. Further, new defences appear—denial of reality and omnipotence—whose function is to neutralise the emotional pain experienced when the object feels threatened or lost. Omnipotent projective identification, a characteristic of the paranoid–schizoid position, is reduced once the depressive position has been consolidated. Klein (1946) describes the depressive position thus:

> With the introjection of the complete object in about the second quarter of the first year marked steps in integration are made. This implies important changes in the relation to objects. The loved and hated aspects of the mother are no longer felt to be so widely separated, and

the result is an increased fear of loss, states akin to mourning and a strong feeling of guilt, because the aggressive impulses are felt to be directed against the loved object. The depressive position has come to the fore. The very experience of depressive feelings in turn has the effect of further integrating the ego, because it makes for an increased understanding of psychic reality and better perception of the external world, as well as for a greater synthesis between inner and external situations. (p. 105)

Infants and children cycle backwards and forwards between these two positions. Unlike Freud, Klein did not believe that pathology could be defined by regressions to, or fixations at, these two positions, because she perceived such fluctuation as developmentally normal if the appropriate means of dealing with the anxieties that arise at each position are operating. Further, both positions remain active throughout adulthood and alternate with fluctuating intensity (Klein, 1935). Klein, like Freud, believed that later psychopathology was a magnified reflection of these early processes, which formed the traumatic core of the unconscious and the critical basis of human existence (Klein, 1945).

With her articulation of the paranoid–schizoid and depressive positions, which are structural, not chronological, concepts, somewhat akin to Freud's use of psychic structures in his structural model, Klein was able to account for the development of the ego, the nature of its relationships with its internal objects via introjection and projection, and the nature of anxiety and guilt. To recapitulate, in this model, anxiety has two main forms—persecutory anxiety, associated with the paranoid–schizoid position, and depressive anxiety, associated with the depressive position. Guilt is understood to be a resolution of the conflict between the life and death instincts. The progression from psychotic to neurotic functioning brings with it the ego's capacity to distinguish internal from external reality and to confront its phantasies with reality, that is, to reality-test. The depressive position might never be fully resolved; at each crisis point in development, a choice must be made to work through the pain of depressive anxiety or to regress to a paranoid–schizoid position to avoid the pain. People might oscillate between the two positions repeatedly throughout life, and the frequency and degree of this oscillation is related to overall mental health.

Even a brief outline of Klein's work would be incomplete without a discussion of the concept of envy, which Klein defines as "an oral-sadistic and anal-sadistic expression of destructive impulses, operative from the beginning of life . . ." (Klein, 1975, p. 176). Klein viewed envy as one of the fundamental emotions that is inevitably revived in the transference in what Klein describes as "memories in feeling"—a concept that has subsequently found expression in a number of later theories (see, for example, Fairbairn, 1946; Girard, 2010; Slochower, 1996; Winnicott, 1945, 1958). The envy is envy for the breast, which is the original source of both emotional and physical sustenance. Envy arises when the infant feels "that the gratification of which he was deprived has been kept for itself by the breast" (Klein, 1975, p. 180). When envy is intense, the capacity for love and gratitude are reduced. Klein distinguishes envy, jealousy, and greed as follows:

> Envy is the angry feeling that another person possesses and enjoys something desirable—the envious impulse being to take it away or to spoil it. Moreover, envy implies the subject's relation to one person only and goes back to the earliest exclusive relation with the mother. Jealousy is based on envy, but involves a relation to at least two people; it is mainly concerned with love that the subject feels is his due and has been taken away, or is in danger of being taken away, from him by his rival. In the everyday conception of jealousy, a man or a woman feels deprived of the loved person by somebody else. Greed is an impetuous and insatiable craving, exceeding what the subject needs and what the object is able and willing to give. At the unconscious level, greed aims primarily at completely scooping out, sucking dry, and devouring the breast: that is to say, its aim is destructive introjection; whereas envy not only seeks to rob in this way, but also to put badness, primarily bad excrements and bad parts of the self, into the mother, first of all into her breast, in order to spoil and destroy her. In the deepest sense this means destroying her creativeness . . . One essential difference between greed and envy . . . would . . . be that greed is mainly bound up with introjection and envy with projection. (p. 181)

For Klein, infantile neurosis arises as a very early defence against psychotic anxieties, which are caused by the projection of destructive drives. For Freud, the infantile neurosis arises in response to the Oedipus complex and fears of castration. Klein proposed that all phases of development occur at much younger ages than in classical theory, thus obviating Freud's structural model and the role and function of regression and fixation. In Kleinian theory, fixation can occur only at the two positions—paranoid–schizoid and depressive; regression refers to the point at which "libido fails to master the death instinct" (Yorke, 1971, p. 148).

For both Sigmund and Anna Freud, the superego emerges from the resolution of the Oedipus complex and is influenced by the child's parents. For Klein, the content and severity of the superego are determined by the quality of the child's sadistic impulses. Drawing on the mechanism of projection, Klein explained that an internal, punitive, forbidding object is created by the child's projection of its aggressive impulses into its internal object. Their respective understanding of the Oedipus complex also differed substantially. For Klein, infants of both sexes become Oedipally attached to the mother; similarly, the father becomes a rival for both sexes during the sadistic-oral period. Girls gradually reduce their interest in the mother's breast and become more interested in the mother's body, which contains the father's penis, and this realisation creates Oedipal conflict; for boys, the fear of castration arises in their desire for their mothers, but for Klein, the fear of castration is also related to much earlier fears of having one's body emptied or destroyed (Klein, 1928).

The nature of the transference in Melanie Klein's work

Klein and Freud shared a similar understooding of the transference. We will review it briefly because of its relevance in accessing and understanding the nature of the earliest object relationships:

> It is characteristic of psycho-analytic procedure that, as it begins to open up roads into the patient's unconscious, his past (in its conscious and unconscious aspects) is gradually . . . revived. Thereby his urge to transfer his early experiences, object-relations and emotions, is reinforced and they come to focus on the psycho-analyst; this implies that the patient deals with the conflicts and anxieties which have been reactivated, by making use of the same mechanisms and defences as in earlier situations. (Klein, 1952b, p. 433)

However, "the mechanisms and defences" revived in the transference are Kleinian rather than Freudian.

I hold that transference originates in the same processes which in the earliest stages determine object-relations. Therefore we have to go back again and again in analysis to the fluctuations between objects, loved and hated, external and internal, which dominate early infancy. We can fully appreciate the interconnection between positive and negative transferences only if we explore the early interplay between love and hate, and the vicious circle of aggression, anxieties, feelings of guilt and increased aggression, as well as the various aspects of objects towards whom these conflicting emotions and anxieties are directed. On the other hand, through exploring these early processes I became convinced that the analysis of the negative transference, which had received relatively little attention in psycho-analytic technique, is a precondition for analysing the deeper layers of the mind. The analysis of the negative as well as of the positive transference and of their interconnection is, as I have held for many years, an indispensable principle for the treatment of all types of patients, children and adults alike. (Klein, 1952b, p. 436)

Melanie Klein's infant

Melanie Klein's infant has suffered a profound and primitive trauma at birth—separation from the mother and the feeling of utter helplessness and rage with its predicament. This original anxiety remains with us throughout life. All later anxieties are related to, and comprise, a form of working through of this traumatic anxiety (Klein, 1948a). While both Freud and Klein concur with respect to the source of this original anxiety, Freud's infant remains powerless and passive in the face of it; Klein's infant does not. Freud's infant does not have an ego at birth, so no response is possible to this original trauma; hence, Freud's infant is doomed to compulsively repeat it, albeit in differing forms and as an attempt at mastery. Freud was primarily engaged in clinical practice with understanding the traumatic neuroses. Klein was more interested in understanding the psychotic pathologies. She argued that although psychotic patients suffer excruciating anxieties, they seek mastery by creatively transforming their terrifying reality into hallucinations and delusions. In the same way, Kleinian infants direct their aggressivity outwards, in the form of oral aggression, which they feel within, in response to their own helplessness and project it on to the breast (Klein, 1948b). This attack protects the infant from the internal attacks of the bad breast (Klein, 1946).

However, this object now becomes a source of anxiety against which infants must defend themselves.

Klein's (1946) infant is aggressive, envious, and orally and anally sadistic. It was this conceptualisation of infancy that aroused so much hostility to her work.

> From the beginning the destructive impulse is turned against the object and is first expressed in phantasied oral-sadistic attacks on the mother's breast, which soon develop into onslaughts on her body by all sadistic means. The persecutory fears arising from the infant's oral-sadistic impulses to rob the mother's body of its good contents, and from the anal-sadistic impulses to put his excrements into her (including the desire to enter her body in order to control her from within) are of great importance for the development of paranoia and schizophrenia. (p. 100)

In a later paper, Klein and colleagues (Klein, Heimann, Isaacs, & Riviere, 1952) link infant feeding problems with "cannabilistic instincts", which both Freud and Abraham (1924) had also discussed in relation to the greed and destructive impulses of the oral-sadistic stage. See, for example, this passage from Freud (1918b):

> . . . the earliest recognizable sexual organisation [is] the so-called 'cannibalistic' or 'oral' phase, during which the original attachment of sexual excitation to the nutritional instinct still dominates the scene . . . Impairment of the nutritional instinct . . . draws our attention to a failure on the part of the organism to master its sexual excitation. In this phase the sexual aim could only be cannibalism-devouring . . . (p. 106)

In describing splitting processes in relation to the object, Klein argued that the infant not only perceives the mother's breast as split into "good" and "bad", but as "fragmented".

> The destructive impulse projected outwards is first experienced as oral aggression. I believe that oral-sadistic impulses towards the mother's breast are active from the beginning of life, though with the onset of teething the cannibalistic impulses increase in strength . . . In states of frustration and anxiety the oral-sadistic and cannibalistic desires are reinforced, and then the infant feels that he has taken in the nipple and the breast in bits. Therefore in addition to the divorce between a good

and a bad breast in the young infant's phantasy, the frustrating
breast—attacked in oral-sadistic phantasies—is felt to be in fragments
. . . (Klein, 1946, p. 104)

When there are difficulties in sucking, the baby feels persecuted by the
breast and "the infant's aggressive impulses towards the breast tend
to turn it in his mind into a vampire-like or devouring object, and this
anxiety could inhibit greed and in consequence the desire to suck".
(Klein, 1952a, p. 97)

However, Melanie Klein presented two quite different perceptions
of the infant, depending on whether she was describing an infant
who was responding to a "good" or "bad" breast. Compare these
passages:

> Throughout my work I have attributed fundamental importance to the
> infant's first object relation—the relation to the mother's breast and to
> the mother—and have drawn the conclusion that if this primal object,
> which is introjected, takes root in the ego with relative security, the
> basis for a satisfactory development is laid. Innate factors contribute
> to this bond. Under the dominance of oral impulses, the breast is
> instinctively felt to be the source of nourishment and therefore, in a
> deeper sense, of life itself. This mental and physical closeness to the
> gratifying breast in some measure restores, if things go well, the lost
> prenatal unity with the mother and the feeling of security that goes
> with it . . . The good breast is taken in and becomes part of the ego,
> and the infant who was first inside the mother now has the mother
> inside himself . . . The breast in its good aspect is the prototype of
> maternal goodness, inexhaustible patience and generosity, as well as
> of creativeness. It is these phantasies and instinctual needs that so
> enrich the primal object that it remains the foundation for hope, trust,
> and belief in goodness. (Klein, 1975, pp. 178–179)

In explicating her concept of projective identification, Klein (1946)
describes the infant thus:

> The phantasied onslaughts on the mother follow two main lines: one
> is the predominantly oral impulse to suck dry, bite up, scoop out and
> rob the mother's body of its good contents. . . . The other line of attack
> derives from the anal and urethral impulses and implies expelling
> dangerous substances (excrements) out of the self and into the mother.
> Together with these harmful excrements, expelled in hatred, split-off

parts of the ego are also projected on to the mother or, as I would rather call it, into the mother. These excrements and bad parts of the self are meant not only to injure but also to control and to take possession of the object. In so far as the mother comes to contain the bad parts of the self, she is not felt to be a separate individual but is felt to be the bad self. (pp. 106–107)

Meares (2000), in attempting to account for the "monstrous attributions" (p. 88) that make up Klein's "frightening world of infantile fantasy" (p. 89), argued that Melanie Klein might have been representing what subsequent authors have called the trauma system in these descriptions of infantile phantasies of the destructive, attacking infant. Like phantasy, early trauma is laid down in an atmosphere of intense negative affect of primitive rage and terror associated with the trauma experience in the absence of reflective function, words, or symbolic representation. The traumatic memory, therefore, consists of negative affect states, ranging from anxiety experienced as a dull and pervasive tension, a lack of safety, or feelings of terror. These feeling states are accompanied by negative self-attributes of worthlessness, badness, and helplessness, which are linked to attributions of the other as powerful, controlling, critical, disaffirming, or mocking. In extreme cases, patients report feeling repulsive, monstrous, or like vermin; the other also takes on monstrous forms, such as witches and devils, that have devastating destructive powers. "The other comes to inhabit the victim . . . self and traumatizer are represented as fused" (Meares, 2000). Meares argues,

A series of negative self-attributes form part of the organisation of the traumatic memory system. They are mingled with negative attributes of the other . . . (p. 87). These images reflect the terror, alienation, and sense of personal disintegration which form the core of memories of severe trauma. Since monstrous attributions are created in a state in which the reflective process is inoperative . . . they are recorded in a memory system which is unconscious. This nightmare world of powerful and frightening feelings . . . has been explored by Melanie Klein . . . who call[s] this . . . experience . . . "unconscious phantasy". (p. 88)

Extreme preverbal trauma is encoded as perceptual representations in procedural memory systems that form part of the trauma memory system of cognitions, emotions, and response tendencies (motor repertoires). When these response tendencies are triggered by contextual cues, individuals literally "act out" the trauma script without being aware of what has triggered their responses, or that they are in the grip of early trauma memories. This process is akin to Freud's "compulsion to repeat" (Freud, 1914g).

> We may say that the patient does not remember anything of what he has forgotten and repressed, but acts it out. He reproduces it not as a memory but as an action: he repeats it without, of course, knowing that he is repeating it. (p. 150)

Critiquing Melanie Klein

Contrary to classical psychoanalytic theory, Klein proposed that the ego was present at birth, and was capable of forming object relationships, experiencing (psychotic) anxiety, and forming and using defence mechanisms. For Klein, the concept "ego"[8] is .akin to the "self" which contains within it, from birth, the life and death instincts, the superego, envy and unconscious phantasies[9] (Yorke, 1971). According to Klein, the basis of all conflict resides in the struggle between the life (libido) and death (destructive and aggressive) instincts. This struggle is triggered by birth trauma that creates persecutory anxiety in which the external world and the mother's breast, as its first representative, are experienced as hostile.

Subsequent theorising about infancy indicate many points of departure from Klein's view; for example, attachment theorists argue for a much stronger role for the environment, including the behaviour of the actual, as opposed to the phantasied parents in infant development (Bowlby, 1940, 1958). The inferred psychological complexity of the newborn and the psychological attribution of adult content to infant minds, including psychotic and persecutory anxiety and awareness of a death instinct, are problematic and have been criticised both within the psychoanalytic literature and in view of recent evidence from infant brain development research (Feldman, 2007; Minagawa-Kawai, Mori, Hebden, & Dupoux, 2008). For example, Fonagy and Target (2003) argued that the intense and disorganising affect observed in infants arises because they have not yet developed the capacity for self-regulation, or, indeed, a template for the regularities in the environment that would make it more manageable and predictable.

Klein identified only a handful of defences—projection, introjection, projective identification, disintegration, spoliation (i.e., spoiling an object through projection of badness into the object as a defence against painful feelings of envy), splitting (of the object into a "good" and "bad" breast, or splitting off painful affect from reparative affect such as gratitude and love), reparation, and the manic defences, in which feelings of dependence on the object are denied. Yorke (1971) expresses puzzlement regarding the operation of Kleinian defences. "What impresses me about these defenses is that they rarely seem to work. No sooner has one dealt with an internal persecutor by projection than one is persecuted by it from outside" (p. 145).

There have also been recent challenges to the very widely accepted concept of splitting that forms such a taken-for-granted role in many psychoanalytic theories (e.g., Klein's "good" and "bad" breast, or Kernberg's "good" and "bad" self-experience). Klein and psychoanalytic theorists generally assume that a perception of "good" and "bad" emerges from the infant's initially undifferentiated affective/bodily experience. From this sense of "pleasure–unpleasure" arises the concept of a good and bad object and a good and bad self. Initially, in the paranoid–schizoid position, these perceptions remain separate and unintegrated and are subject to the action of very complex defences. However, negotiating all these selves and objects requires sophisticated cognitive functioning. For example, the infant would have a great many experiences of the breast in the first weeks and months of life. How does the infant classify an "average" experience of the breast? After a bad experience, an average experience might appear good, but after a good experience, an average experience might appear bad. If, according to Klein, the ego/self exists at birth, would it not have to oversee the "good" and "bad" dichotomies? In other words, would it not precede the split self? Stern (1985) expresses this theoretical dilemma thus:

> How can one postulate a "good self" and "bad self" before there is a self? What would mark the distinction between "good experience" and a "good self"? Or, how do the "good" and "bad" selves interact through the medium of a non-affective self, that is, a cognitive self that

has enough self-coherence and continuity to encompass the "good" and "bad" selves? (p. 251–252)

A related problem is that Melanie Klein's world of "monstrous attributions", described by Meares as possibly representing the unconscious memories laid down in the trauma memory system, is that the infant, at the time that such trauma memories are being established, would not have a sufficient level of cognitive development to characterise their experience in the ways that adult patients who had experienced preverbal trauma describe their experiences retrospectively to their therapists. In her characterisation of infants' mental processes, Klein attributes mental structure, complex fantasies, and defences to the infant, which developmental neuroscience informs us are not developed in the first few months of life (Herba et al., 2010) (see Chapter Six).

There is yet another problem for the Kleinian model—the leap from the pleasure–unpleasure principle of Freud to her good–bad breast dichotomy. Unlike the affective experience of pleasure, which requires no cognitive processing because it is an affective/bodily sensation, Stern (1985) observed that to enable a judgement of good/bad one would also have to infer good or bad intention, an act that cannot be achieved at the level of "core-relatedness" or intrapsychically, but which requires an interpersonal relationship. Although splitting is observed clinically in many psychopathologies, notably in borderline pathology, it is "the product of a post infancy mind capable of . . . symbolic transformations and condensations . . ." (p. 252). These condensations refer to the infant's repeated hedonically toned experiences of the mother, which Stern called "representations of interactions that have generalized" (RIGs) (Stern, 1985, p. 97). Eventually, with sufficient experiences, the superordinate categories of "good" and "bad" will be formed. This process is similar to the Piagetian concept of categorisation (see Chapter Five), in which a young child will gradually learn to sort many different breeds of dog (poodles, Alsatians, fox terriers, etc.) into their superordinate category of "dog". However, this is not a process of splitting, at least initially. It is a process of integration of many experiences into its correct superordinate category.

These theoretical differences must necessarily influence psychoanalytic technique. Yorke (1971) provides a succinct summary, as follows:

One of the major differences, in both adults and children, concerns defense interpretations. Since the classical view is that an impulse cannot be made conscious before the defenses against it are accessible, defense interpretation tends to precede that of id content . . . Kleinians [are] not concerned with defense interpretation . . . id content is always interpreted directly. (p. 151)

Further,

. . . free association is discouraged . . . by constant intervention and by . . . "deep" interpretations . . . based on the assumption that the unconscious is immediately and directly accessible . . . [However,] *interpretations . . . appear to stem from theoretical assumptions rather than from the patient's material.* (pp. 151–152, my italics)

This problem is exacerbated by the fact that Klein, like Freud, did not afford much attention or importance to reality, either to the external environment in general, or to the quality of the care-giving that the child was receiving in particular. Klein's tendency to dismiss the importance of the real world in shaping development might have had its origins in her own traumatic childhood and her (unconscious) need to defend against the pain of her many losses (Marrone & Cortina, 2003). This constitutes one of the major differences between Klein and the attachment theorists, like John Bowlby, who will be discussed later. In similar vein, Klein was much less interested in the quality of the analyst–patient relationship and, hence, the therapeutic alliance did not figure large in her analytic technique (Frosh, 2002), to which we will now turn our attention.

Klein's analytic technique

Recent critics of Klein's work have described Kleinians as "the barmiest of psychoanalysts . . .", yet, who, in times of doubt, "are our guides to the dark side of hatred, jealousy, and hostility" (Margulies, 2002, p. 1042). An excerpt from Klein's account of the first three sessions of her analysis of Dick, a very disturbed four-year-old boy, who was barely articulate, and was probably autistic, demonstrates her technique of "deep" interpretation, which, as observed by Yorke (1971), does not appear to arise from the patient's productions but from her strongly-held theoretical position (Klein, 1930).

I took a big train and put it beside a smaller one and called them 'Daddy-train' and 'Dick-train'. Thereupon he picked up the train I called 'Dick' and made it roll to the window and said 'Station'. I explained: *'The station is mummy; Dick is going into mummy.'* He left the train, ran into the space between the outer and inner doors of the room, shut himself in, saying 'dark' and ran out again directly. He went through this performance several times. I explained to him: *'It is dark inside mummy. Dick is inside dark mummy'* (p. 242). During the third session he . . . pointed to a coal cart and said, "Cut." I gave him a pair of scissors, and he tried to scratch the little pieces of black wood which represented coal, but he could not hold the scissors. Acting on a glance which he gave me, I cut the pieces of wood out of the cart, whereupon he threw the damaged cart and its contents into the drawer and said, "Gone". *I told him that this meant that Dick was cutting faeces out of his mother.* He then ran into the space between the doors and scratched on the doors a little with his nails, *thus showing that he identified the space with the cart and both with the mother's body, which he was attacking* (p. 243) . . . It became clear that in Dick's phantasy *faeces, urine and penis stood for objects with which to attack the mother's body*, and were therefore felt to be a source of injury to himself as well. These phantasies contributed to his *dread of the contents of his mother's body, and especially of his father's penis which he phantasied as being in her womb.* We came to recognize the father's penis and a growing feeling of aggression against it in many forms, the desire to eat and destroy it being especially prominent. For example, on one occasion, Dick lifted a little toy man to his mouth, gnashed his teeth and said 'Tea daddy', by which he meant 'Eat daddy'. He then asked for a drink of water. The *introjection of the father's penis proved to be associated with the dread both of it, as of a primitive, harm-inflicting super-ego, and of being punished by the mother thus robbed* . . . (p. 30, my italics)

Many writers have observed that Kleinian patients learn the analyst's language, as indeed do all psychoanalytic patients, regardless of analytic orientation (Balint, 1968). Balint observed that most people will learn the dominant language of their environment, and, thus, any analysand is capable of learning his analyst's language. However, it is not the analysand's choice if the analysand's hope of being understood by the analyst is to be fulfilled. Morse (1972) further noted that this process of language learning is problematically used to demonstrate the veracity of the psychoanalytic method:

As a matter of logic, preverbal experiences will have to be described by an idiosyncratic language because at that level words have no conventional, shared meaning. The "Kleinian breast" is clearly a thing unto itself . . . In the area of preverbal experience, where words do not have a concise, shared meaning, this learning–confirming process will be especially active . . . rather than being universal, the associations of analysands simply reflect the language they have learned in order to obtain aid and understanding. Thus patients' associations, especially those that deal with preverbal experience where words have no agreed meaning, cannot be taken as proof of the validity of a theory (p. 490).

Analytic language learning can be explained by a behavioural conditioning process called shaping, which involves the identification and reinforcement of successive approximations of the target behaviour. The target behaviour is finally established by reinforcing closer and closer approximations while ceasing to reinforce earlier approximations of the desired behaviour (Martin & Pear, 2003). Learning to talk is an apt example of how shaping occurs in everyday experience. When an infant is just beginning to make sounds parents will reinforce any attempt at communication. As the child develops, his speech sounds are shaped by the care-giver's reinforcement of closer and closer approximations until they resemble intelligible speech. In much the same way, patients learn the "language" of psychoanalysis because it is reinforced by their analysts, often in subtle ways that might be out of the analyst's awareness. Postmodern literary scholars have also expressed similar concerns from a different theoretical perspective.

. . . psychoanalysis is . . . a ritualized encounter that produces certain kinds of discourse, the "intrapsychic" is actually a mode of the interpersonal or even of the cultural . . . Both analysts and patients find in an analysis precisely what they have been trained, consciously and unconsciously, to find . . . patients of Lacanians produce Lacanian symptoms, Kleinian patients, Kleinian ones . . . (Jones, 2003, p. 171)

Klein (1930) herself admitted, with respect to the analysis of Dick that:

In general I do not interpret the material until it has found expression in various representations. In this case, however, *where the capacity to represent it was almost entirely lacking, I found myself obliged to make my interpretations on the basis of my general knowledge, the representations in Dick's behaviour being relatively vague.* (p. 34, my italics)

In most forms of psychoanalysis, interpretations are used spar-
ingly and cautiously until a sound therapeutic alliance has been established. Care is taken not to breach the defences too precipitously for
fear of unleashing unmanageable anxiety, from which the patient
might retreat into impenetrable defences or abandon the therapy altogether. The aim of interpretation is to identify and reduce the defences, thus allowing access to underlying anxiety about unconscious
conflicts. As the defences are interpreted, the ego becomes stronger
and more able to deal with underlying conflicts. One of the major
criticisms of Kleinian technique is that too little attention is paid to
the building of a therapeutic alliance and the importance of the transference is under-emphasised. The focus on the identification and
interpretation of primitive unconscious material needs to occur simultaneously with identification and interpretation of the defences from
the outset of therapy. The aim of Kleinian interpretation is to repair
unconscious splits, a process purportedly aided by the internalisation
of the analytic object, which might prove problematic in the absence
of a therapeutic alliance and positive transference. Another criticism
is the Kleinian focus on the primitive and the internal, with insufficient attention paid to real relationships and events in the patient's
life.

The infant of the Controversies and the British Independent Group

> . . . libido is primarily object-seeking (rather than pleasure-seeking, as
> in the classic theory), and that it is to disturbances in the object-rela-
> tionships of the developing ego that we must look for the ultimate
> origin of all psychopathological conditions. (Fairbairn, 1944, p. 70)

During the period 1920–1940, Anna Freud presided over the Viennese
school of child analysis, known as the "Kinderseminar", which included a large number of eminent psychoanalysts, including Heinz Hartmann, Helen Deutsch, Ernst Kris, and René Spitz. They were an active
group who ran the Viennese Institute of Psychoanalysis, conducted
lectures on psychoanalytic education and child analysis, and published their work in the journal, *The Psychoanalytic Study of the Child*.
They also founded institutions and kindergartens for disadvantaged

children, in which Erik Erikson was actively involved. The advent of the Second World War dispersed this group of primarily Jewish professionals, but they renewed their associations as soon as the war ended. Some of them took the work abroad. Dorothy Burlingham was a key figure in the child analytic scene in London, where she co-founded the Hampstead Clinic with Anna Freud.

Ernest Jones founded the British Psychoanalytic Society in 1919, and in 1920 established the *International Journal of Psychoanalysis*. Melanie Klein joined the English school of psychoanalysis at the invitation of Ernest Jones in 1926. Other eminent members of this group included Alix and James Strachey, Paula Heimann, Joan Riviere, and Susan Isaacs, who, in 1924, became principal of a "revolutionary" school in Cambridge, whose educational philosophy was based on the encouragement of children to study themselves deeply and to express themselves freely, including in sexual matters. The school closed amid scandal and hostility in 1927. After 1946, when Klein's theories became more extreme, her older supporters distanced themselves somewhat, but they were soon replaced by new followers such as Hanna Segal, who was one of Klein's biographers, Herbert Rosenfeld, and Wilfrid Bion. None the less, Riviere paid tribute to Klein for recognising that babies have a mind and engage in psychical processing long before they are able to communicate in ways that adults understand (Geissman & Geissman, 1998).

The term "Controversies" was given to the period 1941–1945, during which there was open hostility between Anna Freud and Melanie Klein and their respective "schools". The details have been recorded in *The Freud–Klein Controversies 1941–1945*, edited by Pearl King and Riccardo Steiner (King & Steiner, 1991). (The interested reader is referred to this text for a detailed coverage.) On Klein's split with Anna Freud, Hanna Segal stated that "neither Anna Freud nor Melanie Klein was driven excessively by personal ambition. They fought because they disagreed. Most splits happen because of analysts' narcissism and grandiosity" (Pick, 2006). This is perhaps a gilding of the lily, given that the two women did not speak to each other at psychoanalytic meetings and maintained this stance for most of their professional lives. Many have argued that there was an underlying sibling rivalry, with each vying for Sigmund Freud's approval. The hostility between them and their respective factions was such that it caused a major rift in the British Psychoanalytic

Society, and there ensued a bitter battle to have Klein expelled. Sadly, Melitta Schmideberg, Klein's daughter, together with her analyst, Edward Glover, were vocal adversaries of Klein's theories and supported those wishing to expel her.

The disagreements centred on the concept of primary narcissism, a period before the development of object relations, as proposed by Freud, and whether object relations were present from birth, as claimed by Klein. We will take up this issue in more detail in later chapters. Klein proposed a much earlier timing for ego development than Freud, which afforded the capacity for unconscious phantasies that Klein viewed as psychic representations of the instincts and the source of introjection and projection. Although these later constructs are generally associated with Kleinian theory, Sigmund Freud had discussed these mechanisms in "Instincts and their vicissitudes" (1915c), in which he described introjection as absorption by the ego of objects associated with pleasure, and projection as the expulsion by the ego of contents associated with pain. Regression, a central construct in Sigmund Freud's theory, was another point of departure between the Freudians and the Kleinians. Freud linked fixation to earlier stages of development and regression to the emergence of mental disorders. However, once Klein had proposed the paranoid–schizoid position, regression became less important in her theorising. She argued that libidinal fixation was not the cause but, rather, the effect of a pathological process (Segal, 1979). In Klein's model, infants fluctuated between pre-genital and genital forms of the Oedipus complex, of which the superego was a part, not an outcome, as suggested by Freud, and this fluctuation was related to anxiety, not fixation or regression (Klein, 1989). Further, Klein argued that her so-called depressive position was reached in infants as young as six months old when psychotic anxieties were resolved. Klein viewed the struggle between the life (Eros) and death (Thanatos) instincts as a central tenet in her theory of infant psychic development. Finally, as discussed above, Klein proposed a theory of female sexuality that followed its own trajectory and was not a "castrated counterpart of masculine sexuality" (Geissman & Geissman, 1998, p. 173).

Klein and Anna Freud were also in conflict regarding the proper technique for child analysis, in particular the role of transference and transference analysis in child analysis. While Anna Freud championed the role of education, reassurance, and support, Klein argued that education, even psychoanalytically orientated education, was not sufficient to correct psychological difficulties in children and that only analysis, using the play technique she developed, would access their anxiety. Klein (1927) believed that play was very important in the lives of children. She subsequently developed play therapy, which she conceptualised as equivalent to a dream-like state or free association in adults—see, for example, *The Psychoanalysis of Children* (1932)—and that the manifest content and meaning of the play had to be analysed in order to reveal its latent content, that is, the symbolic expression of the child's unconscious in the play material (Klein, 1929). Further, in opposition to Anna Freud, Klein argued in "The origins of transference" (1952b) that both the positive and negative transferences needed to be interpreted because "the life and death instincts, and therefore love and hatred, are at bottom in the closest interaction; [therefore] negative and positive transference are basically inter-linked" (Klein, 1975, p. 54).

The Controversies ended in 1946 with the establishment of three schools of psychoanalysis in the British Psychoanalytic Society—the Anna Freud group, the Kleinian group, and the British Independent or Middle group. Kleinians remained focused on child psychoanalysis and the treatment of psychosis, while Anna Freud was more interested in the study of normal children and common childhood disorders, and the effects of early separation on young children in the context of the war and the destruction of Britain's cities, events that resulted in infants and children being separated through parental death or evacuation to safety from the London blitz. Some of these children went to the Hampstead Nurseries, established in 1942 by Anna Freud and Dorothy Burlingham. After the war, a number of other clinics sprang up—the Tavistock Clinic, which espoused Kleinian theories, and the Hampstead Clinic, founded by Anna Freud. The Child Guidance movement, accompanied by Child Guidance Clinics established across the country, also appeared in post-war Britain. These developments were the outward expression of an acceptance of the importance of childhood experiences in psychological well-being.

The British Independent group was so named because it comprised a heterogeneous group of independent thinkers who were not aligned with either the Anna Freudians or the Kleinians in the British Psychoanalytic Society. However, they were unified in their acceptance of Fairbairn's statement, above, that disturbance in object relations is the source of all psychopathology. The key members of the this group were Michael Balint (1949), William Ronald Dodds Fairbairn (1946, 1952, 1958, 1963), Harry Guntrip (1962, 1967, 1973, 1975), Masud Khan (1960, 1963, 1971, 1974, 1981), John Klauber (1976, 1977, 1980), Christopher Bollas (1979, 1981, 1982, 2006), Donald Winnicott, and John Bowlby (see below and Chapter Four). Space does not permit a detailed coverage of all of these contributors to theories of infant and child development; the interested reader is referred to Rayner (1991) and Kohon (1986) for comprehensive reviews.

The British Independents extended and modified Freud's conceptions of repression and pre-Oedipal psychopathology, and further developed and refined object relations theory. They focused their theorising on infant development and the effect of environment and traumata, which they argued were stored in memories that, by virtue of their traumatic nature, become dissociated from the ego or functional self. In contrast to Melanie Klein, the Independents viewed psychopathology as originating in actual pathological objects, which are re-enacted in the therapeutic relationship through the transference, thus permitting a working through of the original trauma with a benign, reparative object/analyst. The analytic relationship was, therefore, viewed as the major vehicle of a successful analytic outcome (McGregor, 2006). Unlike the constitutionally aggressive and destructive baby of Kleinian theory, the baby of the British Independents was perceived as innately social and interactive, who will develop non-traumatically if not thwarted by inadequate parenting. At a meeting of the British Psychoanalytic Society, Bowlby famously asserted, in a reaction against Klein's vision of infants, "But there is such a thing as a bad mother" (Mitchell & Black, 1995, p. 114).

Although each of the British Independents espoused his own theories, there are common themes—for example, the conception that, in contrast to the classical emphasis on intrapsychic mechanisms and phantasy, personality development is a function of relationships between the ego and its objects, both internal and external, and that maintenance of a relationship with the primary care-giving object is necessary for the emotional survival of the infant and young child (Fairbairn, 1946, 1963). Bowlby (1960a, 1963) later observed that no child under ten years of age can tolerate (perhaps even survive) the realisation that his parents do not love him. A depriving and/or rejecting mother awakens an intense longing in the child, who comes to perceive the strength of his need as the reason for her rejection. The child tries to repress his need and adapt himself to his mother's needs (a process later described by Winnicott as impingement and by Brandchaft (2007) as pathological accommodation), which offers hope for the relationship, but at great personal cost to the child.

When early relationships go awry, the result is the development of a damaged, disturbed or distorted self, which struggles to protect the core or true self from annihilation. This damaged self is described in various ways in the different object relations theories: for example, Balint's (1968) "basic fault", Winnicott's (1965b) "false self", McDougall's (1986) "anti-analysand", and Bollas's (1987) "normotic" character, who is "abnormally normal" and who uses manic defences to protect against awareness of a distressed inner life and emotional states. The mechanism for the development of a false self was described by Winnicott (1969a) as "a failure of self-establishment and self-discovery" (p. 711), and by Fairbairn (1944) as a process in which it becomes dangerous for the child to express his

> . . . nascent love of his mother in the face of rejection at her hands: for it is equivalent to discharging his love into an emotional vacuum. Such a discharge is accompanied by an affective experience which is singularly devastating. In the older child this experience is one of intense humiliation over the depreciation of his love . . . At a somewhat deeper level (or at an earlier stage) the experience is one of shame over the display of needs that are disregarded or belittled. In virtue of these experiences of humiliation and shame he feels reduced to a state of worthlessness, destitution or beggardom. His sense of his own value is threatened; and he feels bad in the sense of "inferior". The intensity of these experiences is . . . proportionate to the intensity of his need; and intensity of need itself increases his sense of badness by contributing to it the quality of "demanding too much" . . . his sense of badness is further complicated by the sense of utter impotence which he also experiences. At a still deeper level (or at a still earlier stage) the child's experience is one of . . . exploding ineffectively (with rage and frustration) and being completely emptied of libido. It is thus an experience of disintegration and of imminent psychical death. (Fairbairn, 1944, p. 84)

Daehnert (1998) subsequently identified five functions of the false self. These are to: (i) protect the True Self from mother's impingement and neglect; (ii) maintain connection with mother; (iii) protect mother from the infant's destructiveness; (iv) ward off the child's anxiety about Oedipal conflicts; (v) create a means for the child to disidentify from mother.

The group was critical of impulse psychology, stating that the problems that brought people into therapy were not related to repressed impulses but to damaged relationships of the ego to its internalised objects. When defining his concept of "basic fault", Balint (1968) wanted to

> stress that it is described as a fault, not as a situation, position, conflict, or complex . . . [in which] . . . all the events that happen in it belong to [a] two-person relationship (p. 16) . . . a fault, something wrong with the mind, a . . . deficiency which must be put right. It is not something dammed up for which a better outlet must be found, but something missing . . . perhaps for the whole of the patient's life. An instinctual need can be satisfied, a conflict can be solved, a basic fault can perhaps be merely healed provided the deficient ingredients can be found . . . (pp. 21–22)

As to the cause of the basic fault, Balint ". . . put the emphasis on the lack of 'fit' between the child and the people who represent his environment" (p. 22).

Unlike the Kleinians, who argued that the source of psychopathology lay in the conflict between the life and death instincts, which then transformed into a conflict between love and hate in relation to objects, the Independents argued that the source of psychopathology arose from actual destructive external object relations. Impulses were re-defined as forms of energy attached to these ego structures, not as entities that existed *per se*; put differently, the manner in which a person manages his impulse-tension is a problem of object-relationships (Fairbairn, 1944). To further clarify this central point of object relations theories, self was regarded as reality orientated and, thus, reality constrained from the beginning of life. Fairbairn (1946) argued that "[T]he real libidinal aim is the establishment of satisfactory relationships with objects; and it is, accordingly, the object that constitutes the true libidinal goal" (p. 138). This view has received considerable empirical support from attachment research and developmental psychology, as we shall see in subsequent chapters.

This revised definition and role of impulses and instincts created a problem for Freud's concept of repression, which refers to the ego's function in removing from awareness instinctual energy originating in the id. Fairbairn (1944) argued that what was repressed was neither impulses/instincts nor painful memories, as Freud had proposed, but "bad" internalised objects and those parts of the ego that seek a relationship with these bad objects, in a process akin to dissociation. These complex psychic manoeuvres are necessary because the child needs a "good enough" relationship with his object. If basic relational needs are not met, the infant becomes ambivalent towards his frustrating objects and this frustration unleashes feelings of hatred and rage towards this tantalising but ungiving object, a situation that sets up a cycle of hope and despair (hopelessness). Fairbairn (1952) understood that ambivalence arises in response to experiences of deprivation and frustration with an object that is indispensable to his survival. Given his dependence on this object, the child cannot accept his mother as a bad object and he cannot risk expressing his anger lest he lose her altogether. Therefore, he engages in a defensive internalisation of his mother, which serves the dual roles of allowing the child to preserve her image as safe and loving and also to limit the effects of disappointment and rejection from his "external" or "real" mother. To do this, he must split his internal object and repress its frustrating, rejecting elements, which Fairbairn described as the "internal saboteur". The child now no longer sees his mother as bad. None the less, the child must still interact with his external mother, and must explain to himself why his mother rejects him. He concludes that his mother rejects him because he is bad, unlovable, or too demanding, and if he behaves differently, she might love him. Thus, the mechanism for the development of a false self is established (Armstrong-Perlman, 1991).

Donald Winnicott

"A baby can be fed without love, but lovelessness as impersonal management cannot succeed in producing a new, autonomous human child" (Winnicott, 1971, p. 108).

Like Freud, Winnicott spent his early years until the age of twelve in a household of adoring women—his mother and two older sisters, as well as cooks and housekeepers who managed the well-to-do household of this upper middle-class family. Following a football injury at the age of thirteen, Donald decided that he wanted to study medicine and, after the First World War, he became first a doctor and then a paediatrician at Paddington Green Children's Hospital, where he was to remain for forty years, working primarily with children, with whom he displayed a rare gift. He was known for his extraordinary insights into human nature, and children specifically; he never used drugs to treat children, believing that understanding and corrective relationships would be curative in the majority of cases. He had a long association with the BBC in which he broadcast lectures and discussions about children and parenting that were universally well received by listeners.

The chance discovery of Freud during his medical studies led Winnicott into a ten-year analysis with James Strachey, and an interest in working with psychotic patients. Strachey introduced Winnicott to the work of Melanie Klein (Winnicott, 1977). Winnicott subsequently analysed Klein's son, Erich, and underwent a second analysis with Joan Riviere. He was twice married, the second time to Clare, a social worker with whom he worked during the Second World War. They were a childless couple. During the post-war period, he was active, with Michael Balint, in establishing the Independent or Middle Group within the British Psychoanalytic Society. He was considered a Kleinian by the Anna Freudians and ignored, but he was also rejected by the Kleinians, although he was initially influenced by Klein's ideas, which interested him at first, but which he later retracted, claiming that he could not follow anyone, "not even Freud". Despite his seemingly precarious position with respect to the factions within the British Psychoanalytic Society, he was twice elected its President (Geissman & Geissman, 1998).

Winnicott's work

> There are roughly speaking two kinds of human being, those who do not carry with them a significant experience of mental breakdown in earliest infancy and those who do carry around with them such an experience and who must therefore flee from it, flirt with it, fear it, and to some extent be always preoccupied with the threat of it. (Winnicott, 1989, p. 122)

Winnicott's psychoanalytic focus differed from Sigmund Freud's and Melanie Klein's in that he was less interested in psychopathology and diagnosis and more concerned with the ongoing quality of lived experience, inner reality, one's sense of self as an agentive, purposeful, meaning-seeking being. It is worth noting that several of the British Independents (e.g., Balint, Winnicott, Fairbairn, Guntrip) all had a similar focus and proposed similar theories, using different terminologies, but based on similar clinical practices that were focused on preverbal as opposed to Oedipal issues. Winnicott was selected to represent the British Independent group because of his popular appeal and the fact that some of his metaphors have entered the wider lexicon.

Winnicott (1945) identified three major tasks that needed to be accomplished in infancy. These are (i) integration—"the need to be known in all his bits and pieces by one person" (p. 140); (ii) personalisation—"localization of one's self within one's body", and to create a workable relationship between one's mind and body (p. 140); and (iii) realisation—"an appreciation of time and space, and other properties of reality" (p. 139). To succeed in this enterprise, the infant progresses from a state of undifferentiated unity with the mother: ". . . whenever one finds an infant one finds maternal care, and without maternal care there would be no infant" (Winnicott, 1965b, p. 39), through a transitional phase, involving the gradual development of an understanding of separateness, and a sense of disillusionment in which the infant comes to realise that others are also important in his mother's life. This is accomplished through a process of projection of bad objects, fears, and frustrations into mother and eventual reintrojection of these in a manageable form.

> The object is repudiated, reaccepted, and perceived objectively. This complex process is highly dependent on there being a mother or mother-figure prepared to participate and to give back what is handed out. This means that the mother . . . is in a "to and fro" between being that which the baby has a capacity to find and (alternatively) being herself waiting to be found. (Winnicott, 1968, p. 596)

During this phase, the child makes use of transitional objects that are substitutes for mother, which allow the child to be separated from mother without intolerable anxiety (Winnicott, 1953). Successful negotiation of the transitional period results in the child's progression to relative independence, or, more accurately, to a state of mature dependence.

The new mother's "primary maternal preoccupation" with her infant allows her to be in a state of heightened attunement and, thus, well placed to respond to her baby's needs as they arise. Because the baby is responded to in such an exemplary fashion, that is, in an ideal "holding environment", he develops feelings of omnipotence because mother is (apparently) able to create and fulfil all his wishes. (These early feelings of subjective omnipotence never really leave us—they remain part of our deeply private core selves.) The following text illuminates Winnicott's (1945) understanding of the mother–infant relationship, as well as introducing his concepts of holding, transitional object and dependence:

> In terms of baby and mother's breast (I am not claiming that the breast is essential as a vehicle of mother-love) the baby has instinctual urges and predatory ideas. The mother has a breast and the power to produce milk, and the idea that she would like to be attacked by a hungry baby. These two phenomena do not come into relation with each other till the mother and child live an experience together. The mother being mature and physically able has to be the one with tolerance and understanding, so that it is she who produces a situation that may with luck result in the first tie the infant makes with an external object, an object that is external to the self from the infant's point of view. I think of the process as if two lines came from opposite directions ... If they overlap there is a moment of illusion – a bit of experience which the infant can take as either his hallucination or a thing belonging to external reality. (p. 141)

Eventually, the mother will fail to satisfy her infant's every whim, requiring the infant's feelings of omnipotence to be tempered with objective reality. The transitional space and its transitional objects, such as favourite teddy bears, bunny rugs, and other objects, comfort the child during separations from mother or during maternal failures. Winnicott viewed these objects not only as extensions of the mother, but also of the child's self, who discovers through this transitional process that he can retain some of the original omnipotence of infancy and manage for a time without mother. This space is also creative, playful, experimental, a place where the child learns about the world, both the internal world of his objects and the reality of the external world (Winnicott, 1968, 1971).

Play is immensely exciting. . . . [because of] the precariousness of the interplay of personal psychic reality and the experience of control of actual objects. This is the precariousness of magic itself, magic that arises in intimacy, in a relationship that is being found to be reliable. To be reliable the relationship is necessarily motivated by the mother's love, not by reaction formations (Winnicott, 1968, p. 596).

Out of this play space grows the dual foundational capacities to be alone in the presence of someone and for playing together in a relationship (Winnicott, 1968).

Failure to successfully negotiate these developmental tasks due to the absence of "good enough" maternal responsiveness to the infant's needs results in the development of a "false self", which Winnicott describes in many ways, including as "an internalized environment" and a "social attitude [which] [a]t the extreme of abnormality . . . can easily get itself mistaken for real, so that the real self is under threat of annihilation; suicide can then be a reassertion of the true self" (1965b, p. 133). Winnicott describes the process of necessitating false self development (i.e., psychopathology) in terms of impingement:

In the early development of the human being the environment that behaves well enough (that makes good enough active adaptation) enables personal growth to take place. The self processes then may continue active, in an unbroken line of living growth. If the environment behaves not well enough, then the individual is engaged in reactions to impingement, and the self processes are interrupted. If this state of affairs reaches a quantitative limit the core of the self begins to get protected; there is a hold-up, the self cannot make new progress unless and until the environment failure situation is corrected . . . With the true self protected there develops a false self built on a defence-compliance basis, the acceptance of reaction to impingement. The development of a false self is one of the most successful defence organisations designed for the protection of the true self's core, [but] . . . [w]hile the individual's operational centre is in the false self there is a sense of futility, and in practice we find the change to the feeling that life is worthwhile coming at the moment of shift of the operational centre from the false to the true self, even before full surrender of the self's core to the total ego. From this one can formulate a fundamental principle of existence: that which proceeds from the true self feels real (later good) whatever its nature, however aggressive; that which happens in the individual as a reaction to environmental impingement

feels unreal, futile (later bad), however sensually satisfactory. (Winnicott, 1955, p. 25)

Thus, Winnicott's false self can be understood as a form of adaptation or defensive function that comes into being like the defences in
classical theory, as a means of defending against the contents of the
true self that have come to be experienced as unacceptable in response
to environmental impingements. Mitchell and Black (1995) describe
the false self as a form of disordered subjectivity, in which the "kernel
of genuine personhood is suspended, buffered by an adaptive compliance with the deficient environment" (p. 129) that prevents the baby
from developing a sense of "going-on-being", a phrase coined by
Winnicott to describe what he perceived to be the natural flow of the
infant's experience of needs, appropriate maternal attention, satiation,
and contentment that results in the development of "an affective core
to the pre-representational self" (Stern, 1985, p.7).

There are a number of ways in which impingement occurs: (i) the
child expresses desire and that desire is rebuffed, ridiculed or unfulfilled; (ii) the child is in a state of going-on-being that is not sustained
or supported; (iii) the child is placed in a position of prematurely (i.e.,
before the consolidation of the child's true self) having to negotiate
with the outside world; (iv) assimilation of a "bad object" by the
infant's ego. Following Anna Freud and Hartmann, Winnicott elaborated Freud's concept of primary narcissism by emphasising the role
of the mother as object and the psychological and social environment
in formative narcissistic processes. Winnicott (1955, 1960, 1965b)
argued that narcissism develops within the context of the primary
psychic relationship and that Freud's "shadow"[10] (i.e., a disappointing
or lost object) is assimilated by the infant's ego such that it is recognised as a part of the ego and not as an object, thereby creating an
identity that is constructed through internalising the reflection sent
out by another person. Thus, the object is no longer lost and does not
have to be mourned. Further, the process of assimilation is "forgotten"
and the individual enters into a "primary narcissistic illusion" (Roussillon, 2010), in which the object is taken to be the self's emotional
mirror. The object is not experienced as separate; if the object is "bad"
or lost the self must set up "palliative auto-erotic measures" to deal
with the loss or threat. Winnicott (1972) believed that the ensuing feelings of emptiness were "the effect on the ego of the shadow of an

unresponsive object that remained silent in the face of the self's entreaties, indifferent to the self's urges, perhaps even turning away in hostility" (Rousillon, 2010, p. 826).

The role of psychoanalysis is to restore the "otherness" of the assimilated object. The analytic space exposes the influence of the mirror-object and "reconstructs the characteristic features of the primitive conversation between baby and mother" (Winnicott, 1972, p. 9). The analytic dyad becomes an analogue of the mother–infant dyad; if the normal developmental tasks outlined above could not be accomplished within the mother–infant dyad, they can be accomplished within the analyst–patient dyad. The reliability of the analyst and the analytic setting merge "into the original success situation of primary narcissism" (Geissman & Geissman, 1998, p. 232), where the earliest experiences of maternal care are repeated in the transference as projections that can be interpreted by the analyst. In the same way that the infant builds memories of good maternal care, so the analytic patient who has not experienced maternal reliability or empathy builds confidence in the care of the analyst. This allows the patient to achieve a "continuity of being", a process that was interrupted in infancy by maternal impingements that are experienced by the infant as annihilation of its personal being, against which it defends by the development of a false self that acts as a caretaker and protector of the true self (Winnicott, 1960).

> [T]he true self [is] hidden, protected by a false self. This false self is no doubt an aspect of the true self. It hides and protects it, and it reacts to the adaptation failures and develops a pattern corresponding to the pattern of environmental failure. In this way the true self is not involved in the reacting, and so preserves a continuity of being. This hidden true self suffers an impoverishment, however, that results from lack of experience. The false self may achieve a deceptive false integrity, that is to say a false ego-strength, gathered from an environmental pattern, and from a good and reliable environment; for it by no means follows that early maternal failure must lead to a general failure of child-care. The false self cannot, however, experience life and feel real. (Winnicott, 1956, p. 387)

Two examples will illuminate Winnicott's idea of what it means to feel alive, real, and authentic. In the first example, Winnicott (1986b) quipped to a patient in *Holding and Interpretation: Fragment of an Analysis,* "It seems to have strengthened your whole personality, getting closer to cannibalism and to instincts" (p. 25). In the second example, some young Anglican priests asked him how they would know whether a parishioner was psychiatrically ill and in need of a psychiatrist, or whether he just needed to talk with his priest. Winnicott (1986b) replied:

> If a person comes and talks to you and, listening to him, you feel is boring you, then he is sick and needs psychiatric treatment. But if he sustains your interest, no matter how grave his distress or conflict, then you can help him alright. (p. 1)

In "Metapsychological and clinical aspects of regression within the psycho-analytic set-up", Winnicott (1955) outlined the required therapeutic process which follows from his theory, a process that provides the "good mothering" that was insufficient during the patient's infancy.

1. The provision of a setting that gives confidence.
2. Regression of the patient to dependence. [Note: For Winnicott, the capacity to regress presupposes sufficient care during infancy such that patients have a belief in the possibility of a corrective therapeutic experience.]
3. The patient feeling a new sense of self, and the self hitherto hidden becoming surrendered to the total ego. A new progression of the individual processes that had stopped.
4. An unfreezing of an environmental failure situation.
5. From the new position of ego strength, anger related to the early environmental failure, felt in the present and expressed.
6. Return from regression to dependence, in orderly progress towards independence.
7. Instinctual needs and wishes becoming realizable with genuine vitality and vigour.
8. All this repeated again and again. (p. 22)

To sum up the therapeutic goals and process in Winnicott's (1969a) words:

> [The] false self represent[s] failures of self-establishment and self-discovery. All this makes sense, for me, of the special focus that there is in my work on what I have called transitional phenomena and the study of the minute details . . . that illustrate the gradual build-up of

the individual's capacity to play and the capacity to find and then to use the 'external' world with its own independence and autonomy. (p. 711)

Winnicott placed great importance on the analytic setting, of which the analyst was only a part, in order to (re-)create the mother–infant situation. Subsequently, the importance of the analyst–analytic setting has been recognised in the metaphors for the analytic setting that have been proposed: for example, "nuclear reactor" (Laplanche), "the maternal reverie" (Bion), the "dream space" (Green), and "the improvisational theatre scene" (Bienvenu, 2003; Carignan, 2006). Bienvenu (2003) argues that the components of the analytic situation that foster and contain a process of illusion provide the nexus between the psychoanalytic setting and its therapeutic action. However,

> [f]or the illusionary process to be beneficial to the ego, a parallel process of disillusionment must be set in motion, but in a dose tolerable for the analysand ... [In this process, psychoanalytic truth] migrates from historical truth, via the psychical truth of unconscious fantasies ... toward a conception of truth that emerges from a form of creative intersubjectivity. (Carignan, 2006, p. 995)

As a result of exposing and expunging powerful, and, at times, malevolent or suffocating identifications with internalised parental figures, the unrealised potential, or true self of the patient, can begin to emerge (Winnicott & Khan, 1953). This involves connecting with desires, needs, and feelings for the first time, and knowing that they are one's own.

Winnicott's infant

". . . the child establishing a private self . . . is a sophisticated game of hide-and-seek in which it is a joy to be hidden but a disaster not to be found" (Winnicott, 1965b, p. 186).

Winnicott stated that the passage quoted below had a significant impact on his view of infancy and was perhaps the inspiration for his statement: "There is no such thing as an infant . . ."

> It will be rightly objected that an organisation which was a slave to the pleasure principle and neglected the reality of the external world

could not maintain itself alive for the shortest time, so that it could not have come into existence at all. The employment of a fiction like this is, however, justified when one considers that the infant—provided one includes with it the care it receives from its mother—does almost realise a psychical system of this kind. (Freud, 1911b, p. 219)

Winnicott (1960) subsequently confirmed his position that ". . . at the earliest stages the infant and the maternal care belong to each other and cannot be disentangled" (p. 587). Winnicott acknowledges that the infant is born with inherited potential, but this potential cannot be realised unless the environmental conditions, including, but not limited to, maternal care, are adequate or "good enough". In the course of healthy development, one can expect "the infant ego [to] eventually become free of the mother's ego support, so that the infant achieves mental detachment from the mother, that is, differentiation into a separate personal self" (Winnicott, 1960, p. 588).

In the process of achieving differentiation and separateness, the necessary "structuring of the ego . . . makes anxiety from instinct tension or object loss possible. Anxiety at this early stage is not castration anxiety or separation anxiety; it relates to . . . anxiety about annihilation" (p. 588).

At some very early stage of development, the infant must emerge from "the state of being merged with the mother" (i.e., a state of primary narcissism) and to perceive objects as external to himself. This process can be experienced as traumatic:

The feeling of the mother's existence lasts x minutes. If the mother is away more than x minutes, then the imago fades, and along with this the baby's capacity to use the symbol of the union ceases to be a fact. The baby is distressed, but this distress is soon mended because the mother returns in x + y minutes. But in x + y + z minutes the baby has become traumatized. In x + y + z minutes *the mother's return does not mend the baby's altered state. Trauma implies that the baby has experienced a break in life's continuity, so that primitive defences now become organized to defend against a repetition of "unthinkable anxiety"* or of the acute confusional state that belongs to disintegration of the emerging ego structure. (Winnicott, 1967, p. 369, my italics)

If these traumas are not profound or repetitive, Winnicott's infant becomes actively involved with his environment and engaged in meaning making. He is an intensely relational being who is object seeking and responsive to his primary objects. For Winnicott, unconscious object relations are the foundation of identity and personality:

> . . . the capacity of the individual to be alone . . . is one of the most important signs of maturity in emotional development . . . [it] depends on the existence in the psychic reality of the individual of a good object . . . Being alone in the presence of someone can take place at a very early stage, when the ego immaturity is naturally balanced by ego support from the mother. In the course of time the individual introjects the ego-supportive mother and in this way becomes able to be alone without frequent reference to the mother or mother symbol. (Winnicott, 1958, pp. 417–418)

Winnicott's infant is born with the capacity for social interaction and non-traumatic development; that is, he is not besieged like Freud's and Klein's infants with aggressive and sexual impulses that create conflict. Winnicott's infant, and indeed the infant of the British Middle School, is active, engaged, playful, and responsive to his environment. "The . . . normal child is able to play, to get excited while playing, and to feel satisfied with the game . . . a deprived child . . . is unable to enjoy play . . . (Winnicott, 1958, p. 419).

Critiquing Donald Winnicott

"The absurd is born of this confrontation between the human need and the unreasonable silence of the world" (Camus, 1942, p. 21).

Winnicott's body of work is somewhat difficult to assess because, unlike his predecessors, Sigmund Freud, Anna Freud, and Melanie Klein, he identified new phenomena, or, more accurately, he provided compelling new metaphors and concepts for infant (and indeed, human) experience, but did not develop an adequate structural theory to explain them (Morse, 1972). None the less, one experiences a great deal of intuitive resonance when reading Winnicott, despite being left with questions about his underlying theory. In this critique, I will focus on just two of Winnicott's central constructs: the false self and the transitional space, its objects and symbolic play, because these are the most widely known, the most often quoted, and, in my view, the most in need of clarification. Winnicott proposed that we develop a false self in response to environmental impingement, but the manner in which the self becomes false is not clear. Does the self become false simply by the act of compliance or impingement (a process akin to socialisation at its most benign and abuse or neglect at its most malignant), or is some form of intolerable anxiety (e.g., fear of annihilation) necessary for the construction of a false self as a defensively compliant façade that is eventually experienced as rigid and unreal, giving rise to feelings of fraudulence and futility?

Winnicott proposes that the infant begins life with a true self, a unified (undifferentiated) ego–id structure that is biological in origin, the source of feelings of aliveness and spontaneous gesture, thus confirming his position that object-relationships are present at birth, albeit primitively. It is inevitable that this nascent ego will soon meet with impingement, necessitating the splitting of the ego into a true self (i.e., the unitary primal ego), which is, or becomes, unconscious and remains protected from the world (of impingements), leaving the remaining part of the self, comprising both true and false self aspects, to deal with the world. Continued traumatic impingements motivate a second split, in which the remaining aspects of the true self are defensively split off, leaving only the false self to interact with external reality. Winnicott includes among his list of impingements the offer of the breast when it is not required. Even though the feed from this breast might still be satisfying, because it is a response to impingement, that is, reactive, it cannot feel "real" and, thus, violates the self, giving rise to anxiety because it interrupts the infant's sense of going-on-being. Winnicott does not ascribe agency to the infant, for example, turning away from the offered breast or otherwise refusing to suck on it, behaviours that we will discover are well within the infant's behavioural repertoire and which might mitigate the effects of at least benign or inadvertent maternal impingements. If the offer of the breast when it has not been called for is an impingement, we must ask whether all impingements are traumatic and experienced with anxiety. Winnicott (1945) answers the question, somewhat paradoxically, by observing that objective reality, presumably with all its frustrating or distressing impingements, is, none the less, essential for psychic growth.

> One thing that follows the acceptance of external reality is the advantage to be gained from it. We often hear of the very real frustrations imposed by external reality, but less often hear of the relief and satis-

faction it affords. Real milk is satisfying as compared with imaginary milk, but this is not the point. The point is that in phantasy things work by magic: there are no brakes on magic, and love and hate cause alarming effects. External reality has brakes on it, and can be studied and known, and, in fact, phantasy is only tolerable at full blast when objective reality is appreciated well. The subjective has tremendous value but is so alarming and magical that it cannot be enjoyed except as a parallel to the objective. (Winnicott, 1941, p. 141)

In this passage, Winnicott states that objective reality, presumably a form of impingement (i.e., "very real frustrations"), is essential for the attainment of maturity and personal integration; that is, that impingement is necessary in order to be able to confront and tolerate one's subjectivity or true self.

What are the contents of the two aspects of the true self and how are they in relationship? What process determines which aspects of the true self will be split off in the first split and what remains? If the true self (unitary primal ego) remains hidden and uncontaminated by the external world, as Winnicott claims,

> ... this core never communicates with the world of perceived objects, and . . . the individual person knows that it must never be communicated with, or influenced by external reality ... although healthy persons communicate and enjoy communicating, the other fact is equally true, that each individual is an isolate, permanently non-communicating, permanently unknown, in fact unfound. (Winnicott, 1965b, p. 187, my italics)

and the remaining true self is later split off as a result of further impingements and presumably also becomes unconscious, then only the false self remains to interact with "objective reality", leading to the conclusion that many of us can never feel alive, real, or spontaneous or respond authentically to others. Morse (1972) asks whether such reasoning must render all cultural products manifestations of a false self. Of course, the degree of authenticity, adjustment, or psychopathology attained is relative to the inputs—the level and timing of impingements, the intensity of the repressed elements of self, the amount of environmental support offered subsequently, and so on.

Winnicott is not clear about the relationship between the false self and the superego. If the false self is populated with impinging object introjects with which the infant must comply for survival, is the false self in fact a (punitive) superego? Winnicott's (1956) description of the false self indicates a much more benign function than Freud's super-ego. Compare Freud's concept of the superego and Winnicott's view of the false self. For Freud,

> ... super-ego is ... not simply a residue of the earliest object-choices of the id; it also represents an energetic reaction-formation against those choices. Its relation to the ego is not exhausted by the precept: "You ought to be like this (like your father)." It also comprises the prohibition: "You may not be like this (like your father)". (Freud, 1923b, p. 34)

Winnicott (1956) states that the false self:

> ... develops a fixed maternal attitude towards the true self, and is permanently in a state of holding the true self as a mother holds a baby at the very beginning of differentiation and of emergence from primary identification. (p. 387)

Winnicott's description of the process whereby introjects come to occupy transitional space more closely resembles Freud's superego.

> There is a ... danger, in cases of premature failure of environmental reliability, which is that th[e] potential space may become filled with what is injected into it from someone other than the baby. It seems that whatever is in this space that comes from someone else is *persecutory material, and the baby has no means of rejecting it.* (Winnicott, 1967, p. 371, my italics)

Winnicott (1965b) notes in a discussion of guilt that "[a] false superego develop[s] based in an abnormal way on the intrusion of a very powerful authoritarian influence derived from the environment of early years" (p. 20). Later in the paper he refers to "a more natural superego organisation" (p. 28) but does not elaborate. Still later, in the context of a discussion on the teaching of religion, Winnicott refers to "a personal superego", a "terrifying superego", and "crude superego elements":

> The good alternative [to teaching religion] has to do with the provision of those conditions for the infant and child that enable such things as trust and 'belief in', and ideas of right and wrong, to develop out of the

working of the individual child's inner processes. This could be called the evolution of a personal superego (p. 93) . . . By experience of life and living the child in health becomes ready to believe in something that can be handed over in terms of a personal god. But the personal god idea has no value to a child who has not had the experience of human beings, persons humanizing the terrifying superego formations that relate directly to the infantile impulse and to the fantasy that goes with body functioning and with crude excitements involving instinct . . . (p. 101) . . . We have to provide them in infancy and childhood and adolescence, in home and in school, with the facilitating environment in which each individual may grow his or her own moral capacity, develop a superego that evolved naturally from crude superego elements of infancy, and find his or her own way of using or not using the moral code and general cultural endowment of our age. (p. 105)

It is possible that Winnicott means to infer that the false self and a punitive superego co-exist and serve each other; the harsher the superego, the greater the lack of integration and differentiation, the greater the need for false self functioning. If the harshness of the superego were reduced and the superego came to function as a personal or mature superego, there would be less need for the operation of the false self, which, in turn, might allow greater expression of true self aspects and hence greater integration. Just as there appears to be two processes leading to the repression of the true self, two processes might be needed to rescue the true selves. Removal or reduction of the defensive false self would reveal the true self "of cannibalism and instincts". Resolving conflicts around these primitive instincts would then allow the emergence and expression of the primal ego of aliveness and spontaneous gesture (notwithstanding Winnicott's claim that it can never be known or found!).

Another central concept is the transitional object and the intermediary or potential space, which, according to Winnicott, appear between four and twelve months of age, and whose function is to simultaneously symbolically represent the care-giver and provide support to the infant's task of separating and individuating. For Winnicott (1967), "[t]his potential space is at the interplay between there being nothing but me and there being objects and phenomena outside omnipotent control" (p. 371). The transitional object is, at the same time, both an extension of the child and the child's first "not me" possession, which stands for, or symbolises, the mother's presence

(Winnicott, 1971). The transitional object inhabits this intermediary/potential space between "primary creativity and objective perception" (Varga, 2011, p. 626). Play in this intermediate space provides a safe forum for the child to practise reality and to negotiate the relationship between inner and outer, while not occupying either the subjective or objective worlds. Play, according to Winnicott (1967) ". . . is in fact neither a matter of inner psychic reality nor a matter of external reality" (p. 368). It is difficult to imagine what constitutes such a space, but Winnicott describes it this way:

> It is at the place in space and time where and when the mother is in transition from being (in the baby's mind) merged in with the infant and being experienced as an object to be perceived rather than conceived of. The use of an object (i.e., the first episode of play) symbolizes the union of two now separate things, baby and mother, at the point of the initiation of their state of separateness. A complication exists right from the very beginning of any consideration of this idea, in that it is necessary to postulate that if the use of the object by the baby builds up into anything . . . then there must be the beginning of the setting up in the infant's mind or personal psychic reality of an image of the object (mother). But the mental representation . . . or the imago in the inner world is kept alive by the reinforcement given through the availability of the external separated-off and actual mother, along with her techniques of child-care. (p. 369)

Varga (2011) describes these notions as "abstract and potentially incoherent" (p. 627) and suggests, by extrapolation, that this space could be understood "as the strong presence or proximity of the other" (p. 627) and, thus, represents a form of (constructed) intersubjectivity or affective proximity between child and mother. While the transitional object loses meaning and potency as the child develops, the intermediary space that it occupied continues to be reflected, together with the sense of the other, in cultural pursuits and games. However, achieving the transition from subjective omnipotence to objective perception and the attendant frustration caused by that which is desired and that which is actually available requires first a distinction between "me" (subject) and "not me" (object), which, according to Winnicott, is not present in the infant at the time that this distinction is being learnt, prompting Varga (2011) to observe that "without this distinction, it seems perplexing how the child should ever become aware of the mismatch between inner and outer, self and other" (p. 629). Similarly, if the true self is split off and becomes unconscious as a result of impingements, what constitutes this distinction between "me" and "not me" when such a distinction is made—that is, to which part of "me"/"not me" are the true and false selves assigned? The imputation is that the false self is "me" and the split off true self is "not me". However, my reading of these dichotomies is that one is conscious (me/not me), and the other is not (false/true self) which renders the assertion of any equivalences problematic.

I now return to the relationship between the false self and the intermediary space. How, for example, does the intermediary space operate when only the false self occupies it? Indeed, can a false self "know" and inhabit this intermediary space? How does a child with false self formation react to the reflection of the other on what happens when he is playing in the intermediate space, if indeed he is able to occupy such a space and play there? Winnicott (1958) suggests that deprived children cannot enjoy play, but does not elaborate as to whether they can nevertheless play without enjoyment, although this is perhaps a contradiction, since playing without enjoyment renders the activity something other than play, and invites the question regarding the realm in which this joyless play, which can perhaps be understood as an impingement, takes place.

It seems that "Winnicott discovered data (from the conduct of psychoanalysis) calling for some fundamental reconstruction of psychoanalytic theory, without fully carrying out that reconstruction [himself]" (Morse, 1972, p. 500). Recently, Grossmark (2009) has opined that "reading Winnicott's work often proves to be a difficult task; his writing is often idiosyncratic and dense" (p. 498). Similarly, Varga (2011) observed that "Winnicott was by no means a systematic thinker. Although his work contains countless positive features and several strong ideas . . . many remain notoriously unclear, fragmented and even self-contradictory" (p. 625).

Such criticisms, although more prevalent in recent scholarship, have, in the past, been infrequent. In a provocative review, Hopkins (2011) commented that the analytic community tends to idealise Winnicott, and is, hence, reluctant to comment critically on his personal vulnerabilities, his body of work, and his analytic practice. Instead, Winnicott tends to be described in positive superlatives. For example, in the preface to his book on Winnicott, Tuber (2008) writes,

[T]he clinical acumen and humanity of D. W. Winnicott have always been something to aspire to, something to cherish, and something almost limitless in their usefulness. I write this book, therefore, in large part to pay homage to the man and his work. (p. v)

Winnicott (1969b) himself said that

We get to know a great deal through being involved, but being involved we find it difficult to stand aside, to become detached enough to think . . . to integrate all by the use of available theory and the construction of new theory. (p. ix).

None the less, Winnicott's body of work remains creative, compelling, and current, full of insight and humanity, if a little idiosyncratic and structurally difficult to follow in places. It is perhaps appropriate to view Winnicott and his body of work in an intermediary space between unquestioning homage and critical reflection.

Notes

1. The Psychoanalytic Society of Vienna was founded in 1908, but a group of Freud's students, the kernel of this (later) society began meeting in 1902 in Freud's rooms.
2. Freud did not personally undertake the psychoanalysis of Little Hans. It was accomplished by the boy's father with "coaching" and "instruction" from Freud. See Chapter Two for a detailed discussion.
3. Anna Freud identified nine mechanisms of defence: regression, repression, reaction formation, isolation, undoing, projection, introjections, turning against the self and reversal. To this she added, a tenth, "normal" or adaptive defence—that of sublimation or displacement of instinctual aims. She nominated repression as the most dangerous defence because it had the capacity to "destroy the integrity of the personality".
4. Bion (1962) believed that the experience of emotionally-based knowing and of being known ("K") was as essential as loving and being loved ("L") to psychological integrity. S
5. Available at: www.melanie-klein-trust.org.uk/segalinterview2001.htm
6. Although Freud introduced the concept of the death instinct, he remained sceptical about its nature and its place in psychoanalytic theory.

It may be asked how far I am convinced of the truth of the hypotheses that have been set out in these pages. My answer would be that
I am not convinced myself and that I do not seek to persuade other
people to believe in them. Or, more precisely, I do not know how
far I believe in them. (Freud 1920g, p. 59)

Melanie Klein and her "school" were among the only psychoanalysts
who retained the death instinct as a central concept, with the majority
agreeing with Freud that the concept lacked theoretical plausibility and
clinical utility (Esman, 2008).

7. It is not strictly correct to talk of these two positions as occurring in a
    developmental sequence, as Klein believed that both processes remained
    operative throughout life and that the infant oscillated between the two
    positions.

8. Freud's "ego" was conceived as an organising principle of the mind
    whose task was to manage the other psychic structures and negotiate the
    demands of external reality.

9. Klein's definition of phantasy as the unconscious psychic representatives
    of instinct was different from Freud's much broader conceptualisation of
    fantasy that encompasses hallucinations, delusions, daydreams, memory
    traces, images, and ideation.

10. From Freud's (1917e) Mourning and melancholia, "the shadow of the
    object falls upon the ego" (p. 249).

CHAPTER FOUR

The attached infant: the psychoanalytic legacy

"When the ego finds itself in an excessive real danger which it believes itself unable to overcome by its own strength ... [i]t sees itself deserted by all protecting forces and lets itself die. Here, moreover, is once again the same situation as that which underlay the first great anxiety – state of birth and the infantile anxiety of longing – the anxiety due to separation from the protecting mother"

(Freud, 1923b, p. 58)

I nfant research over the past fifty years has resulted in major revisions to our understanding of psychological development, particularly during infancy (Beebe, 2005; Beebe & Lachmann, 1994; Leon, 1984; Reddy, 1993). These new insights must necessarily change our concepts of the infant, our child rearing practices, psychoanalytic conceptualisations of infancy, and, by extension, the conduct of psychoanalysis (Goldberg, 1988; Sobel & Kirkham, 2006; Wilson, 1997; Wilson, Fel, & Greenstein, 1992). Psychoanalysis has always had a developmental perspective, that is, it is founded on the principle that early experience underlies the development of psychopathology, which is understood to be a manifestation, under conditions of stress, of problematic experiences during infancy and early childhood. However, early psychoanalytic theorising about development was not based on the kind of empirical research that underpins developmental psychology today. It was deduced from the reports of childhood experiences of people undergoing psychoanalysis as adults (Skelton, 2006). Later, infant observation, with its increasingly sophisticated and rigorous research paradigms, has clarified many of the complex issues about the infant's capacities in the first few months of life, including the nature of its first object relationships. These will be discussed in detail later in this chapter. However, a cautionary note is in order here. The methodologies developed for studying infants require inferences on the part of the researcher as to what the observed behaviour of the infant means. Infant mental experience, *per se*, cannot be observed and is, therefore, open to speculation (Hayward & Homer, 2009).

Early theories of attachment diverged on the question regarding to which element of the mother's self or behaviour the infant attached and whether the tie to the mother was based on physiological needs for food and relief of instinctual tensions, or on social needs for proximity, comfort, safety, and recognition; in short, whether attachment was a primary or secondary drive. A related question concerned the timing of object relationships and whether infants pass through phases of primary narcissism (auto-eroticism), autism, merger, or symbiosis before achieving self–other differentiation and the capacity to form object relationships. Because the issues were complex and empirical evidence for competing theories in short supply, the early arguments were essentially theoretical and often internally inconsistent in their attempts to account for all of the observed phenomena. Freud was not unequivocal in his views on auto-eroticism and he increasingly acknowledged, particularly in his later writing, the importance of the infant's psychological tie to its mother. The word "attachment" appears many times in Freud's later writings, and it has various usages, but, in this context, consider the following passages that support his view that attachment is a secondary drive and that self–other (breast) differentiation is not present from birth:

> The first object-cathexes occur in attachment to the satisfaction of the major and simple vital needs, and the circumstances of the care of children are the same for both sexes (Freud, 1933a, p. 118) . . . A child's first erotic object is the mother's breast that nourishes it; love has its

origin in attachment to the satisfied need for nourishment. There is no doubt that, to begin with, the child does not distinguish between the breast and its own body. (Freud, 1940a[1938], p. 188)

Compare these statements with this one, which follows almost immediately in the same publication, which describes the nature and importance of the child's attachment to his mother, and which supports the notion of attachment as a primary drive:

> . . . the root of a mother's importance, unique, without parallel, laid down unalterably for a whole lifetime, as the first and strongest love-object and as the prototype of all later love relations—for both sexes. (1940a[1938], p. 188)

Klein (1959), unlike Freud, believed that object relations were present at birth,

> . . . [The infant has] an innate unconscious awareness of the existence of the mother . . . instinctual knowledge is the basis for the infant's primal relation to the mother . . . the baby looks up to the mother's face, recognizes her footsteps, the touch of her hands, the smell and feel of her breast . . . all of which suggests that some relation, however primitive, to the mother has been established. (p. 248)

However, her emphasis on food, orality, and the mother's breast can be understood in terms of attachment as a secondary drive that satisfies the need for nourishment and relief from the anxiety of helplessness. Notwithstanding, she recognised that attachment also has the character of a primary drive: ". . . the whole of [the infant's] instinctual desires and his unconscious phantasies imbue the breast with qualities going far beyond the actual nourishment it affords" (Klein, 1957, p. 5).

Separation–individuation: Margaret Mahler and Sidney Blatt

Margaret Mahler (1897–1985) and colleagues (Mahler, 1972; Mahler, Pine, & Bergmann, 1975) presented a theory of infant development that was more concerned with separation and individuation—that is, how the infant grows apart from primary care-givers—than attachment, which focuses on how the infant grows together with primary care-givers. Mahler begins with the premise that the infant is not capable of self–other differentiation at birth. The process proposed by Mahler is schematically represented in Figure 1.

Mahler's theory argues that the psychological birth of the infant does not coincide with its physical birth; it can only occur after the "I"–"not-I" understanding emerges, allowing the process of separation from mother, defined by Mahler as emergence from a phase of "normal autism" in which physiological processes dominate and during which infants are perceived to be essentially non-related or objectless, encased in an "autistic shell" that is impervious to external stimuli (Mahler, 1967). From here, the infant moves through the other Mahlerian sub-phases until the achievement of individuation and autonomy. Between two to six months of age, a period of maternal–infant symbiosis occurs (i.e., a state of fusion between infant and mother in which self and not-self are not yet differentiated and during which the "infant behaves and functions as though he and his mother were an omnipotent system—a dual unity within a common boundary" (Mahler, Pine, & Bergman, 1975, p. 44)). After this phase, Mahler describes a four-stage process of development towards separation (from symbiotic fusion with the mother) and individuation (the child's assumption of his own unique characteristics), which she labelled:

- differentiation (5–9 months): the infant "hatches" out of the "symbiotic orbit";

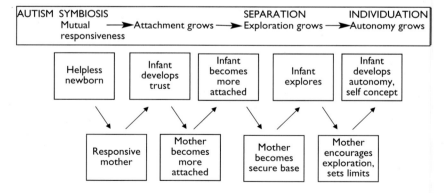

Figure 1. Schematic representation of Mahler's model of attachment, autonomy, and the development of self concept.

- practising (9–15 months): during which rapidly developing motor and cognitive skills support the infant's play and exploration away from mother); *cooperative*
- rapprochement (15–24 months): a period of affective shifts due to a purported ambivalence about separating from mother;
- development of object constancy (24–36 months).

Thus, in Mahler's theory, the infant from birth to about five to six months of age is undifferentiated, passive, and helpless, "beset by libidinal and aggressive drives, protected against external stimulation, and defended against any awareness of separateness" (Demos, 1989, p. 290). The growing awareness of, and interaction with, outer reality results in increasing behavioural, social, and psychic (drive, conflict, defence) complexity (Mahler, Pine, & Bergman, 1975).

Mahler's stage-based theory proposes that problems in the mother–infant interaction during any of the phases of development to autonomy create particular psychopathologies and problems with character development. Recent empirical work in infant observation, to be discussed below, has disconfirmed much of the conceptual underpinnings of Mahler's model, in particular, the fact that infants are impervious to external stimuli; they are, on the contrary, born with cognitive, social, and emotional capacities that render them able to co-construct their experience with their care-givers and their environment. Even at a physical level, infants have five senses that are responsive to external stimuli; they can also feel pain (Franck et al., 2011; Latimer et al., 2011; Riddell et al., 2011; Tramo et al., 2011).

A more recent model of the structural organisation of the developmental process has been offered by Blatt (2008), who proposes that development occurs along the two poles of self-definition and relatedness. Blatt's theory attempts to incorporate Kernberg (1976, 1988) on boundary articulation, Mahler on separation–individuation, Stern (1985) on the development of the self and processes of intersubjectivity, and Piagetian concepts with respect to the cognitive components of development. It is a model of both normal development and psychopathology and comprises eight developmental levels (age at transition to next stage in parentheses) as follows:

1.   Boundary constancy (2–3 months): social smiling and responsiveness;

2.   Recognition constancy (6–8 months): stranger anxiety, specific attachments);
3.   Evocative constancy (16–18 months): sense of object even when out of sight;
4.   Self and object constancy (30–36 months): stable concepts of self and other, use of pronouns;
5.   Concrete operational thought (5 years);
6.   Formal operational thought (11–12 years) (see Piaget, Chapter Five);
7.   Self-identity (late adolescence): sense of individuality and relatedness;
8.   Integrity (mature adulthood): self-in-relation.

Blatt (2008) has also proposed a series of steps that must be negotiated in the separation–individuation process. There are four major divisions within this process.

1.   Either no basic differentiation between self and others or impairments in it.
2.   Establishment and maintenance of object constancy.
3.   Emergence of differentiated and integrated concepts of self and other.
4.   Capacity for empathic reciprocal relationships.

Within these four major achievements of selfhood, there are ten substages that reflect the nuanced and subtle changes that occur over the early lifespan within these four major divisions.

The early psychoanalytic and, indeed, more general view that the infant is merged or undifferentiated requires clarification. Two concepts have potentially been confused in this perception of the infant—those of "absolute dependence" or helplessness at birth, and the state of symbiosis or merger with the mother. Winnicott (1960) attempts to clarify this as follows:

> One half of the theory of the parent–infant relationship concerns the infant, and is the theory of the infant's journey from absolute dependence, through relative dependence, to independence, and, in parallel, the infant's journey from the pleasure principle to the reality principle, and from autoerotism to object relationships. The other half of the theory of the parent–infant relationship concerns maternal care, that is

to say the qualities and changes in the mother that meet the specific and developing needs of the infant towards whom she orientates. (p. 589)

It is possible for the infant to be in a state of absolute dependence with respect to physical and emotional survival at birth, while also possessing, as Klein has argued, and as subsequent infant research has demonstrated, rudimentary object relations and skills and capacities that render the infant a co-constructing partner in the mother–baby dyad. We will return to this issue in the final chapter.

Heinz Kohut

ESTRAGON: We always find something, eh Didi, to give us the impression we exist?

VLADIMIR: Yes, yes, we're magicians. (Samuel Beckett, *Waiting for Godot*, Act 2)

Kohut proposed a theory that represented a radical departure from the libidinal stage-based theories and their derivatives and proposed a model that was less concerned with drives and conflicts than with loss of meaning associated with problematic development that resulted in a "fractured, enfeebled, discontinuous human existence" (Kohut, 1977, p. 238). Kohut's self psychology offers a developmental model as well as a theory of psychopathology and model of therapy that was briefly discussed in Chapter One. In this section, we will focus on the developmental and attachment components in Kohut's theory. A central concept is the self-object, which Kohut conceptualised as an object relationship in which the object is experienced as being a part of or an extension of the subject's self, and in which little or no psychological differentiation occurs (Kohut, 1971). In order for children to grow up as healthy, autonomous adults, Kohut believed that they needed three distinct self-object experiences, each of which contributed to the development of an intrapsychic structure comprising a tripolar self. The self-object needs are for (i) mirroring (related to the grandiose exhibitionistic self), (ii) idealising (related to the internalised idealised parental imago), and (iii) partnering (related to the development of an alter ego).[1] The degree of empathy, the nature of empathy ruptures, and the way in which these ruptures are repaired exert a profound impact on the developing infant self. If the ruptures are not traumatic or prolonged, they result in what Kohut calls "transmuting internalizations", which he described as a gradual internalising of various functions (e.g., self-soothing, self-regulation, pride, persistence) associated with the infant's self-objects. These functions become integrated into the developing child's self structure.

Kohut's self-types are products of the "intersecting matrices of developmental level and structural state" (Brandell, 2010, p. 152). Four have been identified.

1.   The virtual self is the parent's imagined infant who evolves as the parental "selfobjects empathically respond to certain potentialities of the child" (Kohut, 1977, p. 100).
2.   The nuclear self represents the infant's unfolding realisation that he is a separate, agentic self who has a "sense of being an independent center of initiative and perception" (Kohut, 1977, p. 177).
3.   The cohesive self represents the outcome of a healthy developmental process that produces a healthy self structure that allows the individual to live autonomously and adaptively, able to negotiate the "interplay of ambitions, ideals, and talents with the opportunities of everyday reality" (Leider, 1996, p. 143).
4.   The grandiose self is conceptualised as a developmentally normal self-structure of infancy and early childhood "that comes into existence in response to the selfobject's attunement with the child's sense of himself or herself as the center of the universe" (Brandell, 2010, p. 153).

Kohut's theory, like those of his predecessors, has been founded on clinical work with adults and suffers the same methodological problems as other clinical theories of infancy discussed earlier. In particular, the assumption of an undifferentiated, or narcissistic, stage of infancy, experiences of merger with the care-giver, and the characterisation of infantile grandiosity and omnipotence have not been verified in infant observation research (Fonagy & Target, 2003). However, Kohut's conceptualisation of the role of the mother in affect regulation, empathically attuned care-giving, and the notion of "transmuting internalisations" are consistent with the body of empirical work in infant development and with current developmental theory. Kohut did not offer a time frame during which infants acquire self-objects or self-types.

Beyond the psychoanalytic legacy

Psychoanalytically orientated developmental theories, such as Freud's libidinal stage theory, Klein's positions, Mahler's phases, Blatt's developmental levels, and Kohut's selves offer conceptual, theoretical, literary/metaphorical insights into the infant self rather than scientific, empirically grounded knowledge of the gradual unfolding of the self of the human infant. Some of these theories of infant attachment were founded on incorrect premises about the nature of the infant and the infant's capacities. For example, the Freudian notions that the child's attachment to the mother had a sexual origin, that attachment is motivated by helplessness, dependence, and aggression, or that infants are not responsive to external stimuli at birth have all now been disconfirmed by subsequent empirical research that will be discussed in the final chapter. Freud and Klein both remained ambivalent about the nature of attachment and some of their views are consistent with current attachment theory. For example, Freud stated that attachment ". . . cannot be counted among the elementary instinctual components nor can it be classed as belonging to sexuality . . ." (Freud, 1905d, p. 194). Klein (1935) oscillated between a view of attachment as a biologically predetermined link to mother that was separate from the satisfaction of the infant's vital needs, and the view that attachment evolves from the satisfaction of such needs. Stern (1985) sums up as follows:

> Many of the phenomena thought by psychoanalytic theory to play a crucial role in early development, such as delusions of merger or fusion, splitting and defensive or paranoid fantasies, are not applicable to the infancy period—that is, before the age of roughly 18–24 months—but are conceivable only after the capacity for symbolization as evidenced by language emerging when infancy ends. (p. 11)

The notion that infants enter the world in a state of "one great blooming, buzzing confusion" (James, 1981, p. 462) is no longer tenable. Even as recently as 2008, Blatt includes a step in the separation–individuation process in which the infant is characterised as lacking "a sense of physical cohesion or the integrity of separate representations . . . feelings and thoughts are amorphous, undifferentiated or confused" (pp. 258–259). There is now a wealth of research to suggest the opposite. A neonate can get its fingers into its mouth, suck its thumb, stop itself from crying, protect itself by withdrawing certain body parts from pains and irritations, lift its face away from obstacles to breathing, study the visual scene . . . burp, spit up, urinate, defecate, coo, stop crying at the sound of a human voice . . . demonstrate a percept of a human face . . . distinguish sounds basic to speech . . . prefer its mother's voice to the voice of strangers . . . can be conditioned and can modify its behaviour with experience, exchange information among sensory modalities . . . (Konner, 2010, pp. 211–214)

and mimic facial gestures such as tongue protrusion and mouth opening (Meltzoff & Moore, 1997). Further, babies are neurologically equipped to co-construct and make sense of their experiences and relationships. They can detect changes in all sensory domains and integrate information across sensory modalities, remember, recognise and discriminate, imitate, express affect, modulate arousal, and engage in meaningful social interaction with their care-givers. They also react negatively to the cessation of social stimulation when an animated face is replaced by a still face, a phenomenon described as "innate subjectivity" (Nagy, 2008).

Prior to about four months of age, infants react to people in a similar way; that is, they show indiscriminate attachment to most caring figures. However, they can perceptually discriminate aspects of their mothers from other mothers at a much earlier age, within the first days and weeks of life (MacFarlane, 1975). By about four months of age, infants smile and vocalise more with their mothers than other adults, behaviours that indicate that differentiation between the mother and other care-givers is occurring on a social level. Most infants experience separation anxiety and stranger anxiety, commencing from between six and nine months of age (Goubet, Rochat, Marie-Leblond, & Poss, 2006). During this phase, infants will cry when mother leaves, and cling to her when she reappears. Infants will also show a fear of strangers and a reluctance to be held by them. Intense attachment to mother continues to about three years of age, although with increasing mastery over their environments, infants will also attach to other significant figures, such as grandparents, siblings, and day-care workers. Thus, infants develop a "hierarchy of attachment" to several people, but mother is usually at the apex of that hierarchy (Grossmann & Grossmann, 2005). As cognitive development proceeds and person permanence and object permanence develop (i.e., belief that a person or object continues to exist when out of sight), infants learn to accept mother's temporary absences because they now understand that she will return. We will revisit these issues in the next chapter on cognitive development.

Historical influences and the work of the ethologists

Although tracing in greater detail the psychoanalytic origins of attachment theory is a fascinating exercise, space does not permit such an undertaking here. The following brief paragraphs on the precursors to current attachment theory serve as an introduction to the post-psychoanalytic thinking about attachment and the nature of its evolution, and locate the work of two of the most important attachment theorists, John Bowlby and Mary Ainsworth, into its historical and theoretical context. Bowlby's attachment theory, which had its origins in the British object relations tradition, represented a major advance in theory and research into the processes underpinning the early development of human infants as well as understanding the mechanisms and consequences of failures in attachment. It also represented a major methodological advance, in that the hypotheses generated by the theory were testable and, therefore, verifiable or falsifiable.

Bowlby drew on a wide range of disciplines outside psychoanalysis to verify his theories, notably ethology, thereby universalising the appeal and accessibility of his ideas. This position was strengthened when attachment behaviour was observed to follow a similar social clock cross-culturally which was largely independent of differing child-rearing practices during infancy (Konner, 2010). However, throughout its evolutionary history, scholars remain divided as to whether attachment theory is essentially psychoanalytic or evolutionary–ethological (van der Horst, 2011). Bowlby argued that the phenomena observed and documented by Freud were of immense import; however, the theories proposed by Freud to explain these phenomena were problematic (Bowlby, Figlio, & Young, 1986). Bowlby preferred the empirical approach of the natural sciences to the intuitive, hypothetico-deductive methods of psychoanalysis, and he urged his psychoanalytic colleagues to adopt more empirically based approaches to recast psychoanalytic concepts in ethological terms. He quipped that psychoanalytic concepts were too important to be left in the care of psychoanalysts!

Kagan (2011), in his foreword to van der Horst (2011), identified four key influences on Bowlby in his progression towards the articulation of attachment theory and his recognition of the devastating impact of early maternal separation or deprivation on the developing infant that might last a lifetime. In the 1920s, Bowlby was briefly employed in a progressive school for emotionally disturbed children, which was based on Freudian ideas. It was there that he formed his life-long conviction that children deprived of a mother's love were at serious psychological risk for psychopathology. Sadly, the advent of the Second World War provided stark evidence of the effect of parental separation on the psychological well-being of infants and children. On the day of the German invasion of Poland, 734,883 unaccompanied children were evacuated from London into villages and towns in the English countryside. Others were later placed in residential nurseries (if their parents had died in the air raids). Anna Freud and Dorothy Burlingham observed and documented the changed behaviour of such children in the Hampstead nurseries. Early reports of bed-wetting and an array of psychological symptoms in evacuated children led to protests against the evacuations by Donald Winnicott and John Bowlby, among others (van der Horst, 2011).

In the 1930s, hospitals in Britain issued a policy prohibiting visitors, including parents, to their children's wards. The devastating effect on young children in hospital was called the "hospitalisation effect", which included loss of IQ and, in extreme cases, onset of mental retardation, social and emotional withdrawal, separation anxiety, misbehaviour, depression, hopelessness, and despair (Bakwin, Morris, & Bakwin, 1942). In 1946, Bowlby joined the Tavistock Clinic, where he met James Robertson, a social worker who demonstrated in his film (1952),[2] the devastating psychological consequences of hospital policy that forbade mothers to be with their sick children prior to surgery in order to avoid the risk of infection and to reduce the upset to children caused by parental visits. Robertson and Bowlby together identified the typical responses to separation: first, protest (loud, distressed crying and frantic searching for mother), followed by despair (hopelessness and the cessation of search for mother), which was erroneously interpreted by the medical profession to indicate that the child had adjusted to the new environment and was no longer distressed. In the third phase, denial/detachment, the child starts to display more interest in his environment—behaviour interpreted, again erroneously, to mean that the child had "recovered" from the distress of separation (Bowlby, Robertson, & Rosenbluth, 1952).

The third major influence was the work of the ethologists, Konrad Lorenz, Nikolaas Tinbergern, Robert Hinde, and the psychologist Harry Harlow. Although the observational evidence for the detrimental effects of early separation on infant and child development was compelling, there was as yet no coherent theory or experimental evidence to support these observations. Lorenz's (1981) identification of the process of imprinting in goslings in the 1930s as the basis for the development of affectional bonds provided a starting point. Lorenz distinguished between instinctual and learnt behaviours and identified sensitive periods for the expression of instincts or "fixed action patterns". Similarly, Tinbergen (1951), in his book *The Study of Instinct* (an examination of the cause, ontogeny, function, and evolution of instinctual behaviour), distinguished external (i.e., environmental) from internal (i.e., "physiological mechanisms") influences on the expression of innate behaviour. Internal mechanisms determined motivation to express appetitive behaviours such as searching for food or mating rituals, but the external conditions had to be supportive of such expression. Hinde began his scientific career studying birds, but, with Bowlby's encouragement, set up a rhesus monkey colony to study the effects of maternal separation. He was also interested in studying the relative importance of food and warmth as opposed to contact comfort and communication in establishing affectional bonds, which was the primary focus of the work of Harry Harlow in the USA. Hinde demonstrated that infant monkeys separated from both mother and their familiar surroundings suffered the greatest trauma, and slipped rapidly into profound despair, compared with those who were removed either from mother or from their familiar environment. This study disconfirmed Bowlby's contention that protest, despair, and detachment were habitual responses to separation from the mother, regardless of other circumstances (Bowlby, 1960b). In 1973, Lorenz and Tinbergen shared the Nobel prize with Karl von Frisch, for the creation of the new science of ethology, the biological study of animal and human behaviour.

Bowlby used Harlow's (1958; Harlow & Zimmerman, 1996) experiments with cloth and wire surrogate mothers for rhesus monkeys to support his theory of attachment, famously using these experiments to undermine the prevailing psychoanalytic view that all attachment develops through oral gratification. Bowlby argued that the infants' preference for the cloth mother indicated a biological drive that makes contact comfort primarily reinforcing for human and animal infants. Further, Harlow's experiments demonstrated that attachment behaviour could not be explained by learning theory, which proposed that attachment develops as a result of the reinforcing properties of the attachment figure, because birds, monkeys, and human children seek comfort from punishing attachment figures. Accordingly, ethologists concluded that attachment behaviour, like imprinting in birds, is a hard-wired, motivated behavioural system. However, the emergence of different attachment styles is most strongly related to familial environment. Although physiological and temperamental factors influence the degree of separation anxiety, having experienced prior secure attachment mitigates the stress response to separation in timid, highly reactive infants. Conversely, the quality of early attachment relationships has long-term effects on the regulation of the hypothalamic–pituitary–adrenal (HPA) axis as assessed by circulating cortisol (Gunnar, 1998).

While Bowlby remained focused on the nature of the tie between mother and infant, Harlow made significant contributions to the nature of peer and sibling attachments, arguing that there are multiple separate attachment systems that also have evolutionary significance (Vicedo, 2010). For example, deprived, socially isolated monkeys placed with normally developing, younger monkeys gradually develop normal social behaviour, suggesting that children reared in social isolation may survive early deprivation and develop relatively normally. Even severely deprived children can show some recovery if placed in "ideal" care at an early enough age. A series of studies of Romanian orphans showed that if placed before six months of age into good foster families in the UK and Canada, orphans returned to age appropriate cognitive and physical development by four years of age, but with continuing attachment disorders if not placed before four months of age (Audet & Le Mare, 2011; Linville & Lyness, 2007). In contrast, cognitive and social development of Romanian orphans aged between twenty-three and fifty months who remained in Romania was adversely affected for all, most in the severe range (Kaler & Freeman, 1994). These researchers found that deficits were not related to length of time in the orphanage, age at entrance to the orphanage, Apgar scores, or birth weight. However, another study (Fisher, Ames, Chisholm, & Savoie, 1997) reported that the amount of time spent in the orphanage by Romanian orphans adopted to Canada predicted total problems and internalising behaviour disorders on the Child Behavior Checklist. The attentional and social deficits observed in these orphans were associated with smaller amygdalae and hippocampi, as well as dysfunction in the limbic system, confirming that social deprivation has anatomical and physiological as well as emotional, behavioural, and cognitive consequences (Eluvathingal et al., 2006).

Attachment theory

> The tears of the world are a constant quantity. For each one who begins to weep somewhere else another stops. The same is true of the laugh. Let us not then speak ill of our generation, it is not any unhappier than its predecessors. (Samuel Beckett, *Waiting for Godot*)

Attachment theory is an empirically-derived developmental theory that explains how normal development becomes derailed by problematic or impaired attachment relationships in early life. The developmental psychopathology perspective is a useful, heuristic organisational framework through which the development, maintenance, progression or remission of psychological disorders can be understood. It has developed in response to the failure of simpler models to account for the complexities that underpin both normal and pathological development (Cicchetti & Cohen, 1995) and is not complicated by a metapsychology. This model has several major principles, which are summarised below.

1. *Multi-determinism*: many factors in complex interactions contribute to the development to both healthy and abnormal development. Two broad classes of factors, called protective and risk factors, combine to determine both the nature of the difficulties that affect development and the eventual expression and outcome of those difficulties. Protective factors reduce risk and enhance development, while risk factors compromise development and increase risk for psychopathology. For example, the loss of a parent during childhood (risk factor) may be offset to some degree by the availability of alternative secure attachment figures (protective factor). Risk and protective factors have different

effects at different stages of development. For example, behavioural inhibition (that is, shy, avoidant behaviour) towards unfamiliar adults in childhood predicts fear of negative evaluation in adolescents (Vasey & Dadds, 2001). The cumulative risk for development of a psychological disorder is the ratio between risk and protective factors. For example, a young person might be high in negative affectivity as a result of either a genetic vulnerability to anxiety proneness or as a result of inadequate parenting. Repeated stressful exposure to situational demands might increase anxiety, which, in turn, increases the risk of psychopathology.

2. *Multi-finality*: a single factor could be associated with multiple outcomes, depending on the organisation of the system in which those factors operate. For example, a child prone to anxiety is less likely to develop an anxiety disorder if s/he has parents who are attuned to her vulnerabilities and provide needed environmental supports that encourage coping under conditions of stress compared with a child with the same anxiety proneness who has parents who are themselves anxious and who model anxious behaviours to their children.

3. *Equifinality*: a given outcome can be reached by multiple pathways. For example, there are several possible pathways to the development of social anxiety disorder (SAD). SAD might develop slowly in temperamentally shy children, due to a genetic vulnerability such as heightened anxiety sensitivity and behavioural inhibition; it might develop as the result of modelling of anxious behaviours and/or transmission of anxiety-provoking information; it might arise as a result of one or more aversive conditioning experiences in otherwise normally developing children.

The attachment system and the care-giving system together constitute the attachment relationship. Marrone and Cortina (2003) have provided a succinct description of the nine key elements that comprise attachment theory. They are briefly summarised below. Attachment theory is a theory of:

●   *normal developmental processes and of psychopathology*: attachment theory accounts for both normal and psychopathological developmental pathways through the concepts of the secure base and felt security (discussed below);

- *motivation*: infants and young children are motivated to seek protection from attachment figures via the goal-corrected control system of felt security to elicit care when distressed;
- *socio-psychological interactions*: individuals and attachment relationships can only be understood within the socio-cultural framework in which they are embedded;
- *encoding and representation of experience within different memory systems*: Bowlby formulated the concept of internal working models (IWM), which he understood to be abstractions of interpersonal experience (Main, Kaplan, & Cassidy, 1985) that become consolidated during infancy at about the same time (i.e., 9–18 months) that the final stages of object permanence are achieved (Piaget & Cook, 1954a). These are event-based models derived from parental responses to the infant; they are not passively introjected models of the parent *per se*. In Piagetian terms, they are models that are actively constructed by the infant based on the infant's experiences of, and interactions with, the parent and other significant people in the infant's life. IWM are encoded and stored within different memory systems, both verbal (semantic and episodic) and non-verbal (procedural and implicit). Bowlby argued that preverbal experience is encoded in procedural memory; after language develops, memories are encoded and stored semantically (see Chapter Six). In unsatisfactory caregiving environments, such as the experience of unprocessed trauma, or the denial of trauma, these two memory systems become decoupled. "The self that has the readiest access to [episodic memory] . . . is the real self" (Bowlby, 1973, p. 64). Such a statement is clearly synchronous with Winnicott's conceptualisation of the true and false selves (see, for example, Winnicott, 1989);
- *anxiety*: the dominant anxiety in infancy and childhood is fear of loss of the attachment figure (which is a departure from Freud's libido based theory of anxiety, but consistent with his later signal theory of anxiety (Freud, 1926d));
- *affects and emotion*: the most significant and enduring emotions are felt and expressed in relation to attachment figures in early life. It is through these early experiences of felt and expressed affects and emotions that infants learn the meaning and regulation of affective self-states;

- *defence*: defences against anxiety and painful affects that arise in problematic attachment relationships affect internal working models and later interpersonal relationships. Defensive processes might also lead to the dissociation of painful self-states and internal working models leading to feelings of fragmentation;
- *self*: the attachment relationship is the most influential factor in organising early experiences of self, other, and self–other relationships, and, therefore, in characterising the self, self-concept, self-esteem, and capacity for self-regulation;
- *intergenerational transmission of attachment patterns*: people carry their own attachment styles of relating into their relationships with their own children, and each adult state of mind with respect to attachment predicts the nature of attachment in their children. (See below.)

Complex interactions between constitutional, temperamental (e.g., irritability, soothability, flexibility, fearfulness, and response to novelty), environmental, cultural, and familial factors, differences in anxiety proneness and negative affectivity, age at which the child's development has been compromised by the onset of a psychological disorder, the level of developmental competence reached prior to the onset of the disorder, the environmental response to the disorder, and the degree of loss of vital developmental experiences brought about by the disorder all influence its trajectory and outcome (Vasey & Dadds, 2001).

John Bowlby and Mary Ainsworth

John Bowlby (1907–1990) and Mary Ainsworth (1913–1999), who formed a life-long research partnership, were key figures in the development of attachment theory. Bowlby possessed an exceptional intellect and qualified in psychology, medicine, psychiatry, and psychoanalysis. He also had formative experiences as a child that cemented his life-long interest in child development in general and attachment theory in particular. He was the fourth of six children raised by a nanny; he rarely saw his parents. His beloved nanny left the family when he was four and he was sent to boarding school when he was seven years of age, two traumatic attachment experiences that he recalled as "tragic and terrible" (Bowlby, 1973). Although his roots were firmly in psychoanalytic theory (he was analysed by Joan Riviere and supervised by Melanie Klein), Bowlby broke with the psycho-analytic tradition of confirming its own theories using only clinical experience. He argued that psychoanalytic theories needed to be scientifically investigated using the research methods of the natural sciences (Bowlby, 1984). Further, he was insistent that children's psy-chopathologies arose in response to faulty environments and actual relationships with their attachment figures, as opposed to their own fantasies, drives, or Oedipus complex (Bowlby, 1940). Melanie Klein was strongly opposed to his views. Bowlby recalls a case in which Klein forbade him to see the mother of a very disturbed little boy that he was treating. In response, Bowlby (1949) wrote what might be con-sidered the first paper on family therapy. This was followed up with a joint paper by Ainsworth and Bowlby that appeared in the *American Psychologist* in 1991. Bowlby was considered a heretic and ostracised by the psychoanalytic community, although he maintained his psy-choanalytic home within the Middle (later Independent) Group of the British Psychoanalytic Society (Bowlby, Figlio, & Young, 1986).

Bowlby (1958) opens his seminal paper on attachment theory with this statement: "Psychoanalysts are at one in recognizing the child's first object relations as the foundation stone of his personality: yet there is no agreement on the nature and dynamics of this relationship" (p. 350).

Bowlby summarised the four theories of attachment current at that time.

1. *Theory of secondary drive* argued that the child's physiological needs for food and warmth drive the baby's tie to his mother, who is capable of meeting these needs. In time, the baby under-stands that the mother is his source of gratification. Both Sig-mund and Anna Freud were proponents of this theory, which subsequent research has shown to be untenable. For example, Harry Harlow (1906–1981), working with rhesus monkeys, showed that physical contact is the most important element in promoting infant attachment to a care-giver (Harlow & Zimmer-man, 1959). However, both Freuds were equivocal about their theoretical position on attachment as a secondary drive. For example, Anna Freud observed infants and children cling to cruel

mothers, attaching to them regardless of what they offered. This observation led her to speculate that the infant's need for attachment to his mother is instinctual (A. Freud, 1951), a position incompatible with secondary drive theory.

2. *Theory of primary object sucking* refers to the view that infants are hard-wired to suck a human breast, which the baby, in time, learns is attached to his mother, with whom he can develop a relationship.

3. *Theory of primary object clinging* proposes that the need for human contact is the primary motivation for human relationship, and is in infants an in-built need to be in touch with and to cling to a human being, independent of the infant's need for food.

4. *Theory of primary return-to-womb craving* proposes that infants seek to return to the womb. Bowlby dismissed this proposal as "redundant and biologically improbable" (1958, p. 351).

In his initial exposition of the theory, Bowlby believed that attachment behaviour in infancy could be explained by a combination of the theories of primary object sucking and primary object clinging, which he named the theory of component instinctual responses, arguing that an infant's behaviour includes sucking and clinging in addition to following, crying, and smiling, behaviours that serve the function of "reciprocal dynamic binding of mother to child" (p. 351).

Bowlby articulated his attachment theory in a trilogy of books (1969, 1973, 1980) that represent a departure from previous psychoanalytic attachment theories. The critical differences are summarised briefly below.

• Attachment theory represented a major shift from the libidinal stage-based model of development and the fixation–regression model of psychopathology. Bowlby rejected the psychoanalytic concepts of infantile narcissism and the formative role of sexual and aggressive impulses in personality formation (van der Horst, 2011). These models proposed that psychopathology represented a retreat to an earlier stage of development, at which time the particular behaviour currently being exhibited was considered normal for an earlier developmental period (Van Haute & Geyskens, 2007). These models were replaced by a model that conceptualised development as a continuous process in which both normal and pathological development are understood in terms of environmental exigencies, ongoing subjective experiences, and patterns of relating to others that have originated from past experiences but which continue to operate in current relationships (Ravitz, Maunder, Hunter, Sthankiya, & Lancee, 2010; Silk, 2005; Zeanah, Anders, Seifer, & Stern, 1989). Bowlby likened the difference between his conception of development and the psychoanalytic conception to two different types of rail routes. The psychoanalytic conceives of a unitary linear route with various stations (fixations) or reverse movement of the train (regressions) that affect the developmental trajectory. Bowlby's (1973) view is of a railway network in which there are many forks in the track. The direction taken at any fork will depend on both current and past experiences.

- The importance of context in normal and pathological development of children was brought into sharp focus by attachment theory, in which the recursive, mutually reciprocal transactions between individuals and their environments, in particular, the importance of early care-giver–infant interactions replaced the previous focus on intrapsychic mechanisms in psychoanalytic theories, and other reductionistic attempts in genetics and neuroscience to provide a meaningful account of psychological development (Calkins & Hill, 2007).

- Sexuality is decoupled from the attachment system (Marrone & Cortina, 2003). Rather than invoking the Oedipus complex to explain infant sexuality, Bowlby viewed infantile sexuality as a form of exploratory play that is a precursor and prerequisite for mature adult sexuality.

- Bowlby used a descriptive approach to document his observations, rather than a psychoanalytic metapsychology, and a methodology that was prospective, as opposed to the retrospective reconstruction of the psychoanalytic method.

Notwithstanding, Bowlby's attachment theory is grounded in psychoanalytic theory. The advent of object relations theory (Fairbairn, 1952), self psychology (Kohut, 1971), and intersubjective psychoanalysis (Beebe, 2004; Mitchell, 1993) effected a convergence of attachment and psychoanalytic theories, with all acknowledging the reciprocity and complementarity of the attachment and care-giving systems, the interdependence of the mother–child relationship, the role of maternal failure in psychopathological trajectories, the development of a sense of self, the quality of the child's later relationships, and the importance of the social and cultural milieu in shaping development. Thus, Bowlby's ideas have gradually been reintegrated into psychoanalytic theory (Holmes, 2011). The role of unconscious phantasy in development and psychopathology and the absence of a theory of envy remain the major points of contention between the two theories (Holmes, 1996, 2011). Bowlby revolutionised the study of child development when he offered an empirically supported theory that identified attachment processes as universal and normative, which operate over the course of the lifespan and are intergenerationally transmitted. Bowlby argued that the propensity for attachment is hard-wired in both animals and humans, but the nature of the attachment is determined by the care-giving system. Defences are understood to be strategies that deactivate the attachment system and recover emotional distance in order to suppress the activation and awareness of intense unmet attachment needs (Bowlby, 1957).

Bowlby (1973) defined attachment as a biologically based motivational–behavioural system whose goal is to maintain proximity to the attachment figure and to ensure survival of the helpless infant. This system is characterised by four types of behaviour.

1. Maintenance of the infant's physical proximity to its care-giver. The infant will use behaviours such as crying, clinging, crawling, searching, and reaching for the attachment figure to attain physical closeness.

2. Using the attachment figure as a "secure base"[3] (Ainsworth, 1963) from which to explore the environment. Observations of toddlers in parks highlight this function of attachment. With the parent sitting on a park bench, the young child will start to venture further afield, but will maintain some contact with the care-giver through turning, making eye contact, or vocalising. S/he will periodically return to home base to receive reassurance before again venturing out on further explorations. If the attachment figure disappears, exploration will cease immediately and search behaviour for the attachment figure will commence.

3. Return to the attachment figure as a "safe haven" when in danger or alarmed. Unlike some primates, who flee to a place, such as a

burrow, to escape threat, humans seek safety in the company of a person or group with whom they are affiliated. Infants automatically seek their primary attachment figure (usually the mother) when feeling endangered.

4.   Originally conceived as a system whose outcome was protection from present danger, Bowlby (1988) later expanded his view of the role of attachment to include reassurance of the ongoing (emotional) availability of the care-giver. He had observed that a care-giver could be physically available to an infant, but if he were emotionally non-responsive, emotional development and, if severe and prolonged, physical development could be compromised. The final, critical step in the theory of secure attachment was that the infant's or young child's appraisal of the care-giver produced an experience of "felt security", defined as a subjective or internal experience of comfort and safety (Sroufe & Waters, 1977).

Mary Ainsworth (1963) investigated, via observation of mother–infant dyads in controlled conditions, the patterns of communication and relationship between mothers and their infants in order to understand the factors that resulted in either secure or insecure attachment, the outcomes of the child's expectations of the care-giver that became encoded as internal working models of important relationships. Subsequently, she developed a research technique to assess the quality of attachment in infants and young children, called the Strange Situation (Ainsworth, Blehar, Waters, & Wall, 1978). From her observations of infant behaviour in this situation, Ainsworth distinguished secure and insecure attachment, which was based on the mother's degree of sensitivity to the needs of her infant. Later studies showed that paternal sensitivity also promotes secure attachment in infants (Cox, Owen, Henderson, & Margand, 1992). Ainsworth identified three main forms of attachment, to which a fourth was added later by Mary Main (1995).

1.   *Secure attachment*: securely attached infants feel safe to explore and confident that their proximity and comfort seeking behaviour when distressed will be responded to appropriately. Mothers of securely attached infants are sensitive and responsive to their babies' signals, are quick to comfort them when distressed, and

happy to let them explore safely. These mothers are characterised by sensitivity, emotional availability, acceptance, and collaboration with (rather than control of) their infant.

2. *Avoidant attachment (insecure–avoidant)*: avoidant infants show a very different pattern of communication with their care-giver. Unlike securely attached infants, avoidant infants do not acknowledge their mother's presence (i.e., they do not seek proximity) and they do not react with distress when she leaves. They appear calm and more interested in exploring the environment than in making contact with their mothers. Despite the apparent lack of distress, these infants have greatly elevated heart rates and circulating cortisol (stress hormone). These babies had learnt that any attempts to gain comfort and care from their mothers would be futile and, hence, their attachment behaviours had been extinguished. Mothers of avoidant infants were characterised by inhibition of emotional expression, verbal and physical rejection of their infants, aversion to physical contact, and insensitivity to their infants' emotional signals and overtures. As they grow, avoidant children develop IWM that expects rejection if they express a need for proximity and comfort and, therefore, they fear their attachment needs and represent the self as undeserving. Avoidantly attached children engage in defensive processes, such as idealisation, intellectualisation, repression, and denial in order to cope with chronic emotional deprivation (Liotti, 1999).

3. *Ambivalent attachment (insecure–resistant)*: Ainsworth identified two types of ambivalence—one characterised by anger and the other by passivity. Both types of ambivalent infants were too concerned about their mothers' whereabouts to feel free to explore, and both responded with intense distress when she left them. However, when mother returned, angry infants, in turn, reconnected with their mothers but then rejected their approaches. Passive infants, overcome by feelings of misery and helplessness, made only token attempts to regain their mothers' attention. However, both angry and passive infants remained preoccupied with their mothers' whereabouts, even when they were present. Mothers of ambivalent infants were unpredictable in their availability to their children, insensitive to their emotional signals, and discouraged their children's development of autonomy, as evidenced by the inhibition of their exploratory

behaviour. Because parents of ambivalent infants are unpredictable, sometimes available, sometimes neglectful and rejecting, their infants encode both of these response patterns and they come to view themselves as both lovable and undeserving (Attili, 1989).

4.   *Disorganised attachment*: infants showing disorganised attachment had parents who were simultaneously experienced as the safe haven and the source of danger. Following reunion after separation, disorganised infants showed a series of inexplicable and bizarre behaviours that include freezing, collapsing to the floor, and appearing dazed and confused. These behaviours came to be understood as the expression of opposing impulses to simultaneously approach and avoid their mothers. The majority of maltreated infants show this pattern of disorganised attachment, which occurs when the infant experiences the parent as either frightening or frightened or both (for example, parents who are mentally ill, have unresolved PTSD, are substance affected, or are chronically depressed or anxious) (Main, Hesse, & Kaplan, 2005). Disorganised children develop multiple incoherent IWM. In this system, the child might construe the care-giver as frightening and, hence, the cause of their own fear, placing mother in the role of "monster" and self in the role of helpless victim. Alternatively, the child might construe him/herself as the cause of mother's fear and the construal of self and mother is reversed— mother becomes the helpless victim of the child. At times, the parent might be momentarily comforted while in contact with her child; thus, the child construes him/herself as "the omnipotent rescuer of a fragile parent" (Liotti, 1999, p. 765). This sequence prematurely triggers the child's care-giving system, which allows the child to experience comfort from loneliness and distress and to perceive mother as loving and caring.

It will be evident from this discussion that the development of attachment styles is an interpersonal process that unfolds in response to the parents' care-giving style that results in the development of a "relationship . . . between two or more organisms as they become attuned to each other, each providing the other meaningful stimulation and arousal modulation" (Field, 1996, p. 545). The critical features of recent definitions of attachment include its capacity for arousal reduction through the care-giver's prompt response to distress and negative affect, the reinstatement of a sense of security following arousal, and the open and synchronous responsiveness to infant communications (Beebe, 2000; Feldman, Greenbaum, & Yirmiya, 1999; Zeanah, 1996; Zeanah & Fox, 2004).

Infants with secure attachment have mothers who are secure and autonomous with respect to their adult functioning and their experience of their own attachment relationships. For parents who have insecurely attached infants, three distinct patterns of adult states of mind with respect to attachment have been identified, and these mirror the type of disordered attachment in their children. Parents of avoidant infants tend to have a dismissing state of mind in which they minimise or devalue the influence of their own attachment experiences. Accordingly, they have difficulty trusting others. They might sustain long-term relationships, but do not experience emotional intimacy in those relationships. They are, as Bowlby described, compulsively self-reliant and reluctant to feel or express emotions. Instead, such people tend to display excessive physiological arousal, as do avoidant infants, who display little overt distress when their mothers leave, but whose physiological arousal betrays their stress (Spangler & Grossmann, 1993). Dismissing parents ignore or suppress their infants' attachment needs, and such infants learn to live as if they had no such needs. These needs cannot be extinguished, but the use of minimising or deactivating strategies, which support emotional distance, control, and self-reliance suppress the awareness of such needs.

Parents of ambivalent infants have a preoccupied state of mind, so called because their past unsatisfactory attachment experiences continually intrude upon their present life and relationships. They have a history of recurrent trauma or loss that remains unresolved, and they are, hence, too distressed by the past to effectively respond to the attachment behaviours of their children. The emotional life of such parents is governed by feelings of helplessness and fears of abandonment, disapproval, or rejection; hence, they are discouraging of their child's growing autonomy. In contrast to avoidant infants, ambivalent infants use hyper activating strategies that amplify their affect in an attempt to secure the attention of their unreliably available parents.

Parents of disorganised infants are also described as unresolved/disorganised because they suffered repeated and painful trauma while simultaneously having no safe context in which to process and resolve their traumatic experiences. Responses to unresolved trauma include fear, emotional withdrawal, and dissociation.[4] One way that people with such attachment experiences cope is to self-protectively split off unbearable states of mind from others that are more tolerable and able to be integrated into the developing sense of self. Children of such parents will often take on a controlling, parental role in an attempt to manage a frightening situation, in which the parent will unpredictably explode in physical or emotional abuse of their child. Tables 3 and 4 present a summary of attachment styles in infants' and adults' states of mind with respect to attachment in parents.

Attachment failures in infants can be observed in a characteristic apathy and detachment, an increased interest in the physical world, increasing self-absorption, and superficial sociability (Bowlby, 1980). In adults, attachment failures produce feelings of grief that, in the absence of an empathically attuned care-giver, remain unprocessed and unregulated. Authentic relatedness with others is defensively abandoned, at the cost of unbearable states of aloneness. If the attachment failure is prolonged and unrelieved, the infant internalises a failed attachment working model in the form of a punitive superego, which defends against the loneliness (Neborsky, 2006). It is instructive here to include earlier conceptualisations of the superego, which are, in effect, quite similar to the superego of failed attachment. One

Table 3.   Childhood attachment styles.

Secure	Avoidant
In the SST the child expresses protest when mother leaves, but respondspositively to mother's return and is comforted by her.	In the SST the child shows little or no distress when mother leaves and displays little or no visible response upon the care-giver's return.
Ambivalent (insecure-resistant)	**Disorganised**
In the SST the child displays sadness when the mother leaves but upon return is warm to the stranger but is ambivalent and angry with mother.	In SST the child displays bizarre responses to the mother's return. Child appears frozen, dazed or confused and has no coherent strategy to reconnect with mother.

Table 4.   Adult attachment styles.

Secure (autonomous)	Pre-occupied
Positive view of both self and partner. Comfortable with intimacy and independence—able to balance these in relationships.	Positive view of others but negative view of self. Overly dependent on others. Intense feelings of unworthiness and excessive need for approval.
Dismissing	**Unresolved/disorganised**
Compulsive self-reliance with positive self image. Minimise importance ofintimate relationships. May appear hostile and competitive.	Believe they are unlovable and perceive others as uncaring and unavailable. Avoid intimacy because they have difficulty trusting others but crave closeness.

example, from Balint (1968), will suffice to make the point. If we remove the word sexual as a descriptor of early objects, the synergies become apparent.

> . . . the super-ego has been built up . . . of introjections of the stimulating but never fully satisfying [sexual] objects of early infancy, childhood, and puberty . . . super-ego is the sum total of the mental scars left by these objects . . . the individual not only takes in the stimulating but frustrating [sexual] object, but hence-forth feels it an integral part of himself. (p. 4)

Crittenden (1992) modified the attachment system proposed by Bowlby and Main, based on work with a wide range of children, including those who were disadvantaged, non-Western, and maltreated. She retained the three major types of attachment: secure, ambivalent–resistant and avoidant, but renamed the two forms of insecure attachment as coercive and defended, respectively, with a hybrid form of attachment she called defensive–coercive. Crittenden understood disorganised attachment as a transitional process in which the child is "selecting" between the different attachment possibilities. Within Crittenden's three major attachment types, she described ten sub-categories, three secure (secure–comfortable, secure–reserved, secure–reactive); three defended (defended–inhibited, defended–compulsive care-giving, defended–compliant); and three coercive

(coercive–threatening, coercive–disarming, coercive–punitive). These sub-types, each with its own distinct behavioural manifestations, occur in response to different types of parental responding to their children. This system elaborates the protective and defensive mechanisms children use to promote security and proximity to their caregivers. The work of Baumrind (1968, 1971b,c) which identified enduring characteristics of children who had experienced different styles of parenting with respect to the dimensions of warmth and control—authoritarian, rejecting–neglecting, or authoritative—supports Crittenden's sub-types.

Marvin and Britner (2008) have classified Bowlby's attachment model into four phases, as follows: (i) 0–2 months: orientation of signals without discrimination of figure during which newborns respond to social stimuli and elicit responses from caregivers; (ii) 2–6 months: orientation and signals directed toward one or more discriminated figures; (iii) 6–9 months–3 years: maintenance of proximity to discriminated figure by locomotion and signals—relationship represents a goal-corrected partnership. Others have developed other classification themes based on different dimensions of the attachment relationship. For example, Mikulincer & Shaver (2011) have represented attachment styles along two dimensions of anxiety and avoidance, as indicated in Figure 2.

Young (2011) has presented a model that combines the attachment and parenting systems into one schema (Figure 3). It comprises four insecure attachment styles—dependent–clingy has been added to the original three. The frozen–chaotic style in the diagram is equivalent to Main's disorganised–disorientated sub-type. The two dimensions of parenting used in the model—warmth and control—have been adapted from Baumrind's (1991) model of parenting styles. Thus, children of cold and controlling parents develop avoidant–dismissing styles of attachment; children of parents who are cold and indifferent develop disorganised–chaotic attachments; parents who are excessively warm but indifferent have children who are dependent and clingy, while parents who are excessively warm and controlling have children who develop ambivalent–preoccupied styles of attachment. You will notice that the secure domain is skewed towards warmth and control, the right amounts of which was called "authoritative" parenting by Baumrind.

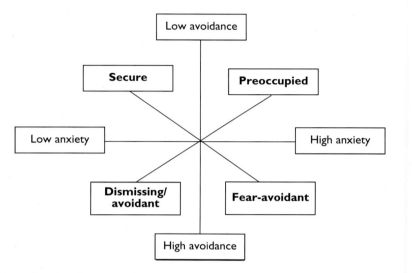

Figure 2. Attachment styles represented as interactions between anxiety and avoidance. *Source:* Mikulincer, M., & Shaver, P. R. (2011). Attachment, anger, and aggression. In P. R. Shaver (Ed.), *Human Aggression and Violence: Causes, Manifestations, and Consequences* (pp. 241–257). Washington, DC: American Psychological Association, with permission.

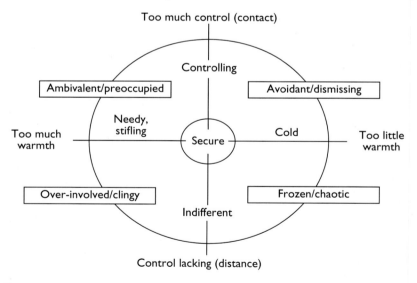

Figure 3. Attachment and parenting systems. *Source:* Young, G. (2011). *Development and Causality: Neo-Piagetian Perspectives.* New York: Springer, with permission.

Mental representations

The concept of "mental representation" is so central to an understanding of all current theories of infant development that it deserves special attention. Today, most psychoanalytic theories subscribe to the proposition that adults recreate or re-enact their early, primary relationships in their subsequent relationships as partners, parents, professionals and psychoanalytic patients (Main, Kaplan, & Cassidy, 1985; Zeanah, Anders, Seifer, & Stern, 1989). What is recreated has variably been called internal representations (Alfasi, 1984), representations of interactions that have generalised (RIGs) (Stern, 1985), object relations (Winnicott, 1986a), subjective world of relatedness (Ainsworth & Bowlby, 1991; Bretherton, 1994b), internal working models of attachment relationships (Fonagy, 1994), mental representations (Beebe, Jaffe, & Lachmann, 2005) and self-representation (Labouvie-Vief, Chiodo, Goguen, Diehl, & Orwoll, 1995). Zelnick and Buchholz (1990) define a mental representation as an "unconscious organizing structure of interactions" that eventually allows the infant to develop a set of "interpersonal expectations" (p. 29) with respect to availability and responsivity of the care-giver. As development progresses, these mental representations expand to include representations of self, other, and social relations, and the implicit rules about how to interact with self and others. The concept of internal representations explains the link between early attachment experiences and later development. They have both predictive and interpretive functions— in both the emotional and cognitive domains—that direct processes of selective attention to (emotional) stimuli, perception of threat, defensive functions, and self-perception, among others (Young, 2011).

Bowlby's concept of internal working models joins two traditions: the Freudian notions of the unconscious and object relations, and the Piagetian cognitive developmental concepts of schemas, egocentrism, and perspective-taking. Mental representations are initially unconscious in the sense that they develop and function spontaneously, without awareness, that is, implicitly, but because of the cognitive component to internal representations, they are capable of being brought into conscious awareness as cognitive development and language progress, or in the course of psychotherapy through processes of self-reflection and mentalising or meta-cognition (Fonagy, 1994).

Beebe and Lachmann (1994) conceptualised "representations [as] relatively persistent, organized classifications about an expected interactive sequence, which are formed by the active process of constructing incoming information" (p. 131) rather than individual representations of self and object, a construct closely related to Stern's representations of interactions that have been generalised (RIGs), discussed below. This view is consistent with Piaget's constructivist theory of cognitive development, which we will discuss in the next chapter. However, care needs to be taken not to neglect the important role of self-regulation, which is influenced not only by reciprocal interactions with a care-giver, but by genetic factors such as infant temperament and cognitive ability, through which these dyadic experiences are interpreted and which contribute to the development of a sense of self. Representations are constructed, interpreted, and transformed in terms of the infant's past experience and current expectations of relationships between the infant and his environment. If there is regularity in these transactions, the universe of the infant becomes expectable and predictable. This pattern recognition underpins the development of the capacity for categorisation, which is fundamental to all aspects of cognitive development, including memory, language, and other symbolic functions, as well as environmental contingencies and understanding the consequences of their behaviour. At the neuropsychological level, self-regulation is underpinned by experience dependent processes of synaptic shaping. Intersecting maturational and environmental impacts on the cortex result in neural pruning, competition, and specialisation that changes both cortical architecture and functioning (Lewis & Todd, 2007).

Many different preverbal domains of infant experience contribute to the encoding and internalisation of representations. These include imagistic, acoustic, visceral, and temporal modes, which might never be translated into linguistic form, but which remain accessible to consciousness. These non-verbal forms of representation are stored in perceptual channels of the sensory apparatus—visual, auditory, olfactory, and kinaesthetic—that Piaget and Cook (1954b,c) described as the sensorimotor stage of cognitive development. These representations might be triggered by environmental stimuli, especially if they have been laid down as part of a trauma system (Meares, 2000). Internal working models are durable across the lifespan. One example of many similar studies showed that maternal perception of her newborn at 4–6 weeks post partum predicted attachment style, using the Adult Attachment Interview, in offspring assessed between thirty and forty years later. Babies whose mothers reported negative perceptions were eighteen times more likely to be classified in one of the three insecure attachment styles compared with infants whose mothers expressed positive perceptions. It was proposed that the mechanism of effect is likely to be the development of a suboptimal mother–infant relationship. Negative mothers are less likely to be attuned or responsive to their infants' mental states, might have greater difficulty attending to and interpreting correctly their infant's signals, and be less able to attenuate their distress (Broussard & Cassidy, 2010).

The intersubjective origins of attachment

Dennett (1987) defines intentionality as the capacity to understand the meaning of one's own and others' behaviour through the attribution of beliefs, desires, thoughts, hopes, and fears to self and others that permits the prediction of future action. The capacity to know the mind of another is a prerequisite for living in an intersubjective world (Giannoni & Corradi, 2006). One of the early infant intersubjective theorists was Daniel Stern, whose seminal work, *The Interpersonal Life of the Infant* (1985), has had a significant impact on our theorising and understanding of infant development.

Stern's (1985) interpersonal theory of self development shares with Margaret Mahler a central focus on the processes underlying the development of a sense of self, but their theoretical origins and therapeutic implications diverge. Mahler's theory resides within a stage-based fixation–regression model, while Stern's is an example of the continuous construction model. Stern emphatically rejects the view that infants are born into a stage of autism or symbiosis, and argues that they never experience "undifferentiation". Stern's proposed model for the development of a sense of self is grounded in the experimental literature that has codified newborn capacities through the application of new and rigorous research designs that began with seminal research on infant perception in the 1960s (Fantz, 1963; Wolff, 1966, 1969). Stern's "stages" are iterative and permeable and unfold in concert with a series of significant biobehavioural shifts in development with respect to physiological, motor, cognitive, and affective development over the first two years of life. Stern's stages are summarised below.

Emergent self (birth to two months)

One of the major new insights from infant research was the realisation that the newborn infant is not always at the mercy of drives and impulses, but engages in lengthy periods of alert inactivity during which significant learning about the world can occur through the infant's calm engagement with environmental stimuli. Neonates are born with a well-developed visuo-motor system and, from the outset, show a preference for human faces over other forms of visual stimuli (Fantz, 1963). Similarly, they prefer human voices to other forms of auditory stimuli (Friedlander, 1970), and the smell of mother's milk over the milk of other lactating mothers (MacFarlane, 1975). Neonates are also cognitively active; they seek sensory stimulation and begin almost immediately to categorise the social world (Gibson, 1983, 1992). As our discussion in the next chapter will show, infants actively engage in constructing their experiences and understanding the world into which they are born. "Infants take sensations, perceptions, actions, cognitions, internal states of motivation, and states of consciousness and experience them directly in terms of intensities, shapes, temporal patterns, vitality affects, categorical affects and hedonic tones" (Stern, 1985, p. 67). Hence, although the first two months of life are "presocial, precognitive, preorganized" (Stern, 1985, p. 37), this is a period of rapid organisation and cognitive and affective learning out of which a sense of self slowly emerges. Infant research has confirmed that ". . . human social relatedness is present from birth . . . [and] does not lean upon physiological need states" (Stern, 1985, p. 44), a position consistent with the British object relations school (Balint, 1949; Fairbairn, 1946).

Core self (two to six months).

A major biobehavioural shift occurs at about two months of age. Infants begin to make direct eye contact, smile, coo, settle into more regular sleep–wake cycles, lift their heads, and show more systematic and complex visual scanning behaviour (Fantz, 1963; Wolff, 1969). What emerges in this period is a "physical self that is experienced as a coherent, wilful, bounded, physical entity with a unique affective life and history belonging to it" (Zeanah, Anders, Seifer, & Stern, 1989, p. 662). The necessary conditions for the emergence of a core self are the presence of self-agency (i.e., experiencing oneself as the author of one's actions), self-coherence (as opposed to fragmentation of the self), self-affectivity (experiencing affects as belonging to experiences of the self), and self-history (developing a sense of continuity as described in Winnicott's (1960, p. 587) notion of "going-on-being"). The integration of these four self-states comprise the core self.

The development of a self-history implies the development of memory and the sense of a self that is continuous in time. There is strong evidence that infants develop motor and perceptual memory, that is, procedural memory, from as young as two months of age, long before memories that are encoded linguistically (Giles & Rovee-Collier, 2011; Rovee-Collier & Cuevas, 2009a,b). The core self of the infant is an active participant in social exchanges with care-givers, and is able to modulate his arousal to keep it at an optimal level (Brazelton & Als, 1979). During this stage of development, there are multiple indicators that the infant perceives a self and another with whom he interacts. In addition, the infant is embedded in a social matrix that is responsible for the infant's well-being. The other can regulate the infant's somatic state (i.e., feelings of hunger and satiation), affect intensity, attachment and felt security, attention, curiosity, and cognitive engagement. As Stern (1985) explains,

> Lived episodes [of being with the other] become the specific episodes for memory, and with repetition they become generalized episodes ... of interactive experience that are mentally represented—that is, representations of interactions that have been generalized, or RIGs. (p. 110)

Whenever a RIG that has influenced self-experience is activated, the infant encounters what Stern describes as an "evoked companion". Stern (1985) was careful to distinguish RIGs and evoked companions from related concepts from psychoanalytic theories:

> The concept of the RIG and evoked companion differs importantly from selfobjects and mergers, in that the integrity of the core sense of self and other is never breached in the presence of an evoked companion. It is also distinct from a "we" experience in that it is felt

as an I-experience with another. Finally, it differs from internalizations in that these in their final form are experienced as internal signals (symbolic cues), rather than as lived or reactivated experiences. (p. 115)

Subjective self (seven to fifteen months)

The transition to the awareness of a subjective self is made when the infant realises that s/he has a mind and that other people also have minds. By approximately nine months of age, the infant realises in rudimentary form that the contents of his own mind can be shared with someone else. This realisation marks the beginning of the development of a theory of mind (Fonagy & Target, 1996). Without a theory of mind, the attainment of intersubjectivity will not be possible (Giannoni & Corradi, 2006). "Theory of mind" theories have been embraced within the discipline of developmental cognitive psychology and will be taken up again in Chapter Five. For intersubjective frameworks to be meaningful, the parties must share the same means of communication, such as gestures, postures, and facial expressions, and attribute the same meaning to these behavioural gestures (Stern, 1985). If these conditions are met in a consistent and predictable manner, these overt behaviours will be associated with their accompanying internal physiological and subjective states. Stern (1985) emphasises that core-relatedness,

> with its establishment of the physical and sensory distinctions of self and other, is the necessary precondition [for the development of an intersubjective self], since the possibility of sharing subjective experiences has no meaning unless it is a transaction that occurs against the surety of a physically distinct and separate self and other. (p. 125)

In the younger infant, only the empathic response is registered; in the (older) intersubjective infant, the empathic process as well as its outcome is experienced, thus paving the way for the experience of psychic intimacy and "the desire to know and be known" (p. 125). Because this period of development is preverbal, the infant–mother dyad relies on three mental states with which to create their interpersonal world: shared attention, joint action (e.g., pointing, gesturing, and following another's gaze to a target object), shared intentions (e.g., expressed in protolinguistic forms such as gestures, postures, alternating eye gaze, actions, and non-verbal vocalisations) and shared affective states. One of the best-known experiments demonstrating the sharing of affective states is the "visual cliff" experiment (Mook, 2004), in which an infant is encouraged to cross a transparent platform to get to its mother on the other side. If the mother has been instructed to smile at the infant on the other side of the visual cliff, the infant will cross the platform and go to its mother. However, if mother is instructed to be fearful, the infant will turn away from the cliff and become distressed (Sorce, Emde, Campos, & Klinnert, 2000). This phenomenon is called social referencing, a process whereby the infant looks to the mother for affective cues about the safety of an uncertain situation before deciding what to do (Rader, 1997). The development of affective attunement is an important step in this process of self-development. It entails the mother's performance of behaviours or vocalisations that express the quality of feeling in a shared affective state with her infant but which does not imitate the exact behavioural expression of that inner state by the infant (Stern, 1985). The attunement could cross domains; for example, an exuberant physical gesture might be responded to by mother with an equivalently exuberant vocal response.

> Attunement is a recasting, a restatement of a subjective state. It treats the subjective state as the referent and the overt behaviour as one of several possible manifestations or expression of the referent . . . attunement [is] an essential step toward the use of symbols . . . (Stern, 1985, p. 161)

Verbal self (15 months+)

> [The emergence of a verbal self] permits the child to begin to construct a narrative of his own life . . . It also makes some parts of our experience less shareable with ourselves and with others. It drives a wedge between two simultaneous forms of interpersonal experience: as it is lived and as it is verbally represented. (Stern, 1985, p. 162)

This is a period of rapid motor, cognitive, and social development. The child begins to be able to work with signs and symbols and, at some point between about 18–24 months of age, undergoes a major cognitive shift whereby the infant is no longer dependent on his senses and motor activity, but can now add language and other symbolic functions (such as symbolic play and deferred imitation) to his toolkit for making sense of the world. Piaget (1954,b,c,d) was the first scientist to codify this stage of cognitive development. We will be covering cognitive development and language acquisition in detail in the next chapter. During the second year of life, infants begin to develop an objective self; they recognise themselves when placed in front of a mirror (Reddy, Williams, Costantini, & Lang, 2010) or when shown a photograph. They develop a core gender identity that is influenced by both neurobiological (e.g., prenatal exposure to testosterone) and socialisation experiences (Hines, 2011), and are capable of responding empathically to others. By nine months of age, infants are capable of affect sharing reactions in response to a pain cry of a peer (Geangu, Benga, Stahl, & Striano, 2011). They are no longer captive to immediate experience—they now have memories upon which they can draw, and have expectations about future events from their past experience.

Stern (1994) subsequently revised and updated his original ideas on the process whereby an infant comes to represent his object-related, interpersonal experience. Stern proposed, based on micro-observations of mother–infant dyads, that moments of meeting or "emergent moments" which evolve into schemas-of-being-with-the-other contribute to interpersonal development. These moments can take several forms, including sensorimotor schemas (sensory motor programmes, see Chapter Five), perceptions–images, symbols–concepts, scripts (a represented sequential account of events), affects, and protonarratives, which represent the experience as a whole. These emergent moments move fluidly through the episode of relating, changing constantly, but laying down the template of the "schema-of-being-with-(m)other". Stern argued that infants necessarily acquire knowledge implicitly, and this way of knowing is reflected in infant learning and therapeutic change. In both mother–infant and analyst–patient dyads, this learning, while goal-directed, is improvised, unpredictable, and non-linear. The process comprises "moments of meeting" in which the dyad co-creates new, implicit, intersubjective understandings that enhance their "way-of-being-with-the-other". These moments of meeting create implicit knowledge; interpretations are a parallel process that results in explicit knowledge (Stern, 1995). This implicit knowledge comprises the infant's developing expectations of the caregiver's availability and responsivity, decision rules about how to interact with others, nascent self-concept, and, as development progresses, cognitive and self-referential beliefs, strategies for self-regulation, and social cognition (i.e., understanding of broader social relationships). Implicit knowledge laid down in infancy can also affect attributions and information-processing (e.g., propensity to perceive threat in relationships and the environment).

Internalisation of dyadic interactions in infancy

A number of current theories (Aleksandrowicz, 2010; Beebe, Jaffe, & Lachmann, 2005) of infant development give primacy to co-constructed dyadic interactions as the cornerstone of psychic structure. Beebe and Lachmann (1994) argue that what is internalised and represented is the dynamic interactive process itself. They provide an empirically based account from a wide array of infant observation studies of mothers and infants interacting in the first year of life that explains the origin, nature, and content of infant mental representations and the processes by which they are formed. There is a long tradition in psychoanalysis, beginning with Freud but crystallised in the object relations theories and formalised in the attachment, intersubjective, and relational schools, that internalised representations of relationships are the foundations of psychic structure that influence personality development, affect psychological health throughout the lifespan, and guide reactions to the object world, both internal and external. Beebe and colleagues (Beebe, 2000; Beebe, 2006; Beebe & Jaffe, 2008; Beebe et al., 2010) and others (Stern, 1985; Stolorow, 2005) showed that mothers and infants together co-construct modes of interaction that become regulated and expected. These interactions are organised around what Beebe and Lachmann (1994) call the three principles of salience, which are discussed below.

The biological substrate of dyadic interactions is now being investigated. Cortisol appears to be a sensitive measure of the quality of the mother–infant interaction and both maternal and infant stress. Optimal mother–infant dyadic interactions that were judged to be supportive of cognitive and socioemotional development resulted in lower levels of cortisol in infants (Letourneau, Watson, Duffett-Leger, Hegadoren, & Tryphonopoulos, 2011). Further, complex relationships have been demonstrated between the hypothalamic–pituitary–adrenal axis (HPA) and sympathetic nervous system (SNS) response measures in mother–infant dyads in a social stress situation (i.e., Strange Situation (Ainsworth, Blehar, Waters, & Wall, 1978)). Mother and infant saliva samples were collected at various times during the stressful situation and tested for cortisol (HPA marker) and salivary alpha-amylase (sAA; SNS marker). Mother and infant stress responses were synchronous, increasing and decreasing in the same pattern over time and in response to changing levels of mother–infant attunement (Laurent, Ablow, & Measelle, 2012).

Ongoing regulations or patterns of interaction

Ongoing regulations or patterns of interaction between infants and their primary care-givers become predictable and expected over time. A shared system of rules gradually develops based on familiarity, repetition, and expectancy between the mother–infant dyad that regulates their joint action and which organises the infant's experience into patterns of mutual and self-regulation. Maternal synchrony with infant affect at three months of age and mutual synchrony at nine months predicts self-control at two years of age (Feldman, Greenbaum, & Yirmiya, 1999). These bidirectional or mutual patterns have been variously called synchrony (Beebe, 2000; Feldman, 2007), proto-conversation (Rochat, Querido, & Striano, 1999), accommodation (Leon, 1984), mutual dialogue (Lyons-Ruth, 1999), reciprocal mutual influence (Beebe & Lachmann, 1988), and co-ordinated interpersonal timing (Crown, Feldstein, Jasnow, Beebe, & Jaffe, 2002). Early representation comprises the storage of these mechanisms of mutual and self-regulation, which can occur in temporal (turn-taking in proto conversation), spatial (facial mirroring, eye gaze), affective (soothing and game-playing), and proprioceptive domains. These effects are moderated by infant temperament; the effects of maternal synchrony were stronger for infants with a difficult temperament (Feldman, Greenbaum, & Yirmiya, 1999).

When the mother–infant dyad is misattuned, the infant's representations become "expectancies of misregulations" (Beebe & Lachmann, 1994, p. 137). Attachment security can be predicted by an inverted U-curve function. Mothers of infants who are securely attached stimulate them with moderate intensities and contingencies. Insecure–avoidant infants have mothers who are over-stimulating, intrusive, and non- or overly contingent, while insecure–resistant infants have mothers who are under-involved, detached, and inconsistent. These forms of regulation affect not only attachment style and other aspects of psychological development, such as the later development of problem behaviours and psychopathology, but also the infant's physical state, such as sleep–wake cycles and other biorhythms (Scher, 2002). The dyadic level of attunement interacts with the baby's constitutional capacities to self-regulate his states of arousal, to shift states when appropriate (e.g., to fall asleep after a period of crying), and to otherwise engage effectively with his environment (Bernier, Carlson, & Whipple, 2010).

In an experimental study of affect mirroring and attunement in infants aged 2–12 months, mothers were observed to attune to six distinct forms of infant behaviour: pleasurable motoric behaviour, effect initiation, focusing, loss of balance, uncontrolled behaviour, and displeasure. The researchers noted that affect attunement was often elicited by infant exploration and play in relation to the non-social world, leading to the conclusion that maternal attunement might have a significant impact on infants' exploratory behaviour and might, therefore, be important for both emotional and cognitive development (Jonsson & Clinton, 2006). In another study of maternal mirroring, four-month-old infants who were empathically mirrored by their mothers showed more attention, smiling, and positive vocalisations than non-mirrored infants, who also showed less awareness of changes in their mothers' behaviour. The authors concluded that unmirrored infants might be less capable of engaging in reciprocal interactions, a deficit that has far-reaching consequences for the quality of attachment relationships (Bigelow & Walden, 2009). Other problematic dyadic interaction sequences between mothers and infants that result in insecure attachment include maternal expression of positive affect that is accompanied by neutral or negative expression in the infant, and low maternal openness, whereby mothers attempt to hide their negative affect from their infants by heightening positive mood (Pauli-Pott & Mertesacker, 2009). Further support for the importance of empathic attunement comes from a review of eighty-eight intervention studies of parents with infants at risk, the goal of which was to enhance parental sensitivity and infants' attachment security. Interventions that improved parental sensitivity also resulted in enhanced infant attachment security, indicating a causal role for parental sensitivity in attachment security (Bakermans-Kranenburg, van IJzendoorn, & Juffer, 2003).

Disruption and repair

Ongoing regulations must be firmly established in order that the infant experiences a disruption or a rupture in the expectable pattern of inter-action. A disruption or rupture represents a violation of the expecta-tion of the pattern of ongoing regulations that can be repaired. Kohut (1984) described this process in his self psychology model of analytic therapy with adults. The repair of disruptions leads to what Kohut called transmuting internalisations that gradually result in a stronger sense of self. Confirmation of expectations results in positive affect in the infant; however, violation of these expectancies produces negative affect in the infant. Dyadic misregulation has also been variously described as disruption, violation of expectancies, mismatch, and disjunction (Beebe & Lachmann, 2002). Most, but not all violations are disruptive and produce negative affect requiring repair. However, some mild violations are necessary to prevent habituation while other violations that occur during spirited play may be experienced posi-tively as novel and exciting (Baumeister & Heatherton, 2004).

Patterns of disruption and repair have been observed in naturalis-tic settings in which the ongoing interactions of matching or mismatching between mothers and their infants are observed unob-trusively, in experimentally induced disruptions (e.g., the "still face" experiment (Tronick, 1989)), and in the study of interactions between clinically disturbed (e.g., depressed) mothers and their infants. Experimental studies of disruption and repair show that reparative functions are necessary for the adaptive organisation of infants' expe-rience. The expectation of repair facilitates the development of secure attachment (Beebe & Lachmann, 1994) in addition to the development of self-efficacy, self-esteem, adaptive coping, and a hopeful, optimistic outlook on life (Tronick, 1989). The reverse is true for infants who experience chronic misattunement. They develop feelings of hope-lessness and helplessness that might follow them into adulthood (Mehler & Argentieri, 1989). For example, depressed mothers are frequently observed to be intrusive and disengaged, and to describe their infants as unresponsive (Dutra, Bureau, Holmes, Lyubchik, &

Lyons-Ruth, 2009; Friedman, Beebe, Jaffe, Ross, & Triggs, 2010). If the depression is prolonged, infants of depressed mothers will also respond to other, more responsive adults with the same depressed disengagement. Such infants appear to internalise a pattern of chronic misregulation, so that episodes that would be experienced as a disruption in securely attached infants would be experienced as expectable in an infant who has internalised a pattern of misregulation. Infants who experience chronic disruption without repair become preoccupied with self-regulation, in particular, the management of their pervasive negative affect and feelings of frustration and deprivation, which renders them vulnerable to the development of psychosomatic symptoms and psychopathology throughout life. For example, individuals who have a history of chronic misattunement with a primary care-giver will often develop a dismissing state of mind with respect to attachment. They maintain a façade of independence and self-sufficiency, and are help-rejecting even though they experience significant symptomatic distress. They deactivate the attachment system and minimise negative experiences as a way of protecting themselves from re-experiencing painful affects and memories of care-givers who have failed them. However, such individuals suffer significant physical and mental health-related symptoms associated with the effort required to sustain their defensive avoidance during periods of increased stress (Muller, 2009). These and other maladaptive interaction patterns become stable by about six months of age (Beebe & Lachmann, 1994). Infants carry these patterns of interaction into new dyadic relationships throughout life, including with intimate partners, friends, colleagues, and their own children. For example, the development of conduct problems and later conduct disorder has been causally linked to misattuned parenting in early infancy, followed by mutually angry and hostile mother–child interchanges when the child is between two and four years of age (Lorber & Egeland, 2011).

The process of disruption and repair has become a central theme in some forms of psychotherapy, in particular the self psychology of Heinz Kohut. While the therapist's aim is to achieve an empathically attuned immersion in the patient's subjective experience, the frequent failures to do so provide the stimulus for the exposure and analysis of the archaic wishes and longings that are activated as a result of the inevitable empathic disruptions that occur in the analytic dyad. In fact, Steinberg (2011) has argued that it is the process of disruption and repair rather than attunement that represents the source of psycho-analytic action.

> [An] overemphasis on the value of attunement can herald a profound forgetting of why the patient comes to treatment . . . Through an on-going analytic process of disruptions and restitutions, patients partake in a great benefit by getting to know from their own bones that they can love and be loved, despite the ubiquitous breakdowns inherent in significant day-to-day relationships. (p. 437)

Heightened affective moments

Infants, from birth, display a wide repertoire of emotional expression that varies in intensity and includes interest or surprise in novelty, happiness, excitement, distress, anger, and disgust (Calkins & Hill, 2007; Pauli-Pott & Mertesacker, 2009). These are observable through facial, vocal, and bodily behaviour. Heightened affective moments refer to interactions that, by virtue of their intensity, stand out from the flow of ongoing regulations, and by virtue of either their chronic-ity or intensity, or an interaction of these dimensions, are influential in the formation of the self. Disruptions and repairs can function as heightened affective moments. There are different types of heightened affective moments: (i) those that occur regularly; (ii) those that are infrequent and not part of daily experience; (iii) those that occur once only. These are usually associated with major trauma, which triggers the release of circulating stress hormones that enhance encoding for strong emotional memory by interacting with neurotransmitters in the amygdala and hippocampus. This neurophysiological process intensifies "flashbulb" memories of situations involving heightened affective moments and might explain emotional conditioning of anxi-ety in such situations (Lupien et al., 2004). Although salient, novel experiences occurring in infancy can be remembered up to two years later, research has not yet established whether such experiences organ-ise internal representations. Heightened negative affective moments might impair cognitive functions such as memory retrieval, although the original memory does not appear to be lost. Emotional state during learning affects the learning process and, hence, the organisa-tion of experience through changes in physiological arousal, affect, cognition, and memory (Lachmann & Beebe, 1993).

A clinical analogue of a heightened affective moment in the psychoanalytic dyad has been described by André (2005); he states that there must necessarily be dissymmetry in the psychoanalytic relationship as a condition for cure. "There can be no analysis between people who agree with (understand/hear) each other" (p. 1). Such agreement is an impediment to analysis because it

> ... creates an illusion of sharing, communication, and symmetry that can mask "enigmatic signifiers" embedded in the analysand's language. A malentendu (or misunderstanding) is a moment when the most ordinary and familiar ... suddenly becomes the most surprisingly strange or "foreign." As an analytic event, it owes less to a lifting of repression than to a sudden eruption of the uncanny. (Carignan, 2006, p. 964)

Mentalisation

> The pathological feeling of alienation ... raises some questions about the apparently banal state of being normal. In fact, when we feel "normal", we have beliefs which allow us to share common and universal meanings ... (Giannoni & Corradi, 2006, p. 271)

Mentalisation has entered the psychological and psychoanalytic lexicons relatively late, but it represents a continuous development of the previous concept of mental representation and its associated concepts discussed in the last section. It is a concept that sits at the intersection of theories of emotion, cognition, attachment, and developmental neuroscience. The term "mentalisation" is closely associated with Fonagy and colleagues (Fonagy, 1989, 1994; Fonagy & Target, 1996, 1997; Fonagy, Moran, Edgcumbe, Kennedy, & Target, 1993), who borrowed the term from cognitive psychology's "theory of mind" research and applied it to attachment theory and psychoanalysis in an attempt to understand "the process of how the brain becomes a mind" (Jurist, 2010, p. 290). Conceptually, it is related to constructs such as "theory of mind", insight, internalisation and representation, but with the explicit characteristic that it involves a process of integration of cognition and affect. Although mentalisation has roots in the biogenetics of individuals, it is not innate. It has its origins in the early cognitive–affective schemas that are established in early attachment relationships and within the social and cultural context and experience. Experimental evidence supports the relationship between mothers' "mind-mindedness", infant attachment security, and children's development of a theory of mind (Laranjo, Bernier, Meins, & Carlson, 2010), indicating that mentalisation is causally related to early attachments.

Insecure forms of attachment and attachment disorders arise when a significant attachment relationship is absent or lost and not replaced (as in the case of maternal death), or as a result of maternal deprivation (mother is insensitive, unresponsive, depressed, neglectful, or abusive) in the absence of other compensating relationships. The effect of attachment failures on behaviour and relationships is cognitively mediated in what Fonagy (2000) describes as a failure to mentalise about experience.

People who cannot mentalise—infants and children who have not yet attained this developmental milestone and those with severe self pathologies such as the narcissistic and borderline personality disorders—engage in forms of cognitive–affective reasoning called psychic equivalence and pretend mode. Psychic equivalence is a process whereby the individual equates the internal and external worlds, believing that what exists in the mind must exist in external reality, and that which exists in the outside world must also exist in the mind. Hence, the projection of fantasy to the outside world results in the experience of the fantasy as reality (Bateman & Fonagy, 2004). A related concept—"pretend mode"—is a mental state that has no referent in physical reality. These two modes are mirror images—psychic equivalence is too real and pretend mode is too unreal. Both are divorced from the real world and the function of the ego. These modes are developmental processes that precede the capacity for reflection and mentalisation, that is, the understanding that thoughts and feelings are mental states that might or might not have an impact on the real world (Bateman & Fonagy, 2004).

Impaired or absent self-reflective function or mentalisation results in somatisation of psychological distress and physical acting out in response to unacknowledged and unverbalised psychic pain (Jurist, 2005; Mitrani, 1993, 1995). Children with early insecure attachments have significantly poorer peer relations, greater moodiness, and more symptoms of depression and anxiety compared with securely attached children (Elicker, Englund, & Sroufe, 1992). Family adversity, child temperament and characteristics, ineffective parenting, and insecure attachment combine in complex ways to influence adaptation throughout the lifespan (McEwen, 2003). Such experiences affect developing brain structures, such as the amygdala, which is involved in the fight/flight response. The amygdala stores unconscious emotional memories. The hippocampus moderates the reactions of the amygdala and interacts with the cortex to store explicit, linguistically retrievable memories (LeDoux, 1996). In children who have suffered severe emotional or relational trauma, the development of these brain structures might be compromised, with the result that the unchecked reactivity of the amygdala will produce extremely intense autonomic reactions in response to relatively minor internal or external triggers (Wallin, 2007). An example of an extreme reaction is dissociation, the psychological equivalent of the physical response to life threatening situations—tonic immobility, or "playing dead". Emotions are, in the first instance, bodily experiences. William James (1884) understood, through personal introspection, that

> . . . emotional brain-processes not only resemble the ordinary sensorial brain-processes, but in very truth are nothing but such processes variously combined . . . the only emotions I propose expressly to consider here are those that have a distinct bodily expression. (p. 11)

Freud came to the same conclusion: "To have heard something and to have experienced something are in their psychological nature two quite different things, even though the content of both is the same" (Freud, 1915e, p. 176).

The nexus between emotion and cognition was subsequently lost in psychology, if not in psychoanalysis, for much of the last century as the disciplines of emotion and cognition developed separately in mainstream psychology. However, the indivisibility of emotional and cognitive processes is increasingly understood, and is no better expressed than in the concept of mentalisation.

It is through the sensitively attuned attachment relationship that emotions are modulated, regulated, and understood. When such a relationship is absent or impaired, so too is the capacity for emotional regulation, including the capacity to accurately identify, name, and understand emotional experience, that is, to mentalise (Fonagy,

Gergely, Jurist, & Target, 2004). Gunderson (in Bateman & Fonagy, 2004) defines it thus:

> . . . a sense of self develops from observing oneself being perceived by others as thinking or feeling. The stability or coherence of a child's sense of self depends upon sensitive, accurate and consistent responses to him and observations about him by his caretakers. By internalizing perceptions made by others about himself, the infant learns that his mind does not mirror the world, his mind interprets the world. This is termed a capacity to mentalize, meaning the capacity to know that one has an agentive mind and to recognize the presence and importance of mental states in others. (p. vi)

Put simply, mentalisation (also called reflective function and self-reflective function) is the ability to make use of the mental representation of one's own and others' emotional states in order to perceive and interpret human behaviour in terms of intentional mental states such as goals, desires, wishes, and emotion (Fonagy, Target, Gergely, Allen, & Bateman, 2003). Two component processes are prerequisites to the development of the capacity to mentalise: emergence of a sense of an agentive self and awareness of one's own and other's mental states. Empathic mirroring in interactions with attachment figures provides the training ground for the development of awareness of mental states, because the infant learns about emotional states from the outside in (Vygotsky, 1997).

Without the capacity to mentalise, emotions are experienced as somatic sensations (e.g., pounding heart, sweating, dry mouth, trembling, etc.) or physical symptoms (e.g., headache, gastrointestinal complaints, muscle tension, etc.) and are never fully comprehensible to the person experiencing these states. Emotional experiences that are too painful or traumatic, or are judged to be unacceptable to the primary attachment figure, are split off or separated from other emotional states that are more "acceptable" to the care-giver or tolerated by the individual, and which can, therefore, be integrated into one's sense of self. The intolerable affects remain dissociated, undeveloped, and stored somatically, that is, in the body (Wallin, 2007).

Individuals whose early attachment experiences were unsatisfactory develop multiple internal working models, some of which are defensively dissociated from others and from awareness, creating the risk of rapid shifts from manageable to overwhelming states of mind.

Hence, failure of attachment relationships can undermine the development of cortical structures that are associated with both affect regulation and mentalisation. The result is chronic hyper-arousal, such as that seen in severe anxiety, which cannot be modulated by mentalising or seeking comfort from an attachment figure (Schore, 2003). Such hyper-arousal is experienced outside of one's control, because the disturbed attachment experiences have resulted in the lack of a stable sense of self with the capacity for symbolic representation of one's own mental states. Hence, their affect remains intense, confusing, poorly labelled or understood, and, above all, unregulated.

Jurist (2010) has argued that the cognitive sciences, from which the concept of mentalisation originated, have focused too much on cognitions and human rationality, while psychoanalysis has been more concerned with emotion and motivation and the role of the unconscious in hindering self-knowledge and knowledge of others, but neglected the role of cognition in human development and action. The capacity for affect regulation is necessary for the development of mentalisation. Once mentalisation is established, the capacity for mentalised affectivity—the ability to reflect on, regulate, and find meaning in one's affects—emerges. Figure 4 represents the relationship between these constructs.

Fonagy's research on mentalisation has highlighted the strong connection between early experiences of trauma and deficits in mentalising and the implications that this relationship has on the treatment of trauma-based disorders, such as post traumatic stress disorder and borderline personality disorder (Fonagy, 1989). Indeed, the aims of psychotherapy can be articulated in terms of enhancing the capacity for affect regulation; that is, learning to tolerate, understand,

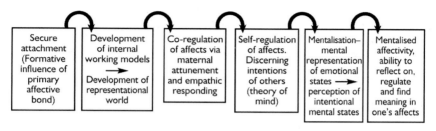

Secure attachment (Formative influence of primary affective bond)	Development of internal working models → Development of representational world	Co-regulation of affects via maternal attunement and empathic responding	Self-regulation of affects. Discerning intentions of others (theory of mind)	Mentalisation– mental representation of emotional states → perception of intentional mental states	Mentalised affectivity, ability to reflect on, regulate and find meaning in one's affects

Figure 4. Relationship between secure attachment and the development of the capacity for mentalised affectivity.

and contain negative affects, a process that leads to meaning-making. Therapy then becomes a process "of working through the manifestations of our representational world in current affective experience" (Jurist, 2010, p. 297), whereby we identify, process, express, and make sense of our affects with a reflective other (therapist), so that we can "attain a sense of familiarity . . . and comfort with [our] own internal life" (Jurist, 2010, p. 298).

The nature and outcome of early traumatic experience

Freud's original trauma–affect model (i.e., trauma is caused by external events such as child sexual abuse whose associated affects have not been expressed and worked through) is really not far removed from current models arising from infant research that have re-focused attention on the effect of the environment, in particular the psychological environment, described as the intersubjective or relational matrix (Mitchell, 1993) into which infants are born that can have both enhancing and devastating effects on development (Beebe, 2000, 2006; Beebe & Jaffe, 2008; Winnicott, 1986a). The more subtle shift within this re-focus has been the changing view of what experiences constitute trauma. As with many complex psychological issues, Freud (1926d) presaged this change, although his original conceptualisation of trauma was event based (e.g., death of a parent; sexual abuse). However, he later revised his theory of anxiety, distinguishing between traumatic (primary) anxiety—which he defined as a state of psychological helplessness in the face of overwhelmingly painful affect, such as fear of abandonment or attack—and signal (secondary) anxiety, which is a form of anticipatory anxiety that alerts us to the danger of re-experiencing the original traumatic state by repeating it in a weakened form, so that measures to protect against retraumatisation can be taken. In these definitions of anxiety, Freud is not talking about single, discrete events that cause the trauma, but a generalised fear of an anticipated experience, a position much closer to post-classical Freudians, attachment theorists, and relational and intersubjective theorists (Diamond, 2004).

Spitz (1965), in his book, *The First Year of Life*, said, "I cannot emphasize sufficiently how small a role traumatic events play in [infant] development" (p. 139). Most traumatic experiences of childhood are now understood to be caused by the chronic misattunements of parents and their failure to meet the basic psychological needs of their infants (Bateman & Fonagy, 2004). This view closely aligns with Spitz's view that adverse affective climates created by problematic mother–infant interchanges were traumatogenic. Wallin (2007) distinguishes between "large-T trauma", which involves the experience of natural disasters such as floods, fires, tsunamis, war, social dislocation, suffering repeated physical or sexual abuse, actual abandonment, or parental mental illness or severe substance abuse, and "small-t trauma", which takes an abundance of forms and has varying descriptors: for example, "shock trauma", "retrospective trauma" (a trauma that acts retroactively in memory) (A. Freud, 1972), "strain trauma" (which overtaxes the resources of the psychic apparatus) (Kris, 1956a, p. 73), "cover trauma" (analogous to cover memories) (Kris, 1956b), "silent trauma" (which has no obvious outward manifestation) (Hoffer, 1952), "cumulative trauma" (Khan, 1963), "secondary trauma" (Sandler, 1967), "relational trauma" (Bond, 2010; Brandchaft, 2002; Schore, 2009), and "pathological accommodation" (Brandchaft, 2007; Taerk, 2002), in which repeated, severe and unrepaired disruptions to the relationship between parent and child occur, but which are likely to remain undetected and invisible to the outside world, since such families often appear to function very well. Winnicott's (1974) concept of impingement is apposite. By impingement he meant

> . . . a pattern developed in which the continuity of being was interrupted by the patient's infantile reactions to impingement, these being environmental factors that were allowed to impinge by failures of the facilitating environment . . . to understand this it is necessary to think not of trauma but of nothing happening when something might profitably have happened. It is easier for a patient to remember trauma than to remember nothing happening . . . (p. 45)

Mitchell and Black (1995), in their description of traumatising empathic failures ". . . as attention becom[ing] prematurely diverted to survival, to the parents' needs, to the self-distorting adaptation to the external world" (p. 210) capture Winnicott's concept of impingement and Brandchaft's idea of pathological accommodation.

In Freud's structural model, unconscious wishes compete with each other and with conscious wishes for expression and gratification. Repressive forces that prevent the satisfaction of instinctual needs press for consciousness, thereby creating conflict and anxiety. Today, the source of psychopathology is no longer considered to be due to horizontal splits between the id's sexual and aggressive drives, the containing forces of the superego's guilt, and the ego's anxiety about the conflict, as classical psychoanalysis postulates, but to aborted developmental processes that create vertical splits between different self-states that have not been integrated because they contain unbearable psychic pain that has been defensively dissociated (Kohut, 1971; Kohut & Wolf, 1978). This view is not too different from Breuer's original thoughts about the altered states of consciousness that he observed in his hysterical patients (Freud (with Breuer, 1895d)) or Winnicott's notion of true- and false-self organisations that have been very widely applied in the literature (Cassimatis, 1984; Daehnert, 1998; Dorpat, 1999; Giovacchini, 1993a,b; Newman, 1996; S. Stern, 1992; Tagliacozzo, 1989; Winnicott, 1965a).

With the central focus of self psychology on the actual trauma perpetrated by parents on their children, Kohut was described as "the most powerful dissident . . . on the contemporary psychoanalytic scene" (Gedo, 1986, p. 99). In addition, the therapeutic techniques of self psychology were understood to have developed in reaction to the

> iatrogenic effects of "classic" psychoanalytic technique . . . neutrality, anonymity, abstinence, long silences, exclusive reliance on interpretation with virtual elimination of the "impurities" of the emotional relationship. Being impossible in theory as well as in practice, it became *tout court* a negative emotional relationship, i.e., a chronic narcissistic injury. It is not a coincidence that many Kohutian analyses were second analyses after orthodox analytic failures. (Migone, 1994, p. 90)

In other words, classical psychoanalytic therapy represented a chronic failure in attunement that was experienced as traumatising by the patient. The nature and role of trauma in psychopathology was, therefore, one of the key differences that opened up between Freud's classical psychoanalysis and most of its subsequent offshoots, beginning with object relations theory ("libido is not primarily pleasure-seeking, but object-seeking" (Fairbairn, 1952, p. 137)), ego psychology, self psychology, attachment-based psychotherapies, and the intersubjective approaches, which all replaced the focus on conflictual internal drives with the identification and working through of faulty early relationships through a reparative therapeutic relationship that is regarded as critical to therapeutic action.

With the redefinition of trauma as a failed interpersonal process, usually between the mother and her infant, rather than as a discrete event, the question arises as to how such events are encoded, remembered, or recalled. The memory for early trauma is unlikely to be encoded verbally, because the failure occurred early in the child's life, often before the development of language, which, therefore, renders the experience unavailable to declarative (episodic) or explicit memory. Rather, little "t" trauma is stored as a procedural or implicit memory in the form of bodily sensations, affects, impulsive behaviour, or defensive processes that are triggered under conditions in which the traumatising experience is repeated in some form in current life. Such experiences may be re-enacted in the therapeutic situation, which allows them to become current and conscious and, therefore, accessible to change (Westen, 1999). People who have suffered this kind of trauma grow up with serious self-pathologies that have characteristic commonalities and subjective experiences. These include feelings of discontinuity, fragmentation, incoherence, and chaos, and intensely painful affects that might be described as feeling lifeless or dead. Gergely (2007) has enumerated four aspects of self-experience that are damaged in these severe, preverbal self-pathologies. They are: (i) an inability to monitor or understand one's emotional states, that is, the capacity for accurate self-perception of one's emotional states is impaired; (ii) consequently, since perception of one's emotional states are misperceived and distorted, there is an inability to self-regulate emotional states, with the result that feelings of guilt, shame, humiliation, and self-hate can overwhelm coping resources; (iii) without an ability to mentalise about one's own emotional states, there is also an inability to mentalise about the minds or emotional states of others in relation to the self, rendering the capacity to sustain meaningful intimate relationships difficult if not impossible; (iv) finally, many people with severe self-pathology suffer from psychic equivalence (i.e., the inability to differentiate subjective emotional states from reality). These commonly identified features of people presenting for therapy are a further source of evidence about how environmental failures occur and the effects of those failures on the developing person.

Generational transmission of attachment
and lifelong effects of attachment security

"The . . . commitment of a parent to sustain an infant through a period of dependency is amongst the most important aspects of natural selection" (Seso-Simic, Sedmak, Hof, & Simic, 2010, p. 148)

How are attachment systems transmitted from parents to children? Demos (1999) argues that a mother's ability to respond empathically to her infant's distress signals depends on her own attachment history and the way in which her distress was managed by her own mother and, subsequently, by herself. In the case of trauma, and in the absence of repair of traumatic misattunements or frank abuse, defences are erected to protect the self from the retraumatising affective dysregulation were these experiences to break through the defences. This incapacity to bear or feel these dissociated affects of terror, rage, and helplessness renders such mothers incapable of responding in a helpful way with their own distressed infants. Because their family of origin experiences have not been metabolised or processed, they cannot be mentalised, a perquisite to understanding or responding in a helpful, soothing way towards their distressed infants. Because abused parents cannot tolerate these affective states in themselves, when they detect them (unconsciously) in their infants, they might become angry and, in some cases, abusive. Parents project their unbearable self-images into their children, who, in turn, develop negative self-perceptions (formerly described as a punitive superego) that are very difficult to modify in therapy. Thus, "trauma is passed on by traumatized parents traumatizing their own children" (Demos, 1999, p. 219). This process is not inevitable; not all parents who were abused as children abuse their own children. A number of intervening factors, such as intelligence, temperamental flexibility that allows people to manage their internal affective states in a more adaptive manner than dissociation or projection, compensatory attachment experiences later in life, or working through the trauma in therapy are all experiences that can break the generational transmission of trauma.

A child's attachment security can be predicted with a high degree of concordance from their mother's state of mind with respect to attachment. Attachment security is stable through to adulthood, indicating its importance in providing a secure foundation for later development. Table 5 shows the relationship between parental states of

Table 5.   Adult–child attachment relationships.

1.	Secure parents ⟶	secure infants
2.	Preoccupied parents ⟶	ambivalent infants
3.	Dismissing parents ⟶	avoidant infants
4.	Disorganised/unresolved parents ⟶	disorganised infants

mind with respect to attachment and attachment type most frequently seen in their offspring.

A combination of quality of parent–child interactions and genetic factors (shared genes between parents and their children) mediate this intergenerational transfer of attachment quality (Ein-Dor, Mikulincer, Doron, & Shaver, 2010). These patterns of transmission are not automatic; maternal sensitivity can block the transmission of attachment type, particularly when there is a mismatch in mother–infant attachment styles (Atkinson et al., 2005).

On average, in western cultures such as the USA, about 65% people are securely attached, 20% are avoidant, and 15% are anxious. These distributions remain relatively constant across the lifespan, from infancy to adulthood (van IJzendoorn & Sagi, 1999). However, cross-cultural differences in attachment styles have been observed. For example, in a German sample, avoidant attachment was more common than secure attachment; in Japanese and Israeli kibbutz infants, resistant attachment was much more frequently observed than in the USA samples (Bretherton, 1985).

Attachment quality is multi-determined and includes the social context into which both parents and their children are born. Interestingly, the quality of maternal care-giving predicts attachment quality more accurately for younger children, indicating that other factors come into play as children get older. One of these factors is child-rearing practices. Baumrind (1971a) identified three patterns of child rearing: authoritarian (emotionally cold parents set rigid rules and strict limits), permissive (emotionally distant parents set few rules and show poor limit setting), and authoritative (emotionally warm parents negotiate rules and set flexible limits). Children with authoritative parents are more likely to become socially competent, happy, and high achieving compared with children with parents who are permissive or authoritarian (Steinberg, Darling, & Fletcher, 1995).

Innate characteristics of parents, their early life experiences, including relationships with their own care-givers, interact with current life
experiences, such as a supportive or abusive partner or financial stress,
to influence the level of psychosocial adjustment achievable, their ability to cope, and the emergence of psychopathology. All of these factors
contribute to the quality of parenting that they are able to provide for
their children. The quality of attachment is determined by the quality
of parenting and by the presence and quality of compensatory relationships that are available to the child. Object relations (i.e., internal
working models or mental representations of relationships) and available resources, both material and personal, determine the way in
which experiences are appraised, and these factors form the basis for
the development of the coping repertoire of the individual. From this
repertoire, behavioural attempts to cope with challenges emerge, and
the outcome of this coping behaviour is either resilience (positive
coping under conditions of risk) or vulnerability (maladaptive coping,
including the development of psychopathology). The child then trans-
fers these experiences into their parenting of the next generation of
children. Kenny (2000) has developed a schematic representation that
attempts to integrate the developmental, attachment, and coping literatures to include all the factors responsible for the trajectories of
resilience and vulnerability. The model is presented in Figure 5.

The attachment system remains active during adulthood and
continues to exert a significant influence on psychological and social
functioning. Adults respond to perceived threats with activation of the
mental representations of attachment figures laid down in infancy and
childhood, as a means of coping and regulating emotions (Ein-Dor,
Mikulincer, Doron, & Shaver, 2010). When these attachment systems
are faulty, their activation at times of stress and crisis is likely to result
in emotional dysregulation. Such systems are not able to support the
mitigation of distress or the attainment of felt security. Instead, distress
is intensified and alternative, secondary attachment strategies involving either hyper-activation or deactivation of the attachment system
are triggered (Main, Hesse, & Kaplan, 2005). People who experience
attachment-related anxiety, that is, anxious attachment, in which the
predominant concern is the unavailability of the attachment figure in
times of need, will hyper-activate the attachment system in order to
attract the attention of the emotionally absent care-giver. In contrast,
those who experience attachment-related avoidance, that is, an

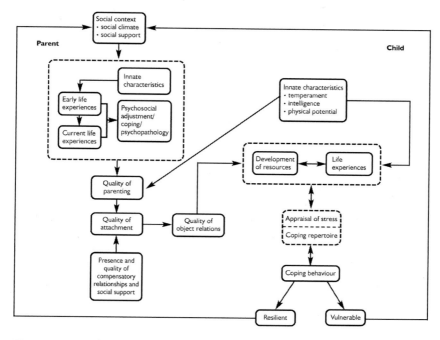

Figure 5. A model of the generational transmission of resilient and vulnerable behaviour. Source: Kenny, D. T. (2000). From psychological foundations of stress and coping: a developmental perspective. In: D. T. Kenny, J. G. Carlson, F. J. McGuigan, & J. L. Sheppard (Eds.), *Stress and Health: Research and Clinical Applications* (pp. 73–104). Ryde, NSW: Gordon Breach Science/Harwood Academic.

avoidant attachment style, distrust their attachment figures and will deactivate the attachment system in favour of dealing independently with danger or threat (Ein-Dor, Mikulincer, Doron, & Shaver, 2010). Those who are securely attached demonstrate a strong sense that they can manage the threat and seek support from others to aid their own coping efforts. Anxiously attached individuals will catastrophise about the severity of the threat and will become insistent about their need for support to deal with it. Avoidantly attached individuals will minimise the threat and attempt to cope with it alone (Cassidy & Shaver, 2008).

Notes

1. See Chapter Four for a description of the parental relationship and how these self-object experiences are reflected in the therapeutic relationship.

2.   René Spitz had earlier written the script for a similar film, *Grief: A Peril in Infancy* (1947), whose caption read "Give mother back to baby".

3.   The notion of a "secure base" originated with William Blatz, on whose theory Mary Ainsworth conducted her PhD—see Blatz, W. (1944). *Understanding the Young Child*. Oxford: Morrow; Blatz, W. (1954). Out of the mouth of babes . . . What is man . . .? *Bulletin of the Institute of Child Study*, *16*(2): 3–6; Blatz, W. (1957). Positive mental health. *Bulletin of the Institute of Child Study*, *19*(4): 1–3. Blatz, W. (1966). *Human Security: Some Reflections*. Oxford: University of Toronto Press.

4.   Most contemporary theories conceptualise the dissociating effect of trauma on the development of the self, as did Pierre Janet, who proposed that self-understanding is a creative act of meaning-making in which new experiences are constantly integrated into the cognitive–affective schemata that comprise one's perception of "self". Intolerable experiences become *ideés fixes*, are split off from normal consciousness, and cannot be integrated within accessible memory structures (Janet, P. (1907). *The Major Symptoms of Hysteria*. New York: Macmillan).

CHAPTER FIVE

The cognitive infant

"Thought is an unconscious activity of the mind"

(Alfred Binet, in Piaget, 1954e, p. 251)

T he terms cognitive–developmental theory and Jean Piaget are almost synonymous. No coverage of cognitive development in infancy and childhood would be complete without a review of Piaget's work. A tribute to Jean Piaget published in the journal *Psychological Science* (1996) provides a good starting point for gaining an understanding of Piaget's profound insights and the breadth and depth of their influence on all branches of developmental psychology. Piaget was committed to the development of a biological theory of knowledge, which eventually assumed the title "genetic epistemology". Piaget believed that knowledge unfolded spontaneously and embryonically as opposed to teaching, which he viewed as externally driven by teachers or parents. Piaget viewed didactic teaching as limited and lacking in creativity. He argued that development explains learning, a position that is contrary to the widely held opinion that development is the sum of discrete learning experiences (Piaget, 2003b). Brainerd (1996) summarised the essence of Piagetian theory thus:

[Piaget concluded that] logic is inherent in action and that the roots of logic are therefore to be found in the organisation of action. It was this conclusion that formed the basis for Piaget's hypothesis that even the most sophisticated forms of human reasoning are motor activities carried out on a symbolic plane. (p. 192)

This conviction resulted in Piaget's intensive study of the non-verbal expressions of intelligence in infants and young children, using research paradigms based on the manipulation of concrete materials, and an analysis of children's explanations or incorrect answers to cognitive challenges, methods that have subsequently formed the basis for thousands of studies in cognitive development. It is interesting to note in passing the synergies between Freud's "body ego" and Piaget's notion of sensorimotor intelligence, concepts that align with later theories of embodied cognition that propose that representations formed in the motoric, somatosensory, affective, and interoceptive systems play an important role in both cognition and social cognition, the capacity to discern beliefs, intentions, wishes, emotions, and desires in others (Goldman & de Vignemont, 2009).

Piaget had some revolutionary ideas about children's mental processes; for example:

1. Children actively construct their understanding of the world through processes of assimilation, accommodation, organisation, and adaptation, a process resulting in equilibration (see Figure 6).
2. Children are not passive imitators or responders to environmental stimuli. They do not internalise "passive copies of external objects and events" (Flavell, 1996, p. 201); rather, they create dynamic schemas to represent their experience. These schemas are organised action systems that are initially applied operatively (i.e., the infant operates on the environment guided by the schema). Eventually, schemata become more figurative; they are internal matches to external "configurations", thus transforming into symbolic thought.
3. Children's cognitive behaviour is intrinsically motivated, not controlled by external motivations such as social reinforcement. The need for adaptation and equilibration is hard-wired.
4. All cognitive development occurs via a process of equilibration, commencing with cognitive equilibrium at the current level of functioning, followed by cognitive disequilibrium due to a failure

of assimilation. Equilibration is motivated by observation of discrepant phenomena not previously observed, which resolves, by application of accommodation, into cognitive equilibrium at a new, higher level of functioning that accommodates the previously discrepant phenomena (Flavell, 1996). Assimilation and accommodation, acting together, result in equilibration, the transitional mechanism leading to development. Of course, maturation has a key role to play, and as the child matures, processes of meta-cognition and reflective abstraction support further development.

Piaget struggled with the tension between two competing theories of cognitive development: (i) the constructivist view that states that infants and young children actively construct their understanding of the world by acting upon it; and (ii) the stage-based view that states that cognitive development unfolds in a fixed and invariant sequence of stages that are relatively impervious to external influences. Piaget wanted to integrate these two perspectives into a single theoretical framework. Hence, Piaget's theory is both constructivist and stage-based, whereby each stage is developmentally grounded and genetically determined, changing with maturation and experience from simple reflex-based schemas to symbolic and logical cognitive structures. It is also a structural theory, arguing that cognition is built on mental structures that are described in each of his stages of cognitive development. Piaget identified both stage-like progressions in the acquisition of cognition and variation due to contextual factors such as arousal state, maturation, experience, nature of the task, and environmental conditions, among others (Fischer & Hencke, 1996). He assumed, like the early psychoanalytic theorists, that infants could not distinguish between self and others or object from action (Piaget, 1927). We will revisit this issue in Chapter Six. For now, we will begin with Piaget's stage-based cognitive developmental theory before considering other issues in cognitive development and theories that followed Piaget.

Piaget's stages of cognitive development

Most theories of cognitive development commence at birth. However, there is now evidence that learning begins *in utero*. The human foetus can detect light, respond to sound through systematic changes in foetal heart rate and movement, move synchronously with music, and show memory traces for these *in utero* experiences after birth. Foetuses also experience pain, discriminate the voices of their mothers and show a preference for their native language at birth (Derbyshire, 2010), so they are not entering the world as "empty vessels" to be filled. Piaget (1942, 1947; Piaget & Cook, 1954a,b,c,d,e; Piaget & Inhelder, 1969) identified four stages of cognitive development based on the different ways that children of different ages and cognitive capacity construct reality. Piaget argued that thought precedes language in the early stages of development and that the child's language development is dependent on his/her level of cognitive development. In other words, development in the use of language reflects underlying development in cognitive capacity. Table 6 summarises the four stages of cognitive development in Piaget's theory.

All perceptual and cognitive theories of development assume that children are born with some capacity to process information. The newborn is capable of perceiving stimulation; his senses—vision, hearing, touch, taste, and smell—are all operating to some degree. Reflexes, such as the eye blink or the knee jerk are also present at birth and are automatic responses to stimulation. More complex reflexes such as rooting, sucking, and swallowing are needed for survival, since they are co-ordinated in the act of obtaining sustenance from the breast. It is through these sensory and reflexive capacities that infants begin to interact with their environments. Piaget called this first stage of development the sensorimotor stage, to reflect his view that children solve problems using their sensory systems and motoric activity rather than the symbolic processes (including language) that characterise the other three major periods of development. Through repeated activities such as sucking and grasping, the infant gradually develops schemas or organised patterns of behaviour. These schemas become organised into more complex schemas and a process of adaptation occurs that allows information to be assimilated into the new schema or to be accommodated in the event that new knowledge replaces old, less appropriate schemas for the new object. Feedback from the environment determines which schemas are maintained and elaborated and which fade into disuse. In this process, combinations of visual, auditory, tactile, olfactory, and motor representations of objects are combined to form more complex, complete, and permanent

Table 6. Piaget's stages of cognitive development.

Stage	Approximate ages	Characteristics
Sensorimotor	Birth to 1½–2 years	Reflexes modified through sensory and motor experience to form behavioural schemas that child applies to objects he can perceive directly. Period ends with the achievement of object permanence and the beginning of representational thinking.
Preoperational	½/2–6/7 years	Use of symbolic thought, including language, to understand the world. Child engages in other semiotic functions such as art, symbolic play and delayed imitation of previously observed behaviour.
Concrete operational	6/7–11/12 years	Begins to solve problems logically but can apply mental operations to concrete objects or events only. Understands concepts of conservation, number, and classification.
Formal operations	11/12–adulthood	Hypothetical problems can be solved by applying the same rules that apply to concrete problems. Can "operate on operations" as well as objects. Understands multiple perspectives, and issues such as ethics, politics, and social sciences become interesting.

representations of objects (and people) in the real world. Figure 6 summarises this process.

Piaget's sensorimotor period is divided into six sub-stages, as outlined in Box 1.

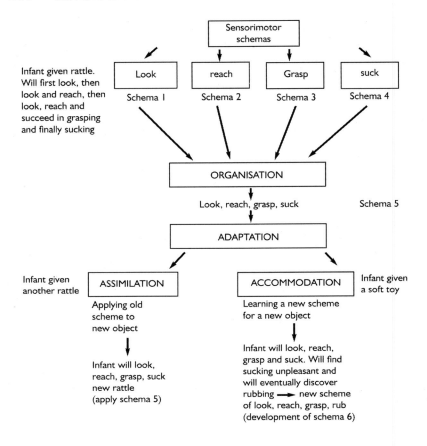

Figure 6. Schematic representation of the processes involved in the development of cognitive capacity.

People continue to organise and adapt their experiences through-out life. Organisation and adaptation apply equally to the older child's operations—the mental equivalents of behavioural schemas—as they do to the infant's behavioural schemas. These operations become more complex as the child grows and matures. Piaget identified three major changes in operations over the early lifespan, which he defined as preoperational, concrete operational, and formal operational. It is useful to present the whole of Piaget's stage theory here, even though concrete and formal operations post-date infancy and childhood, which is the main focus of this book.

Box 1:   Piagetian sub-stages of the sensorimotor period

1. *Modification of reflexes (0–1 month)*
- Reflexes become efficient and more voluntary movements replace them
2. *Primary circular reactions (1–4 months)*
- Repetition of interesting body movements that were discovered by accident (e.g., baby puts fist in his mouth and sucks it; he calms down and continues to suck).
3. *Secondary circular reactions (4–10 months)*
- Repetition of interesting external events that were discovered by accident— not yet inventing new behaviour (e.g., infant squeezes rubber duck and it quacks; infant squeezes duck again and again).
- Secondary circular reactions indicate causality but the infant is unaware of the need for a physical or spatial connection between a cause and its consequences and is insensitive to causes located outside his own body.
4. *Coordination of secondary reactions (10–12 months)*
- Combining schemes to obtain a goal. Infant shows continued orientation towards a specific goal. Previous behaviours only are joined together; there is no novelty.
5. *Tertiary circular reactions (12–18 months)*
- Varying repetition for novelty (e.g., infant throws spoon on the floor, then throws food, then throws bowl). Child learns about properties of objects and actions. Actions are not merely to obtain some goal. Novel actions develop by trial and error.
- Beginning of cause–effect understanding with respect to physical causality. The infant is aware of causes that originated outside his own body; search for causes but limited to those closely associated in time and space; begins to infer causes and anticipate effects.
6. *Beginning of representational thought (18–24 months)*
- Thinking prior to acting (e.g., infant puts down toy before trying to open a door). Child examines old schemes mentally, rather than trying them in a trial-and-error fashion.
- Begins with word meanings that are unstable and idiosyncratic
- Semiotic functions become established that presage transition into the preoperational stage of development. These include: (i) search for hidden objects; (ii) delayed imitation; (iii) symbolic play (pretending, make believe, drama); (iv) language development (child can describe past and future events, use of words becomes more conventional, language controls child's behaviour, language helps control and organise child's environment); (v) mental images/representations; (vi) drawing.

A critical and central skill acquired at the end of the sensorimotor period is object permanence, defined as the understanding that objects (and people) continue to exist when out of sight. Object permanence is necessary for more complex schema development and for memory. Absence or poorly developed object or person permanence explains the lack of distress in infants in the first few months of life when mother leaves, and the capacity of other care-givers to attend to the child's needs without protest from the infant. Box 2 outlines the six sub-stages in the development of object permanence.

Box 2:   Six substages in the development of object permanence

1. 0–2 months	*No expectations of searching.* Child looks at objects in visual field; if object leaves visual field, infant stops looking.
2. 2–4 months	*Passive expectation.* For a short while infant will gaze at a location where object disappeared.
3. 4–8 months	*Search for partially covered objects.* Infant can anticipate the trajectory of the object and look for it at its landing place; will reach for a partially covered object. If it disappears completely, infant will stop reaching.
4. 8–12 months	*Search for completely covered objects.* Infant will search for objects that others have caused to disappear but cannot do so successfully if a series of movements (displacements of the object) are involved.
5. 12–18 months	*Search after visible displacements.* Can handle displacements, will search for an object where last seen, provided infant has observed the displacements.
6. 18+ months	*Search (and find objects) after hidden displacements.* Final stage of object permanence; retains memory for object position and can retrieve it.

A similar sequence also characterises the development of infants' understanding of the permanence and uniqueness of their mothers, although babies with secure attachments to their mothers develop person permanence at a younger age than they develop object permanence.

Preoperational thinking

Each of the four stages in Piaget's theory of cognitive development is characterised by distinctive cognitive processes. While the sensorimotor period is essentially non-verbal, the rapid development of language in the preoperational period has allowed researchers to identify the interesting features of the cognitive processes of young children that are distinctly different from adult cognition. Piaget's theory contends that preoperational reasoning is organised around different principles from the propositional logic used by older children and adults. These principles are summarised in Box 3.

Box 3:   Cognitive features of preoperational children

1. *Inability to conserve*
The idea that amount is conserved when shape changes is not understood. Not until 6–8 years do children realise that amount remains the same despite changes in shape or height of container.

2. *Change*
Difficulty understanding gradual transformations relating to age and time.

3. *Centration*
Focusing or centring on one feature of a situation to the exclusion of all others, and the inability to reconcile conflicting or complementary facts spontaneously (e.g., a child centres on the height of water in two containers, but ignores their width, when deciding if the amount of water is the same in each).

4. *Classification*
Ability to sort objects into categories or classes is not developed until 5–6 years, although experience, SES, and intelligence influences age at which this skill is acquired.

5. *Cause and effect*
Because of centration, cannot focus on the relationship between events and does not understand chance (e.g., as we are walking, the clouds are moving; so, walking makes the clouds move).

6. *Egocentrism*
The child's ideas of the world are limited by his own perspective and experience: for example, will try to comfort his crying mother by bringing her his teddy bear.

7. *Animism*
Idea that everything in the world is alive, like me. Piaget defined animism as a child's mistaken belief that non-living things are alive or have attributes of animals or people (e.g., the sun was angry with the clouds, so chased them away).

8. *Artificialism*
Belief that living things can be made from blocks, sand, clay. Artificialism was Piaget's term for the belief that natural phenomena are all ultimately products of human engineering.

9. *Realism*
Attribution of tangible, material qualities to events like dreams, words, or wishes which actually have no concrete physical existence.

10. *Syncretic reasoning* (from the Greek, *synkretismos*, meaning combined beliefs)
Objects are classified according to a limited and changing set of criteria, resulting in the tendency to fuse unrelated details. For example, a doll with a pink dress will be classified with a pink car because they are both pink.
11. *Transductive thinking*
The tendency to reason from one particular fact or specific instance to another: for example, a log floats because it is big; a leaf floats because it is small.

Box 4 presents a description provided by a preoperational child of how to prepare a turkey for Thanksgiving (a national celebration that occurs each November in the USA) (Martel, 1974) and contains many of the features of preoperational thinking. Perhaps you can try to identify which of the eleven features above are contained in the account below.

Box 4: The preoperational world of a preoperational child—her description of the preparations required for a Thanksgiving dinner

A whole Turkey

    1 big bag full of a whole turkey (get the kind with no feathers on, not the kind the Pilgrims ate)
    A giant lump of stuffin'
    1 squash pie
    1 mint pie
    1 little fancy dish of sour berries
    1 big fancy dish of a vegetable mix
    20 dishes of all different candies; chocolate balls, cherry balls, good'n plenties and peanuts

Get up when the alarm says to and get busy fast. Unfold the turkey and open up the holes. Push in the stuffin' for a couple hours. I think you get stuffin' from that Farm that makes it. I know you have to pin the stuffin' to the turkey or I suppose it would get out. And get special pins or use big long nails. Get the kitchen real hot, and from there on you just cook turkey. Sometimes you can call it a bird, but it's not. Then you put the vegetables in the cooker—and first put one on top, and next put one on the bottom, and then one in the middle. That makes a vegetable mix. Put 2 red things of salt all in it and 2 red things of water also. Cook them to just ½ of warm. Put candies all around the place and Linda will bring over the pies. When the company comes put on your red apron.

Concrete operations and the cognitive shift

A number of significant changes occur in the cognitive development of children entering Piaget's third stage of cognitive development. The cognitive shift (from preoperational to concrete operational thinking) occurs between five and seven years, during which the child learns to reason logically so that their thinking becomes more like the thinking of adults. However, children in the concrete operational stage can only apply their logic to the physical world, not yet to abstract concepts. They develop the ability to conserve mass, number, and size (they realise that changing the form of a substance does not change the amount, volume, or weight of the substance). Children in this stage can also classify objects, seriate (arrange objects from smallest to largest), and make transitive inferences (i.e., apply previously learned rules or relationships to solve new problems). These skills combine to enable children to develop numeracy and to apply arithmetic rules to solve problems. Children in this stage can make longer-term plans, seek intellectual rewards, develop vocabulary, and increase selective attention and short term memory.

Formal operations

Recent research on brain development shows that the brain continues to grow throughout adolescence and into the early twenties, prompting some researchers to advocate an extension of adolescence to the mid-twenties (de Souza Favaro & de Andrade, 2011; Seginer & Shoyer, 2012). Typical brain development is comprised of several stages, including proliferation (an increase in the brain's grey matter, which consists of neuronal cell bodies in the regions of the brain involved in muscle control, sensory perception such as seeing and hearing, memory, emotions, and speech); migration of neurons; creation of dendritic and synaptic connections, dendritic pruning and programmed cell death, which involves the elimination of unused nerve fibres and stimulation and strengthening of "preferred" connections with the process of myelination, the covering of nerve fibres with myelin, a substance that insulates the nerve fibres and makes them more efficient in conducting sensory, pain, and cognitive stimuli (Schumann & Nordahl, 2011)). Myelination begins in infancy (Deoni et al., 2011), and the process is completed during adolescence. The development of formal operational thinking is associated with the activation of these processes in the prefrontal cortex of the brain, the last part of the brain to undergo development; it is responsible for skills such as organising thoughts, weighing consequences, assuming responsibility, and interpreting emotions.

Not everyone achieves formal operations, the capacity for hypothetical, logical, and abstract thought (Kuhn, 2008). Formal operational thinkers have the capacity for hypothetico–deductive reasoning, the ability to detect logical flaws in arguments, recognise that problems might have more than one solution, think abstractly about concepts such as justice, gravity, and religion, construct and test hypotheses, deal simultaneously with different aspects of a problem, think about the future, and about the process of thinking itself (i.e., metacognition) (Piaget, 2008). People who have intellectual disabilities and those who have suffered significant educational or sensory deprivation are unlikely to reach this stage of cognitive development. Some cultures do not require or value the intellectual skills demonstrated in formal operations and, hence, do not support their development (Oesterdiekhoff, 2007).

Formal operational adolescents apply their cognitive skills to personal self-reflection and, because this is a new and intense process consuming much emotional and cognitive energy, adolescents can often appear self-centred. Because adolescents are focused on themselves, their thoughts, and expanding sense of intellectual power, they come to perceive themselves as being "centre stage" (Moshman, 2011). These adolescent characteristics are now understood to constitute one aspect of identity formation (Martin & Sokol, 2011). Formal operational adolescents are often characterised by four qualities, presented in Box 5.

Box 5:   Characteristics of formal operational thinking

1.   *Adolescent egocentrism*
Tendency to focus on oneself to the exclusion of others; belief that no one can understand what they are thinking, feeling, or experiencing because these are unique and not previously experienced by others, especially parents; heightened sensitivity to actual or perceived criticism, self-criticism, and self-doubt.

2.   *Invincibility fable*
Arising from adolescent egocentrism, the erroneous belief that one is not subject to the negative consequences of common risky behaviours, such as unprotected sex, substance abuse, reckless driving, and thrill-seeking activities.

(continued)

(continued)

3.   Personal fable

The egocentric belief that one is destined to achieve greatness through outstanding accomplishments in one's chosen field; sometimes accompanied by the fantasy that one's parents are inadequate and inferior and possibly not one's biological parents.

4.   Imaginary audience

The egocentric belief that others are constantly thinking or talking about them, or if present, scutinising them, leading adolescents to pay exaggerated attention to their appearance.

Self-centredness notwithstanding, many adolescents are concerned with social justice issues beyond their own experiences and become involved in causes and organisations in order to make a contribution to society. This demonstrates characteristics in opposition to adolescent egocentrism, although it is their egocentrism that allows adolescents to believe that they can influence outcomes in the wider community (Schwartz, Maynard, & Uzelac, 2008). Post formal adult reasoning, in those adults who reach this stage of cognitive development, by contrast to the characteristics outlined above, is usually either inductive or deductive. Induction occurs when a series of specific instances is understood to imply a general rule. Deduction occurs when a specific proposition is inferred from a general fact or principle. Without the organising framework of at least the stage of concrete operations, the young child is less sensitive to contradictions than the older thinker.

A note about egocentrism

Piaget first identified egocentrism in preschool children. He defined it as the inability to distinguish subject from object, which was demonstrated by egocentric or "absolutist" speech or collective monologue, and the inability to take the perspective of others (Piaget, 1927). Piaget subsequently revised this view when he observed the phenomenon in infancy (Piaget, 1936). Piaget believed that children remained egocentric until adolescence and perhaps beyond, but there is now strong evidence from experiments in the post-Piagetian era that have consistently also identified skills such as mental representation, metacognition (Robertson, 2010; Robson, 2010), and empathy in children at ages much earlier than previously believed (Bandstra, Chambers, McGrath, & Moore, 2011; Rieffe, Ketelaar, & Wiefferink, 2010). The early appearance of these skills must necessarily relate to attachment experiences including, in particular, maternal attunement, with children experiencing secure attachment showing more capacity for these skills and at an earlier age than insecurely attached children (See Chapter Four).

Piaget (2003a,b) later expanded the conceptualisation of egocentrism and decentration to incorporate concepts like autoregulation, equilibrium, and equilibration. The developmental task with respect to egocentrism is to decentre, both cognitively and affectively. In the sensorimotor period, the child progresses from self at the centre of the universe to a rudimentary empathy; in the preoperational period, the child does not yet differentiate the needs of self from other and gradually develops an understanding that there are different minds; in the concrete operational stage, the child progresses from an exclusive focus on friends to an appreciation that rules are grounded in mutual expectations. In the formal stage, adolescents prepare to enter the adult world but without a planned future and with an overvalued self. They progress to the capacity to act with consistency across thought and action, to plan, evaluate, and imagine a future. Kesselring and Muller (2011) clarified the concept of egocentrism into three component stages: (i) lack of perspective-taking; (ii) lack of co-ordination in perspective- taking; (iii) decentration (co-ordinated perspective-taking leading to reflective abstraction). The shift from egocentrism to decentration is motivated by cognitive challenges or perturbations that are at first resisted, then incorporated and integrated.

Cognition and affect

In concluding this brief exposition on Piaget, I would like to finish with two less well known aspects of his theory: the role of affect in cognitive development (Labouvie-Vief, Gruhn, & Studer, 2010; Piaget & Cook, 1954a; Piaget & Inhelder, 1969) and his exposition of the affective unconscious and the cognitive unconscious (Piaget, 1973). In his paper "The affective unconscious and the cognitive unconscious", Piaget stated "I am persuaded that a day will come when the psychology of cognitive functions and psychoanalysis will have to fuse in a general theory which will improve both ..." (Piaget, 1973, p. 250). Piaget further argued that just as psychoanalysts believe that the source of affects remains largely unknown, so do the deep structures of cognition, the schemata, classifications, operations, and propositional logic: "... though the ego is conscious of the contents of its thought, it knows nothing of the innermost mechanism which directs its thought" (p. 251). Piaget viewed this phenomenon as universal across the lifespan and not restricted to children. He cited the early mathematicians, who obeyed certain mathematical laws in their argumentation that were not articulated until hundreds of years later, and Aristotle, whose philosophical arguments were cogent, but who never articulated the logic of relations. Piaget concluded:

> If our previous hypotheses are correct, we shall be able to parallel, stage by stage, the intellectual structures and the levels of emotional development. Since no structure exists without dynamic, and since, respectively, a new form of energizing regulation must correspond to any new structure, a certain type of cognitive structure must correspond to each new level of emotional behaviour. (Piaget, 1954, unpublished, cited in Young, 2011, p. 58)

Piaget elaborated the relationship between affect and cognition as follows:

1.   During the preoperational period, "intuitive emotions" appear, including early social feelings and prototypical moral concerns.
2.   During the concrete operational period, the child experiences "interiorized social emotions" with accompanying autonomous moral feelings.
3.   During the formal operational period, "ideological feelings" emerge, including the development of collective ideals and the assignment to the self of a role and goals in society (Piaget, 1954, unpublished, cited in Young, 2011, p. 59).

Piaget carried his argument further by hypothesising a process that he described as cognitive repression. Since becoming conscious consists of reconstructing on a higher level an action that was already organised at a lower level, why, he asked, do certain sensorimotor schemata become conscious via their conversion into representations or verbal explanations, while others remain out of awareness, or attract incorrect explanations, even when an action has been success-ful in achieving its end? Piaget argued that even when the imple-mented sensorimotor schema was successful, but was in conflict with a previously held conscious idea, the (new) schema cannot be inte-grated into the system of current concepts and is effectively blocked or repressed to avoid cognitive discomfort. Of course, the very young child might simply not understand what he did (because of the complex physics involved) and resorts to an explanation that is intel-ligible to him. In Piaget's model, we only need to become conscious of action schemata if there is a maladaptation or contradiction or a conflict between more than one possibility of achieving the action outcome. If we are behaving adaptively with good functional outcomes, like running up and down the stairs, or playing a well prac-tised piece of music, our actions are automatic and we do not need to become conscious of how we accomplished them. This is, in fact, the theory, derived much later, of skilled motor performance (Milton, Solodkina, Hluŝtík, & Smalla, 2007). Becoming conscious does not simply refer to an emergent awareness of a phenomenon; both affec-tive and cognitive consciousness requires some form of reconstruction or reorganisation. It is a dynamic process in which the present, both cognitive and affective, is determined by a past that is always being reconstructed in the present. I hasten to add that Piaget did not view this relationship as causal, that is, cognitions do not cause affects, or affects cognitions; rather, "affective and cognitive mechanisms remain interrelated though distinct" because affects "are based on energies and cognitions on structures" which he believed to be intrinsic (Piaget, 1954a, p. 261). Piaget understood that emotional development involved the evolution of complex representations from simple struc-tures in much the same way as complex cognitive structures evolved from simple schemas. Once stabilised, these structures become "crys-tallized cognitive–emotional structures" that are linked to the self and the other in time and space so that the structures and their content are not controlled by their physical presence in the here and now (Labouvie-Vief, Gruhn, & Studer, 2010). Subsequent cognitive theo-rists have argued for the indissociability of cognition and affect and refer to cognitive–affective structures and concepts like social cogni-tion (Deater-Deckard & Mullineaux, 2010; Russ, 2006). Piaget also recognised, but did not elaborate, the importance of the social context in which these cognitive and emotional structures unfold. More recent theorists have argued that culture, which provides conceptual and symbolic frameworks, becomes embodied in the developing child, who reworks these cultural–symbolic representations into a more personalised social representation within their cognitive–affective structures (Nicolopoulou & Weintraub, 2009). A comment by Klin and Jones (2007) is apposite:

> There is more than a cognitive unconscious i.e., learning that takes place as a result of sensorimotor explorations of the physical world; there is also a social–affective unconscious i.e., learning that takes place as a result of sensorimotor explorations of the social world. (p. 12)

Finally, cognitive performance and emotional responsiveness on Piagetian sensorimotor tasks in infants aged two to thirteen months are mediated by individual differences in attention to the task and self-regulation; level of development is a moderating factor in this relationship (Lewis, Koroshegyi, Douglas, & Kambe, 1997).

Critique of Piaget's cognitive developmental theory

Piaget was a giant in the field of cognitive developmental theory who proposed most of the foundational ideas upon which the theory still relies. However, no theory is without flaws, so, in this section, we will briefly review these. Two of the major criticisms of Piaget are that he underestimated the capacities of very young children, and that he did not give proper emphasis to the role of culture and education in children's cognitive development, in particular the central role of social interaction (Gopnik, 1996). However, many of his basic tenets and propositions about stage-like progression are still receiving support in the empirical literature (Desrochers, 2006), so the edifice of his theory is by no means being dismantled in this section.

Object permanence

While Piaget thought that object permanence did not develop before about ten months of age, Baillargeon (1987) demonstrated its presence in infants aged 14–16 weeks using an ingenious experiment in which infants were habituated to a solid screen that rotated back and forth through a 180° arc. Following this, a box was placed behind the screen and the infants were shown two events. In one, the screen was rotated until it reached the occluded box (possible event); in the other, the screen rotated through a full 180° arc, as though the box were not behind it (impossible event). Infants who habituated quickly looked longer at the impossible event, suggesting that they understood that the box continued to exist after it was occluded by the screen, and that the screen could not rotate through a space occupied by an occluded box. Since memory is required for object permanence, the experiment also demonstrated greater capacity for memory in young infants than previously thought, as well as some understanding of some of the space and time properties of the physical world.

Infant memory

Current psychoanalytic and other developmental theories rest on the premise that infants have a capacity for long-term memory. If, as claimed by analytic and attachment based theories, infant behaviours and experiences affect later adjustment, the infant must be able to encode and retrieve, in some form, their early experiences. Resistance to the idea that preverbal infants can remember their experiences has been reinforced by the notion of infantile amnesia (the finding that adults rarely recall events that occurred prior to 3–4 years of age) and evidence from neuroscience that brain mechanisms required for long-term memory are functionally immature in infancy (Rovee-Collier, 1997; Rovee-Collier & Cuevas, 2009a,b). Previous understanding that memory is unidimensional, depends on the development of particular neural circuitry, and can only be verified by verbal report has given way to current scholarship that recognises memory as "multidimensional, multilayered and multimodal" (Paley & Alpert, 2003, p. 330).

Infants display an impressive capacity for memory. Study paradigms using the mobile conjugate reinforcement paradigm, in which infants learn to operate a mobile hanging above them in their cribs by kicking their foot, which is tied by a ribbon to the mobile, provide evidence for the existence of implicit and explicit memories in the preverbal infant. The paradigm implements a subsequent non-reinforcement phase, during which the ribbon is detached. The number of foot kicks counted during this phase constituted a test for the immediate retention of the memory of the mobile (Howe, 2000). In a delayed recognition task, intervals of three minutes or greater were used to assess longer-term memory for the mobile. By using different retrieval cues as memory probes during different time length delays, it was possible to ascertain which attributes of the mobile (e.g., specific details or general features, focal or contextual cues) were accessible to the original memory representation following initial encoding (Rovee-Collier & Cuevas, 2009; Rovee-Collier & Hayne, 1987). Use of different "reminders" (i.e., a component of the original stimulus complex that was presented during training) recovered different kinds of memory traces, that is, features that were encoded in the memory trace and which remained functional after different time delays to re-presentation. Reactivation of the encoded memory was considered to be indicative of implicit memory, while delayed recognition was considered analogous to explicit memory. However, target memories could only be retrieved if the infant re-encountered stimuli that matched attributes stored in the original representation. This is known as "encoding specificity" (Tulving, 1983).

Functional memory processing appears to be quite similar in three- and six-month-old infants, although six-month-olds show more rapid retrieval and modification of memories and less context dependence than three-month-olds, indicating that cue, context, and the training event are stored together in memory and that the cue and the context must be activated simultaneously in order for the memory to be retrieved (Shields & Rovee-Collier, 1992). Small deviations in contexts and cues can be tolerated without affecting memory retrieval, which also depends on the time to retrieval (Hayne, Rovee-Collier, & Borza, 1991). Using a deferred imitation technique, 14–16-month-old infants showed impressive deferred imitation capacity. They were able to reproduce target behaviours (i.e., specific manipulations with specific objects) that they had observed two and four months earlier during a brief exposure (Meltzoff, 1995). Following a series of studies on long-term memory retrieval, Perris, Myers, and Clifton (1990) concluded that at three years of age, children can remember aspects of a single experience that occurred when they were six months old.

These and many similar experiments have confirmed that the infant's representational system is far more advanced than Piaget and, indeed, many infant researchers previously assumed. In summary, a large body of research only touched upon here indicates that infants' memories are enduring and specific. Retrieval and modification of memories become more rapid between three months and six months of age, with increasing dependence on contextual cues to facilitate retrieval. As memories become less accessible, reliance on contextual support increases. Infants aged 14–16 months display long-term retention, supporting the existence of explicit memory at these ages. Contextual specificity acts as a protective mechanism for early memories and might account, at least in part, for infantile amnesia (Nadel & Zola-Morgan, 1984). Memory retrieval only occurs under conditions in which infants encounter stimuli that are virtually identical to those experienced during training. Experiments using deferred imitation assessed age-related changes in infant declarative memory over the first two years. When infants were tested for their ability to reproduce actions twenty-four hours after adult modelling, changes in context or in the object disrupted the performance of younger (six months) but not older (12–18 months) infants. The age-related improvement in representational flexibility might partially account for infantile amnesia and its gradual lessening as the child grows (Hayne, Boniface, & Barr, 2000).

Developmental advances in perception and attention decrease the probability that an identical stimulus would be encountered several years later to aid retrieval (Hildreth & Rovee-Collier, 2002; Hsu & Rovee-Collier, 2006). Additionally, the acquisition of language could render the linguistically competent individual unable to access memories comprising only perceptually-based attributes. Very young infants display memory dissociations between implicit and explicit memory, calling into question the primacy of conscious recollection as the defining characteristic of explicit memory (Rovee-Collier, 1997). Similarly, Freud's dynamic unconscious (Maldonado, 2011), accounts of psychoanalytic treatment (Slochower, 1996), and trauma research (Meares, 2000) indicate that experiences that cannot be explicitly recalled still exert an influence on one's current behaviour. We will return to this in the final chapter, where we consider the equivalence of the psychoanalytic concept of the unconscious and the notion of implicit memory. For now, we will examine this evidence as a possible explanation for infantile and childhood amnesia.

*Principles of infant memory development that
might account for infantile amnesia*

There are four general principles of memory development during infancy that involve mechanisms—encoding, retention, and retrieval—derived from the study of adult memory that could account, at least in part, for infantile and childhood amnesia. These are summarised from the discussion above and from Hayne (2004).

Principle 1: Older infants encode information faster

Newborns can encode information about their environment and distinguish that information from novel information that they encounter subsequently. The speed of encoding increases with age, especially during the first year of life.

Principle 2: Older infants remember longer

Infants of the same age show uniform performance in long-term retrieval on the mobile conjugate reinforcement paradigm. When infants aged between two and eighteen months were tested for retention at varying time intervals from training, the maximum duration of retention increased linearly with age. Infants aged two months retained their learning for twenty-four hours, while eighteen-month-old infants remembered for an average of thirteen weeks. Increasing retrieval and retention capacity is observed throughout early childhood, up to four years of age.

Principle 3: Older infants use a wider range of retrieval cues

In infancy, memory retrieval only occurs when the same cues and contexts are present at both the time of encoding and the time of retrieval (Encoding specificity hypothesis). As infants develop, reliance on the same cues and contexts becomes less rigid during memory retrieval, and retrieval can occur when some of the original cues have been changed during retrieval. The older the child, the more changes can occur without disrupting retrieval.

*Principle 4: Forgotten memories can be retrieved
through the presentation of a reminder*

Infants show rapid forgetting in the absence of training (i.e., repeated exposures) and reminders. When training and reminders are added, memory retrieval improves. A single reminder presented at the end of a retrieval episode significantly improves longer-term retention of the event. Infants initially trained at six months accurately retained the original memory until at least two years of age if they sporadically received reminders in the time interval between acquisition and retrieval testing. They also showed increased speed of retrieval, decreased exposure time to the reminders, and the ability to use a wider range of cues to aid retrieval.

Implications for childhood amnesia

Infants as young as six months old demonstrate the capacity for declarative or explicit memory, thus ruling out the assertion that infant and childhood amnesia is a result of the inability to encode information. Infants show a gradual continuous change in the capacity to encode, retain, and retrieve information that is a linear function of age, thus ruling out any hypothesis based on proposals of discontinuous, stage-like transitions in memory processing. It is likely that the explanation lies in an efficiency hypothesis: as infants grow, they become faster at encoding, form richer mental representations of the (training) event, require fewer cues to retrieve the memories, retain memories longer, and retrieve memories when stimulus novelty is introduced in the retrieval situation. Assessment of forgetting indicates that infant retention improves between six and ninety-one times over the first two years of life (Hartshorn et al., 1998; Herbert & Hayne, 2000). Taken together, efficiency in remembering and propensity to forget during infancy might, at least partially, account for infant and childhood amnesia.

Much of the period of childhood amnesia (up to 3–4 years of age) is characterised by limited language. Thus, the lack of language has much intuitive appeal as an explanation for childhood amnesia. However, for a range of reasons, including the similar results obtained from studies of memory in animals, who do not have language, absence of language is not an adequate explanation for this phenomenon. Even when language does develop in the latter part of infancy, infants are not yet able to use language in the service of memory (Simcock & Hayne, 2002). Because encoding, retention, and retrieval are implicated in childhood amnesia, it is possible that language serves indirect functions in memory and amnesia. First, encoding memory linguistically is efficient and increases both the quality and duration of retention. Second, the use of language-based retrieval cues increases the efficiency of retrieval, and allows for the encoding of meta-cues across situations that share common features but which are not identical. Thus, Hayne (2004) argues that language is a retrieval cue like other cues that are used to aid memory retrieval. Other child-hood developments, including the development of a sense of self and a theory of mind, might make further contributions to the efficiency of memory storage and retrieval, which, in turn, reduce childhood amnesia. These issues are taken up in the last section of this chapter.

The role of the environment in cognitive development

Piaget's (2003b) theory of cognitive development was essentially rationalist and constructivist (i.e., the child generates his own intel-lectual activity) and neglected the influence of the environment and culture on children's learning. Although Piaget attempted to reconcile these two sets of influences in his early writings (he explicitly acknow-ledged the influence of peers on children's communication), he under-estimated the effects of interactions with adults on children's developing cognition and the social transmission of knowledge. It seems truistic to state that children use multiple sources to generate knowledge, including both their own sensorimotor and intellectual strategies, as well as the assimilation of knowledge transmitted by significant others, and through the social transmission of knowledge that occurs simply by being part of a social system (Elbers, 1986). Both systems are observable in children's cognitions, on the one hand reflecting the social and cultural standards in their environment, and, on the other, demonstrating a rejection of adult input because they are actively engaged in solving their own intellectual problems. This latter phenomenon is most obvious in language development, during which children use incorrect language structures, such as over-generalised plurals (e.g., I have two foots) or incorrect past tense rules (e.g., I goed to sleep) that could not have been transmitted by adults. Further, chil-dren develop domain-specific expertise that can only be explained by a combination of innate propensities to develop expertise in that domain and exposure to environmental conditions that foster and develop that expertise. Children might, therefore, function at a higher level cognitively in one domain if they have acquired expertise through extensive practice and experience. Child musicians and athletes are examples. One characteristic of domain-specific expertise is that problem-solving becomes more efficient because children can rely on their memory of behavioural patterns and ways of responding as they build up automatic templates with over-learned solution procedures that allow them to bypass complex reasoning processes (Flavell, 1992). For example, a child prodigy in piano memorises all the scale and arpeggio patterns of all twelve tonal keys in Western classical music. When confronted with a concerto that begins with running scale passages, s/he does not have to read the score note by note, or pause to work out fingering, because these templates have been well established through practice and can be extracted at the appropriate time. Information processing theories argue that development is an outcome of increasingly efficient capacities to process such information.

Stage theories

Siegler (1994) addresses the major weaknesses of stage theories of cognitive development—their failure to specify how change occurs and the variability in the process of change. He argued that evolutionary theory is an analogy for cognitive development: "evolution is the product of interactions among mechanisms that produce variability . . . that select among varying entities . . . and that preserve the lessons of the past" (p. 17). He conceptualises cognitive development as changes in the distribution of ways of thinking (i.e., strategies), rather than as sudden shifts from one way of thinking to another. Halford (1993) also attempted to define and explain children's mental models, skills, and strategies. He characterises mental models as "representations that are active while solving a problem and that provide the workspace for inference and mental operations" (p. 23). Like Siegler, Halford is interested in process and change in cognition, but their approaches are different, making for interesting comparisons. The essential element in Halford's theory is not the development of strategies, but the development of understanding, which he defines as ". . . a mental model that represents the structure of the concept or phenomenon" (p. 238). Since knowledge is necessary for understanding, the process through which knowledge is acquired (i.e., learning) is an essential part of the theory. Halford identifies two types of learning—basic learning and induction, and acquisition of mechanisms for building cognitive skills and strategies. For example, children as young as three years of age understand that thinking is different from talking, an understanding that Piaget believed was not possible even in 6–7-year-old children, whom he claimed construed thinking as synonymous with speech. Refer to Chapter One for a discussion of other issues related to stage-based theories.

Cognitive structures

Piaget proposed a number of new concepts to explain his theory of cognitive development. Many of these concepts were useful to progress our understanding of cognitive development in infants and children and remain so today. Others are no longer current in their original form. Space permits only a brief mention of the many revolutionary ideas that comprise Piagetian theory; for example, his concepts of schemas, assimilation–accommodation, equilibration (i.e., the application and co-ordination of operations or causal explanations that require inferences in order to understand the logic of an interaction), constructivism (i.e., the child actively constructs his knowledge of the world), structuralism (i.e., cognitive totalities that underlie human intelligence), essentialism (i.e., there are essential properties in children's reasoning at particular ages), and dynamism (i.e., the sensorimotor precursor of psychological causality). Subsequent research has shown that Piaget's core construct, constructivism, is much more important in children's cognitive development than even Piaget imagined. For example, children will construct new strategies for solving problems even when they already know a successful strategy for that particular problem or have been taught alternative strategies by adults. Further, strategy failure is not the motivation for strategy construction (Siegler, 1994, 1996); rather, it appears to be an intrinsic feature of cognitive development and represents a form of cognitive play that is intrinsically rewarding to children. However, Siegler (1996) cautioned against a search for essentialism in children's stages of cognitive development. He noted that variability is the rule rather than the exception, and that the same children can generate different strategies and solutions to the same problems from one proximal presentation to the next, and that the reasoning can show greater or lesser maturity at different presentations. He suggested a more fruitful direction would be to explore the conditions under which particular forms of reasoning occur, including the nature of the problem to be solved and the child's past experience with similar problems. There are also a number of other controversies and omissions in the theory: for example, the question of domain specific development, quantitative *vs.* qualitative developmental changes in cognition, the mechanisms of transition between stages, the effects of practice, experience, and expertise, the existence of natural domains and constraints, and the role of sociocultural influences (Young, 2011).

Theories of cognitive development after Piaget

A relational metaframe views antimonies as coordinates not to be split, and reality as neither out there or internal to the sensori–perceptual–cognitive apparatus of the organism, but constituted in the interactive, superordinate, grounded, participatory relations of the individual in context, especially the social one. All related divisions such as mind–body, nature–nurture, continuity–discontinuity, and stability–instability are artificially imposed heuristics with limited advantages and limiting disadvantages. (Young, 2011, p. xi)

Like Freud, Piaget's ideas have been variously endorsed, revoked, tested, modified, and reincorporated into current models of child cognition in a group of theories collectively termed neo-Piagetian. This is a rich field and there are many (perhaps too many) theories, and perhaps too many of them are stage-based. However, as the rather grand quote under the title of this section indicates, they must share a relational metatheory and metaframe to qualify for inclusion. These new wave cognitive theories must account for development beginning from the reflexive behaviour of the foetal period to the self-reflective assessment of the value of our lives as we face death, ideally in old age. This is a tall order, and I am not convinced that any stage-based theory, however complex, interactionist, and recursive, can adequately account for this transition. However, I will outline a few of these theories below and you can make up your own mind about their adequacy.

You will recall our discussion in Chapter Four on the shift in classical psychoanalytic theorising to an intersubjective framework to better understand emotional development and attachment. Young (2011) puts cognitive development on a similar footing. Like the inter-subjectivists, his theoretical approach implies integration across all levels of organisation, from the biological and physiological to the societal, cultural, and historical. Young presents a (self-evident) view that development is predicated on individual–context interactions. With respect to this criterion, Freud would perhaps have qualified for inclusion, given that his developmental model included, at the very least, biological (id instincts and impulses), organismic (personal/temperamental factors) (ego), and environmental (superego) interactions. Other theoretical approaches have been less inclusive; for example, behaviourism privileged environment (i.e., conditioning models), ethology privileged biological factors (e.g., imprinting), and Piaget focused on the personal (constructivism). Developmental advances on these models, such as social learning theory (Bandura, 1977) and attachment theory (see Chapter Four) are more inclusive and explanatory. Neo-Piagetian, ecological, information processing, and developmental systems theories are some of the more recent multi-systemic approaches to understanding human development.

Many of the neo-Piagetian theories maintain the essential integrity of the Piagetian model and are quite similar to each other. The stages in these modified theories refer to the same or similar concepts as those in Piaget's model, but the names and number of stages within each model varies. Some of the key neo-Piagetian theorists are Case (1988, 1992), Fischer (1980), Biggs (1992; Biggs & Collis, 1991) and Young (2011). Each has developed an integrated model of cognitive socio-affective correspondence, and all have argued for an integrated model of human development, both in terms of its hierarchical organisation and in terms of its biological, cognitive, and affective modalities. It is self-evident that biology, cognition, and affect are interrelated, interactive, and recursive. Freud knew this very well. He discovered early that bringing conflicting ideas into conscious awareness was not sufficient for cure; the therapist also had to arouse its accompanying affect. In rather colourful language, Freud explains the issue thus:

> Informing the patient of what he does not know because he has repressed it is only one of the necessary preliminaries to the treatment. If knowledge about the unconscious were as important for the patient

as people inexperienced in psycho-analysis imagine, listening to lectures or reading books would be enough to cure him. Such measures, however, have as much influence on the symptoms of nervous illness as a distribution of menu-cards in a time of famine has upon hunger. (Freud, 1910k, p. 225)

Neonates engage in sensory scanning and orientating (proto-cognition) behaviours; for example, locating and latching on to mother's nipple. They very soon develop representations of salient objects in their immediate environment, such as their mother's face, voice, and smell, which eventually result in an integrated representation of mother. These early orientating behaviours are associated with sensations, motor feedback, and affects. Sucking milk from mother might be associated with both negative (e.g., distress and frustration if feeding was delayed, colic, etc.) and positive (e.g., when they feel sated and satisfied) affects. As this sequence is repeated over many iterations, memory develops, first procedural and later declarative. As for the associated affects, the contents of those memories can be positively or negatively valenced. These memory traces eventually solidify into mental representations about which the child has both thoughts (cognitions/memories) and feelings (affects).

Case's (1988) and Fischer's (1980) models are similar. Case changed the names of the (Piagetian) stages and added a stage before Piaget's sensorimotor stage as follows: orientating, sensorimotor, (inter)relational, dimensional, and vectorial. Case identified four emotions in the newborn orientating phase—contentment, distress, engagement (interest), and disengagement (boredom). By the end of this phase, the affects of pleasure, delight, fear, and rage appear. The infant in the orientating stage engages in what Case refers to as attachment-related precursor behaviours. Passive attachment behaviours appear in the next stage, beginning with preferential smiling at the primary care-giver. These behaviours are followed by active attachment behaviours in the form of seeking and expressing distress to a departing care-giver.

In addition, Case elaborated the processes related to the development of a sense of self through these recursive developmental stages, from the nascent self-related experiences of earliest infancy, progressing to the appearance of a sense of personal agency in which infants recognise their limbs as being under their control, to a realisation that mother-and-self and self-and-object pairs are interlinked and cause action–reaction sequences, resulting in the emergence of an implicit "I" self (cf. William James) as an agent in the object world. At the same time, the "me" self appears as an object of conscious reflection, demonstrated by self-recognition when placed in front of a mirror. Following these achievements, co-operative and pretend play emerges. These are followed by more systematic social behaviour and understanding that one is a member of a social network of parents and siblings.

Fischer (1980) argued that children of the age at which the Oedipus complex is proposed in psychoanalytic theory do not yet grasp the individual social roles fulfilled by the members of their families, and offers an alternative explanation to that of Freud. Very young children do not understand the concepts of child and adult, girl and woman, boy and man; they certainly do not grasp the concepts of husband and wife and their relational complementarity. Perhaps children can understand that they are like their same-sex parent, but they do not understand that their parents do not stay the same age while they themselves age. Finally, children of Oedipal age cannot hold in mind two categorisations simultaneously—that of parent and child (age) and that of male and female (sex). If they focus on the sex dimension and ignore age, it is possible for them to think that they are interchangeable with their same-sex parent. This results in confused beliefs about their social net until representational thought develops and allows them to categorise two dimensions simultaneously, so that they now recognise that they have a male parent and a female parent and that they are either female or male children, thus finally understanding that they cannot be a substitute for the same-sex parent. Hence, there is a plausible, cognitively based explanation for Oedipal-like behaviour in young children.

Biggs (1992) offers a five-stage model of cognitive development quite similar to Piaget's, comprising sensorimotor, iconic, concrete–symbolic, formal, and post-formal stages, each with a different form of knowing that is characteristic. In the sensorimotor stage, the knowing is tacit (and tactile); during the iconic stage, the knowing is intuitive; in the concrete–symbolic stage, the knowing is declarative, while formal and post-formal stages evince theoretical and metatheoretical ways of knowing, respectively. Each form of knowing within each stage is at first unistructural, progressing to multistructural and then relational as the child prepares to enter the next stage of development.

Flavell (1992) threw down the gauntlet to post-Piagetian researchers (and indirectly to psychoanalytic conceptions of infancy) with his revised upward estimate of competence in infants and young children and his revised downward estimate of cognitive competence in adults.

> ... [R]ecent research suggests that infants can perceptually discriminate most of the speech sounds used in human language, discriminate between small numerosities (e.g., sets of two vs. three objects), distinguish causal from non causal event sequences, understand a number of basic properties of objects including object permanence, distinguish between animate agents and inanimate objects, detect intermodal correspondences, imitate facial gestures, form concepts and categories, and recall past events. As precocious infant abilities continue to be discovered, the difference between infant and post-infant competencies, although still substantial, seems less and less discontinuous and qualitative. Similarly, young children also turn out to be not as incompetent ... precausal, preoperational, and so on as we once thought. ... [T]heir understanding of numbers and mental states ... is more advanced than previously believed. ... [E]ven 2-year-olds are non-egocentric in the sense that they realise that another person will not see an object they see if the person is blindfolded or is looking in a different direction ... Finally, adult cognition is less developmentally advanced than we had assumed. (p. 999)

Flavell (1999) provides an excellent overview of the "new wave" of cognitive developmental research and theory building, which includes theory theory, a contemporary constructivist theory based on the idea that "cognitive development is the result of the same mechanisms that lead to theory change in science" (Gopnik, 1996, p. 221); modular theories that assert that representations of the world are a product of innate structures (i.e., modules) that, once externally triggered, create invariant cognitive structures related to that module. Examples of modular theories include perception and the acquisition of the semantics and syntax of a language (see, for example, Chomsky's (2006, 2011) proposition of innate universal grammar), simulation theory (Hesslow, 2012), and information processing theories (Gopnik, 2011; Halford & Andrews, 2011) that argue that improvements in information processing ability (that is, how we build and use representations, what we attend to and remember), and strategies we use to solve problems explains development. Space permits only the briefest of coverage, but the interested reader is referred to Young (2011) for a comprehensive account. I will focus this section on three core areas—symbolic development, theory of mind theories, and integrative developmental systems theories.

Symbolic development figures prominently in many post-Piagetian theories of cognitive development. DeLoache (1995) studied the way in which very young children make the symbol-referent connection and how they begin to use symbols as sources of information and as the basis for reasoning and problem solving. She reports on a series of experiments that resulted in the development of a theory of symbolic development, the Model Model, in which representational insight is the core element. The age at, and degree to which, children develop representational insight varies according to the characteristics of the symbol (salience), the symbol-referent relationship (iconicity), the symbol user (experience), and the social context (instruction). The development of symbolic sensitivity is posited as the process underlying symbolic development.

"Theory of mind" theories describe the ability to infer and understand the thoughts, feelings, and motivations of others. Surprisingly, reasoning about beliefs and desires has been demonstrated in infancy much earlier than previously believed (Caron, 2009). Leslie, Friedman, and German (2004) propose a "theory of mind" mechanism (ToMM) that is specialised for learning about one's own and others' mental states. To explain the nature of this mechanism, they use the analogy of the development of the concept of colour.

> . . . [C]oncepts are introduced into the cognitive system by a mechanism, analogously to the way that color concepts are introduced by the mechanisms of color vision. The child does not build theories of what color is nor discover theories of particular colors. Instead the mechanisms of color vision serve to introduce color representations and to lock the representations to appropriate referents in the world. In this vein . . . we investigate . . . the core inferential mechanisms of belief–desire reasoning, [which they argue is] a modular–heuristic process of domain-specific learning. (p. 528)

The false belief task and visual fixation study designs and their many variants have been used as the experimental paradigms to explore early belief–desire reasoning and the presence of knowledge and attribution in infancy. These studies generally show that 13–15-month-old infants are sensitive to others' false beliefs, thereby demonstrating a representational theory of mind (Caron, 2009). However, in reviewing available evidence, Sodian (2011) distinguishes between the capacity to attribute motivational states such as goals and dispositions and the presence of a representational theory of mind, demonstrated by the infant's understanding of false belief. For example, using a non-verbal object transfer task based on the general violation of expectation paradigm, fifteen-month-old infants could master different belief-inducing situations in a highly flexible way, using both visual and manual information as the basis for belief induction (Trauble, Marinovic, & Pauen, 2010). Sodian concluded that the capacity for attribution has been demonstrated in the first year of life. Although there is growing evidence that older infants demonstrate a representational theory of mind, the claim that infants less than twelve months of age have a representational theory of mind is still unresolved.

Young (2011) proposed a developmental systems theory framework that rejects splits in human development throughout the lifespan, such as those outlined in the opening chapter between nature and nurture, continuity and discontinuity, and stability and change. In his system, development at all levels, from cells to soma, psyche, and culture is regulated through mutually influential connections among all levels of the developmental system, which remains plastic (i.e., capable of change) throughout the lifespan. Other developmental theorists have expressed similar views. Baltes' (1987) model was discussed in Chapter One. In similar vein, and in contrast to Piaget's view of how schema are built and elaborated, Demos (1989) argued that

> [T]he infant does not begin with simple, uncoordinated perceptual functions, such as a visual schema and an auditory schema, and gradually construct more complex units, such as visual-auditory schema, as Piaget . . . argued, but rather begins with a highly complex perceptual system that operates across modalities in an abstract way. With experience and time the infant fills in the details of specific characteristics of objects, but is aware from the beginning of their three dimensionality, of their contours, speed, location, and permanence. (p. 287)

Young's (2011) five level model (i.e., reflexive, sensorimotor, peri-operational, abstract, and collective intelligence) of cognitive develop-ment, by which he meant "a cognitive–emotional symbiotic fusion", represents what he describes as "post modern intelligence" (p. xiv). Each level has five sub-stages: co-ordination, hierarchisation, system-atisation, multiplication, and integration, which recur cyclically during progression through each level of cognitive development. These sub-stages have neurological underpinnings that have evolved through a "particular evolutionary pressure" (p. xiv). Further, for each of these sub-stages Young (2011) has identified the need for a different mode of parenting: during the reflexive period, essentially physical parenting is required; this is followed by attachment-promoting parenting during the sensorimotor stage, educational parenting in the perioperational period, and parenting to promote community linkage in the abstract and collective intelligence stages. Young also maps Erik Erikson's psychosocial stages, or, more accurately, a modified, neo-Eriksonian model with considerably more sub-stages than the eight proposed in the original model, on to his neo-Piagetian model.

Language development

There are two major theories of language development, the behav-ioural and nativist. In *Verbal Behaviour*, Skinner (1957) argued that chil-dren's language learning is governed by the same processes of imita-tion and reinforcement that underpin all learning. The basic criticism of the behavioural explanation is that a language possesses an infinite variety of words, forms, and structures, and it is not reasonable to assume that children learn each of these separately, as unique stimu-lus-response associations. Second, children use grammatical forms they do not hear adults using, for example, "She goed to school", or "Me want it", so they could not have imitated these expressions from adults and they are more likely to receive corrective feedback rather than reinforcement for uttering them. Chomsky (1980) proposed his nativist theory to account for the shortcomings in Skinner's theory. He suggested that we have a biologically based, innate mechanism, which he termed the "language acquisition device" (LAD), that helps chil-dren acquire the rules of language. In support of the existence of this "device", Chomsky pointed to the linguistic interchangeability of newborns (that is, newborns can discriminate all the sounds of every world language until the sounds of their dominant language takes precedence), and the rapidity of language acquisition in infancy and early childhood. Because all of the world's languages, including sign language, share common functional features, Chomsky argued that they share an underlying "universal grammar" that supports the development of rules and forms of specific languages, a process he called culture-specific transformational grammar.

The LAD is understood to be linked to some form of genetically endowed brain circuitry to explain the "deep structure" of language, which is triggered by environmental stimuli. A number of studies have identified language universals in the world's approximately 4,000 languages (Konner, 2010). Other pieces of evidence support the view for a biologically brain-based genetic programme for language development. These include (i) the brain is lateralised at birth in language-related areas; (ii) bilingual children reared from infancy with two languages are able to keep the two language codes separate by twelve months of age (Kovács & Mehler, 2009); (iii) children in very different physical, social, and cultural environments show strong similarities in acquisition and timing of acquisition of grammatical structures, which suggests a central role for the developing brain; (iv) identical twins show more similar pronunciation, grammatical errors, and verbal comprehension than non-identical twins (Lewis & Thompson, 1992); (v) the timing of the different phases of language acquisition is the same universally; for example, babbling peaks at eight months of age and this is followed by a sharp rise in vocabulary development. Chomsky was never able to specify either the exact characteristics of the "language acquisition device" or how it worked, but subsequent research has localised language acquisition to particular areas and circuits (e.g., Broca's area) supported by the growing maturity of the brain, such as increased fibre density and myelination (Bergen & Woodin, 2011; Deoni et al., 2011; Dubois et al., 2008; Lewis & Carmody, 2008).

Infant communication, emergence of a sense of self, and the capacity for self-regulation

> . . . the analysand's . . . style of speaking, rather than conveying meaning, becomes an uncanny object for the analyst . . . the analytic

situation re-creates elements of the enigmatic encounter between infant and adult . . . the analytic endeavor comes closest to the process of learning to speak when these primitive forms of psychic life encoded in the analysand's language are questioned . . . Analysis can be a revival or an invention of these forms. (Carignan, 2006, p. 955)

Language, like a sense of self, develops in the intersubjective space between mother and child. Characteristics of non-shared environments, such as level of maternal attunement, can exert strong effects on language competence. There is evidence, at least in the Western world, that supports the contention that early non-verbal interactions, including behaviours such as mutual gaze, gaze following, gaze alternation, shared attention to objects and jointly pointing at objects, between mothers and their infants are necessary (but not sufficient) for language to emerge (Akhtar & Gernsbacher, 2008; Herold & Akhtar, 2008). Additionally, mothers naturally and spontaneously use "motherese", commonly called "baby talk", with their infants, a language system that highlights the sounds and structures of the language in an exaggerated way that supports both language learning and secure attachment (Schleidt, 1991). As with most mother–infant interactions, the infant contributes to the language learning–communication partnership. Newborns have communicative intent. Crying in the human infant is a cross-cultural universal that is essential for survival. At birth it indicates primarily physical distress, such as pain and hunger, but is later associated with social distress, such as separation anxiety. Researchers have identified three distinct crying patterns that convey unhappiness, frustration, and pain. Cross-cultural differences in maternal response to infant crying produces different outcomes; that is, infant crying is responsive to maternal attention, proximity, and carrying (Konner, 2010). The decline in crying is due to brain maturation and the appearance of other signal systems, such as smiling and non-crying vocalisations. At about five to six weeks of age, babies will coo (utter vowel sounds) in response to seeing faces or hearing voices. At twenty weeks, the baby will babble (combine consonants and vowels) and by twenty-four weeks, distinct sound combinations are discernible (ba-ba, da-da, ma-ma, etc.). At eight months, the baby will babble in conversation and "take his turn" in the interchange. Between 10–12 months, babies can adjust their intonation to communicate happiness, distress, commands, and questions.

First words appear soon after—those that are most important appear first, not those heard most often. Once vocabulary starts to develop, babies use holophrases (single words that express intent, e.g., "milk", "go", etc.) to communicate. Vocabulary development increases rapidly once the infant is able to mentally represent his world. By eighteen months, the child might have between 3–50 words in his vocabulary, and by two years the child is using two word sentences, such as "More juice", "All gone", and "What that?" (Chomsky, 2006).

Language learning is both a cognitive and an emotional process that involves the emotional attachment of the child to his primary communication partners. There is enormous reward value for the infant in the growing capacity to successfully communicate needs, wants, and emotions to those who are best placed to respond appropriately. Because language is intrinsically motivated by the attuned responsiveness of the care-giver, language becomes imbued with emotional significance. As language develops, it supports the growing sense of self-awareness as both an "I" and a "me" in the Jamesian (James, 1981) sense of the terms: "I" as a subjective, aware, and agentive self, and "me" as the object of my self-reflection, the outcome of which is the development of self-concept and self-esteem. The "I" self constructs the "me" self with increasing complexity as the infant moves through various stages of development (Harter, 2003, 2006a,b,c). Indeed, the capacity for self-representation has been closely associated with cognitive development and maturation of the left temporo–parietal junction that is also involved in language development (Lewis & Carmody, 2008). Stern (1985) ascribed the emergence of a "verbal self" to this process (see Chapter Four). Similarly, Meissner (2008a,b) viewed language acquisition as evidence of the emergent self:

> [T]he mental activities involved in the thinking process and the forming of words and sentences and the bodily mediated processes and actions involved in speech production are reflective of an underlying integrated concept of mind–body (brain) organisation within an overriding self-system. (p. 28)

Ogden (1990) summarised the relationship between language acquisition and the development of a sense of self as follows:

The achievement of symbol formation proper allows one to experience oneself as a person thinking one's thoughts and feeling one's feelings. In this way, thoughts and feelings are experienced to a large degree as personal creations that can be understood (interpreted). Thus, for better or worse, one develops a feeling of responsibility for one's psychological actions (thoughts, feelings, behavior). (p. 71)

Thus, ". . . speech provides for flexible self-regulation of . . . psychological activity" (Luria, 1964, p. 143) and permits the child to commence structuring a self-narrative (Stern, 1985). Importantly, it supports the development of executive function, a cognitive–affective processing system involving processes such as verbal self-regulation and self-instruction, attentional control, working memory, planning, self-monitoring, response control/inhibition, ability to change mental set (i.e., cognitive flexibility) and delay gratification; in short, the ability to control one's thoughts and actions (Young, 2011). Development of the prefrontal cortex is closely associated with the development of executive function (Wolfe & Bell, 2007). Infants as young as ten months of age use attentional control to regulate emotional reactivity (Bell, Greene, & Wolfe, 2010).

The achievement of self-regulation, a component of executive function, is one of the major developmental tasks of infancy and early childhood. Self-regulation is simultaneously a cognitive, affective, and relational process that requires a balance between action and inhibition of action. It commences in infancy with the development of increasing control of arousal and attentional processes and proceeds through childhood in the development of effortful, deliberate, conscious, voluntary control. Many of these higher order processes are controlled by language (Jacques & Marcovitch, 2010). Eventually, some of these control mechanisms will become automatic and unconscious. However, while some forms of cognitive and emotional regulation are carried out by executive processes, which are subject to voluntary control, other forms of regulatory behaviour are under the control of more primitive subcortical processes and occur automatically. There are reciprocal feedback loops between these two systems, with cortical processes modulating subcortical activities, and subcortical activities regulating cortical activity by

tuning its activities to the demands and opportunities provided by the environment. Cortical controls buy us time, as needed for planning and intelligent action. Subcortical controls provide energy, focus, and direction as needed for relevant emotion-guided behaviour. (Lewis & Todd, 2007, p. 406)

There are at least eight separate models that attempt to explain the development of self-regulation in early childhood (Friedman, Miyake, Robinson, & Hewitt, 2011; McClelland & Tominey, 2011). They are summarised below:

1. Psychoanalytic: as the ego develops through nurturing interactions with the environment, it is increasingly able to manage conflicts between id and superego and to negotiate with the "real" world.
2. Behavioural: the young child becomes responsive to contingencies of reinforcement, learns to self-instruct, and to delay gratification.
3. Social learning: the child internalises "expected" standards of behaviour through processes of social learning (e.g., modelling, imitation, vicarious reinforcement, self-evaluation, and self-reinforcement).
4. Social cognition: the child develops the ability to control self and events in the environment through direct experiences of controlling self and environment, which leads to self-attributions of control.
5. Vygotskian: the child is endowed with innate curiosity and strives for independence, which, with development, is achieved via use of internalised language that directs thoughts and actions.
6. Piagetian: the child is innately curious and creative and interested in interacting with the environment. The process of equilibration motivates resolution of cognitive conflicts. Progression through stage-based cognitive developmental processes supports the development of cognitive capacity and self-regulation of learning and emotion.
7. Neo-Piagetian: the child has an innate interest in problem-solving, which becomes increasingly focused on particular domains of interest (based on gene–environment interactions), supported by increasing information processing capacities.
8. Information processing: the child is a strategist who develops an increasingly complex array of strategies, collectively called executive function, with which to negotiate the world.

More recent models have called for a better integration of cognitive and emotional components in developmental models of self and self-regulation (Sokol, Müller, Carpendale, Young, & Iarocci, 2010). Young (2011) has ascribed corresponding "emotional regulation stages" to each of his five stages of cognitive development derived from Piaget. He observes that even in the early stage of sensorimotor development, the infant engages in reactive emotional regulation by disengaging from dyadic interaction and looking away when fatigued or bored. From here, emotional regulation becomes increasingly intentional and purposive. Note, for example, the pleasure the child generates for himself during tertiary circular reactions. With the advent of language, a major cognitive achievement, the capacity for emotional regulation improves dramatically for the reasons outlined above. A satisfactory endpoint for emotional regulation during childhood includes the capacity for adaptive, context-sensitive, self-reflection prior to action.

CHAPTER SIX

The modern infant: enter developmental neuroscience

"The ego begins as a 'state' ego, rather than a body ego"

(Sander, 1962, p. 20)

Developmental neuroscience and infant observation jointly provide a foundation upon which theorising about infant development can be progressed, verified, modified, or rejected. Advances in our understanding of the unconscious, primarily via developments in cognitive and memory research, the development of attachment theory and its underlying neurobiology, and infant observation methods have each been pivotal in integrating the scientific investigation of human development and behaviour, psychoanalytic theory and practice, and the study and understanding of infancy. An integration of the apparently diverse disciplines of neuroscience, psychoanalysis, and infant research offers the best hope of understanding infancy and, indeed, the infant that resides within all of us. In this final chapter, we will work at the intersections of these three disciplines to develop a nuanced, scientifically verifiable conceptualisation of the human infant.

Sander's (1962) comment above is a good starting point for this discussion because it acknowledges the infant's capacity for inner experience from birth. Beginning with the repertoire of affective states on the sleep-wake continuum, the infant organises and internalises his conscious experiences or "states", which represent configurations of the functioning of the organism during particular experiences. The term "state" appears frequently in infant research literature in its various forms, depending on which part of the system is involved; for example, mental states (Fonagy, 1989), emotional states (Tomkins, 1991), self-states (Yerushalmi, 2001), and interpersonal states or representations of interactions that have generalised (RIGs) (Stern, 1985) or "schemas-of-being-with-another" (Stern, 1994, 1995).

In this chapter, we will explore the evolving understanding of infancy from the perspective of the most recent research into infant capacities and interpersonal behaviour, and the effects of human neurobiology on these emerging capacities and behaviours.

The changing view of infancy

> If one speaks of the developing infant as described by Anna Freud as driven, or the Kleinian infant as rageful and paranoid, or the Kohutian baby as ambitious but also seeking mirroring, the baby of infant research is seen as a relatively more active part of a relational interpersonal system. (Morgan, 1997, p. 320)

Psychoanalysis has always been a developmental theory, in that both normal and pathological development is attributed to early life experiences. Pathology represents failures in early object relationships and emergence of symptoms is understood to express problematic relationships with internal objects, or, as Stern (1985) prefers, representations of interactions that have generalised (RIGs). Early psychoanalytic developmental theory was based on clinical work with adults, not on direct observation or research with infants. The challenge for psychoanalytic theory in the past fifty years has been to review its tenets about early development in light of the vast literature now available in developmental psychology and developmental neuroscience.

Accordingly, understanding development in the psychoanalytic sense has undergone a number of iterations since Freud (1905d) first proposed his psychosexual stage theory, which described successive stages of libidinal development through the oral, anal, phallic, and genital phases. With the advent of the concept of internal objects and the theory of object relations, psychosexual stage theory was considered inadequate, and, indeed, wrong. However, stage theories are inherently attractive and a number of stage theories based on changes in responsiveness between mother, infant, and environment have been proposed. Examples include Anna Freud's developmental lines (A. Freud, 1963, 1981); Klein's paranoid–schizoid and depressive positions, to which Ogden added a third mode of experience, the autistic contiguous mode (Ogden, 1989a,b); Mahler's and Blatt's separation–individuation process (Mahler, Pine, & Bergmann, 1975; Blatt, 2008); Erikson's eight stages of man (Erikson, 1980a); and Winnicott's (1953) notion of transitional phenomena and the stage of concern, among others. While each of these theories has merit, they must now be balanced against empirical findings of the observed infant. For example, contrary to Winnicott's statement that ". . . there is no such thing as a baby, there is indeed a baby with a functioning set of unique social, experiential and organisational capacities and there is a mother with her unique history and capacities" (Demos, 2007, p. 152).

Demos (2007) and others (Dawson-Tunik, Fischer, & Stein, 2004; Hayslip, Neumann, Louden, & Chapman, 2006; Krettenauer, 2011) have been critical of stage-based theories of development and their underlying assumptions of the unfolding of a linear, universal, invariant sequence of developmental stages that are guided by a genetic blueprint. Stage-based theories assume that later stages are more complex and integrated than earlier stages, and necessarily assume that earlier stages are somehow a deficient or partial expression of what is to come. In contrast, current developmental theories view the course of development as fluid, reversible, and responsive to life experiences (Quartz & Sejnowski, 1997). Current theories are underpinned by a dialectical view that at any stage of life, each person influences, and is influenced by, the response of others, and that these encounters affect development because human brains are plastic and capable of change throughout the lifespan (Erickson, 1968). For example, a successful psychotherapy or a successful marriage can establish new internalised working models of secure attachment that compete with old, insecure templates, and these can modulate the impact of early trauma. Conversely, previously securely attached individuals who are exposed to successive overwhelming traumata, such as war, loss of loved ones, displacement, immigration, and detention, that over-whelm coping resources make the person vulnerable to severe psychopathology and risk of self harm.

Mahler (1963, 1967) presented a similar analysis of development during infancy, proposing that the quality of the ongoing interchanges between a mother and her infant were instrumental in the shift from dependence to autonomy. Other developmental theories have tried to pinpoint the age or stage of development at which the infant moves from dependence to autonomy. For example, both Freud and Erikson nominated the achievement of toilet training as the period marking the shift from dependence to autonomy; Mahler proposed that auton-omy began when the infant starts walking at around twelve months; Spitz argued that the critical shift occurred during the second year of life when the word "no" entered the child's vocabulary. Research on infant capacities (e.g. Beebe, Lachmann, & Jaffe, 1997) shows that infants demonstrate autonomy in their interpersonal relationships in the first weeks and months after birth, including the capacity to initi-ate and terminate social interaction with their care-givers.

Contrary to the assumption of stage-based theories, development at the beginning of life is neither deficient nor incompetent and begins neither in a state of undifferentiation nor with a set of discrete capac-ities that are not integrated. Case (1988) identified four emotional states in the newborn—contentment, distress, engagement, and disengagement. From birth, neonates strive for equilibrium and, if achieved, respond with quiescence (e.g., endogenous smile or engage-ment). In contrast, if the neonate experiences disequilibrium, s/he responds with irritability or fussiness, disengagement, or disgust. Relief of the disequilibrium (e.g., being offered a nipple when thirsty) will produce states of relief and contentment (Young, 2011). As early as one month of age, infants have been observed to actively explore, attend to, and recognise objects. New emotions appear—interest, boredom/disappointment, rage, joy/delight, wariness/aversion).

By sixteen weeks of age, infants can use features such as size, shape, and colour to identify objects (Bower, 1971a,b; Bower & Paterson, 1972). Two-month-old infants can learn complex discrimi-nations to gain a milk reward or light stimulation (Papousek, 1967a,b, 1969). Further, stage theories assume that the attainment of the high-est stage of a particular developmental sequence indicates that the individual has reached an ideal endpoint representing optimal functioning. Krettenauer (2011) noted the inherent difficulty of defining the highest stage of a particular developmental sequence and the problem that so few people appear to reach these ideal endpoints. For example, in Piaget's theory, the endpoint of formal operational thinking is not achieved by a significant minority of adolescents, the point at which the theory ends. Subsequent additional higher stages, such as dialectical reasoning, have been proposed to account for more sophisticated adult reasoning abilities observed in some late adolescents and adults (Hui, Fok, & Bond, 2009; Wu & Chiou, 2008). Stage-based theories tend to regard homogeneity as an ideal and treat individual variation and idiosyncrasies as noise. They have difficulty accounting for the process of change, that is, progression from one stage to the next, and they undervalue the role of context and lived experience in development.

Demos (2007) proposed a dynamic systems perspective of human development, arguing that it is a more heuristic, evidence-based approach that places individual variation at the centre of development. This approach recognises the critical roles of context and affect in the developmental unfolding of the human infant, and that lived experience, genetics, and biology each make important contributions to developmental outcomes. In this model, early infant competencies are "continually elaborated over time in dynamic, creative and highly idiosyncratic ways" (p. 140). The human organism is born with a strong tendency toward psychic coherence and a need for agency. These initial capacities are required for survival and adaptation and motivate other systems, such as the attachment system (Ghent, 2002). These dynamic, self-organising characteristics, together with appropriate experiences in the social and physical world, account for the development of psychic structure (i.e., mind) that comprises consciousness, memory, affects, cognition, and language (Demos, 2007).

At the neurobiological level, mental activity is represented by the rapid development of increasingly complex neural networks and interconnections between networks. The neurological system is constantly active at all levels of complexity, from the firing of a single neuron to neurotransmitter activity at the synapse, to integrated networking between larger neural networks, to conscious experience (Demos, 2007). Activity at the micro-level combines to represent neurally incoming sensory or motor stimulation. At birth, the distribution of neurons is complete. The brain is dependent on incoming experience to build these neurons into neural networks, thus making the context of brain development critically important (Johnson, 2010; Johnson & Gilmore, 2000). The process of myelination (i.e., the wrapping of axons in fatty sheaths that enhance conduction of neural impulses in the human cerebral cortex) provides a useful template for understanding how neurobiology and experience operate in complex reciprocal ways to progress behavioural development. Myelination commences during gestation and is regionally specific from birth. The speed of myelination of specific nerve regions predicts functional increases in that region. For example, myelination of the corticospinal tracts predicts the advances in neuromuscular function in the first twelve months of life (Izard, Dehaene-Lambertz, & Dehaene, 2008). These processes unfold according to a genetically determined maturational sequence (Giedd et al., 1999). Severe environmental deprivation in specific functions, however, such as being raised in darkness, impairs myelination in the specific nerve region affected, in this case, optic nerve neurons (McMullen, Andrade, & Stahl, 2004; Wu & Chiou, 2008). In contrast, stimulation of specific behavioural functions, such as that which occurs in professional musicians who have been practising since childhood, produces greater white matter density (Bengtsson et al., 2005).

Morgan (1997) identified five key characteristics of infants that have been verified by empirical research. These are as follows.

Newborns are interpersonally competent. Although sociality *per se* emerges between the second and third months of life, it is not directed specifically at primary care-givers until about five to six months of age. However, infants actively interact with their care-givers from birth in a process of reciprocal mutual influence. They are responsive to social referencing cues and adjust their behaviour accordingly (Carver & Vaccaro, 2007; Repacholi, Meltzoff, & Olsen, 2008). A number of theories have suggested that babies pass through autistic (Mahler, 1967; 1972; Mahler, Pine, & Bergmann, 1975), autistic–contiguous (Ogden, 1989a,b), auto-erotic (Nagera, 1964), fused, merged (Ogden, 2004) or symbiotic states (Mahler, Pine & Bergman, 1975) before emerging with a differentiated sense of self and other. This issue has been constantly revisited over the past 100 years in both infant research and psychoanalysis, but has never been put to rest (Alperin, 2001). Note the typical quote below that asserts the position is commonplace and taken for granted.

It is by now a commonplace of child psychology that in the earliest stage of life an infant and his mother cannot be seen as two separate individuals, but rather as a single unit, or dual unity, as Mahler (1963, 1968) calls it. (Mohacsy, 1976, p. 501)

These positions are no longer tenable in light of infant research showing the opposite, that is, that babies are from birth imitators, observers, learners, communicators, and interpersonal partners (Giles & Rovee-Collier, 2011; Lyons-Ruth, 1999; Rovee-Collier & Cuevas, 2009a,b). Neonates engage in active intermodal mapping (AIM), a process that unites perception with execution of a motor plan, which permits imitation from birth (Meltzoff & Moore, 1994) and beginning of "like me" perceptions, which form the basis for social cognition (Meltzoff, 2007a,b; Meltzoff & Brooks, 2008). By six weeks of age, infants show deferred imitation. When confronted with a non-responsive face, they will reproduce a tongue protrusion they had imitated twenty-four hours earlier, purportedly in an attempt to ascertain whether the passive face before them is the same as the person whom they had imitated the day before. Imitation rapidly becomes more complex, with cooing games indicating the presence of social expectations by two to three months of age (Caron, 2009).

Research also shows that infants in the first two months of life actively engage and negotiate with their mothers around their sleep–wake and feeding–eliminating cycles. Infants whose care-giver–infant relationship was disrupted after the first ten days of life showed dysregulation in the organisation of basic biological functions, leading the authors to conclude that early regulation of biological functions is the outcome of mutual negotiation between the infant and his caregiver (Sander, 1988). Thus, far from being fused, merged, undifferentiated, or "radically egocentric" (Piaget, 1954a), the infant enters the world with self–other equivalences that are innately specified and experientially elaborated (Meltzoff, 2007a,b). Intersubjectivity is primordial, not developmental. Varga (2011) concludes:

The findings concerning neonatal imitation reveal the equi-primordiality of our own sense of an embodied self and a sense of others . . . the intermodal translation is operative from the very beginning . . . no "translation" or transfer is necessary because it is already accomplished in the embodied perception itself, and is already intersubjective (Gallagher, 2005, p. 80). These abilities make obvious that two earlier conceptions of the lack of intersubjectivity in infancy, the one proposing a selfless state, and the other Winnicottian position proposing infant omnipotence, are mistaken. The infant finds itself always already engaged with the intersubjective world. (pp. 631–632)

Infant development proceeds in a process of continuous unfolding of increasingly complex organisation. Development is not stage based or dotted with points of fixation and regression; it is additive and iterative rather than linear or step-wise (Morgan, 1997). The use of stages to describe development is more a reflection of the need of researchers for heuristic devices for managing large quantities of data rather than a reflection of the actual process of development. Behaviours reflecting the concepts of fixation and regression, once central to early psychoanalytic theory and practice, are now conceptualised as an individual's attempts to respond adaptively to challenging life experiences.

Infants are interdependent and interactive with their care-givers, rather than driven by instincts or governed by phantasies. I do not need to press the point further than to refer the reader back to Chapter Four, in which attachment theory is discussed at length and developmental outcomes are explained in terms of attachment styles.

Systems of interaction build psychic structure. The work of Beebe and colleagues and Stern (1985), also discussed in Chapter Four, has highlighted the central role of ongoing regulations or patterns of interaction, their disruption and repair, and heightened affective moments in building psychic structure in the developing infant. In current theory, psychic structure does not refer to the edifices of the id, ego, or super-ego, but to internalised objects and representations of interpersonal interactions. Bowlby's (1973) "working model of attachment" and Stern's (1985) RIGs are two examples of psychic structure as it is currently conceptualised.

The need for affect regulation, rather than drives, motivates behaviour. The infant is born with the capacity to experience positive (rewarding) and negative (punishing) affects, which he encodes both neurologically and in memory. The infant is, therefore, motivated to increase positive affects, decrease or manage negative affects, and to minimise affect inhibition. "The goal of re-experiencing positive affect and avoiding or escaping from negative affect is one kind of lawful dynamic that [operates] in development" (Demos, 1989, p. 296). These motivations enhance learning of environmental contingencies that lead to positive and negative affects and to organising behaviour to influence outcomes (Tronick, 2002; Tronick & Beeghly, 2011).

> Infants appear to be just as attracted to the expectation of a pleasurable outcome that accompanies success as they are motivated to avoid the negative affect experienced with too much incongruence, dissonance, or the inability to discover the contingencies and adjust their own behavior accordingly. (Papousek, Papousek, & Koester, 1986, p. 99)

Infant temperament

Infant temperament has been mentioned several times throughout this book, mostly for its appearance as a predictor of characteristics of later development in many developmental studies. The contribution of infant temperament to both attachment quality and later developmental problems is difficult to assess because of the complex interrelationships between genes, biology, and the physical and social environment. Some researchers attribute a major role to temperament (e.g., Kagan, 2004; Kagan & Snidman, 2004; Kagan, Snidman, Kahn, & Towsley, 2007) while others emphasise the importance of sensitive maternal responsiveness in mitigating the possible negative effects of a difficult infant temperament on development (e.g., Beebe et al., 2010; Jonsson & Clinton, 2006).

A number of recent studies have explored the effect of infant temperament on maternal responsiveness and mood, and its converse, the effect of maternal responsiveness and other environmental factors on infant temperament. Studies show that infant temperament, environment, and maternal characteristics interact in complex ways; for example, easy temperament reduces risk of later behavioural problems, but only in lower risk environments (Derauf et al., 2011). Similarly, maternal sensitivity during distress, but not during free play, predicted attachment security in six-month-old infants, while infant temperament was found to be unrelated to attachment security (Leerkes, 2011).

A recent study involving 296 mothers of healthy newborns born at term showed that maternal post-partum anxiety and depression were significantly related to a number of dimensions of mother-rated infant temperament assessed on the Early Infancy Temperament

Questionnaire, including infant activity, rhythmicity, approach, distractibility, overall temperamental difficulty, and adaptability and intensity. Researchers observed a dose-response relationship between maternal mood and infant temperament. Higher scores on anxiety and depression were significantly associated with maternal ratings of more difficult infant temperament. It is, of course, possible that depressed and anxious mothers are more likely to perceive their infants as difficult than mothers who are not depressed and anxious (Britton, 2011). However, other evidence supports the general contention that various measures of infant temperament, physiological reactivity, and self-regulation in the first days and months of life predict behavioural problems and internalising disorders in childhood. The effects of these early constitutional factors are exacerbated in children who are born into families with low cohesiveness and less focus on play in early childhood (Dale et al., 2011).

A related question about infant temperament is whether it is stable across the lifespan. Longitudinal studies are needed to assess this. In one such study, infant temperament, in particular the dimensions of positive and negative affectivity, and attention were assessed at four and twelve months using the Infant Behaviour Record (IBR) from the Bayley Scales for Infant Development (BSID). The degree to which these measures predicted temperament at six years was examined with the Dimensions of Temperament Survey-Revised (DOTS-R) in seventy-two full-term babies. Measures were also taken of motor performance, orientation, and autonomic nervous system (ANS) stability of newborns at three and thirty days. Motor performance, orientation, and ANS stability of the neonate at three and thirty days predicted positive and negative affectivity at four months. State regulation at three days predicted attention, and ANS stability at three days predicted negative affectivity at twelve months. In turn, negative affectivity at twelve months predicted persistence and attention at six years. This study points to the enduring impact of early negative affectivity and autonomic reactivity on the development of temperament from birth to six years (Canals, Hernandez-Martinez, & Fernandez-Ballart, 2011).

Probably the most researched dimension of infant temperament is behavioural inhibition, also called slow-to-warm-up temperament in infancy, which shows stability across the first six years of life (Persson-Blennow & McNeil, 1988). Slow-to-warm-up infants became shy six-year-old children. However, beyond this age, the incidence of shyness did not differ in this group compared with children with easy or moderately easy temperaments. However, maternal sensitivity and support reduced the later degree of shyness in their slow-to-warm-up infant sons (Grady, Karraker, & Metzger, 2012).

Integration of neuroscience, psychoanalysis, and attachment theory

> We shall not cease from exploration
> And the end of all our exploring
> Will be to arrive where we started
> And know the place for the first time.
>
> (T. S. Eliot, Little Gidding,
> No. 4 from *Four Quartets*)

Freud was initially trained as a medical doctor and then as a neurologist before embarking on his project of psychoanalysis. From the outset, Freud (1950[1895]), in his *Project for a Scientific Psychology*, believed that there was a biological substrate that corresponded to the psychological processes he observed in his psychoanalytic work and which he hoped would one day be found. His dream is now closer to being realised with the advent of neuroscience, the discipline of developmental psychology, and the sophisticated research methods and technologies that have been brought to bear on these complex questions. We will begin by considering some of these biologically relevant findings: the role of neuropeptides in attachment, the role of mirror neurons and the construct of embodied simulation in mentalisation and empathy, the micro-communications that occur between mothers and infants that have clarified the impact of early maternal attunement on healthy development, and the nature of intersubjectivity.

The neurobiology of attachment

There are structures at every biopsychosocial level—cells, brains, bodies, dyads, families, cultures—that prepare and organise life in relationship with other people who recognize, respond, and communicate together. (Seligman, 2009, p. 503)

Attachment, a complex system that is evident in most mammals as well as humans, is now understood to be an evolutionary process with its own neurobiological and neurochemical as well as psychosocial origins that interact to ensure survival and reproduction (Carter & DeVries, 1999). Our discussion in Chapter Four on attachment focused primarily on its psychological dimensions and the psychosocial conditions that determine the quality of the attachment relationship between mother and infant. However, the development of this highly selective psychological relationship is mirrored by a complex biology that is the subject of this discussion.

Much of our understanding of the biological strata underlying attachment behaviours has come from animal studies that have identified sets of highly predictable, complementary maternal and newborn interactions that ensure a pattern of contingent behaviours that supports survival, development, and reproduction (Harlow, 1978; Van der Horst, 2011). Recent human studies have left us in no doubt about the relationship between the human organism's neurobiology, attachment behaviours, and the essentially intersubjective nature of human sociality (Seligman, 2009). There is a large body of research and scholarship in this area (Chernus, 2007; Fonagy, Luyten, & Strathearn, 2011; Kjellmer & Winberg, 1994; Lacy & Hughes, 2006; Schore, 1994; Swain, Lorberbaum, Kose, & Strathearn, 2007) and its implications for psychoanalytic theory and practice (Brockman, 2001; Forsyth, 1997; Glucksman, 1995).

Maternal behaviour has wide-ranging influences on the development of newborns. These include quality of attachment, security in interpersonal relationships, stress reactivity, social cognition, and memory for socially relevant information and, upon reaching adulthood, capacity as a parent (Strathearn, 2007; Swain et al., 2007). These outcomes are mediated by neurobiological effects on the attachment system, which can be broadly categorised into four main areas: (i) stress reactivity; (ii) the neuropeptides, oxytocin and vasopressin; (iii) the dopaminergic system underpinning stimulus-reward learning; (iv) mirror neurons.

Stress reactivity

The cortisol-mediated stress system operates from birth. Infant temperament, the quality of care-giving and the interactions between temperament and care-giving affect the reactivity of the stress system (Gunnar & Cheatham, 2003). Numerous animal studies have demonstrated a relationship between animal maternal behaviours (e.g., licking, grooming, and nursing) in the first few days following birth and subsequent lower stress reactivity in offspring at both the behavioural and neurochemical level (e.g., reduced production of the stress hormones, corticotrophin and corticosterone) (Strathearn, 2007). In human infants, different maternal soothing behaviours with different levels of infant distress have differential effects on infant stress reactivity. For example, one study showed that feeding and pacifying maternal responses were only effective at lower levels of infant distress and that a combination of maternal holding, rocking, and vocalising were necessary to ease infant reactivity across all intensities of distress (Jahromi, Putnam, & Stifter, 2004).

Denenberg (1964) showed that daily stimulation or stress in the first three weeks following birth in rat pups resulted in permanent alteration of their physiology and behaviour. Early stress and separation also altered mothers' behaviours; these changes are now thought to account for the observed changes in their offspring's physiology and behaviour. Normal maternal behaviour that includes soothing touch and other forms of tactile stimulation, passive contact, and feeding regulates the activity of the hypothalamic–pituitary–adrenal (HPA) axis, which, in turn, affects gene expression, prompting Konner (2010) to state that "maternal care can reach into the genome of the young" (p. 365). In human infants, differences in quality of early maternal care is also associated with alterations in brain structure and the genetic structure of DNA in such a way that the brain's ability to modulate reactions to stressors is impaired (Weaver et al., 2004). Even short separations of infants from their mothers has significant behavioural and physiological sequelae, including prolonged protest, increased activity, distressed crying, and physiological changes such as increased heart rate, changes in body temperature, and increased activation of the HPA axis. Children who have experienced prolonged separations, for example, children raised in orphanages or children reared by depressed mothers, develop enlarged amygdala, which appears to be an early marker of biological sensitivity to quality of maternal care (Lupien et al., 2011).

Cortisol is a sensitive measure of both maternal and infant stress. For example, mothers with pre-term infants have higher cortisol levels than mothers of full-term infants. Optimal mother–infant dyadic interactions that were judged to be supportive of cognitive and socioemotional development resulted in lower levels of cortisol in infants (Letourneau, Watson, Duffett-Leger, Hegadoren, & Tryphonopoulos, 2011). Complex relationships exist between HPA and sympathetic nervous system (SNS) response measures in mother–infant dyads in a social stress situation (i.e. Strange Situation (Ainsworth, Blehar, Waters, & Wall, 1978)). Mother and infant saliva samples were collected at various times during the stressful situation and tested for cortisol (HPA marker) and salivary alpha-amylase (sAA; SNS marker). Mother and infant stress responses were synchronous, increasing and decreasing in the same pattern over time and in response to changing levels of mother–infant attunement (Laurent, Ablow, & Measelle, 2012).

Fonagy, Luyten, and Strathearn (2011) have identified a complex relationship between the neurobiology of attachment, the capacity for mentalisation, and stress reactivity. Oxytocin reduces the neuroendocrine response to stress and enhances maternal bonding and attunement to the infant, thereby enhancing maternal mentalisation, which, in turn, promotes secure attachment and the capacity for mentalisation in her child. A capacity for mentalisation is protective against social stress. Figure 7 represents these relationships.

Activation and deactivation of the attachment system is associated with activation and deactivation of affect and arousal regulation systems (Weinberg, 2006). Indeed, arousal regulation that occurs in the midbrain is a complex neurochemical process involving excitation and inhibition of interactive neural systems. This system might play a central role in regulating a number of other higher-order functions, including cortical function, attention, cognition, stress reactivity, and performance. The response in these systems varies according to varying levels of arousal. At some point, the level of arousal becomes intolerable and this results in a switch from cortical (mentalised execu-

Figure 7. The relationship between oxytocin, mentalisation, attachment, and stress reactivity in mother–infant pairs.

tive function) to subcortical (automatic) functioning, with a consequent decrease and then loss of ability to mentalise. Early parenting experiences and early exposure to stress and trauma could contribute to this threshold of responsiveness in this arousal regulatory system (Mayes, 2000, 2006). You will recall that different attachment styles are associated with different levels of activation of the attachment system: dismissing styles are associated with deactivation of the attachment system and preoccupied styles with hyper-activating strategies. Evidence from neuroimaging studies supports the view that attachment history affects the point at which stress becomes intolerable, which turns the

> mentalizing system from planned, controlled and organized cognition to automatic processing with narrow, poorly sustained attention and increased vigilance for attachment disruptions such as rejection and abandonment. (Fonagy, Luyten & Strathearn, 2011, p. 55)

The effects of being reared by a chronically depressed mother reach beyond attachment deficits into physical, physiological, cognitive, and social deficits, beginning in infancy. Such infants show increased latencies to habituate to their mothers' faces and voices and show no visual preference for their mothers compared with strangers (Hernandez-Reif, Field, Diego, & Largie, 2002). Newborns of depressed mothers suck for twice as long as newborns of non-depressed mothers, indicating early difficulty with arousal dysregulation, overactivity, or greater need for compensatory hedonic behaviour (Hernandez-Reif, Field, & Diego, 2004). There are other major differences between newborns of depressed mothers, many beginning prenatally. These include retarded foetal growth (Diego et al., 2009); changes in prenatal dopamine (Field et al., 2008a) and serotonin levels (Field et al., 2008b); higher cortisol and norepinephrine levels (Konner, 2010); sleep disturbance (Field et al., 2007); and greater arousal and less attentiveness to face and vocal stimuli by neonates of depressed mothers on the Brazelton Neonatal Behavioral Assessment Scale (Hernandez-Reif, Field, Diego, & Ruddock, 2006), among a great many other differences too numerous to discuss here.

Oxytocin and vasopressin

Two neuropeptides—oxytocin and vasopressin—have been implicated in a number of affiliative responses in both animals and humans, including pair-bonding, mating, maternal (care-giving) behaviours and attachment (Marazziti et al., 2008). Oxytocin is also involved in the stress response, as outlined in the previous section (Bartz & Hollander, 2006). Oxytocin is a neuropeptide found only in mammals (Marazziti et al., 2006). It is associated with uterine contractions during childbirth and the "let down" response in the breasts of lactating mothers (Feldman, Weller, Zagoory-Sharon, & Levine, 2007). High concentrations of oxytocin during pregnancy are associated with stronger maternal bonding, as evidenced by the expression of positive affect towards her infant, extended gaze, affectionate touch, maintenance of proximity, and close monitoring of her newborn (Feldman, Weller, Zagoory-Sharon, & Levine, 2007). Oxytocin has been identified as the necessary and sufficient condition for the onset of maternal behaviours in the rat. It is also essential for pair bonding; when an oxytocin agonist is administered, monogamous female prairie voles mated normally but showed no interest in their mate (Insel, 2003).

Oxytocin and vasopressin receptors are dense in brain regions associated with attachment and other social behaviours and these act on receptors in the limbic system (Heinrichs, von Dawans, & Domes, 2009). Oxytocin is synthesised in the hypothalamus and distributed into brain areas responsible for attachment and other social behaviour; it is, therefore, implicated in a myriad of functions in the social–emotional domain (Carter & DeVries, 1999; Feldman, Gordon, Schneiderman, Weisman, & Zagoory-Sharon, 2010; Feldman, Weller, Zagoory-Sharon, & Levine, A., 2007; Freed, 2008; Gordon, Zagoory-Sharon, Leckman, & Feldman, 2010; Marazziti et al., 2006; Marazziti et al., 2008; Pedersen, 2004). For example, increases in oxytocin levels result in increases in a range of behaviours associated with the attachment system, including enhanced sensitivity to social cues, improved social memory, heightened care-giver sensitivity to the infant's mental state, heightened approach behaviours and physical proximity, decreased social avoidance, enhanced attachment feelings in offspring towards their parents (Freed, 2008), greater partner support and reduced reactivity to social stress. These effects of oxytocin are mediated by its role in the down regulation of the HPA axis (Carter & DeVries, 1999).

Laboratory studies with healthy humans have also confirmed the anxiety attenuating effects of oxytocin, with those receiving both intranasal oxytocin and social support showing the lowest salivary cortisol in response to a psychosocial stressor (Heinrichs, Baumgartner, Kirschbaum, & Ehlert, 2003). Given that oxytocin is associated with both affiliative behaviours and reduced anxiety and fear responding in human subjects, there is considerable potential for the exploration of its therapeutic effects in psychological disorders that are characterised by social deficits, anxiety, and fear (Bartz & Hollander, 2006).

Lactating mothers have a lower risk of child maltreatment that is hypothesised to be associated with the increased oxytocin release during breastfeeding and the close social contact with their infants (Martorell & Bugental, 2006). Recent research has identified a link between oxytocin levels, the capacity for attachment-related mentalisation and facilitation of the development of the child's theory of mind (Fonagy, Luyten, & Strathearn, 2011). Corollary findings support the role of oxytocin in both attachment and mentalisation. Women who experienced emotional abuse or neglect in early life and maltreated children show both reduced oxytocin and impaired mentalisation, lack of appropriate empathy for emotionally distressed children, and poorer understanding of emotion in facial expressions. Further, maltreated children engaged in less symbolic and dyadic play, referred less frequently to their own internal states, and had delayed theory of mind understanding (Fonagy, Luyten, & Strathearn, 2011).

Vasopressin appears to have a stronger role in male affiliative and social behaviour, such as aggression, courtship, and male pair bonding. In contrast to the calmative, fear-modulating effects of oxytocin, vasopressin has anxiogenic effects, and appears to be associated with increased vigilance, arousal, and activation (Heinrichs, von Dawans, & Domes, 2009). Elevated levels of vasopressin have been observed in personality disordered individuals with a history of interpersonal violence and aggression. Sex differences in the effects of vasopressin have also been noted. In men, vasopressin heightened perception of threat in neutral male facial expressions and heightened autonomic reactivity to threatening faces, while in women, it increased perceptions of friendliness in female facial expressions (Coccaro, Kavoussi, Hauger, Cooper, & Ferris, 1998). Paradoxically, vasopressin has also been implicated in altruistic behaviour, pair-bonding, and decreased quality in marital relationships (Walum et al., 2008). The influence of these two neuropeptides on social behaviour is complex and is still being worked out. As Bartz and Hollander (2006) observed,

Research implicates oxytocin and vasopressin in the neurobiology of attachment; however . . . these neuropeptides are only two of many players and other agents including dopamine, endogenous opiods, ACTH and gamma-aminobutyric acid are also likely involved in this process. (p. 524)

In combination, oxytocin and vasopressin simultaneously activate the reward–attachment system and deactivate neurobiological systems that interfere with attachment (e.g., social avoidance, defensive behaviour).

Dopamine

Dopamine has been implicated in the process of social bonding via the dopaminergic-mediated stimulus–reward learning system involving the midbrain, limbic system, amygdala, hippocampus, and the frontal reward regions, in particular, the orbitofrontal cortex (Seso-Simic, Sedmak, Hof, & Simic, 2010). The firing of dopaminergic neurons increases during pleasurable activities, such as eating, engaging in sexual activity, and while bonding with a child. Deep brain stimulation of a human subject in the region of the brain that contains dopaminergic fibres resulted in feelings of elation and euphoria (Moan & Heath, 1972). Further, drugs that facilitate dopamine transmission result in assignment of reward properties to previously neutral stimuli (Wise, 2004). Positive events that were unexpected increase neuronal activity in this system, while negative events that were unexpected result in a decrease in the rate of neuronal activity in this system (Strathearn, 2007). The dopaminergic system is also implicated in mother–infant interactions in rats. Maternal exposure to their pups activates dopamine release while lesions in the pathways mediating dopamine release result in disruptions to maternal behaviour (Insel, 2003). Dopamine release is also associated with mating and pair bonding. In the prairie vole, a monogamous rodent, mating facilitates partner preference, which is, in turn, associated with a signficant increase in dopamine release. Further, dopamine agonists block the development of partner preference, leading the researchers to conclude that the dopamine activation of D2 receptors is necessary for the mediation of social attachments in female voles (Gingrich, Liu, Cascio, Wang, & Insel, 2000). Oxytocin and vasopressin might be responsible for the specificity of dopamine effects with respect to social attachment formation, such as maternal behaviour towards infants and pair bonding with mates by linking social signals to these reward pathways (Insel, 2003). Finally, recent neurobiological models of drug addiction have identified a possible pathway for the influence of maternal deprivation on the development of addiction. The dopaminergic system of adult rats who were separated at birth from their mothers and subsequently either handled or not handled was activated by either the injection of psychostimulant drugs or stress induction. Maternally separated, non-handled rats displayed hyperactive behaviour when placed in an unfamiliar setting and dose-dependent higher sensitivity to cocaine-induced locomotor activity than non-separated, handled rats. In addition, the maternally deprived rats showed neuro-anatomical anomalies in their dopamine transporter sites. The researchers concluded:

> ... these findings provide compelling evidence that disruptions in early postnatal rearing conditions can lead to profound and lasting changes in the responsiveness of mesocorticolimbic dopamine neurons to stress and psychostimulants, and suggest a neurobiological basis for individual differences in vulnerability to compulsive drug taking. (Brake, Zhang, Diorio, Meaney, & Gratton, 2004, p. 1863)

Mirror neurons

"Neural mirroring solves the problem of other minds, how we can access and understand the minds of others and makes intersubjectivity possible, thus facilitating social behaviour" (Iacoboni, 2009, p. 653).

Mirror neurons were a serendipitous discovery in the 1990s by a group of Italian researchers, who noticed that neurons in the premotor cortex (an area involved in planning and co-ordinating motor behaviours) of monkeys fired not only when they were performing a motor action, but also when they were observing the action being performed (Rizzolatti & Craighero, 2004). It was subsequently observed that the neural circuits activated by a human subject performing actions, expressing emotions, and experiencing sensations are automatically activated in an observer of those actions, emotions, and sensations. It has been proposed that this neural mechanism of "embodied simulation" provides the biological substrate underpinning social cognition and the development of a "theory of mind" (Gallese, Eagle, & Migone, 2007). Mirror neurons have now been implicated in a range of complex human functions including motor behaviour, language development, bonding and attachment, and the ability to respond to others with empathy (Seso-Simic, Sedmak, Hof, & Simic, 2010).

There are two types of mirror neurons: strictly congruent mirror neurons that fire during observation of the exact action that they code motorically, and broadly congruent mirror neurons that fire during the observation of an action that achieves the same, or a logically related, goal to the action that had been coded motorically. This capacity implies that metacognition is operating in the domain of purposeful actions; that is, the intention or outcome of the action is integrated with the movement before it begins. The assignment of an intention does not appear to be conscious—it occurs by default, once the activation of an embodied simulation has occurred. This also suggests that mirror neurons are shaped by experience; certain actions imply particular intentions. Further, actions embedded in contexts produce stronger firing in the premotor cortex, suggesting that this area of the brain is responsible for both action recognition and discerning action intention (Gallese, Eagle, & Migone, 2007).

Broadly congruent mirror neurons are important in social interactions because direct imitation of others' behaviours in social settings would attract a negative reaction from one's social partners. Mirror neurons cross sensory modalites and fire when a characteristic sound of an action is heard in the absence of any visual input about the action being performed. The auditory properties of mirror neurons have relevance for language development. In addition, studies have shown that mirror neurons fire in the premotor cortex when people read action-based sentences or listen to another person reading these sentences (Iacoboni, 2009). These findings indicate that the neural structures involved in action execution are also involved in understanding the semantic content of the same actions when read or verbally described (Glenberg & Kaschak, 1997).

In the discussion that follows, we will focus on the role of mirror neurons in empathy and early maternal communication. Infants experience the world affectively via their sensorimotor system (Damasio, 1994). Pairing of affective experiences with behavioural responses results in the automation of these responses—these affects are embodied; that is, "the sensorimotor system . . . support[s] the reconstruction of what it would feel like to be in a particular emotion, by means of simulation of the related body state" (Gallese, Eagle, & Migone, 2007, p. 142). There is evidence from fMRI studies that at least for some emotions (e.g., disgust), experiencing and witnessing that same emotion on the face of another person activates the same brain structure—the anterior insula (Wicker et al., 2003). Similar findings have been observed for touch. Being touched on one's body activates the same neural networks activated by observing the body of some-one else being touched (Blakemore, Bristow, Bird, Frith, & Ward, 2005). Similar results have been obtained for pain. The same neural structures activate during subjective pain experiences and when witnessing the pain of others or being given symbolically mediated knowledge of the same pain experience of one's own and others' pain reactions, a process also explained by embodied simulation, whereby the individual maps the vicarious (observed) pain experience somato-topically on to his or her own sensorimotor system (Jackson, Meltzoff, & Decety, 2005). Embodied simulation is non-conscious and pre-reflexive; it is not the result of the deliberate and conscious cognitive effort required in mental simulation during which one imaginatively places oneself in the shoes of the other, generating introspectively what one believes to be the other's mental state (Gordon, 2005).

Newborns as young as eighteen hours can reproduce mouth and facial movements modelled by an adult. This indicates that newborns are capable of "active intermodal mapping" (Meltzoff & Moore, 1977, 1994, 1997); that is, they can translate visual information into motor action. This ability suggests that there is an "innate sensorimotor neural mechanism of automatic embodied simulation" (Gallese, Eagle, & Migone, 2007, p. 146) that might form the neural basis for intersubjective processes such as empathy, synchrony, communica-tion, and mentalisation. However, some degree of maturation needs to occur before infants can infer intent. For example, twelve-month-old infants can anticipate the goal of an observed motor act only when they achieve the motor competence to perform that same act (Sommerville & Woodward, 2005), suggesting that complex social cognitive skills such as goal detection are based on experiential know-ledge that allows the infant to "mentalise" the intention of an observed other. This evidence has led some researchers to argue that experience is, at its core, intersubjective.

> Intersubjectivity is constituted at the very beginnings of perception
> and proprioception . . . The basic elements of becoming oneself by
> being with others are in the first place, movement, time, space, all
> coordinated in social interaction . . . personality arises in our disposi-
> tion to collaborate. . . (Seligman, 2009)

The first year of life is critical for the establishment of secure attachment between a mother and her infant. Because the infant is preverbal, the mother must find ways of communicating her understanding of the infant's needs and feeling states through empathy and attuned responding. Part of this process involves imitation/mirroring of the infant's facial expressions, which represents the first social dialogue that supports the development of the infant "self". The mother's capacity to respond empathically to her infant (i.e., to correctly interpret and respond to her child's emotions) is associated with her capacity for reflective function (Fonagy & Target, 1999; Giannoni & Corradi, 2006). Both of these capacities have now been shown to be associated with activation of the mirror neuron system when a mother interacts with her infant (Iacoboni, 2009). Lenzi and colleagues (2009) have demonstrated that mirror neurons in the frontal cortex, anterior insula, amygdala, and limbic system activate during maternal observation of her own infant. The activation is greater when observing her own infant compared with the observation of another, unrelated infant. Further, mirror neurons showed greater activation in mothers with higher reflective function, thus providing strong evidence that the mirror neuron system is one of the biological substrates of the maternal capacities required for the development of secure attachment in her infant. Dysfunctions in the mirror neuron system have been strongly associated with developmental disorders that involve the severe social deficits observed in the autism spectrum disorders. Even when higher functioning autistic children are observed to imitate equally well with normally functioning control children, children with autism showed no or reduced mirror neuron activity and the level of activity was significantly associated with the severity of social deficits (Dapretto et al., 2006).

I will conclude this section on a cautionary note. As exciting as these findings on mirror neurons appear to be, we must exercise care not to equate brain with mind or to seek confirmation of infant capacities or unconscious psychological processes from neuroscientific evidence alone. A number of problematic assumptions have resulted in equivalence errors. First, the correspondence assumption states that brain activity is associated with mental activity in a straightforward way; that is, we know what the mind is doing when we know what the brain is doing because there is a correspondence between brain activity and mental activity. Second, the shared experience assumption states that brain activity in the same local regions of the brain in observing–observed pairs of individuals does not necessarily equate to the same subjective experience for those individuals; third, the directness assumption states that the observer's brain activity provides direct access to the mind of the other (Vivona, 2009). These cautions notwithstanding, evidence is accumulating that there exists in the human brain a complex neural network for empathy (Iacoboni, 2007). Space has permitted only a short exposition of the evidence and the interested reader is referred to the following references (Baird, Scheffer, & Wilson, 2011; Cattaneo & Rizzolatti, 2009; Iacoboni, 2009; Iacoboni & Dapretto, 2006; Keysers & Gazzola, 2006; Whitehead, 2009) for a more detailed treatment.

Unconscious and implicit processes

> The discovery of implicit memory has extended the concept of the unconscious and supports the hypothesis that this is where the emotional and affective – sometimes traumatic – presymbolic and preverbal experiences of . . . mother–infant relations are stored. (Mancia, 2006, p. 83)

The concept of the unconscious is a cornerstone of the psychoanalytic edifice, yet from the outset, Breuer and Freud experienced great resistance to the acceptance of the role of the unconscious in human behaviour, first because of the semantic difficulties it created,

> The objections that are raised against 'unconscious ideas' existing and being operative seem for the most part to be juggling with words. No doubt 'idea' is a word belonging to the terminology of conscious thinking, and 'unconscious idea' is therefore a self-contradictory expression. But the physical process which under lies an idea is the same in content and form (though not in quantity) whether the idea

rises above the threshold of consciousness or remains beneath it. It would only be necessary to construct some such term as 'ideational substratum' in order to avoid the contradiction and to counter the objection. (Breuer, 1893, p. 223)

and second, because it challenged the cherished notion of free will. Freud described it thus:

... human megalomania will have suffered [a] ... wounding blow from the psychological research of the present time which seeks to prove to the ego that it is not even master in its own house, but must content itself with scanty information of what is going on unconsciously in its mind ... (Freud, 1916–1917, p. 285)

It is, therefore, remarkable that the idea of the unconscious has become both commonplace and scientifically indisputable in just over 100 years, leading Le Doux (1996) to declare that ". . . unconscious processing is the rule rather than the exception" (p. 71). A great many cognitive and affective processes, including memory, cognition, affect, motivation, and attitudes can be implicit (Wilson, Lindsey, & Schooler, 2000).

In mainstream psychology texts, we see the terms unconscious/ implicit/tacit knowledge and unconscious/implicit cognition, among others (Augusto, 2010). The idea of the unconscious is so fundamental to an understanding of both infant development and psychoanalysis that it warrants special attention. Freud was fascinated with the unconscious:

The strangest characteristic of unconscious (repressed) processes ... is due to their entire disregard of reality-testing; they equate reality of thought with external actuality, and wishes with their fulfilment – with the event – just as happens automatically under the dominance of the ancient pleasure principle. Hence also the difficulty of distinguishing unconscious phantasies from memories that have become unconscious. But one must never allow oneself to be misled into applying the standards of reality to repressed psychical structures, and on that account, perhaps, into undervaluing the importance of phantasies in the formation of symptoms on the ground that they are not actualities, or into tracing a neurotic sense of guilt back to some other source because there is no evidence that any actual crime has been committed. (Freud, 1911b, p. 225)

Freud understood the unconscious to contain ideas that are, paradoxically, not only not able to be thought about, but which remain completely unavailable to thought. Despite this, these hidden ideas exert a profound effect on daily life. Freud's unconscious is the locus of dynamic psychic activity, the place where wishes, impulses, and drives reside, a place not beholden to the realities of logic or time or the constraints of socially acceptable behaviour. It is a dynamic reservoir of archaic phantasies that "proliferate in the dark" (Freud, 1915d, p. 149), an "infantile and anti-social Utopia" (Frosh, 2003, p. 14) that exerts "upward" pressure for expression. Freud described it thus:

> The actual traumatic moment . . . is the one at which the incompatibility forces itself upon the ego and at which the latter decides on the repudiation of the incompatible idea. That idea is not annihilated by a repudiation of this kind, but merely repressed into the unconscious. When this process occurs for the first time there comes into being a nucleus and centre of crystallisation for the formation of a psychical group divorced from the ego – a group around which everything which would imply an acceptance of the incompatible idea subsequently collects. The splitting of consciousness . . . is accordingly a deliberate and intentional one. At least it is often introduced by an act of volition; for the actual outcome is something different from what the subject intended. What he wanted was to do away with an idea, as though it had never appeared, but all he succeeds in doing is to isolate it psychically. (Freud (with Breuer), 1895d, p. 123)

The concept of repression is essential to an understanding of Freud's unconscious: Freud understood ". . . the very great extent to which repression and what is unconscious are correlated" (Freud, 1915d, p. 148). In fact, he viewed repression as "the prototype of the unconscious" (Freud, 1923b, p. 15), that is, as a mental process that creates the unconscious.

There have been many reworkings of Freud's vision of the unconscious. In Chapter Four, we explored some of these changes in the discussion of mentalisation and what constitutes and causes trauma.

Space does not permit a full exposition of the shift from Freud's dynamic unconscious to the intersubjectivists' relational unconscious, to Bion's and Grotstein's (2009) symbolic, meaning-making unconscious that "supplies the external world with metaphors and poetic images" (Bohleber, 2011, p. 288), or Newirth's (2003) "generative unconscious", which they conceive as the source of subjectivity. Newirth's conceptualisation invokes Winnicott's "true self" and Bollas's "unthought known". In the final analysis, all of these conceptualisations are metaphors containing implicit theories and world views that guide clinical practice (Appelbaum, 2011). Most of these reworkings do, however, represent a similar shift in the conceptualisation of the contents of the unconscious from Freud's repressed instinctual representatives to dissociated, unformulated self-states that are enacted in interpersonal relationships. These self-states are derived from, and represent, internalised object relationships operating at various levels of psychological organisation, ranging from archaic to highly structured (Bohleber, 2011). Stolorow (1992a,b) argues that these structures contain, not the forbidden impulses, drives, and phantasies of classical psychoanalysis, but intolerable affects that could not be integrated because of the absence of a responsive enough environment.

> Such unintegrated affect states become the source of lifelong inner conflict, because they are experienced as threats both to the person's established psychological organisation and to the maintenance of vitally needed ties. Thus affect-dissociating defensive operations are called into play, which reappear in the analytic situation in the form of resistance. A defensive self-ideal is often established, which represents the self purified of the "offending" affect states that were perceived as intolerable . . . and the inability to fully embody this affectively purified ideal then becomes a continual source of shame and self-loathing. *It is in the defensive walling off of central affect states, rooted in early derailments of affect integration, that the origins of what has traditionally been called the "dynamic unconscious" can be found.* (Stolorow, Brandchaft & Atwood, 1987, pp. 91–92, my italics)

Thus, the dynamic unconscious contains intolerable affects that have been defensively dissociated to protect against retraumatisation. The intersubjective unconscious is fluid in the sense that these defensive processes are responsive to the nature of the care-giving environment and to psychotherapy—greater attunement results in less affective dissociation in fewer affective domains.

The proposition that much of our mental life is unconscious and comprises unconscious thoughts, feelings, and motives has now found robust support in the experimental literature (Fisher & Greenberg, 1995; Westen, 1998, 1999). Much of this evidence has come from cognitive and memory research (de Houwer, 2006), which has identified distinct neuroanatomical correlates of two distinct processes— implicit and explicit—in thought and memory. For example, the hippocampus is essential for explicit, but not for implicit, memory, which is more closely associated with the amygdala, particularly in fear conditioning. The term "explicit" defines processes that are conscious, that is, able to be thought about, articulated, and acted upon. The term "implicit" denotes those processes that cannot be consciously retrieved or articulated, but are, none the less, expressed in other non-verbal systems such as the sensory, somatic (i.e., psychosomatic illness), or behavioural (i.e., acting out without awareness). Westen (1999) argued that while there is ample evidence for the existence of unconscious processes, the classical view of the unconscious

> . . . has outlived its usefulness, because there are many different kinds of unconscious processes that serve different functions, and many of these processes have very different neuroanatomical substrates. To the extent that psychoanalysis maintains its essentially functionalist approach—defining structures in terms of functions, and focusing on the functions of symptoms, thoughts, memories, defenses . . .—the experimental delineation of unconscious processes with different functions will require a change in both our language and our conceptualization. (p. 1064)

Freud was primarily concerned with the dynamic unconscious and its contents and effects on psychic functioning. Subsequent psychoanalytic thinkers modified the contents of Freud's unconscious in the ways that have just been discussed. However, Freud had a broader view of unconscious processes that is less well known outside psychoanalytic writing; he was also aware of more universal, benign, unconscious processes that constitute normal functioning and which align more closely with the findings of experimental psychology as we will see below.

Unconscious memory

"We are all much more expert unconsciously than consciously, because expertise implies automatization of processes that once required conscious attention" (Westen, 1999, p. 1097).

Freud (1901b) was aware of different forms of memory and their complex operations.

> Remembering in adults ... makes use of a variety of psychical material. Some people remember in visual images; their memories have a visual character. Other people can scarcely reproduce in their memory even the scantiest outlines of what they have experienced ... in the case of childhood memories: they are plastically visual even in people whose later function of memory has to do without any visual element. Visual memory accordingly preserves the type of infantile memory ... (p. 47)

Experimental and clinical memory research has identified a number of ways of remembering, presaged by Freud in the quote above. Memory is now described as a process that is activated by either external or internal retrieval cues (Rustin & Sekaer, 2004). Hence, "each memory is an amalgam of the memory itself and the retrieval cue" (p. 70). Compare this explanation of memory with that offered by Freud in 1901:

> One is ... forced by various considerations to suspect that in the so-called earliest childhood memories we possess not the genuine memory-trace but a later revision of it, a revision which may have been subjected to the influences of a variety of later psychical forces. Thus the "childhood memories" of individuals come in general to acquire the significance of "screen memories" and in doing so offer a remarkable analogy with the childhood memories that a nation preserves in its store of legends and myths. (p. 47)

Freud (1899a) defined a "screen memory" as follows:

> A recollection ... whose value lies in the fact that it represents in the memory impressions and thoughts of a later date whose content is connected with its own by symbolic or similar links, may appropriately be called a "screen memory". (p. 316)

and the process whereby the original memory is affected or influenced by the screen memory (retrieval cue):

> Anyone who has investigated a number of people psychologically by the method of psycho-analysis will in the course of his work have collected numerous examples of every kind of screen memory. However, the reporting of these examples is made extraordinarily difficult owing to the nature of the relations . . . between childhood memories and later life. In order to show that a childhood memory is to be regarded as a screen memory, it would often be necessary to present the complete life history of the person in question. Only rarely is it possible to lift a single screen memory out of its context in order to give an account of it. (Freud, 1901b, p. 48).

Memories can be broadly divided into two main categories: explicit memories (also called declarative memories), which are are memories that have been symbolised and can be recalled and verbalised, and implicit memories (also called procedural or non-declarative memories), which are memories that have never been experienced in symbolic form (Atallah, Frank, & O'Reilly, 2004). Explicit memory can be categorised into semantic memory that stores words and concepts, and episodic memory that stores specific events (Tulving, 1972, 1983, 1985). Implicit memory comprises subsystems for priming, associative learning, and non-associative learning, together with procedural memory skills and habits. Implicit memory involves the kind of "know how" that is required to hit a ball with a tennis racquet, peel potatoes, play the piano, or perform any motor programme. Some forms of procedural memory can be made conscious or explicit, such as the strategies used to solve mathematical problems, or particular forms of social knowledge such as knowing the subtle differences between how you greet your friends and your parents. Paradoxically, thinking too much about (i.e., making conscious) how one performs a skilled motor sequence or other implicitly known behaviours can interfere with its execution (Altenmüller, Wiesendanger, & Kesselring, 2006).

Explicit and implicit memories differ in quality along a number of dimensions. For example, implicit memories are remembered and stored as *Gestalt*, or whole memories, that cannot be divided into components. This tends to make them both robust and inflexible because

the memory is perceptually bound; it is remembered in the circumstances under which it was laid down (Rovee-Collier & Cuevas, 2009).
Put differently,

> ... procedural knowledge is a set of procedures, instructions, even
> algorithms, or just structures or patterns that are implementable rather
> than describable. Subjects act in a goal-directed and often skilled way
> without being aware that they do so, and, when probed, without being
> able to say what it is they draw on. (Augusto, 2010, p. 118)

Compare this definition of procedural knowledge with Freud's notion
of one of the functions of the unconscious:

> We know what is meant by ideas "occurring" to one – thoughts that
> suddenly come into consciousness without one's being aware of the
> steps that led to them, though they, too, must have been psychical acts.
> It can even happen that one arrives in this way at the solution of some
> difficult intellectual problem which has previously for a time baffled
> one's efforts. All the complicated processes of selection, rejection and
> decision which occupied the interval were withdrawn from conscious-
> ness. (Freud, 1940b[1938b], p. 283)

Implicit (procedural) memory is present at birth and appears to be
operating to some degree in the last trimester of pregnancy. In addition to the sensory and motor forms of implicit memory, there is a
third form, relational: that is, as discussed throughout this book, the
feeling shapes of being-with-another (Bendit, 2011; Mancia, 2006).
Infants build networks implicitly, based on their ongoing interactions
with their parents and other significant others that Stern and colleagues (1998) called "implicit relational knowing", or "representations of interactions that have generalized". The durability and
robustness of implicit memories explain, at least in part, the durable
nature of our internal representations, the beliefs, attitudes, and interpersonal behaviours regarding self and others that have formed
outside awareness in the early part of the lifespan. They are also holis-
tic and inflexible—that is, they are stored as a whole or *Gestalt* and
tend not be understood in terms of their component parts. They
cannot be recalled and are difficult to modify even when variations are
introduced in reality. Further, there is some degree of independence
between knowledge/memories acquired implicitly compared with

those formed under overt, explicit conditions. Many semantic and episodic memories are laid down on a single trial, compared with implicit relational memories, which require many repetitions over time to be encoded.

Bendit (2011) has proposed that chronic maternal misattunements during infancy are coded first implicitly, and, later, as language develops, in semantic memory as facts of the kind "nobody cares" or "nobody responds", "I'm not important" or "I don't matter" (p. 26). The experiences thus coded cannot be consciously remembered and, therefore, are unlikely to be responsive to cognitive therapies such as cognitive reframing. These semantic memories cause intense emotional pain. If the pain is unrelieved and unmitigated over time, suicide becomes an option. Subsequent experiences of emotional pain trigger the original unbearable self-state without any recall of their origins, thus giving the present situation the same emotional intensity as the original experience against which the person-as-infant felt helpless. Any form of emotional unresponsiveness from important people is likely to be sufficient to trigger the original abandonment/annihilation fears produced in the original situation during infancy. These representations, or ways of knowing, are re-enacted in subsequent adult relationships, and in the psychoanalytic relationship, where they can be understood and reworked. Rustin and Sekaer (2004) argue that the psychoanalyst acts as a retrieval cue for these implicit memories, or relational ways of knowing, but the process renders the memory a co-constructed product of the analyst–patient dyad. Memories thus constructed or co-constructed, transformed, or embellished build new networks leading, one hopes, to positive psychological change.

Associative memory is a form of implicit memory. In its broadest definition, it refers to learning in which a new response becomes associated with a particular stimulus. It is most closely allied with modes of learning called classical and instrumental (operant) conditioning (Martin & Pear, 2003). Conditioning is a process whereby people and animals learn about the relationships between events. In classical conditioning, the association between a stimulus and response is learnt simply by their temporal contiguity; in operant conditioning, the association is learnt because of the outcome of a particular response to a particular stimulus; that is, if the response is rewarded, it is more likely to recur; if it is punished, it is less likely to recur. Building associative memories occurs in two stages—attention and

binding (Wichert, 2011)—and requires hippocampal/cortical interactions to ensure stability (Lesburgueres, Gobbo, Alaux-Cantin, Hambucken, Trifilieff, & Bontempi, 2011).

In the context of our discussion on unconscious processes, we are
interested to know how infants acquire associative memories, the
content of these memories, their durability and retrievability, and how
they affect subsequent development. The discussion of infant memory
in Chapter Five highlighted infants' impressive capacity to remember
non-traumatic memories. In this section, we will briefly discuss their
capacity to remember traumatic memories. As discussed in Chapter
Four, we know that infants store affectively charged experiences in
specific brain structures that are engraved in procedural memory in a
process akin to that for non-traumatic memories. The amygdala, until
recently, was associated primarily with affective functions, in particular, fear processing, but has now been shown to be involved in
processes such as attention and associative learning. It is also involved
in the physiological response to conditioned fear (Gazzaniga, Ivry, &
Mangnun, 2002), while the hippocampus is involved in the associative
learning component (Squire & Zola-Morgan, 1991). (For a detailed
review, see Phelps, 2006.) Emotion generally enhances memory processes, but negative emotion appears to disrupt associative memory
retrieval via hyperactivation of the amygdala during encoding of
negatively valenced associations (Okada et al., 2011).

Emotional conditioning, including fear conditioning, does not
require conscious awareness of the temporal association between
stimuli and responses (LeDoux, 1996); neither is language necessary
for this form of infant learning/memory because other systems—
behavioural, visual, somatic, somatosensory—also store infant (preverbal) experiences. These appear to be persistent and indelible and
generally occur outside the awareness of the association between the
current behaviour and past trauma.

Research supports the psychoanalytic contention that infant experiences are accessible as affective or perceptually based states via the
transference in people undergoing psychoanalysis. In a review of nine
studies that reported on infant trauma that had access to accurate
third party accounts of events, Paley and Alpert (2003) concluded that
traumas occurring between birth and three years of age might be
encoded, stored, and expressed in both verbal and non-verbal forms.
These include behavioural re-enactments (i.e., spontaneous expres-

sions of trauma linked to behaviours in everyday activities (Burgess, Hartman, & Baker, 1995)), trauma-specific fears, post-traumatic play, phobias, fear avoidance reactions, nightmares, repetitive, compulsive behaviours, and obsessional thoughts. Sugarman (1992) described the therapy of a twenty-six-month-old girl who had survived a plane crash at sixteen months of age. During her first session, she re-enacted the trauma by crashing a toy plane. Children can impose a verbal description of a non-verbal trauma once they acquire the language to do so (Gaensbauer, 1995). ". . . behavior cannot be understood without taking consciousness into account and that conscious experience cannot be fully understood without taking unconscious psychological processes into account" (Shevrin & Dickman, 1980, p. 432).

Priming refers to the process that activates stored information, making it accessible to people in a way that influences their perception and cognition. Priming is a form of unconscious perception (Kouider & Dehaene, 2007). It is examined in experiments during which a stimulus (e.g., picture of a cat) is presented that will activate associated networks related to cat, such as Siamese, tiger, lion, etc., thereby revealing the underlying or latent structure of associative networks for the primed word or image (Kunde, Kiesel, & Hoffmann, 2003). Priming effects have been observed even when the stimulus prime has been presented subliminally, that is, the subject has no conscious recognition of the fact that they have been primed (Sweatt, 2003). The defence mechanism of displacement is a psychoanalytic analogy of this process. For example, a female who has had a problematic relationship with her mother presents for therapy complaining about authority conflicts with her female supervisors at work. An associative network has been activated or primed with respect to female bosses who reproduce the problematic dealings she had with her authoritarian mother, with whom she was fearful and compliant. Figure 8 provides a graphical summary of the various forms of memory discussed above.

Freud (1900a) used the term "preconscious" to describe processes stored in memory that were readily retrievable, rational, reality-orientated, and linked to language, a description akin to explicit memory. Westen (1999) argued that the concept needed to be refined to distinguish between implicit procedural knowledge, defined as unconscious thoughts such as beliefs, fantasies, networks of association, and representations that are currently activated and, therefore, accessible, from unconscious thoughts that are not currently active, some of

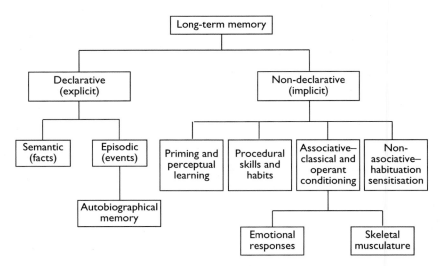

Figure 8.   Explicit and implicit cognitive neuroscience and the study of memory (adapted from Milner, Squire, & Kandel, 1998, p. 451).

which might never become active because they are associated with severe conflict or painful affect. If these threaten to become accessible, defence mechanisms are activated to prevent full expression, although residual behaviour may alert an attuned therapist to their existence. Implicit procedural knowledge is not stored semantically and, therefore, cannot influence conscious thought as do activated, unconscious beliefs or attitudes. In a reformulation of the preconscious–unconscious Freudian structure, Westen (1999) proposed that:

> Information is encoded in memory along networks of association whether or not the information is conflictual, and these networks can influence thought and behavior to the extent that they become activated unconsciously . . . all thought, memory and perception, including our most complex cognitive processes, may actually involve activation of networks of association, where the units or "nodes" on those networks may be as small as a single neuron or set of neurons. (p. 1071)

Unconscious affect

Mainstream psychology now accepts the proposition that affective processes can be unconscious and that people defend against their entry into consciousness using unconscious defence mechanisms

(Spezzano, 1993). Research on unconscious memory has informed our understanding of how memories/phantasies laid down in infancy arise and are transformed through retrieval cues triggered by subsequent experiences, and which are eventually recreated in the analyst–patient relationship where they become once again available for scrutiny and meaning-making (Maldonado, 2011).

People with a variety of neurological conditions, such as split brain patients (whose two hemispheres have been surgically disconnected), and those with hippocampal damage, Korsakoff's syndrome, and prosopagnosia (loss of ability to recognise faces) all suffer impairments in explicit memory but show emotional memory for people and events. Consistent findings of this nature have led to the proposal that the neural circuitry for affective learning and cognitive learning might be distinct (Custers & Aarts, 2005).

Psychoanalysts have long talked of the difference between cognitive insight and emotional insight, with the latter involving a reactivation of the associational network, not just cognitive knowledge of its existence. Breuer (1893) expressed it thus:

> . . . [T]here seems to be no theoretical difficulty in . . . recognizing unconscious ideas as causes of pathological phenomena . . . [W]hen the intensity of an unconscious idea increases it enters consciousness *ipso facto*. Only when its intensity is slight does it remain unconscious. What seems hard to understand is how an idea can be sufficiently intense to provoke a lively motor act . . . and at the same time not intense enough to become conscious . . . the clarity of our ideas, and consequently their capacity . . . for [becoming] conscious is determined . . . by the feelings of pleasure or unpleasure which they arouse, by their quota of affect. When an idea immediately produces lively somatic consequences, this implies that the excitation engendered by it flows off into the paths concerned in these consequences . . . precisely because this idea has physical consequences, because its sums of psychical stimuli have been 'converted' into somatic ones, it loses the clarity which would otherwise have marked it out in the stream of ideas. Instead of this it is lost among the rest. (p. 224)

It is perhaps a little paradoxical that learning theory and conditioning processes provide another source of evidence for unconscious affect. For example, a "mere exposure effect" (Kleeman, 2011) has been identified in studies of dichotic listening in which two different acoustic signals are presented through headphones to each ear of the research participants, who were instructed to attend to only one channel. Although they were unable to recognise the content of the unattended channel, when it was replayed later and they were asked to rate their preference among several options, they chose the tones that they had previously heard but not registered cognitively, thus indicating an affective preference for the familiar sounds. Similar effects have been observed with aversive stimuli. For example, participants were first exposed to nonsense syllables that were paired with mild electric shock until a conditioned anxiety response developed with presentation to the syllables alone. When participants were later subliminally exposed to the same nonsense syllables, they registered higher levels of arousal, even though the participants were unaware that they had been exposed to the syllables that had formerly been paired with electric shock (Lazarus & McCleary, 1951). A large number of subsequent studies have confirmed this mechanism of affective learning with respect to stimuli that people had not consciously perceived (de Gelder, Vroomen, & Pourtois, 2002). No great leap of logic is required to see the relevance of this type of unconscious affective learning in early relationships and how the associative networks established for this learning can prime positive or negative feelings to significant others throughout life.

Previous studies of unconscious affect obtained similar results. In one study, participants were presented with neutral and taboo words and the latency of recognition response was recorded. Taboo words were recognised more slowly than neutral words; further, during presentation of the taboo words, skin conductance (a measure of arousal) rose before the words were consciously recognised (McGinnies, 1949). These results support a preconscious stage of processing in which affective content is evaluated unconsciously (Bargh, 1997). Many studies have reported that emotionally-charged, anxiety-laden stimuli have slower response times compared with other forms of stimuli, even when presented at speeds near the threshold for conscious perception (Shevrin, 1996).

The relationship between unconscious affect, the use of defences to keep the affect out of consciousness, and physiological reactivity has been demonstrated in a number of studies. Of particular relevance to this discussion is a study by Dozier and Kobak (1992), who documented the psycho-physiological costs of lack of attunement to one's own affective states in people with a dismissing state of mind with respect to attachment. Subjects completed the Adult Attachment Interview, during which time skin conductance was monitored while they recalled memories of separation, rejection, and threat involving their parents. The more emotionally avoidant strategies used in their recollections were associated with greater physiological reactivity. Another study demonstrating the effect of implicit affect (distress) on health compared self-report methods that are based on our conscious awareness of our cognitive and emotional processes with clinical assessments and tests of early memory. Self-report measures have been unable to differentiate those who are genuinely psychologically healthy from those who maintain "a facade or illusion of mental health based on denial and self-deception (Cousineau & Shedler, 2006, p. 427). They are, therefore, restricted by the limited information yielded by this method; one cannot tell if one does not know. Clinically derived assessment procedures, such as early memory narratives that assess implicit psychological processes (Shedler, Mayman, & Manis, 1993), can identify defensive denial of distress, reports of "illusionary mental health" (p. 1117) and associations between denial and physiological reactivity.

Westen (1999) drew the following conclusions from this body of research: (i) affective processing occurs unconsciously with and without the aid of defences; (ii) people use defences to keep unconscious threatening thoughts and affects out of awareness; (iii) people might not be able to articulate their feelings because they might not want to know, or they have not had to make, the link to (unconscious) associations that gave rise to their affects. This is because associative networks that link affects and mental representations are built without conscious awareness. In this way, infants build networks, based on their ongoing interactions with their parents and significant others that Stern and colleagues (1998) called implicit relational knowing or "representations of interactions that have generalized". It is these representations, or ways of knowing, that are re-enacted in the psychoanalytic relationship and reworked.

Non-verbal and non symbolic processes and the concept of embodiment

The first forms of human communication are non-verbal—the urgent cry of the distressed infant who is hungry, cold, wet, in pain, or in need of contact comfort. Gradually, over the first three years of life, early, primitive forms of communication give way to verbal and other forms of symbolic communication, but the need for parental action or gratification persists. There has been an increasing emphasis on the importance of these early, preverbal stages of development in contemporary psychoanalysis (Fonagy & Target, 2003; Gergely, 1992; Green, Crenshaw, & Kolos, 2010; Wilson et al., 1992) and the recognition of the existence of both symbolic and non-symbolic codes of mental functioning (Lecours, 2007). Primacy has, therefore, been assigned to non-verbal experience as the foundation on to which conscious, linguistic experience is superimposed. Proponents argue that non-verbal experience must necessarily be located centre stage, because

> . . . a nonverbal stream of experience exists alongside, and is distinct from, experience that is structured linguistically . . . [this] implies that unless language is grounded in something non linguistic, we cannot do justice to unconscious dynamics, dialogical complexity, and truth claims. (Zeddies, 2002, p. 4)

Non-symbolic codes could persist into adulthood for those who have suffered severe psychological trauma in childhood, particularly at the earliest stages of prelinguistic development. The inability to symbolise is accompanied by the use of primitive defences—compulsion to repeat, splitting, projective identification, dissociation, fragmentation—and affects that are unmentalised and unregulated (White, 2011). Freud (1915d) recognised these two codes of mental functioning by describing how conscious ideas could be split into "word presentations" and "thing presentations", which he understood to be the sensory experience of a phenomenon after the linguistic component had been repressed. Non-symbolic codes can be expressed in motoric, visceral or sensory systems. Stern (2010) argued that

> Psychoanalysis traditionally privileges the explicit, verbalizable meaning of psychodynamic forces that are interpretable (p. 660) . . . [but] [l]anguage and abstract forms of thought build on earlier modes of making and representing meaning . . . (p. 658) . . . the deepest level of meaning . . . is the level of lived engagements with others around central developmental needs, as these engagements are represented in

implicit, procedural forms of memory . . . abstractions are secondary
. . . this level of *enactive representation* encodes the most profound
aspects of human experience . . . (pp. 660–661, my italics)

An ingenious study assessed the way in which psychologically
defensive processes might find expression in basic motor responding,
that is, whether such defences can be said to be "embodied". Participants were assessed with respect to their attachment style and then
asked to push or pull a lever in response to lexical stimuli presented
on a computer display. Those participants with an avoidant attachment style pushed the lever away from themselves at faster latencies
in response to the lexical stimulus "mum" than those with secure
attachment. The researchers concluded that ". . . avoidant motives are
automatically primed when attachment-related stimuli are processed,
and that these tendencies manifest themselves in basic, motor-specific
ways" (Fraley & Marks, 2011, p. 243).

Language and conceptual understanding are linked, but the question regarding the nature of this relationship between language and
concepts is still being worked out. How do we derive meaning from
sensory inputs? How are these inputs coded in infants before they
acquire language in such a way that they continue to affect perception,
behaviour, and relationships into adulthood, a claim that appears as
a given in most psychoanalytic literature (Panhofer, 2011)? Do linguistic and non-linguistic data share processing mechanisms and, if so,
at what level of processing? These are large questions that I must
address in a small space. There are varying views of this relationship.
An early theory argued that language constrains both perception
and concept formation (e.g., Whorf, 1956). Embodied, simulationist
theories argued the opposite, that in order to understand a concept,
we must mentally simulate its referent (i.e., imagine the sensory-
motor programme associated with the concept), a view that supports
Piaget's notion of the origin of cognition in sensorimotor schemata.
Recent research has pointed to the importance of perceptual simulation in the development of language and reading comprehension
(Engelen, Bouwmeester, de Bruin, & Zwaan, 2011). None the less,
cognitive science has, for the most part, adhered to "disembodied"
theories of cognition, arguing that while cognitive processing is
informed by sensorimotor processes and enacted by motor systems,
sensory and motor systems do not constitute the cognitive system
(Adams, 2010).

More recent theorising argues that not only do sensorimotor processes contribute to cognitive development, they might, in fact, constitute them (Laakso, 2011). Challenges to this position come from researchers who argue that concepts and language might actually be processed by separate modular processors, while still others argue that language processors might use non-linguistic information in processing, if available (Spivey, Tyler, Eberhard, & Tanenhaus, 2001; Tanenhaus, Spivey-Knowlton, Eberhard, & Sedivy, 1995). However, a series of methodologically robust studies has recently concluded that conceptual and linguistic meanings are "extracted . . . in remarkably independent channels" (Endress & Potter, 2012, p. 1). The interested reader is referred to Shapiro (2011) for a comprehensive coverage of this still hotly debated area in cognitive science.

I have used the phrases, "embodied emotion", "embodied cognition", "embodied simulation", and "embodied symbolisation" in various places in this book and in the previous discussion without lingering over the origin or meaning of the word "embodied". I will, therefore, conclude with a brief overview of this concept. We have all had "gut feelings" that we have trusted in our decision making about events and people. It is a lay term for the notion of embodied knowledge that we can neither articulate nor explain, yet we are willing to back in making important decisions. Bechara and Damasio (2005) have called this gut feeling the somatic marker hypothesis (SMH). This hypothesis proposes that during the process of decision making, somatic and emotional changes occur that are encoded and stored in memory and later triggered when we are placed in a similar decision-making situation. In other words, an association between cognitive processing during decision making and biological processes develops that is learnt and stored in the ventromedial prefrontal cortex (VMPFC). These associated emotions and somatic states can be triggered and experienced consciously or unconsciously, in which case they tend to bias decision making for reasons that the individual cannot explain. These somatic markers can aid future adaptive learning, particularly in situations where the outcome is likely to be negative; they act as a warning signal against a particular behavioural choice (Carter & Pasqualini, 2004), in much the same way as Freud proposed with his concept of signal anxiety. In a review of the concept and its supportive empirical evidence, Dunn, Dalgleish, and Lawrence (2006) concluded that "while presenting an elegant theory of how emotion influences decision-making, the SMH requires additional empirical support to remain tenable" (p. 239).

From a developmental perspective, the notion of embodiment is understood as part of the process of the development of a theory of mind in the child, which begins with the infant's "understanding" of another person as a process of sensorimotor, perceptual, emotional, and non-conceptual embodied practices. These practices are the infant's introduction, and constitute their primary access, to the minds of others. These practices remain operative even after we attain theory of mind abilities (Gallagher, 2001; Gibbs, 2006). Young (2011) proposes that the infant commences by constructing a "cognition–emotion body of the other" and notes that the benefit of such conceptualisations

> ... includes in a concept related to theory of mind the sensorimotor, embodied notion of early intelligence [as well as] an understanding of early mentalizations and representations about the other as being heavily corporal, action-oriented, and grounded in the physical. That is, from infancy onward, we do not create schemes and concepts just about the other as a developing mind but also about the other as a developing socioaffective person in a body. (p. 340)

I hope that I have demonstrated in this chapter that there are remarkable confluences between psychoanalytic theory and developmental science, with each serving the other well. There are also synergies between different levels of discourse in different disciplines that all further our understanding of how personhood emerges, what constitutes "good enough" environments that allow each new person to thrive, and what is needed to repair environments that were not good enough to support the emergent mind. The psychoanalytic imagination emerged from history, literature, philosophy, and theology. Beginning with the retrospective clinical analysis of adult patients and a concept of the irrational unconscious, it has partnered with empirical sciences and developmental psychology to develop a nuanced, evidence-based understanding of its original precepts, with modifications as indicated by research.

The baby in mind

The infant of developmental neuroscience and modern psychoanalysis is, from birth, a social being who is attuned, intersubjective, and intentional. Social cognition evolves over the first days, months, and years of life, beginning with neonatal imitation and progressing to the development of a theory of mind. Development is fluid, reversible, and responsive to life experiences. Human infants express a strong tendency toward psychic coherence and a need for agency; infants actively attend to, explore, and recognise objects, seek to resolve disequilibrium, and respond to the restoration of equilibrium with contentment. Context and affect interact with genetics and biology in complex ways to support the development of multiple dynamic, self-organising systems, of which the attachment system is primary, through which psychic structure (i.e., mind) that comprises consciousness, memory, affects, cognition, and language emerges.

One of the major lessons of recent scholarship in developmental psychology is the importance of the relational perspective in understanding development in infancy and early childhood.

> In the relational perspective of social cognition, intersubjectivity is considered primordial, and developing cognition is considered as differentiated out of intersubjectivity by way of interpersonal interactions. The relational viewpoint perceives the child as socially engaged . . . from early in life so that, out of the matrix of social interactions, conceptions of self and other gradually differentiate . . . beginning with experiences embodied in sensorimotor actions. (Young, 2011, p. 332)

The primordial intersubjectivity referred to here should not be confused with earlier psychoanalytic notions of the merged, autoerotic, undifferentiated, autistic-contiguous states of newborns that do not ascribe to the infant any of the capacities that have been shown to be present just hours and days after birth. Through the capacity for active intermodal matching, the newborn has immediate access to the actions and intentions of others. Thus, the perception that others are "like me" is the foundation on which a sense of self, social cognition and intersubjectivity develop (Meltzoff, 2007a,b).

If Freud were to write a revised edition of his *Project for a Scientific Psychology* (1950[1895]), he would be well pleased with the progress made in the intervening century in identifying the biological substrate of the psychological processes that so fascinated him over his long creative life, as well as confirming some of his profound psychological insights. Such was his vision and prescience, I think he would recognise the infant of attachment theory and developmental neuroscience as the natural heir of his Oedipal infant.

REFERENCES

Abraham, K. (1924). A short study of the development of the libido, viewed in the light of mental disorders. In: *Selected Papers on Psycho-Analysis*. London: Hogarth.

Abrams, S. (2001). Summation-unrealized possibilities: comments on Anna Freud's *Normality and Pathology in Childhood*. *Psychoanalytic Study of the Child*, 56: 105–119.

Adams, F. (2010). Embodied cognition. *Phenomenology and the Cognitive Sciences*, 9(4): 619–628.

Adler, A. (1925). The practice and theory of individual psychology, P. Radin (Trans.). *Psychoanalytic Review*, 12(1): 124–126.

Adler, A. (1929). Understanding human nature, W. B. Wolfe (Trans.). *Psychoanalytic Review*, 16(1): 102–103.

Ainsworth, M. D. (1963). The development of mother–infant interaction among the Ganda. In: B. M. Foss (Ed.), *Determinants of Infant Behaviour* (Vol. 2, pp. 67–112). New York: Wiley.

Ainsworth, M. D., & Bowlby, J. (1991). An ethological approach to personality development. *American Psychologist*, 46(4): 331–341.

Ainsworth, M. D., Blehar, M. C., Waters, E., & Wall, S. (1978). *Patterns of Attachment: A Psychological Study of the Strange Situation*. Hillsdale, NJ: Lawrence Erlbaum.

Akhtar, N., & Gernsbacher, M. A. (2008). On privileging the role of gaze in infant social cognition. *Child Development Perspectives, 2*(2): 59–65.

Aleksandrowicz, D. R. (2010). Early emotional development and the developmental matrix. *Archives of Psychiatry and Psychotherapy, 12*(1): 15–23.

Alfasi, G. (1984). The effect of infancy research on psychoanalytic theory and practice. *PsycCRITIQUES, 29*(7): 553–554.

Alperin, R. M. (2001). Barriers to intimacy: an object relations perspective. *Psychoanalytic Psychology, 18*(1): 137–156.

Alpert, A. (1959). Reversibility of pathological fixations associated with maternal deprivation in infancy. *Psychoanalytic Study of the Child, 14*: 169–185.

Altenmüller, E., Wiesendanger, M., & Kesselring, J. (Eds.). (2006). *Music, Motor Control and the Brain*. Oxford: Oxford University Press.

American Psychiatric Association (2000). *Diagnostic and Statistical Manual of Mental Disorders (DSM-IV-TR)*. Arlington, VA: American Psychiatric Association.

Appelbaum, J. (2011). Should psychoanalysis become a science? *American Journal of Psychoanalysis, 71*(1): 1–15.

Appignanesi, L., & Forrester, J. (1993). *Freud's Women*. London: Virago Press.

Arlow, J. A. (1985). The concept of psychic reality and related problems. *Journal of the American Psychoanalytic Association, 33*: 521–535.

Arlow, J. A. (1996). The concept of psychic reality—how useful? *International Journal of Psychoanalysis, 77*: 659–666.

Armstrong-Perlman, E. M. (1991). The allure of the bad object. *Free Associations, 2*(3): 343–356.

Atallah, H. E., Frank, M. J., & O'Reilly, R. C. (2004). Hippocampus, cortex, and basal ganglia: insights from computational models of complementary learning systems. *Neurobiology of Learning and Memory, 82*: 253–267.

Atkinson, L., Goldberg, S., Raval, V., Pederson, D., Benoit, D., Moran, G., Poulton, L., Myhal, N., Gleason, K., & Leung, E. (2005). On the relation between maternal state of mind and sensitivity in the prediction of infant attachment security. *Developmental Psychology, 41*(1): 42–53.

Attili, G. (1989). The psychology of character and temperament in Italy: a historical review and recent trends. In: G. A. Kohnstamm (Ed.), *Temperament in Childhood* (pp. 581–596). Oxford: John Wiley.

Atwood, G. E., & Stolorow, R. D. (1984). *Structures of Subjectivity: Explorations in Psychoanalytic Phenomenology*. Hillsdale, NJ: Analytic Press.

Audet, K., & Le Mare, L. (2011). Mitigating effects of the adoptive care-giving environment on inattention/overactivity in children adopted from Romanian orphanages. *International Journal of Behavioral Development*, 35(2): 107–115.

Augusto, L. M. (2010). Unconscious knowledge: a survey. *Advances in Cognitive Psychology*, 6: 116–141.

Baillargeon, R. (1987). Object permanence in 3 and a half and 4 and a half month old infants. *Developmental Psychology*, 23: 655–664.

Baird, A. D., Scheffer, I. E., & Wilson, S. J. (2011). Mirror neuron system involvement in empathy: a critical look at the evidence. *Social Neuroscience*, 6(4): 327–335.

Baker, J. E. (2001). Mourning and the transformation of object relationships: evidence for the persistence of internal attachments. *Psychoanalytic Psychology*, 18(1): 55–73.

Bakermans-Kranenburg, M. J., van IJzendoorn, M. H., & Juffer, F. (2003). Less is more: meta-analyses of sensitivity and attachment interventions in early childhood. *Psychological Bulletin*, 129(2): 195–215.

Bakwin, A. N., Morris, R., & Bakwin, H. (1942). *Psychologic Care During Infancy and Childhood*. New York: D. Appleton-Century.

Bálint, A. (1949). Love for the mother and mother-love. *International Journal of Psychoanalysis*, 30: 251–259.

Balint, M. (1949). Early developmental states of the ego. Primary object love. *International Journal of Psychoanalysis*, 30: 265–273.

Balint, M. (1968). *The Basic Fault: Therapeutic Aspects of Regression*. London: Tavistock.

Balsam, R. H. (2010). Where has Oedipus gone? A turn of the century contemplation. *Psychoanalytic Inquiry*, 30(6): 511–519.

Baltes, P. B. (1987). Theoretical propositions of lifespan developmental psychology: on the dynamics between growth and decline. *Developmental Psychology*, 23: 611–626.

Bandstra, N. F., Chambers, C. T., McGrath, P. J., & Moore, C. (2011). The behavioural expression of empathy to others' pain versus others' sadness in young children. *Pain*, 152(5): 1074–1082.

Bandura, A. (1977). *Social Learning Theory*. Englewood Cliffs, NJ: Prentice-Hall.

Baranger, M., & Baranger, W. (2008). The analytic situation as a dynamic field. *International Journal of Psychoanalysis*, 89(4): 795–826.

Bargh, J. (1997). The automaticity of everyday life. In: R. S. Wyer (Ed.), *The Automaticity of Everyday Life: Advances in Social Cognition* (Vol. 10, pp. 1–61). Mahwah, NJ: Lawrence Erlbaum.

Barrington, C. (2004). Bringing medieval children out of the shadows. Accessed at: http://muse.jhu.edu/journals/childrens_literature/v032/32.1barrington.pdf

Bartz, J. A., & Hollander, E. (2006). The neuroscience of affiliation: forging links between basic and clinical research on neuropeptides and social behavior. *Hormones and Behavior, 50*(4): 518–528.

Bateman, A., & Fonagy, P. (2004). *Psychotherapy for Borderline Personality Disorder*. Oxford: Oxford University Press.

Baumeister, R. F., & Heatherton, T. F. (2004). Self-regulation failure: an overview. In: R. M. Kowalski (Ed.), *The Interface of Social and Clinical Psychology: Key Readings* (pp. 51–69). New York: Psychology Press.

Baumrind, D. (1968). Authoritarian vs. authoritative parental control. *Adolescence, 3*(11): 255–272.

Baumrind, D. (1971a). Current patterns of parental authority. *Developmental Psychology Monograph, 4* (1, Part 2).

Baumrind, D. (1971b). Current patterns of parental authority. *Developmental Psychology, 4*(1): 1–103.

Baumrind, D. (1971c). Harmonious parents and their preschool children. *Developmental Psychology, 4*(1, Pt. 1): 99–102.

Baumrind, D. (1991). The influence of parenting style on adolescent competence and substance use. *Journal of Early Adolescence, 11*: 56–95.

Baysinger, C., Plubell, P., & Harlow, H. (1973). A variable-temperature surrogate mother for studying attachment in infant monkeys. *Behavior Research Methods & Instrumentation, 5*(3): 269–272.

Bechara, A., & Damasio, A. R. (2005). The somatic marker hypothesis: a neural theory of economic decision. *Games and Economic Behavior, 52*(2): 336–372.

Beckett, S. (1954). *Waiting for Godot*. St Louis, MO: Demco Media, Turtleback Books, 2001.

Beckett, T. (1969). A candidate's reflections on the supervisory process. *Contemporary Psychoanalysis, 5*(2): 169–179.

Beebe, B. (2000). Coconstructing mother–infant distress: the microsynchrony of maternal impingement and infant avoidance in the face-to-face encounter. *Psychoanalytic Inquiry, 20*(3): 421–440.

Beebe, B. (2005). Mother–infant research informs mother–infant treatment. *Psychoanalytic Study of the Child, 60*: 7–46.

Beebe, B. (2006). Co-constructing mother–infant distress in face-to-face interactions: contributions of microanalysis. *Infant Observation, 9*(2): 151–164.

Beebe, B., & Jaffe, J. (2008). *Dyadic Microanalysis of Mother–Infant Communication Informs Clinical Practice*. New York: Cambridge University Press.

Beebe, B., & Lachmann, F. M. (1988). Mother–infant mutual influence and precursors of psychic structure. *Progress in Self Psychology, 3*: 3–25).

Beebe, B., & Lachmann, F. M. (1994). Representation and internalization in infancy: three principles of salience. *Psychoanalytic Psychology, 11*(2): 127–165.

Beebe, B., & Lachmann, F. M. (2002). *Infant Research and Adult Treatment: Co-constructing Interactions*. New York: Analytic Press/Taylor & Francis Group.

Beebe, B., Jaffe, J., & Lachmann, F. (2005). A dyadic systems view of communication. In: *Relatedness, Self-definition and Mental Representation* (pp. 23–42). New York: Routledge/Taylor & Francis Group.

Beebe, B., Jaffe, J., Markese, S., Buck, K., Chen, H., Cohen, P., Bahrick, L., Andrews, H., & Feldstein, S. (2010). The origins of 12-month attachment: a microanalysis of 4-month mother–infant interaction. *Attachment & Human Development, 12*(1–2): 6–141.

Beebe, B., Knoblauch, S., Rustin, J., Sorter, D., Jacobs, T. J., & Pally, R. (2005). *Forms of Intersubjectivity in Infant Research and Adult Treatment*. New York: Other Press.

Beebe, B., Lachmann, F. M., & Jaffe, J. (1997). Mother–infant interaction structures and presymbolic self- and object representations. *Psychoanalytic Dialogues, 7*(2): 133–182.

Beebe, B., Rustin, J., Sorter, D., & Knoblauch, S. (2003). An expanded view of intersubjectivity in infancy and its application to psychoanalysis. *Psychoanalytic Dialogues, 13*(6): 805–841.

Beebe, J. (2004). Can there be a science of the symbolic? *Journal of Analytic Psychology, 49*(2): 177–191.

Bell, M. A., Greene, D. R., & Wolfe, C. D. (2010). Psychobiological mechanisms of cognition–emotion integration in early development. In: S. D. Calkins (Ed.), *Child Development at the Intersection of Emotion and Cognition* (pp. 115–132). Washington, DC: American Psychological Association.

Bendit, N. (2011). Chronic suicidal thoughts and implicit memory: hypothesis and practical implications. *Australasian Psychiatry, 19*(1): 25–29.

Bengtsson, S. L., Nagy, Z., Skare, S., Forsman, L., Forssberg, H., & Ullen, F. (2005). Extensive piano practicing has regionally specific effects on white matter development. *Nature Neuroscience, 8*(9): 1148–1150.

Bergen, D., & Woodin, M. (2011). Neuropsychological development of newborns, infants, and toddlers (0 to 3 years old). *Handbook of Pediatric Neuropsychology* (pp. 15–30). New York: Springer.

Bergmann, M. S. (2010). The Oedipus complex and psychoanalytic technique. *Psychoanalytic Inquiry, 30*(6): 535–540.

Bernier, A., Carlson, S. M., & Whipple, N. (2010). From external regulation to self-regulation: early parenting precursors of young children's executive functioning. *Child Development, 81*(1): 326–339.

Bernstein, A. E. (1989). Analysis of two adult female patients who had been victims of incest in childhood. *Journal of the American Academy of Psychoanalysis and Dynamic Psychiatry, 17*(2): 207–221.

Bienvenu, J. (2003). Healing through the search for truth: the well-tempered analytic situation. *Canadian Journal of Psychoanalysis, 11*(2): 399–420.

Bierman, K. L., Bruschi, C., Domitrovich, C., Fang, G. Y., & Miller-Johnson, S. (2004). Early disruptive behaviors associated with emerging antisocial behavior among girls. In: M. Putallaz (Ed.), *Aggression, Antisocial Behavior, and Violence Among Girls: A Developmental Perspective* (pp. 137–161). New York: Guilford Press.

Bigelow, A. E., & Walden, L. M. (2009). Infants' response to maternal mirroring in the still face and replay tasks. *Infancy, 14*(5): 526–549.

Biggs, J. B. (1992). Modes of learning, forms of knowing, and ways of schooling. In: A. Demetriou, M. Shayer, & A. Efklides (Eds.), *Neo-Piagetian Theories of Cognitive Development: Implications and Applications for Education* (pp. 30–51). London: Routledge.

Biggs, J. B., & Collis, K. F. (1991). Multimodal learning and the quality of intelligent behavior. In: H. A. H. Rowe (Ed.), *Intelligence: Reconceptualization and Measurement* (pp. 57–76). Hillsdale, NJ: Lawrence Erlbaum.

Bion, W. R. (1959). Attacks on linking. *International Journal of Psycho-analysis, 40*: 308–315.

Bion, W. R. (1962). *Learning from Experience.* London: William Heinemann.

Bion, W. R. (1963). *Elements of Psycho-Analysis.* London: Heinemann.

Blakemore, S.-J., Bristow, D., Bird, G., Frith, C., & Ward, J. (2005). Somatosensory activations during the observation of touch and a case of vision-touch synaesthesia. *Brain and Cognition, 128*: 1571–1583.

Blatt, S. J. (2008). Developmental antecedents of relatedness and self-definition. In: *Polarities of Experience: Relatedness and Self-definition in Personality Development, Psychopathology, and the Therapeutic Process* (pp. 43–70): Washington, DC: American Psychological Association.

Blomfield, O. H. (1987). Human destructiveness: an essay on instinct, foetal existence and infancy. *International Review of Psychoanalysis, 14*: 21–32.

Bogin, B. (1999). Evolutionary perspective on human growth. *Annual Review of Anthropology, 28*: 109–153.

Bohleber, W. (2011). The dynamic unconscious in the analytic relationship. *International Journal of Psychoanalysis, 92*(2): 285–288.

Bollas, C. (1979). The transformational object. *International Journal of Psychoanalysis, 60*(1): 97–107.

Bollas, C. (1981). Treatment of primitive mental states. *International Journal of Psychoanalysis, 62*: 251–255.

Bollas, C. (1982). On the relation to the self as an object. *International Journal of Psychoanalysis, 63*: 347–359.

Bollas, C. (1987). *The Shadow of the Object: Psychoanalysis of the Unthought Known*. New York: Columbia University Press.

Bollas, C. (2006). Perceptive identification. *Psychoanalytic Review, 93*(5): 713–717.

Bond, A. H. (2010). New aspects of infantile trauma. *PsycCRITIQUES, 55*(36). Accessed at: doi:Electronic Collection: 2010–13180–001.

Bonomi, C. (1997). *Freud and the Discovery of Infantile Sexuality: A Reassessment*. Lanham, MD: Jason Aronson.

Bornstein, M. H., Putnick, D. L., Heslington, M., Gini, M., Suwalsky, J. T. D., Venuti, P., & Zingman de Galperin, C. (2008). Mother–child emotional availability in ecological perspective: three countries, two regions, two genders. *Developmental Psychology, 44*(3): 666–680.

Boswell, J. (1988). *The Kindness of Strangers: The Abandonment of Children in Western Europe from Late Antiquity to the Renaissance*. Chicago, IL: University of Chicago Press.

Bower, T. (1971a). The object in the world of the infant. *Scientific American, 225*(4): 30–38.

Bower, T., Broughton, J., & Moore, M. (1971b). Development of the object concept as manifested in changes in the tracking behavior of infants between 7 and 20 weeks of age. *Journal of Experimental Child Psychology, 11*(2): 182–193.

Bower, T. G., & Paterson, J. G. (1972). Stages in the development of the object concept. *Cognition, 1*(1): 47–55.

Bowlby, J. (1940). The influence of early environment in the development of neurosis and neurotic character. *International Journal of Psychoanalysis, 21*: 154–178.

Bowlby, J. (1949). The study and reduction of group tensions in the family. *Human Relations, 2*: 123–128.

Bowlby, J. (1957). An ethological approach to research in child development. *British Journal of Medical Psychology, 30*: 230–240.

Bowlby, J. (1958). The nature of the child's tie to his mother. *International Journal of Psychoanalysis, 39*: 350–373.

Bowlby, J. (1960a). Grief and mourning in infancy and early childhood. *Psychoanalytic Study of the Child, 15*: 9–52.

Bowlby, J. (1960b). Separation anxiety. *International Journal of Psychoanalysis, 41*: 89–113.

Bowlby, J. (1963). Pathological mourning and childhood mourning. *Journal of the American Psychoanalytic Association, 11*: 500–541.

Bowlby, J. (1969). *Attachment and Loss: Attachment* (Vol. 1). London: Hogarth.

Bowlby, J. (1973). *Attachment and Loss: Separation, Anxiety and Anger* (Vol. 2). London: Hogarth.

Bowlby, J. (1980). *Attachment and Loss: Loss, Sadness and Depression* (Vol. 3). London: Hogarth.

Bowlby, J. (1981). Psychoanalysis as a natural science. *International Review of Psychoanalysis, 8*: 243–256.

Bowlby, J. (1984). Psychoanalysis as a natural science. *Psychoanalytic Psychology, 1*(1): 7–21.

Bowlby, J. (1988). *A Secure Base: Clinical Applications of Attachment Theory*. London: Routledge.

Bowlby, J., Figlio, K., & Young, R. M. (1986). An interview with John Bowlby on the origins and reception of his work. *Free Associations, 1*(6): 36–64.

Bowlby, J., Robertson, J., & Rosenbluth, D. (1952). A two-year-old goes to hospital. *Psychoanalytic Study of the Child, 7*: 82–94.

Brainerd, C. J. (1996). Special section: psychological science celebrates the centennial of Jean Piaget. *Psychological Science, 7* (4): 191–225.

Brake, W. G., Zhang, T. Y., Diorio, J., Meaney, M. J., & Gratton, A. (2004). Influence of early postnatal rearing conditions on mesocorticolimbic dopamine and behavioural responses to psychostimulants and stressors in adult rats. *European Journal of Neuroscience, 19*(7): 1863–1874.

Brandchaft, B. (2002). Reflections on the intersubjective foundations of the sense of self: Commentary on paper by Steven Stern. *Psychoanalytic Dialogues, 12*(5): 727–745.

Brandchaft, B. (2007). Systems of pathological accommodation and change in analysis. *Psychoanalytic Psychology, 24*(4): 667–687.

Brandell, J. R. (2010). Contemporary psychoanalytic perspectives on attachment. *Psychoanalytic Social Work, 17*(2): 132–157.

Brazelton, T. B., & Als, H. (1979). Four early stages in the development of mother–infant interaction. *Psychoanalysis Study of the Child*, 34: 349–369.

Breazeale, D. (Ed. & Trans.) (1979). *Philosophy and Truth: Selections from Nietzsche's Notebooks of the Early 1870s*. Atlantic Highlands, NJ: Humanities Press.

Bretherton, I. (1985). Attachment theory: retrospect and prospect. *Monographs of the Society for Research in Child Development*, 50(1/2): 3–35.

Bretherton, I. (1994a). The origins of attachment theory: John Bowlby and Mary Ainsworth. In: R. D. Parke, P. A. Ornstein, J. J. Reiser, & C. Zahn-Waxler (Eds.), *A Century of Developmental Psychology* (pp. 431–471): Washington, DC: American Psychological Association.

Bretherton, I. (1994b). Infants' subjective world of relatedness: moments, feeling shapes, protonarrative envelopes, and internal working models. *Infant Mental Health Journal*, 15(1): 36–41.

Breuer, J. (1893). Theoretical. In: *Studies on Hysteria. S.E.*, 2: 183–251. London: Hogarth.

Britton, J. R. (2011). Infant temperament and maternal anxiety and depressed mood in the early postpartum period. *Women & Health*, 51(1): 55–71.

Brockman, R. (2001). Toward a neurobiology of the unconscious. *Journal of the Americal Academy of Psychoanalysis and Dynamic Psychiatry*, 29(4): 601–615.

Bronfenbrenner, U. (1979). *The Ecology of Human Development: Experiments by Nature and Design*. Cambridge, MA: Harvard University Press.

Broussard, E. R., & Cassidy, J. (2010). Maternal perception of newborns predicts attachment organization in middle adulthood. *Attachment & Human Development*, 12(1–2): 159–172.

Burgess, A. W., Hartman, C. R., & Baker, T. (1995). Memory presentations of childhood sexual abuse. *Journal of Psychosocial Nursing and Mental Health Services*, 33: 9–16.

Burlingham, D. (1967). Empathy between infant and mother. *Journal of the American Psychoanalytic Association*, 15: 764–780.

Calkins, S. D., & Hill, A. (2007). Caregiver influences on emerging emotion regulation: biological and environmental transactions in early development. In: J. J. Gross (Ed.), *Handbook of Emotion Regulation* (pp. 229–248). New York: Guilford Press.

Campbell, S. B., Spieker, S., Burchinal, M., & Poe, M. D. (2006). Trajectories of aggression from toddlerhood to age 9 predict academic and social functioning through age 12. *Journal of Child Psychology and Psychiatry*, 47(8): 791–800.

Camus, A. (1942). *The Myth of Sisyphus*. J. O'Brien, (Trans.). Harmondsworth: Penguin Classics, 2006.

Canals, J., Hernandez-Martinez, C., & Fernandez-Ballart, J. D. (2011). Relationships between early behavioural characteristics and temperament at 6 years. *Infant Behavior & Development, 34*(1): 152–160.

Carignan, L. (2006). Canadian Journal of Psychoanalysis. *Psychoanalytic Quarterly, 75*(3): 955–967.

Caron, A. J. (2009). Comprehension of the representational mind in infancy. *Developmental Review, 29*: 69–95.

Carr, A., & O'Reilly, G. (2007). Lifespan development and the family life-cycle. In: A. Carr (Ed.), *The Handbook of Intellectual Disability and Clinical Psychology Practice* (pp. 50–91). New York: Routledge/Taylor & Francis.

Carter, C., & DeVries, A. (1999). Stress and soothing: an endocrine perspective. In: M. Lewis & D. Ramsay (Eds.), *Stress and Soothing* (pp. 3–18). Mahwah, NJ: Lawrence Erlbaum.

Carter, S., & Pasqualini, M. C. (2004). Stronger autonomic response accompanies better learning: a test of Damasio's somatic marker hypothesis. *Cognition and Emotion, 18*(7): 901–911.

Carver, L. J., & Vaccaro, B. G. (2007). 12-month-old infants allocate increased neural resources to stimuli associated with negative adult emotion. *Developmental Psychology, 43*(1): 54–69.

Case, R. (1988). The whole child: toward an integrated view on young children's cognitive, social and emotional development. In: A. D. Pellegrini (Ed.), *Psychological Bases for Early Education* (pp. 155–184). New York: Wiley.

Case, R. (1992). Neo-Piagetian theories of child development. In: R. J. Sternberg (Ed.), *Intellectual Development* (pp. 161–196). New York: Cambridge University Press.

Cassidy, J., & Shaver, P. R. (Eds.). (2008). *Handbook of Attachment: Theory, Research, and Clinical Applications* (2nd edn). New York: Guilford Press.

Cassimatis, E. G. (1984). The 'false self': existential and therapeutic issues. *International Review of Psychoanalysis, 11*: 69–76.

Cattaneo, L., & Rizzolatti, G. (2009). The mirror neuron system. *Archives of Neurology, 66*(5): 557–560.

Chen, Z., & Hancock, J. E. (2011). Cognitive development. In: A. S. Davis (Ed.), *Handbook of Pediatric Neuropsychology* (pp. 49–59). New York: Springer.

Chernus, L. A. (2007). The remarkable explanatory power of neurobiology: a validation and synthesis of psychoanalytic theory, infant observation, and clinical social work practice. *Psychoanalytic Social Work*, *14*(1): 77–93.

Chess, S., & Thomas, A. (1996). *Temperament*. New York: Routledge.

Chickering, A. W., & Reisser, L. (1993). *Education and Identity* (2nd edn). San Francisco, CA: Jossey-Bass.

Chomsky, N. (1980). *Rules and Representations*. Oxford: Basil Blackwell.

Chomsky, N. (2006). *Language and Mind* (3rd edn). New York: Cambridge University Press.

Chomsky, N. (2011). Language and other cognitive systems. What is special about language? *Language Learning and Development*, *7*(4): 263–278.

Chused, J. F. (2007). Little Hans "analyzed" in the twenty-first century. *Journal of the American Psychoanalytic Association*, *55*(3): 767–778.

Cicchetti, D., & Cohen, D. J. (1995). Perspectives on developmental psychopathology. In: D. Cicchetti & D. J. Cohen (Eds.), *Developmental Psychopathology: Theory and Methods* (Vol. 1, pp. 3–20). New York: Wiley.

Coccaro, E. F., Kavoussi, R. J., Hauger, R. L., Cooper, T. B., & Ferris, C. F. (1998). Cerebrospinal fluid vasopressin levels: correlates with aggression and serotonin function in personality-disordered subjects. *Archives of General Psychiatry*, *55*(8): 708–714.

Colicos, M. A., & Syed, N. I. (2006). Neuronal networks and synaptic plasticity: understanding complex system dynamics by interfacing neurons with silicon technologies. *Journal of Experimental Biology*, *209*: 2312–2319.

Cousineau, T. M., & Shedler, J. (2006). Predicting physical health: Implicit mental health measures versus self-report scales. *Journal of Nervous and Mental Disease*, *194*(6): 427–432.

Cox, M. J., Owen, M. T., Henderson, V. K., & Margand, N. A. (1992). Prediction of infant–father and infant–mother attachment. *Developmental Psychology*, *28*: 474–483.

Crittenden, P. M. (1992). Quality of attachment in the preschool years. *Development and Psychopathology*, *4*: 209–241.

Crown, C. L., Feldstein, S., Jasnow, M. D., Beebe, B., & Jaffe, J. (2002). The cross-modal coordination of interpersonal timing: six-week-olds infants' gaze with adults' vocal behavior. *Journal of Psycholinguistic Research*, *31*(1): 1–23.

Custers, R., & Aarts, H. (2005). Positive affect as implicit motivator: on the nonconscious operation of behavioral goals. *Journal of Personality and Social Psychology*, *89*: 129–142.

Dadds, M. R., Davey, G. C. L., & Field, A. P. (2001). Developmental aspects of conditioning processes in anxiety disorders. In: M. W. Vasey &

M. M. Dadds (Eds.), *The Developmental Psychopathology of Anxiety* (pp. 205–230). New York: Oxford University Press.

Daehnert, C. (1998). The false self as a means of disidentification: a psychoanalytic case study. *Contemporary Psychoanalysis, 34*(2): 251–271.

Dale, L. P., O'Hara, E. A., Schein, R., Inserra, L., Keen, J., Flores, M., & Porges, S. W. (2011). Measures of infant behavioral and physiological state regulation predict 54-month behavior problems. *Infant Mental Health Journal, 32*(4): 473–486.

Damasio, A. (1994). *Descartes' Error: Emotion, Reason and the Human Brain*. New York: Avon Books.

Dapretto, M., Davies, M. S., Pfeifer, J. H., Scott, A. A., Sigman, M., Bookheimer, S. Y., & Iacoboni, M. (2006). Understanding emotions in others: mirror neuron dysfunction in children with autism spectrum disorders. *Nature Neuroscience, 9*(1): 28–30.

Darkwa, O. K., & Mazibuko, F. N. (2002). Population aging and its impact on elderly welfare in Africa. *International Journal of Aging and Human Development, 54*(2): 107–123.

Dawson-Tunik, T. L., Fischer, K. W., & Stein, Z. (2004). Do stages belong at the center of developmental theory? A commentary on Piaget's stages. *New Ideas in Psychology, 22*(3): 255–263.

Deater-Deckard, K., & Mullineaux, P. Y. (2010). Cognition and emotion: a behavioral genetic perspective. In: S. D. Calkins (Ed.), *Child Development at The Intersection of Emotion and Cognition* (pp. 133–152). Washington, DC: American Psychological Association.

Debiec, J., Diaz-Mataix, L., Bush, D. E., Doyere, V., & Ledoux, J. E. (2010). The amygdala encodes specific sensory features of an aversive reinforcer. *Nature Neuroscience, 13*(5): 536–537.

de Gelder, B., Vroomen, J., & Pourtois, G. (2002). Covert affective cognition and affective blindsight. In: B. de Gelder, E. de Haan, & C. Heywood (Eds.), *Out of Mind: Varieties of Unconscious Processes* (pp. 205–221). Oxford: Oxford University Press.

de-Graaf-Peters, V. B., & Hadders-Algra, M. (2006). Ontogeny of the human central nervous system: what is happening when? *Early Human Development, 82*(4): 257–266.

de Houwer, J. (2006). What are implicit measures and why are we using them? In: R. W. Wiers & A. W. Stacy (Eds.), *The Handbook of Implicit Cognition and Addiction* (pp. 11–28). Thousand Oaks, CA: Sage.

DeLoache, J. S. (1995). Early understanding and use of symbols: the model model. *Current Directions, 4*(4): 109–113.

Demos, E. V. (1989). A prospective constructionist view of development. *Annual of Psychoanalysis, 17*: 287–308.

Demos, E. V. (1999). The search for psychological models: commentary on papers by Stephen Seligman and by Robin C. Silverman and Alicia F. Lieberman. *Psychoanalytic Dialogues, 9*(2): 219–227.

Demos, E. V. (2007). The dynamics of development. In: C. Piers (Ed.), *Self-Organizing Complexity in Psychological Systems* (pp. 135–163). Lanham, MD: Jason Aronson.

Demos, E. V. (2008). Basic human priorities reconsidered. *Annual of Psychoanalysis, 36*: 246–265.

Denenberg, V. H. (1964). Critical periods, stimulus input, and emotional reactivity: a theory of infantile stimulation. *Psychological Review, 71*(5): 335–351.

Dennett, D. (1987). *The Intentional Stance.* Cambridge, MA: MIT Press.

Deoni, S. C. L., Mercure, E., Blasi, A., Gasston, D., Thomson, A., Johnson, M., Williams, S. C., & Murphy, D. G. (2011). Mapping infant brain myelination with magnetic resonance imaging. *Journal of Neuroscience, 31*(2): 784–791.

Derauf, C., LaGasse, L., Smith, L., Newman, E., Shah, R., Arria, A., Huestis, M., Haning, W., Strauss, A., Grotta, S. D., Dansereau, L., Lin, H., & Lester, B. (2011). Infant temperament and high-risk environment relate to behavior problems and language in toddlers. *Journal of Developmental and Behavioral Pediatrics, 32*(2): 125–135.

Derbyshire, S. W. (2010). Foetal pain? *Best Practice & Research Clinical Obstetrics & Gynaecology, 24*(5): 647–655.

Dervin, D. (1988). Freud's baby and ours: notes toward a psychohistory of psychoanalysis. *Journal of Psychohistory, 16*(1): 79–87.

de Souza Favaro, S. M., & de Andrade, L. M. B. (2011). Study of adolescence extension. One vision of parents and sons. *Acta Psiquiatrica y Psicologica de America Latina, 57*(1): 39–49.

Desrochers, S. (2006). Beyond Piagetian cognitive milestones. *Intellectica, 44*(2): 249–251.

Diamond, D. (2004). Attachment disorganization: the reunion of attachment theory and psychoanalysis. *Psychoanalytic Psychology, 21*(2): 276–299.

Diego, M. A., Field, T., Hernandez-Reif, M., Schanberg, S., Kuhn, C., & Gonzalez-Quintero, V. H. (2009). Prenatal depression restricts fetal growth. *Early Human Development, 85*(1): 65–70.

Dorpat, T. (1999). Inauthentic communication and the false self. *Psychoanalytic Review, 86*(2): 209–222.

Dozier, M., & Kobak, R. (1992). Psychophysiology in attachment interviews: converging evidence for deactivating strategies. *Child Development, 63*(6): 1473–1480.

Dubois, J., Dehaene-Lambertz, G., Soares, C., Cointepas, Y., Le Bihan, D., & Hertz-Pannier, L. (2008). Microstructural correlates of infant functional development: example of the visual pathways. *Journal of Neuroscience, 28*(8): 1943–1948.

Dunn, B. D., Dalgleish, T., & Lawrence, A. D. (2006). The somatic marker hypothesis: a critical evaluation. *Neuroscience and Biobehavioral Reviews, 30*(2): 239–271.

Dutra, L., Bureau, J.-F., Holmes, B., Lyubchik, A., & Lyons-Ruth, K. (2009). Quality of early care and childhood trauma: a prospective study of developmental pathways to dissociation. *Journal of Nervous and Mental Disease, 197*(6): 383–390.

Edgcumbe, R. (2000). *Anna Freud: A View of Development, Disturbance, and Therapeutic Techniques*. London: Routledge.

Ein-Dor, T., Mikulincer, M., Doron, G., & Shaver, P. R. (2010). The attachment paradox: how can so many of us (the insecure ones) have no adaptive advantages? *Perspectives on Psychological Science, 5*(2): 123–141.

Elbers, E. (1986). Theory building in developmental psychology: children's theories and developmental theory. *Advances in Psychology, 36*: 365–403.

Elicker, J., Englund, M., & Sroufe, L. A. (1992). Predicting peer competence and peer relationships in childhood from early parent–child relationships. In: R. D. Parke & G. W. Ladd (Eds.), *Family–Peer Relationships: Modes of Linkage* (pp. 77–106). Hillsdale, NJ: Erlbaum.

Eliot, T. S. (1968). *Four Quartets*. Boston, MA: Harcourt.

Eluvathingal, T. J., Chugani, H. T., Behen, M. E., Juhász, C., Muzik, O., Maqbool, M., Chugani, D. C., & Makki, M. (2006). Abnormal brain connectivity in children after early severe socioemotional deprivation: a diffusion tensor imaging study. *Pediatrics, 117*(6): 2093–2100.

Endress, A. D., & Potter, M. C. (2012). Early conceptual and linguistic processes operate in independent channels. *Psychological Science, 23*(2): 1–11.

Engelen, J. A., Bouwmeester, S., de Bruin, A. B., & Zwaan, R. A. (2011). Perceptual simulation in developing language comprehension. *Journal of Experimental Child Psychology, 110*(4): 659–675.

Erikson, E. H. (1968). *Identity: Youth and Crisis*. New York: W. W. Norton.

Erikson, E. H. (1980a). *Identity and the Life Cycle*. New York: W. W. Norton.

Erikson, E. H. (1980b). On the generational cycle: an address. *International Journal of Psychoanalysis, 61*: 213–223.

Esman, A. H. (2008). *From Death Instinct to Attachment Theory: The Primacy of the Child in Freud, Klein, and Heimann*: Philippe Van Haute and

Tomas Geyskens. New York: Other Press (2007) (Review). *Psychoanalytic Quarterly, 77(3):* 967–970.

Fairbairn, W. D. (1944). Endopsychic structure considered in terms of object-relationships. *International Journal of Psychoanalysis, 25:* 70–92.

Fairbairn, W. D. (1946). Object-relationships and dynamic structure. *International Journal of Psychoanalysis, 27:* 30–37.

Fairbairn, W. D. (1952). *Psychoanalytic Studies of the Personality.* London: Tavistock.

Fairbairn, W. D. (1958). On the nature and aims of psycho-analytical treatment. *International Journal of Psychoanalysis, 39:* 374–385.

Fairbairn, W. D. (1963). Synopsis of an object-relations theory of the personality. *International Journal of Psychoanalysis, 44:* 224–225.

Fantz, R. (1963). Pattern of vision in newborn infants. *Science, 140:* 296–297.

Feldman, R. (2007). On the origins of background emotions: from affect synchrony to symbolic expression. *Emotion, 7(3):* 601–611.

Feldman, R., Gordon, I., Schneiderman, I., Weisman, O., & Zagoory-Sharon, O. (2010). Natural variations in maternal and paternal care are associated with systematic changes in oxytocin following parent–infant contact. *Psychoneuroendocrinology, 35(8):* 1133–1141.

Feldman, R., Greenbaum, C. W., & Yirmiya, N. (1999). Mother–infant affect synchrony as an antecedent of the emergence of self-control. *Developmental Psychology, 35(1):* 223–231.

Feldman, R., Weller, A., Zagoory-Sharon, O., & Levine, A. (2007). Evidence for a neuroendocrinological foundation of human affiliation: plasma oxytocin levels across pregnancy and the postpartum period predict mother–infant bonding. *Psychological Science, 18(11):* 965–970.

Ferenczi, S. (1933). Thalassa: a theory of genitality. *Psychoanalytic Quarterly, 2:* 361–364.

Field, A. P. (2006). Is conditioning a useful framework for understanding the development and treatment of phobias? *Clinical Psychology Review, 26(7):* 857–875.

Field, T. (1996). Attachment and separation in young children. *Annual Review of Psychology, 47:* 541–561.

Field, T. (2002). Prenatal effects of maternal depression. In: S. H. Goodman & I. H. Gotlib (Eds.), *Children of Depressed Parents: Mechanisms of Risk and Implications for Treatment* (pp. 59–88). Washington, DC: American Psychological Association.

Field, T., Diego, M., Hernandez-Reif, M., Figueiredo, B., Deeds, O., Ascencio, A., & Kuhn, C. (2008a). Prenatal dopamine and neonatal behavior and biochemistry. *Infant Behavior & Development, 31(4):* 590–593.

Field, T., Diego, M., Hernandez-Reif, M., Figueiredo, B., Deeds, O., Ascencio, A., & Kuhn, C. (2008b). Prenatal serotonin and neonatal outcome: brief report. *Infant Behavior & Development*, *31*(2): 316–320.

Field, T., Diego, M., Hernandez-Reif, M., Figueiredo, B., Schanberg, S., & Kuhn, C. (2007). Sleep disturbances in depressed pregnant women and their newborns. *Infant Behavior & Development*, *30*(1): 127–133.

Fischer, K. W. (1980). A theory of cognitive development: the control and construction of a hierarchy of skills. *Psychological Review*, *87*: 477–531.

Fischer, K. W., & Hencke, R. W. (1996). Infants' constructions of actions in context of Piaget's contribution to research on early development. *Psychological Science*, *7*(4): 204–210.

Fisher, L., Ames, E. W., Chisholm, K., & Savoie, L. (1997). Problems reported by parents of Romanian orphans adopted to British Columbia. *International Journal of Behavioral Development*, *20*(1): 67–82.

Fisher, S., & Greenberg, R. P. (1995). *Freud Scientifically Reappraised: Testing the Theories and Therapy*. New York: John Wiley.

Flavell, J. H. (1992). Cognitive development: past, present and future. *Developmental Psychology*, *28*(6): 998–1005.

Flavell, J. H. (1996). Piaget's legacy. *Psychological Science*, *7*(4): 200–203.

Flavell, J. H. (1999). Cognitive development: children's knowledge about the mind. *Annual Review of Psychology*, *50*: 21–45.

Fliegel, Z. O. (1973). Feminine psychosexual development in Freudian theory—a historical reconstruction. *Psychoanalytic Quarterly*, *42*: 385–408.

Flom, R., Lee, K., & Muir, D. (Eds.). (2007). *Gaze-Following: Its Development and Significance*. Mahwah, NJ: Lawrence Erlbaum.

Fonagy, P. (1989). On tolerating mental states: theory of mind in borderline personality. *Bulletin of the Anna Freud Centre*, *12*(2): 91–115.

Fonagy, P. (1994). Mental representations from an intergenerational cognitive science perspective. *Infant Mental Health Journal*, *15*(1): 57–68.

Fonagy, P. (2000). Attachment and borderline personality disorder. *Journal of the American Psychoanalytic Association*, *48*(4): 1129–1146.

Fonagy, P., & Target, M. (1996). Playing with reality: I. Theory of mind and the normal development of psychic reality. *International Journal of Psychoanalysis*, *77*: 217–233.

Fonagy, P., & Target, M. (1997). Attachment and reflective function: their role in self-organization. *Development and Psychopathology*, *9*: 679–700.

Fonagy, P., & Target, M. (1999). An interpersonal view of the infant. In: P. Fonagy (Ed.), *Psychoanalysis and Developmental Therapy* (pp. 3–31). Madison, CT: International Universities Press.

Fonagy, P., & Target, M. (2003). *Psychoanalytic Theories: Perspectives from Developmental Psychopathology*. Philadelphia, PA: Whurr.

Fonagy, P., Gergely, G., Jurist, E., & Target, M. (2004). *Affect Regulation, Mentalization, and the Development of the Self*. New York: Other Press.

Fonagy, P., Luyten, P., & Strathearn, L. (2011). Borderline personality disorder, mentalization, and the neurobiology of attachment. *Infant Mental Health Journal*, 32(1): 47–69.

Fonagy, P., Moran, G. S., Edgcumbe, R., Kennedy, H., & Target, M. (1993). The roles of mental representations and mental processes in therapeutic action. *Psychoanalytic Study of the Child*, 48: 9–48.

Fonagy, P., Target, M., Gergely, G., Allen, J. G., & Bateman, A. W. (2003). The developmental roots of borderline personality disorder in early attachment relationships: a theory and some evidence. *Psychoanalytic Inquiry*, 23(3): 412–459.

Forsyth, D. W. (1997). Proposals regarding the neurobiology of oedipality. *Psychoanalytic Contemporary Thought*, 20(2): 163–206.

Fox, N. A., & Reeb-Sutherland, B. C. (2010). Biological moderators of infant temperament and its relation to social withdrawal. In: K. H. Rubin (Ed.), *The Development of Shyness and Social Withdrawal* (pp. 84–103). New York: Guilford Press.

Fraley, R., & Marks, M. J. (2011). Pushing mom away: embodied cognition and avoidant attachment. *Journal of Research in Personality*, 45(2): 243–246.

Franck, L. S., Ridout, D., Howard, R., Peters, J., & Honour, J. W. (2011). A comparison of pain measures in newborn infants after cardiac surgery. *Pain*, 152(8): 1758–1765.

Frank, G. (1999). Freud's concept of the superego: review and assessment. *Psychoanalytic Psychology*, 16(3): 448–463.

Freed, P. (2008). Oxytocin and trust. *Neuro-Psychoanalysis*, 10(1): 103–104.

Freud, A. (1929). On the theory of analysis of children. *International Journal of Psychoanalysis*, 10: 29–38.

Freud, A. (1936a). *The Ego and Mechanisms of Defence*. London: Karnac.

Freud, A. (1936b). *Normality and Pathology in Childhood*. London: Karnac.

Freud, A. (1951). Observations on child development. *Psychoanalytic Study of the Child*, 6: 18–30.

Freud, A. (1953). A two-year-old goes to hospital—scientific film by James Robertson. *International Journal of Psychoanalysis*, 34: 284–287.

Freud, A. (1960). Discussion of Dr. John Bowlby's paper. *Psychoanalytic Study of the Child*, 15: 53–62.

Freud, A. (1963). The concept of developmental lines. *Psychoanalytic Study of the Child*, 18: 245–265.

Freud, A. (1965). Diagnostic skills and their growth in psycho-analysis. *International Journal of Psychoanalysis, 46*: 31–38.

Freud, A. (1968). Willie Hoffer, M.D., Ph.D. *Psychoanalytic Study of the Child, 23*: 7–11.

Freud, A. (1969). John, seventeen months: nine days in a residential nursery by James and Joyce Robertson. *Psychoanalytic Study of the Child, 24*: 138–143.

Freud, A. (1971). The infantile neurosis: genetic and dynamic considerations. *Psychoanalytic Study of the Child, 26*: 79–90.

Freud, A. (1972). *Problems of Psychoanalytic Technique and Therapy*. London: Hogarth Press.

Freud, A. (1981). The concept of developmental lines—their diagnostic significance. *Psychoanalytic Study of the Child, 36*: 129–136.

Freud, A. (1982). The past revisited. *Annual Review of Psychoanalysis, 10*: 259–265.

Freud, S. (with Breuer, J.) (1895d). *Studies on Hysteria. S.E., 2*. London: Hogarth.

Freud, S. (1896a). Heredity and the aetiology of the neuroses. *S.E., 3*: 141–156. London: Hogarth.

Freud, S. (1896b). The aetiology of hysteria. *S.E., 3*: 187–221. London: Hogarth.

Freud, S. (1898a). Sexuality in the aetiology of the neuroses. *S.E., 3*: 259–285. London: Hogarth.

Freud, S. (1899a). Screen memories. *S.E., 3*: 299–322. London: Hogarth.

Freud, S. (1900a). *The Interpretation of Dreams. S.E., 4–5*. London: Hogarth.

Freud, S. (1901b). *The Psychopathology of Everyday Life. S.E., 6*. London: Hogarth.

Freud, S. (1905d). *Three Essays on the Theory of Sexuality. S.E., 7*: 123–246. London: Hogarth.

Freud, S. (1907c). The sexual enlightenment of children. *S.E., 9*: 129–140. London: Hogarth.

Freud, S. (1909b). *Analysis of a Phobia in a Five-Year-Old Boy. S.E., 10*: 1–150. London: Hogarth.

Freud, S. (1910k). 'Wild' psycho-analysis. *S.E., 11*: 219–228. London: Hogarth.

Freud, S. (1911b). Formulations on the two principles of mental functioning. *S.E., 12*: 213–226. London: Hogarth.

Freud, S. (1912b). The dynamics of transference. *S.E., 12*: 97–108. London: Hogarth.

Freud, S. (1914d). On the history of the psycho-analytic movement. *S.E., 14*: 1–66. London: Hogarth.

Freud, S. (1914g). Remembering, repeating and working-through. *S.E.*, *12*: 145–156. London: Hogarth.

Freud, S. (1915c). Instincts and their vicissitudes. *S.E.*, *14*: 109–140. London: Hogarth.

Freud, S. (1915d). Repression. *S.E.*, *15*: 141–158. London: Hogarth.

Freud, S. (1915e). The unconscious. *S.E.*, *14*: 159–215. London: Hogarth.

Freud, S. (1916–1917). *Introductory Lectures on Psycho-Analysis*. *S.E.*, *16*: 241–463. London: Hogarth.

Freud, S. (1917e). Mourning and melancholia. *S.E.*, *14*: 237–258. London: Hogarth.

Freud, S. (1918b). *From the History of an Infantile Neurosis*. *S.E.*, *17*: 1–124. London: Hogarth.

Freud, S. (1920g). *Beyond the Pleasure Principle*. *S.E.*, *28*: 1–64. London: Hogarth.

Freud, S. (1923b). *The Ego and the Id*. *S.E.*, *19*: 1–66. London: Hogarth.

Freud, S. (1924c). The economic problem of masochism. *S.E.*, *19*: 155–170. London: Hogarth.

Freud, S. (1925j). Some psychical consequences of the anatomical distinction between the sexes. *S.E.*, *19*: 241–258. London: Hogarth.

Freud, S. (1926d). *Inhibitions, Symptoms and Anxiety*. *S.E.*, *20*: 75–126. London: Hogarth.

Freud, S. (1930a). *Civilization and its Discontents*. *S.E.*, *21*: 59–145. London: Hogarth.

Freud, S. (1931b). Female sexuality. *S. E.*, *21*: 223–243. London: Hogarth.

Freud, S. (1933a). *New Introductory Lectures on Psycho-Analysis*. *S. E.*, *22*: 1–182. London: Hogarth.

Freud, S. (1940a[1938]). *An Outline of Psycho-Analysis*. *S.E.*, *23*: 139–208. London: Hogarth.

Freud, S. (1940b[1938]). Some elementary lessons in psycho-analysis. *S.E.*, *23*: 279–286. London: Hogarth.

Freud, S. (1950)[1895]. *Project for a Scientific Psychology*. *S.E.*, *1*: 281–391. London: Hogarth.

Freud, W. E. (1981). The setting: to be in touch. *Journal of Child Psychotherapy*, *7*: 141–143.

Friedlander, B. Z. (1970). Receptive language development in infancy. *Merrill-Palmer Quarterly*, *16*: 7–51.

Friedman, D. D., Beebe, B., Jaffe, J., Ross, D., & Triggs, S. (2010). Microanalysis of 4-month infant vocal affect qualities and maternal postpartum depression. *Clinical Social Work Journal*, *38*(1): 8–16.

Friedman, N. P., Miyake, A., Robinson, J. L., & Hewitt, J. K. (2011). Developmental trajectories in toddlers' self-restraint predict individual differences in executive functions 14 years later: a behavioral genetic analysis. *Developmental Psychology, 47*(5): 1410–1430.

Frieze, I. H., Parsons, J. E., Johnson, P. B., Ruble, D. N., & Zellman, C. L. (1978). *Women and Sex Roles: A Social Psychological Perspective.* Oxford: W. W. Norton.

Fromm, E., & Narváez, F. (1968). The Oedipus complex: comments on 'The case of little Hans'. *Contemporary Psychoanalysis, 4*(2): 178–187.

Frosh, S. (2002). *Key Concepts in Psychoanalysis.* New York: New York University Press.

Frosh, S. (2003). Psychoanalysis, Nazism and 'Jewish science'. *International Journal of Psychoanalysis, 84*(5): 1315–1332.

Gadamer, H.-G. (1975). *Truth and Method.* New York: Crossword.

Gaensbauer, T. J. (1995). Trauma in the preverbal period: symptoms, memories, and developmental impact. *Psychoanalytic Study of the Child, 50*: 122–149.

Gallagher, S. (2001). The practice of mind: Theory, simulation or primary interaction. *Journal of Consciousness Studies, 8*: 83–103.

Gallese, V., Eagle, M. N., & Migone, P. (2007). Intentional attunement: mirror neurons and the neural underpinnings of interpersonal relations. *Journal of the American Psychoanalytic Association, 55*(1): 131–176.

Gazzaniga, M. S., Ivry, R. B., & Mangnun, G. R. (2002). *Cognitive Neuroscience* (2nd edn). New York: W. W. Norton.

Geangu, E., Benga, O., Stahl, D., & Striano, T. (2011). Individual differences in infants' emotional resonance to a peer in distress: self–other awareness and emotion regulation. *Social Development, 20*(3): 450–470.

Gedo, J. E. (1986). *Conceptual Issues in Psychoanalysis. Essays in History and Method.* Hillsdale, NJ: Analytic Press.

Geissmann, C., & Geissmann, P. (1998). *A History of Child Psychoanalysis.* London: Routledge.

Gergely, G. (1992). Developmental reconstructions: infancy from the point of view of psychoanalysis and developmental psychology. *Psychoanalysis & Contemporary Thought, 15*(1): 3–55.

Gergely, G. (2007). The social construction of the subjective self: the role of affect mirroring, markedness, and ostensive communication in self-development. In: L. Mayes, P. Fonagy, & M. Target (Eds.), *Developmental Science and Psychoanalysis: Integration and Innovation* (pp. 45–82). London: Karnac.

Gesell, A. (1940). *The First Five Years of Life: A Guide to the Study of the Preschool Child.* New York: Harper & Bros.

Ghent, E. (2002). Wish, need, drive: motive in the light of dynamic systems theory and Edelman's selectionist theory. *Psychoanalytic Dialogues*, 12(5): 763–808.

Giannoni, M., & Corradi, M. (2006). How the mind understands other minds: cognitive psychology, attachment and reflective function. *Journal of Analytic Psychology*, 51(2): 271–284.

Gibbs, R. W. (2006). *Embodiment and Cognitive Science*. New York: Cambridge University Press.

Gibson, E. J. (1983). Perceptual phenomena and perceptual meanings in infants and young children. In: *Issues in Cognition: Proceedings of a Joint Conference in Psychology* (pp. 87–102): Washington, DC: National Academy of Sciences and American Psychological Association.

Gibson, E. J. (1992). How to think about perceptual learning: twenty-five years later. In: *Cognition: Conceptual and Methodological Issues* (pp. 215–237): Washington, DC: American Psychological Association.

Giedd, J. N., Blumenthal, J., Jeffries, N. O., Castellanos, F. X., Liu, H., Zijdenbos, A., & Rapoport, J. (1999). Brain development during childhood and adolescence: a longitudinal MRI study. *Nature Neuroscience*, 2(10): 861–863.

Giles, A., & Rovee-Collier, C. (2011). Infant long-term memory for associations formed during mere exposure. *Infant Behavior & Development*, 34(2): 327–338.

Gingrich, B., Liu, Y., Cascio, C., Wang, Z., & Insel, T. R. (2000). Dopamine D2 receptors in the nucleus accumbens are important for social attachment in female prairie voles (Microtus ochrogaster). *Behavioral Neuroscience*, 114(1): 173–183.

Giovacchini, P. L. (1993a). Schizophrenia, the pervasive psychosis: paradoxes and empathy. *Journal of the America Academy of Psychoanalysis and Dynamic Psychiatry*, 21(4): 549–565.

Giovacchini, P. L. (1993b). [Review of] *Broken Structures: Severe Personality Disorders and Their Treatment*. Salman Akhtar. Northvale, NJ: Jason Aronson, 1992. *Psychoanalytic Review*, 80(3): 496–498.

Girard, M. (2010). Winnicott's foundation for the basic concepts of Freud's metapsychology? *International Journal of Psychoanalysis*, 91(2): 305–324.

Glenberg, A. M., & Kaschak, M. P. (1997). Grounding language in action. *Psychonomic Bulletin & Review*, 9: 558–565.

Glucksman, M. L. (1995). Psychodynamics and neurobiology: an integrated approach. *Journal of the Americal Academy of Psychoanalysis and Dynamic Psychiatry*, 23(2): 179–195.

Goldberg, A. (Ed.). (1988). *Frontiers in Self Psychology* (Vol. 3). Hillsdale, NJ: Analytic Press.

Goldhaber, D. E. (1986). *Life-Span Human Development*. Fort Worth, TX: Harcourt College.

Goldman, A., & de Vignemont, F. (2009). Is social cognition embodied? *Trends in Cognitive Sciences, 13*(4): 154–159.

Gopnik, A. (1996). The post-Piaget era. *Psychological Science, 7*(4): 221–225.

Gopnik, A. (2011). The theory theory 2.0: probabilistic models and cognitive development. *Child Development Perspectives, 5*(3): 161–163.

Gordon, I., Zagoory-Sharon, O., Leckman, J. F., & Feldman, R. (2010). Oxytocin and the development of parenting in humans. *Biological Psychiatry, 68*(4): 377–382.

Gordon, R. M. (2005). The doom and gloom of divorce research: comment on Wallerstein and Lewis (2004). *Psychoanalytic Psychology, 22*(3): 450–451.

Goretti, G. R. (2007). Projective identification: a theoretical investigation of the concept starting from 'Notes on some schizoid mechanisms'. *International Journal of Psychoanalysis, 88*(2): 387–405.

Goubet, N., Rochat, P., Marie-Leblond, S., & Poss, S. (2006). Learning from others in 9–18-month-old infants. *Infant and Child Development, 15*(2): 161–177.

Grady, J. S., Karraker, K., & Metzger, A. (2012). Shyness trajectories in slow-to-warm-up infants: relations with child sex and maternal parenting. *Journal of Applied Developmental Psychology, 33*(2): 91–101.

Green, E. J., Crenshaw, D. A., & Kolos, A. C. (2010). Counseling children with preverbal trauma. *International Journal of Play Therapy, 19*(2): 95–105.

Greenberg, J., & Mitchell, S. A. (1983). *Object Relations in Psychoanalytic Theory*. Cambridge, MA: Harvard University Press.

Grogan-Kaylor, A., & Otis, M. D. (2007). The predictors of parental use of corporal punishment. *Family Relations: Interdisciplinary Journal of Applied Family Studies, 56*(1): 80–91.

Grossmann, K. E., & Grossmann, K. (2005). Universality of human social attachment as an adaptive process, from www.brown.edu/Departments/Human_Development_Center/Roundtable/Grossman2.pdf

Grossmark, R. (2009). Review of Attachment, Play, and Authenticity: A Winnicott Primer. *Psychotherapy: Theory, Research, Practice, Training, 46*(4): 498–499.

Grotstein, J. (2009). *". . . But at the Same Time and on Another Level . . .": Psychoanalytic Theory and Technique in the Klein /Bionian Mode* (Volume 1). London: Karnac.

Gruhn, W. (2002). Phases and stages in early music learning. A longitudinal study on the development of young children's musical potential. *Music Education Research, 4*(1): 51–71.

Grünbaum, A. (1982a). Can psychoanalytic theory be cogently tested "on the couch"? Part I. *Psychoanalytic Contemporary Thought, 5*(2): 155–255.

Grünbaum, A. (1982b). Can psychoanalytic theory be cogently tested "on the couch"? Part II. *Psychoanalytic Contemporary Thought, 5*(3): 311–436.

Gunnar, M. R. (1998). Quality of early care and buffering of neuro-endocrine stress reactions: potential effects on the developing human brain. *Preventive Medicine: An International Journal Devoted to Practice and Theory, 27*(2): 208–211.

Gunnar, M. R., & Cheatham, C. L. (2003). Brain and behavior interfaces: stress and the developing brain. *Infant Mental Health Journal, 24*(3): 195–211.

Gunnar, M. R., Kryzer, E., Van Ryzin, M. J., & Phillips, D. A. (2011). The import of the cortisol rise in child care differs as a function of behavioral inhibition. *Developmental Psychology, 47*(3): 792–803.

Guntrip, H. (1962). The manic–depressive problem in the light of the schizoid process. *International Journal of Psychoanalysis, 43*: 98–112.

Guntrip, H. (1967). The concept of psychodynamic science. *International Journal of Psychoanalysis, 48*: 32–43.

Guntrip, H. (1973). Science, psychodynamic reality and autistic thinking. *Journal of the American Academy of Psychoanalytic and Dynamic Psychiatry, 1*(1): 3–22.

Guntrip, H. (1975). My experience of analysis with Fairbairn and Winnicott—(How complete a result does psycho-analytic therapy achieve?). *International Review of Psycho-Analysis, 2*: 145–156.

Halford, G. S. (1993). *Children's Understanding: The Development of Mental Models*. Mahwah, NJ: Lawrence Erlbaum.

Halford, G. S., & Andrews, G. (2011). Information-processing models of cognitive development. In: U. Goswami (Ed.), *The Wiley-Blackwell Handbook of Childhood Cognitive Development* (2nd edn, pp. 697–721). New York: Wiley-Blackwell.

Hall, G. S. (1920). Preface. In: S. Freud, *A General Introduction to Psychoanalysis* (p. v). New York: Boni & Liveright.

Harlow, H. F. (1958). The nature of love. *American Psychologist, 13*: 673–685.

Harlow, H. F. (1978). The nature of love. In: E. R. Hilgard (Ed.), *American Psychology in Historical Perspective* (pp. 459–481). Washington, DC: American Psychological Association.

Harlow, H. F., & Zimmerman, R. (1959). Affectional responses in the infant monkey. *Science, 130*: 421–432.

Harlow, H. F., & Zimmermann, R. R. (1996). Affectional responses in the infant monkey. In: L. D. Houck (Ed.), *Foundations of Animal Behavior:*

Classic Papers with Commentaries (pp. 376–387). Chicago, IL: University of Chicago Press.

Harter, S. (2003). The development of self-representations during childhood and adolescence. In: M. R. Leary (Ed.), *Handbook of Self and Identity* (pp. 610–642). New York: Guilford Press.

Harter, S. (2006a). The development of self-esteem. In: M. H. Kernis (Ed.), *Self-esteem Issues and Answers: A Sourcebook of Current Perspectives* (pp. 144–150). New York: Psychology Press.

Harter, S. (2006b). The self. In: N. Eisenberg (Ed.), *Handbook of Child Psychology: Social, Emotional, and Personality Development* (6th edn, pp. 505–570). Hoboken, NJ: John Wiley.

Harter, S. (Ed.). (2006c). *Developmental and Individual Difference: Perspectives on Self-Esteem*. Mahwah, NJ: Lawrence Erlbaum.

Hartley, S., Ojwang, P., Baguwemu, A., Ddamulira, M., & Chavuta, A. (2005). How do carers of disabled children cope? The Ugandan perspective. *Child: Care, Health and Development, 31*(2): 167–180.

Hartmann, H. (1939). *Ego Psychology and the Problem of Adaptation*. New York: International Universities Press.

Hartshorn, K., Rovee-Collier, C., Gerhardstein, P. C., Bhatt, R. S., Wondoloski, T. L., Klein, P., Gilch, J., & Campos-de-Carvalho, M. (1998). Ontogeny of long-term memory over the first year-and-a-half of life. *Developmental Psychobiology, 32*: 69–89.

Havighurst, R. J. (1972). *Developmental Tasks and Education*. Chicago, IL: University of Chicago Press.

Hay, D. F. (2005). The beginnings of aggression in infancy. In: R. E. Tremblay (Ed.), *Developmental Origins of Aggression* (pp. 107–132). New York: Guilford Press.

Hayne, H. (2004). Infant memory development: implications for childhood amnesia. *Developmental Review, 24*(1): 33–73.

Hayne, H., Boniface, J., & Barr, R. (2000). The development of declarative memory in human infants: age-related changes in deferred imitation. *Behavioral Neuroscience, 114*(1): 77–83.

Hayne, H., Rovee-Collier, C. K., & Borza, M. A. (1991). Infant memory for place information. *Memory and Cognition, 19*: 378–386.

Hayslip, B., Neumann, C. S., Louden, L., & Chapman, B. (2006). Developmental stage theories. In: J. C. Thomas (Ed.), *Comprehensive Handbook of Personality and Psychopathology, Personality and Everyday Functioning* (pp. 115–141). Hoboken, NJ: John Wiley & Sons.

Hayward, E. O., & Homer, B. D. (2009). Review of infants' sense of people: precursors to a theory of mind. *Infant and Child Development, 18*(4): 370–372.

Heidegger, M. (1962). *Being and Time*, J. Macquarrie & E. Robinson (Trans.). London: SCM Press.

Heimann, P. (1952). Preliminary notes on some defence mechanisms in paranoid states. *International Journal of Psychoanalysis, 33*: 208–213.

Heinrichs, M., Baumgartner, T., Kirschbaum, C., & Ehlert, U. (2003). Social support and oxytocin interact to suppress cortisol and subjective responses to psychosocial stress. *Biological Psychiatry, 54*(12): 1389–1398.

Heinrichs, M., von Dawans, B., & Domes, G. (2009). Oxytocin, vasopressin, and human social behavior. *Frontiers in Neuroendocrinology, 30*(4): 548–557.

Heisenberg, W. (1958). *The Physicist's Conception of Nature.* New York: Harcourt, Brace.

Herba, C. M., Roza, S. J., Govaert, P., van Rossum, J., Hofman, A., Jaddoe, V., & Tiemeier, H. (2010). Infant brain development and vulnerability to later internalizing difficulties: the Generation R study. *Journal of the American Academy of Child & Adolescent Psychiatry, 49*(10): 1053–1063.

Herbert, J., & Hayne, H. (2000). Memory retrieval by 18–30-month-olds: age-related changes in representational flexibility. *Developmental Psychology, 36*(4): 473–484.

Hernandez-Reif, M., Field, T., & Diego, M. (2004). Differential sucking by neonates of depressed versus non-depressed mothers. *Infant Behavior and Development, 27*: 465–476.

Hernandez-Reif, M., Field, T., Diego, M., & Largie, S. (2002). Depressed mothers' newborns show inferior face discrimination. *Infant Mental Health Journal, 23*: 643–653.

Hernandez-Reif, M., Field, T., Diego, M., & Ruddock, M. (2006). Greater arousal and less attentiveness to face/voice stimuli by neonates of depressed mothers on the Brazelton Neonatal Behavioral Assessment Scale. *Infant Behavior & Development, 29*(4): 594–598.

Herold, K. H., & Akhtar, N. (2008). Imitative learning from a third-party interaction: relations with self-recognition and perspective taking. *Journal of Experimental Child Psychology, 101*(2): 114–123.

Hesslow, G. (2012). The current status of the simulation theory of cognition. *Brain Research, 1428*: 71–79.

Hildreth, K., & Rovee-Collier, C. (2002). Forgetting functions of reactivated memories over the first year of life. *Developmental Psychobiology, 41*(3): 277–288.

Hines, M. (2011). Gender development and the human brain. *Annual Review of Neuroscience, 34*: 69–88.

Hinshelwood, R. D. (1991). *A Dictionary of Kleinian Thought*. University of California: Jason Aronson.

Hoffer, W. (1952). The mutual influences in the development of ego and id earliest stages. *Psychoanalytic Study of the Child*, 7: 31–41.

Hoffman, I. Z. (2007). Reply to Jon Mills (2006): an open letter to the members of Division 39. *Psychoanalytic Psychology*, 24(2): 401–405.

Hoffman, L. W. (1981). *Foundations of Family Therapy: A Conceptual Framework for Systems Change*. New York: Basic Books.

Holmes, J. (1996). Bowlby, Fairbairn, and Sutherland: the Scottish connection in psychotherapy. *Free Associations*, 6(3): 351–378.

Holmes, J. (2011). Attachment in the consulting room: towards a theory of therapeutic change. *European Journal of Psychotherapy and Counselling*, 13(2): 97–114.

Hopkins, L. B. (2011). Cocreated idealization in the Winnicott/Khan analysis: commentary on paper by Joyce Slochower. *Psychoanalytic Dialogues*, 21(1): 28–32.

Howe, M. L. (2000). Problems in the measurement of long-term retention and its development. In: *The Fate of Early Memories: Developmental Science and the Retention of Childhood Experiences* (pp. 119–132): Washington, DC: American Psychological Association.

Hrdy, S. B. (1999). *Mother Nature: A History of Mothers, Infants, and Natural Selection*. New York: Ballantine Books.

Hsu, V. C., & Rovee-Collier, C. (2006). Memory reactivation in the second year of life. *Infant Behavior & Development*, 29(1): 91–107.

Huesmann, L., Eron, L. D., & Dubow, E. F. (2002). Childhood predictors of adult criminality: are all risk factors reflected in childhood aggressiveness? *Criminal Behaviour and Mental Health*, 12(3): 185–208.

Hui, C. M., Fok, H. K., & Bond, M. H. (2009). Who feels more ambivalence? Linking dialectical thinking to mixed emotions. *Personality and Individual Differences*, 46(4): 493–498.

Hunt, D. (1970). *Parents and Children in History: The Psychology of Family Life in Early Modern France*. New York: Basic Books.

Iacoboni, M. (2007). Face to face: the neural basis of social mirroring and empathy. *Psychiatric Annals*, 37(4): 236–241.

Iacoboni, M. (2009). Imitation, empathy, and mirror neurons. *Annual Review of Psychology*, 60: 653–670.

Iacoboni, M., & Dapretto, M. (2006). The mirror neuron system and the consequences of its dysfunction. *Nature Reviews Neuroscience*, 7(12): 942–951.

Insel, T. R. (2003). Is social attachment an addictive disorder? *Physiology & Behavior*, 79(3): 351–357.

Isaacs, S. (1948). The nature and function of phantasy. *International Journal of Psychoanalysis, 29*: 73–97.

Izard, V., Dehaene-Lambertz, G., & Dehaene, S. (2008). Distinct cerebral pathways for object identity and number in human infants. *Plos Biology, 6*(2): e11.

Jackson, P. L., Meltzoff, A. N., & Decety, J. (2005). How do we perceive the pain of others? A window into the neural processes involved in empathy. *NeuroImage, 24*: 771–779.

Jacobson, E. (1964). *The Self and the Object World*. New York: International Universities Press.

Jacques, S., & Marcovitch, S. (2010). Development of executive function across the life span. In: W. F. Overton (Ed.), *The Handbook of Life-Span Development: Cognition, Biology, and Methods* (pp. 431–466). Hoboken, NJ: John Wiley & Sons.

Jaenisch, R., & Bird, A. (2003). Epigenetic regulation of gene expression: how the genome integrates intrinsic and environmental signals. *Nature Genetics, 33*: 245–254.

Jahromi, L. B., Putnam, S. P., & Stifter, C. A. (2004). Maternal regulation of infant reactivity from 2 to 6 months. *Developmental Psychology, 40*(4): 477–487.

James, W. (1884). What is an emotion? *Mind, IX*: 188–206.

James, W. (1981)[1890]. *The Principles of Psychology*. Cambridge, MA: Harvard University Press.

Johnson, M. H. (2010). Understanding the social world: a developmental neuroscience approach. In: *Child Development at the Intersection of Emotion and Cognition* (pp. 153–174): Washington, DC: American Psychological Association.

Johnson, M. H., & Gilmore, R. O. (2000). Infancy: biological processes. In: *Encyclopedia of Psychology, Vol. 4* (pp. 263–268).Washington, DC: American Psychological Association.

Jones, N. A., Field, T., & Almeida, A. (2009). Right frontal EEG asymmetry and behavioral inhibition in infants of depressed mothers. *Infant Behavior & Development, 32*(3): 298–304.

Jones, R. A. (2003). Between the analytical and the critical: implications for theorizing the self. *Journal of Analytic Psychology, 48*(3): 355–370.

Jonsson, C.-O., & Clinton, D. (2006). What do mothers attune to during interactions with their infants? *Infant and Child Development, 15*(4): 387–402.

Juri, L. J. (Ed.). (2003). *Revisiting Freud in the Light of Attachment Theory: Little Hans' Father – Oedipal Rival or Attachment Figure?* London: Whurr.

Jurist, E. L. (2005). Mentalized affectivity. *Psychoanalytic Psychology*, 22(3): 426–444.

Jurist, E. L. (2010). Mentalizing minds. *Psychoanalytic Inquiry*, 30(4): 289–300.

Kagan, J. (2004). Developmental perspectives. In: L. J. Haas (Ed.), *Handbook of Primary Care Psychology* (pp. 95–103). New York: Oxford University Press.

Kagan, J., & Snidman, N. (2004). *The Long Shadow of Temperament.* Cambridge: Belknap Press/Harvard University Press.

Kagan, J., Snidman, N., Kahn, V., & Towsley, S. (2007). The preservation of two infant temperaments into adolescence: II. The longitudinal study. *Monographs of the Society for Research in Child Development*, 72(2): 10–18.

Kahane, C. (1992). Freud's sublimation: disgust, desire and the female body. *American Imago*, 49(4): 411–425.

Kaler, S. R., & Freeman, B. J. (1994). Analysis of environmental deprivation: cognitive and social development in Romanian orphans. *Journal of Child Psychology and Psychiatry*, 35(4): 769–781.

Katz, J. (1963). On primary gain and secondary gain. *Psychoanalytic Study of the Child*, 18: 9–50.

Keller, H., Yovsi, R. D., & Voelker, S. (2002). The role of motor stimulation in parental ethnotheories: the case of Cameroonian NSO and German women. *Journal of Cross-Cultural Psychology*, 33(4): 398–414.

Kellogg, N. D., Committee on Child Abuse & Neglect. (2009). Clinical report—the evaluation of sexual behaviours in children. *Pediatrics*, 124(3): 992–998.

Kenny, D. T. (2000). Psychological foundations of stress and coping: a developmental perspective. In: D. T. Kenny, J. G. Carlson, F. J. McGuigan, & J. L. Sheppard (Eds.), *Stress and Health: Research and Clinical Applications* (pp. 73–104). Ryde, NSW: Gordon Breach Science/ Harwood Academic.

Kenny, D. T. (2001). Cognitive-developmental theory. In: C. Jones (Ed.), *Readers' Guide to the Social Sciences* (Vol. 1, pp. 230–231). London: Fitzroy Dearborn.

Kernberg, O. F. (1976). *Object-relations Theory and Clinical Psychoanalysis.* New York: Jason Aronson.

Kernberg, O. F. (1988). Psychic structure and structural change: an ego psychology-object relations theory viewpoint. *Journal of the American Psychoanalytic Association*, 36(Suppl): 315–337.

Kernberg, O. F. (1994). Validation in the clinical process. *International Journal of Psychoanalysis*, 75: 1193–1200.

Kesselring, T., & Müller, U. (2011). The concept of egocentrism in the context of Piaget's theory. *New Ideas in Psychology, 29*(3): 327–345.

Keysers, C., & Gazzola, V. (2006). Towards a unifying neural theory of social cognition. *Progress in Brain Research, 156*: 379–401.

Khaleque, A. (2003). Attachment and lifespan development: a review of the adult attachment literature. *Psychological Studies, 48*(1): 28–35.

Khan, M. R. (1960). Regression and integration in the analytic setting— a clinical essay on the transference and counter-transference aspects of these phenomena. *International Journal of Psychoanalysis, 41*: 130–146.

Khan, M. R. (1963). The concept of cumulative trauma. *Psychoanalytic Study of the Child, 18*: 286–306.

Khan, M. R. (1971). Infantile neurosis as a false-self organization. *Psychoanalytic Quarterly, 40*: 245–263.

Khan, M. R. (1974). *The Privacy of the Self*. London: Hogarth Press.

Khan, M. R. (1981). From masochism to psychic pain. *Contemporary Psychoanalysis, 17*: 413–421.

Kim-Cohen, J., Caspi, A., Taylor, A., Williams, B., Newcombe, R., Craig, I. W., & Moffitt, T. E. (2006). MAOA, maltreatment, and gene–environment interaction predicting children's mental health: new evidence and a meta-analysis. *Molecular Psychiatry, 11*: 903–913.

King, P., & Steiner, R. (1991). *The Freud–Klein Controversies 1941–45* (Vol. 11). London: Tavistock/Routledge.

Kjellmer, I., & Winberg, J. (1994). The neurobiology of infant–parent interaction in the newborn: an introduction. *International Forum on Psychoanalysis, 3*(3): 195–196.

Klauber, J. (1976). Some little-described elements of the psychoanalytical relationship and their therapeutic implications. *International Review of Psycho-Analysis, 3*: 283–290.

Klauber, J. (1977). Analyses that cannot be terminated. *International Journal of Psychoanalysis, 58*: 473–477.

Klauber, J. (1980). Formulating interpretations in clinical psychoanalysis. *International Journal of Psychoanalysis, 61*: 195–201.

Kleeman, A. (2011). Collective aesthetics and the mere exposure effect. In: M. Callies (Ed.), *Bi-Directionality in the Cognitive Sciences: Avenues, Challenges, and Limitations* (pp. 159–170). Amsterdam: John Benjamins.

Klein, G. S. (1959). Consciousness in psychoanalytic theory: some implications for current research in perception. *Journal of the American Psychoanalytic Association, 7*: 5–34.

Klein, M. (1927). The psychological principles of infant analysis. *International Journal of Psychoanalysis, 8*: 25–37.

Klein, M. (1928). Early stages of the Oedipus conflict. *International Journal of Psychoanalysis, 9*: 167–180.

Klein, M. (1929). Personification in the play of children. *International Journal of Psychoanalysis, 10*: 193–204.

Klein, M. (1930). The importance of symbol-formation in the development of the ego. *International Journal of Psychoanalysis, 11*: 24–39.

Klein, M. (1932). *The Psycho-Analysis of Children*. International Psycho-Analytical Library, 22. London: Hogarth Press.

Klein, M. (1935). A contribution to the psychogenesis of manic–depressive states. *International Journal of Psychoanalysis, 16*: 145–174.

Klein, M. (1940). Mourning and its relation to manic–depressive states. *International Journal of Psychoanalysis, 21*: 125–153.

Klein, M. (1945). The Oedipus complex in the light of early anxieties. *International Journal of Psychoanalysis, 26*: 11–33.

Klein, M. (1946). Notes on some schizoid mechanisms. *International Journal of Psychoanalysis, 27*: 99–110.

Klein, M. (1948a). A contribution to the theory of anxiety and guilt. *International Journal of Psychoanalysis, 29*: 114–123.

Klein, M. (1948b). *The Importance of Symbol-Formation in the Development of the Ego: Contributions to Psycho-Analysis*. London: Hogarth Press.

Klein, M. (1952a). On observing the behaviour of young infants. In: *Envy and Gratitude and Other Works 1946–1963*. The International Psycho-Analytical Library, 104. London: Hogarth Press and the Institute of Psycho-Analysis, 1975.

Klein, M. (1952b). The origins of transference. *International Journal of Psychoanalysis, 33*: 433–438.

Klein, M. (1957). Le tendenze criminali nei bambini normali. *Rivista Psicoanalisi, 3*(1): 3–18.

Klein, M. (1975). *Envy and Gratitude and Other Works 1946–1963*. International Psycho-Analytic Library, 104. London: Hogarth Press and the Institute of Psycho-Analysis.

Klein, M. (1989). The Oedipus complex in the light of early anxieties (1945). In: R. Britton, M. Feldman, & E. O'Shaugnessy (Eds.), *The Oedipus Complex Today: Clinical Implications* (pp. 11–82): London: Karnac.

Klein, M., Heimann, P., Isaacs, S., & Riviere, J. (1952). *Developments in Psychoanalysis*. London: Hogarth Press and the Institute of Psycho-analysis.

Klin, A., & Jones, W. (2007). Embodied psychoanalysis? Or, on the confluence of psychodynamic theory and developmental science. In: L. C.

Mayes (Ed.), *Developmental Science and Psychoanalysis: Integration and Innovation*. London: Karnac.

Kohon, G. (1986). *The British School of Psychoanalysis: The Independent Tradition*. London: Free Association Books.

Kohut, H. (1971). *The Analysis of Self*. New York: International Universities Press.

Kohut, H. (1977). *The Restoration of the Self*. New York: International Universities Press.

Kohut, H. (1984). *How Does Analysis Cure?* Chicago, IL: University of Chicago Press.

Kohut, H., & Wolf, E. S. (1978). The disorders of the self and their treatment: an outline. *International Journal of Psychoanalysis, 59*: 413–425.

Kolb, B., & Whishaw, I. Q. (1998). Brain plasticity and behavior. *Annual Review of Psychology, 49*: 43–64.

Konner, M. (2010). *The Evolution of Childhood: Relationships, Emotion, Mind*. Cambridge, MA: Belknap Press/Harvard University Press.

Kouider, S., & Dehaene, S. (2007). Levels of processing during non-conscious perception: a critical review of visual masking. *Philosophical Transactions of the Royal Society B, 362*: 857–875.

Kovács, A. M., & Mehler, J. (2009). Cognitive gains in 7-month-old bilingual infants. *Proceedings of the National Academy of Sciences, 106*(16): 6556–6560.

Krettenauer, T. (2011). The issue of highest stages in structural-developmental theories. In: A. H. Pfaffenberger (Ed.), *The Postconventional Personality: Assessing, Researching, and Theorizing Higher Development* (pp. 75–86). Albany, NY: State University of New York Press.

Kris, A. O. (1987). Fixation and regression in relation to convergent and divergent conflicts. *Bulletin of the Anna Freud Centre, 10*(2): 99–117.

Kris, E. (1956a). The recovery of childhood memories in psychoanalysis. *Psychoanalytic Study of the Child, 11*: 54–88.

Kris, E. (1956b). The personal myth—a problem in psychoanalytic technique. *Journal of the American Psychoanalytic Association, 4*: 653–681.

Kuhn, D. (2008). Formal operations from a twenty-first century perspective. *Human Development, 51*(1): 48–55.

Kunde, W., Kiesel, A., & Hoffmann, J. (2003). Conscious control over the content of unconscious cognition. *Cognition, 97*: 223–242.

Laakso, A. (2011). Embodiment and development in cognitive science. *Cognition, Brain, Behavior: An Interdisciplinary Journal, 15*(4): 409–425.

Labouvie-Vief, G., Chiodo, L. M., Goguen, L. A., Diehl, M., & Orwoll, L. (1995). Representations of self across the life span. *Psychology of Aging, 10*(3): 404–415.

Labouvie-Vief, G., Gruhn, D., & Studer, J. (2010). Dynamic integration of emotion and cognition: equilibrium regulation in development and aging. In: M. E. Lamb (Ed.), *The Handbook of Life-Span Development, Social and Emotional Development* (Vol. 2, pp. 79–115). Hoboken, NJ: John Wiley & Sons.

Lachmann, F. (2010). Addendum; afterthoughts on Little Hans and the universality of the Oedipus complex. *Psychoanalytic Inquiry, 30*(6): 557–562.

Lachmann, F. M., & Beebe, B. (1992). Reformulations of early development and transference: implications for psychic structure formation. In: F. M. Lachmann & B. Beebe (Eds.), *Interface of Psychoanalysis and Psychology* (pp. 133–153). Washington, DC: American Psychological Association.

Lachmann, F. M., & Beebe, B. (1993). Interpretation in a developmental perspective. *Progress in Self Psychology, 9*: 45–52.

Lacy, T. J., & Hughes, J. D. (2006). A systems approach to behavioral neurobiology: integrating psychodynamics and neuroscience in a psychiatric curriculum. *Journal of the Americal Academy of Psychoanalysis and Dynamic Psychiatry, 34*(1): 43–74.

Laranjo, J., Bernier, A., Meins, E., & Carlson, S. M. (2010). Early manifestations of children's theory of mind: the roles of maternal mind-mindedness and infant security of attachment. *Infancy, 15*(3): 300–323.

Latimer, M., Jackson, P., Johnston, C., & Vine, J. (2011). Examining nurse empathy for infant procedural pain: testing a new video measure. *Pain Research & Management, 16*(4): 228–233.

Laurent, H. K., Ablow, J. C., & Measelle, J. (2012). Taking stress response out of the box: stability, discontinuity, and temperament effects on HPA and SNS across social stressors in mother–infant dyads. *Developmental Psychology, 48*(1): 35–45.

Lazarus, R. S., & McCleary, R. A. (1951). Autonomic discrimination without awareness: a study of subception. *Psychological Review, 58*(2): 113–122.

Lecours, S. (2007). Supportive interventions and nonsymbolic mental functioning. *International Journal of Psychoanalysis, 88*(4): 895–915.

LeDoux, J. (1996). *The Emotional Brain: The Mysterious Underpinnings of Emotional Life*. New York: Simon and Shuster.

LeDoux, J. (1998). *The Emotional Brain: The Mysterious Underpinnings of Emotional Life*. London: Weidenfeld & Nicolson.

Leerkes, E. M. (2011). Maternal sensitivity during distressing tasks: a unique predictor of attachment security. *Infant Behavior & Development, 34*(3): 443–446.

Leider, R. (1996). The psychology of the self. In: E. Nersessian & R. Kopff (Eds.), *Textbook of Psychoanalysis* (pp. 127–164). Washington, DC: American Psychiatric Press.

Lenzi, D., Trentini, C., Pantano, P., Macaluso, E., Iacoboni, M., Lenzi, G., & Ammaniti, M. (2009). Neural basis of maternal communication and emotional expression processing during infant preverbal stage. *Cerebral Cortex, 19*(5): 1124–1133.

Leon, I. G. (1984). Psychoanalysis, Piaget and attachment: the construction of the human object in the first year of life. *International Journal of Psychoanalysis, 11*(3): 255–278.

Lesburgueres, E., Gobbo, O. L., Alaux-Cantin, S., Hambucken, A., Trifilieff, P., & Bontempi, B. (2011). Early tagging of cortical networks is required for the formation of enduring associative memory. *Science, 331*(6019): 924–928.

Leslie, A. M., Friedman, O., & German, T. P. (2004). Core mechanisms in 'theory of mind'. *Trends in Cognitive Sciences, 8*(12): 528–533.

Letourneau, N., Watson, B., Duffett-Leger, L., Hegadoren, K., & Tryphonopoulos, P. (2011). Cortisol patterns of depressed mothers and their infants are related to maternal–infant interactive behaviours. *Journal of Reproductive and Infant Psychology, 29*(5): 439–459.

Levinson, D. J. (1978). *The Seasons of a Man's Life*. New York: Knopf.

Lewis, B. A., & Thompson, L. A. (1992). A study of developmental speech and language disorders in twins. *Journal of Speech & Hearing Research, 35*(5): 1086–1094.

Lewis, M., & Carmody, D. P. (2008). Self-representation and brain development. *Developmental Psychology, 44*(5): 1329–1334.

Lewis, M. D., & Todd, R. M. (2007). The self-regulating brain: cortical–subcortical feedback and the development of intelligent action. *Cognitive Development, 22*(4): 406–430.

Lewis, M. D., Koroshegyi, C., Douglas, L., & Kampe, K. (1997). Age-specific associations between emotional responses to separation and cognitive performance in infancy. *Developmental Psychology, 33*(1): 32–42.

Lichtenstein, H. (1970). Changing implications of the concept of psychosexual development—an inquiry concerning the validity of classical psychoanalytic assumptions concerning sexuality. *Journal of the American Psychoanalytic Association, 18*: 300–318.

Linville, D., & Lyness, A. P. (2007). Twenty American families' stories of adaptation: adoption of children from Russian and Romanian institutions. *Journal of Marital and Family Therapy, 33*(1): 77–93.

Liotti, G. (1999). Understanding the dissociative processes: the contribution of attachment theory. *Psychoanalytic Inquiry, 19*(5): 757–783.

Lipina, S. J., & Colombo, J. A. (2009). Effects of poverty on development II: Cognitive neuroscience perspectives. In: *Poverty and Brain Development During Childhood: An Approach from Cognitive Psychology and Neuroscience.* (pp. 75–91). Washington, DC: American Psychological Association.

Lobb, M. S. (2009). Sexuality and love in a psychotherapeutic setting: from the death of Oedipus to the emergence of the situational field—a Gestalt therapy development. *International Journal of Psychotherapy, 13*(1): 5–16.

Lorber, M. F., & Egeland, B. (2009). Infancy, parenting and externalizing psychopathology from childhood through adulthood: developmental trends. *Developmental Psychology, 45*(4): 909–912.

Lorber, M. F., & Egeland, B. (2011). Parenting and infant difficulty: testing a mutual exacerbation hypothesis to predict early onset conduct problems. *Child Development, 82*(6): 2006–2020.

Lorenz, K. (1965). *Evolution and Modification of Behavior.* Chicago, IL: University of Chicago Press.

Lorenz, K. (1981). *The Foundations of Ethology.* New York: Springer.

Lupien, S. J., Fiocco, A., Wan, N., Maheu, F., Lord, C., Schramek, T., & Tu, M. T. (2004). Stress hormones and human memory function across the lifespan. *Psychoneuroendocrinology, 30*(3): 225–242.

Lupien, S. J., Parent, S., Evans, A. C., Tremblay, R. E., Zelazo, P. D., Corbo, V., & Seguin, J. R. (2011). Larger amygdala but no change in hippocampal volume in 10-year-old children exposed to maternal depressive symptomatology since birth. *Proceedings of the National Academy of Sciences of the United States of America, 108*(34): 14324–14329.

Luria, A. R. (1964). Factors and forms of aphasia. In: A. V. S. D. Reuck & M. O'Connor (Eds.), *Disorders of Language* (pp. 143–161). Boston, MA: Little, Brown.

Lyons-Ruth, K. (1999). The two-person unconscious: intersubjective dialogue, enactive relational representation, and the emergence of new forms of relational organization. *Psychoanalytic Inquiry, 19*(4): 576–617.

MacFarlane, J. (1975). Olfaction in the development of social preference in the human neonate. In: H. Hofer (Ed.), *Parent–Infant Interaction* (pp. 103–112). Amsterdam: Elsevier.

Mahler, M. S. (1963). Thoughts about development and individuation. *Psychoanalytic Study of the Child, 18*: 307–324.

Mahler, M. S. (1967). On human symbiosis and the vicissitudes of individu ation. *Journal of the American Psychoanalytic Association, 15*: 740–763.

Mahler, M. S. (1972). On the first three phases of the separation–individuation process. *International Journal of Psychoanalysis, 53*: 333–338.

Mahler, M. S., Pine, F., & Bergman, A. (1975). *The Psychological Birth of the Human Infant*. New York: Basic Books.

Mahon, E. J. (2001). Anna Freud and the evolution of psychoanalytic technique. *Psychoanalytic Study of the Child, 56*: 76–95.

Main, M. (1995). Attachment: overview and implications for clinical work. In: S. Goldberg, R. Muir & J. Kerr (Eds.), *Attachment Theory: Social, Developmental and Clinical Perspectives* (pp. 404–474). Hillsdale, NJ: Analytic Press.

Main, M., Hesse, E., & Kaplan, N. (2005). Predictability of attachment behaviour and representational processes. In: K. E. Grossman, K. Grossman, & E. Waters (Eds.), *Attachment from Infancy to Adulthood: Lessons from Longitudinal Studies* (pp. 245–304). New York: Guildford Press.

Main, M., Kaplan, N., & Cassidy, J. (1985). Security in infancy, childhood, and adulthood: a move to the level of representation. *Monographs of the Society for Research in Child Development, 50*(1–2): 66–104.

Malan, D. H. (1979). *Individual Psychotherapy and the Science of Psychodynamics* (2nd edn). Oxford: Butterworth-Heinemann.

Malan, D. H., & Osimo, F. (1992). *Psychodynamics, Training, and Outcome in Brief Psychotherapy*. Oxford: Butterworth-Heinemann.

Maldonado, J. L. (2011). The dynamic unconscious in the analytic relationship. *International Journal of Psychoanalysis, 92*(2): 280–283.

Mallants, C., & Casteels, K. (2008). Practical approach to childhood masturbation—a review. *European Journal of Pediatrics, 167*(10): 1111–1117.

Mancia, M. (2006). Implicit memory and early unrepressed unconscious: their role in the therapeutic process (how the neurosciences can contribute to psychoanalysis). *International Journal of Psychoanalysis, 87*(1): 83–103.

Marazziti, D., Bani, A., Casamassima, F., Catena, M., Consoli, G., Gesi, C., Iovieno, N., Massei, G. J., Muti, M., Ravani, L., Romano, A., Roncaglia, I., & Scarpellini, P. (2006). Oxytocin: an old hormone for new avenues. *Clinical Neuropsychiatry: Journal of Treatment Evaluation, 3*(5): 302–321.

Marazziti, D., Del Debbio, A., Roncaglia, I., Bianchi, C., Piccinni, A., & Dell'Osso, L. (2008). Neurotrophins and attachment. *Clinical Neuropsychiatry: Journal of Treatment Evaluation, 5*(2): 100–106.

Margulies, A. (2002). Review essay on Judith L. Mitrani's "Ordinary People and Extra-ordinary Protections: A post-Kleinian Approach to the Treatment of Primitive Mental States". *Journal of the American Psychoanalytic Association, 50*: 1042–1051.

Marrone, M., & Cortina, M. (2003). Introduction: reclaiming Bowlby's contribution to psychoanalysis. In: M. Cortina & M. Marrone (Eds.), *Attachment Theory and the Psychoanalytic Process* (pp. 1–24). London: Whurr.

Martel, J. G. (1974). *Smashed Potatoes: A Kid's-Eye View of the Kitchen.* Boston, MA: Houghton Mifflin.

Martin, G., & Pear, J. (2003). *Behaviour Modification: What It Is and How to Do It* (7th edn). Englewood Cliffs, NJ: Prentice Hall.

Martin, J., & Sokol, B. (2011). Generalized others and imaginary audiences: a neo-Meadian approach to adolescent egocentrism. *New Ideas in Psychology, 29*(3): 364–375.

Martorell, G. A., & Bugental, D. B. (2006). Maternal variations in stress reactivity: implications for harsh parenting practices with very young children. *Journal of Family Psychology, 20*(4): 641–647.

Marvin, R. S., & Britner, P. A. (2008). Normative development: the ontogeny of attachment. In: J. Cassidy & P. R. Shaver (Eds.), *Handbook of Attachment: Theory, Research and Clinical Applications* (pp. 269–294). New York: Guildford Press.

Masur, C. (2009). Parent–infant psychotherapy. *Journal of the American Psychoanalytic Association, 57*(2): 467–473.

Mayes, L. C. (2000). A developmental perspective on the regulation of arousal states. *Seminars in Perinatology, 24*(4): 267–279.

Mayes, L. C. (2006). Arousal regulation, emotional flexibility, medial amygdala function, and the impact of early experience: comments on the paper of Lewis et al. *Annals of the New York Academy of Sciences, 1094*: 178–192.

McClelland, M. M., & Tominey, S. L. (2011). Introduction to the special issue on self-regulation in early childhood. *Early Education and Development, 22*(3): 355–359.

McDougall, J. (1986). *Theater of the Mind.* New York: Basic Books.

McEwen, B. S. (2003). Early life influences on life-long patterns of behavior and health. *Mental Retardation and Developmental Disabilities Research Reviews, 9*(3): 149–154.

McGinnies, I. (1949). Emotionality and perceptual defense. *Psychological Review, 56*: 244–251.

McGregor, J. C. (2006). A British Independent analyst at work. *Journal of the American Psychoanalytic Association, 54*(2): 633–641.

McLafferty, C. L. (2006). Examining unproven assumptions of Galton's nature–nurture paradigm. *American Psychologist, 61*(2): 177–178.

McMullen, C. A., Andrade, F. H., & Stahl, J. S. (2004). Functional and genomic changes in the mouse ocular motor system in response to light deprivation from birth. *Journal of Neuroscience*, (1): 61–69.

Meares, R. (2000). *Intimacy and Alienation: Memory, Trauma and Personal Being*. New York: Brunner-Routledge.

Mehler, J. A., & Argentieri, S. (1989). Hope and hopelessness: a technical problem? *International Journal of Psychoanalysis, 70*: 295–304.

Meissner, W. W. (2008a). The role of language in the development of the self. II: Thoughts and words. *Psychoanalytic Psychology, 25*(2): 220–241.

Meissner, W. W. (2008b). The role of language in the development of the self. III: The significance of pronouns. *Psychoanalytic Psychology, 25*(2): 242–256.

Meltzoff, A. N. (1995). What infant memory tells us about infantile amnesia: long-term recall and deferred imitation. *Journal of Experimental Child Psychology, 59*: 497–515.

Meltzoff, A. N. (2007a). 'Like me': a foundation for social cognition. *Developmental Science, 10*(1): 126–134.

Meltzoff, A. N. (2007b). The 'like me' framework for recognizing and becoming an intentional agent. *Acta Psychologica, 124*(1): 26–43.

Meltzoff, A. N., & Brooks, R. (2008). Self-experience as a mechanism for learning about others: a training study in social cognition. *Developmental Psychology, 44*(5): 1257–1265.

Meltzoff, A. N., & Moore, M. K. (1977). Imitation of facial and manual gestures by human neonates. *Science, 198*: 75–78.

Meltzoff, A. N., & Moore, M. K. (1994). Imitation, memory, and the representation of persons. *Infant Behavior & Development, 17*: 83–99.

Meltzoff, A. N., & Moore, M. K. (1997). Explaining facial imitation: a theoretical model. *Early Development & Parenting, 6*: 179–192.

Menninger, K. A., & Holtzman, P. S. (1973). *Theory of Psychoanalytic Technique* (2nd edn). New York: Basic Books.

Messinger, D., & Fogel, A. (2007). The interactive development of social smiling. In: R. Kail (Ed.), *Advances in Child Development and Behavior* (Vol. 35, pp. 327–366). San Diego, CA: Elsevier Academic Press.

Midgley, N. (2006). Re-reading "Little Hans": Freud's case study and the question of competing paradigms in psychoanalysis. *Journal of the American Psychoanalytic Association, 54*(2): 537–559.

Migone, P. (1994). The problem of "real" trauma and the future of psychoanalysis. *International Forum of Psychoanalysis, 3*(2): 89–95.

Mikulincer, M., & Shaver, P. R. (2011). Attachment, anger, and aggression. In: P. R. Shaver (Ed.), *Human Aggression and Violence: Causes,*

Manifestations, and Consequences (pp. 241–257). Washington, DC: American Psychological Association.

Miller, M., Gelfand, J., & Hinshaw, S. P. (2011). Attention-deficit/hyperactivity disorder. In: A. S. Davis (Ed.), *Handbook of Pediatric Neuropsychology* (pp. 565–579). New York: Springer.

Milton, J., Solodkina, A., Hluštík, P., & Smalla, S. L. (2007). The mind of expert motor performance is cool and focused. *NeuroImage, 35*(2): 804–813.

Milner, B., Squire, L. R., & Kandel, E. R. (1998). Cognitive neuroscience and the study of memory. *Neuron, 20*(3): 445–468.

Minagawa-Kawai, Y., Mori, K., Hebden, J. C., & Dupoux, E. (2008). Optical imaging of infants' neurocognitive development: recent advances and perspectives. *Developmental Neurobiology, 68*(6): 712–728.

Mitchell, J. (2004). The importance of sibling relationships in psychoanalysis. *International Journal of Psychoanalysis, 85*(2): 557–561.

Mitchell, S. A. (1993). *Hope and Dread in Pychoanalysis*. New York: Basic Books.

Mitchell, S. A. (1995). Commentary on "Contemporary structural psychoanalysis and relational psychoanalysis". *Psychoanalytic Psychology, 12*(4): 575–582.

Mitchell, S. A., & Black, M. J. (1995). *Freud and Beyond: A History of Modern Psychoanalytic Thought*. New York: Basic Books.

Mitrani, J. L. (1993). "Unmentalized" experience in the etiology and treatment of psychosomatic asthma. *Contemporary Psychoanalysis, 29*: 314–342.

Mitrani, J. L. (1995). Toward an understanding of unmentalized experience. *Psychoanalytic Quarterly, 64*: 68–112.

Moan, C. E., & Heath, R. G. (1972). Septal stimulation for the initiation of heterosexual behavior in a homosexual male. *Journal of Behavior Therapy and Experimental Psychiatry, 3*(1): 23–30.

Model, E. (1994). Parental pathology and its impact on contact. *Bulletin of the Anna Freud Centre, 17*(3): 224–228.

Mohacsy, I. (1976). Fusion and anxiety: children's drawings and Renaissance art. *Journal of the American Academy of Psychoanalysis and Dynamic Psychiatry, 4*(4): 501–514.

Mook, D. (2004). *Classic Experiments in Psychology*. Westport, CT: Greenwood Press.

Moore, B. E., & Fine, B. D. (1990a). *Psychoanalytic Terms and Concepts*. New Haven, CT: American Psychoanalytic Association and Yale University Press.

Moore, B. E., & Fine, B. (1990b). Development. In: B. E. Moore & B. Fine (Eds.), *Psychoanalytic Terms and Concepts* (pp. 55–57). New Haven, CT: Yale University Press: American Psychoanalytic Association.

Morgan, A. C. (1997). The application of infant research to psychoanalytic theory and therapy. *Psychoanalytic Psychology*, *14*(3): 315–336.

Morse, S. J. (1972). Structure and reconstruction: a critical comparison of Michael Balint and D. W. Winnicott. *International Journal of Psychoanalysis*, *53*(4): 487–500.

Moshman, D. (2011). *Adolescent Rationality and Development: Cognition, Morality, and Identity* (3rd edn). New York: Psychology Press.

Muller, R. T. (2009). Trauma and dismissing (avoidant) attachment: intervention strategies in individual psychotherapy. *Psychotherapy: Theory, Research, Practice, Training*, *46*(1): 68–81.

Müller, T. (2004). On psychotic transference and countertransference. *Psychoanalytic Quarterly*, *73*(2): 415–452.

Munakata, Y., Casey, B. J., & Diamond, A. l. (2004). Developmental cognitive neuroscience: progress and potential. *Trends in Cognitive Sciences*, *8*(3): 122–128.

Music, G. (2011). *Nurturing Natures: Attachment and Children's Emotional, Sociocultural and Brain Development*. New York: Psychology Press.

Nadel, L., & Zola-Morgan, S. (1984). Infantile amnesia: a neuro-biological perspective. In: M. Moscovitch (Ed.), *Advances in the Study of Communication and Affect: Infant Memory* (Vol. 9, pp. 145–172). New York: Plenum.

Nagera, H. (1964). Autoerotism, autoerotic activities, and ego development. *Psychoanalytic Study of the Child*, *19*: 240–255.

Nagy, E. (2008). Innate intersubjectivity: newborns' sensitivity to communication disturbance. *Developmental Psychology*, *44*(6): 1779–1784.

Najeeb, S. (2011). The complexities of non-verbal communication: different perspectives. Psychoanalytic seminar series, Sydney Institute of Psychoanalysis, Sydney.

Nasio, J.-D., Pettigrew, D., & Raffoul, F. (2010). *Oedipus: The Most Crucial Concept in Psychoanalysis*. Albany, NY: State University of New York Press.

Neborsky, R. J. (2006). Brain, mind and dyadic change processes. *Journal of Clinical Psychology*, *62*(5): 523–538.

Nelson, C. A. (1994). Neural bases of infant temperament. In: *Temperament: Individual Differences at the Interface of Biology and Behavior* (pp. 47–82): Washington, DC: American Psychological Association.

Neu, J. (2000). *A Tear Is An Intellectual Thing*. Oxford: Oxford University Press.

Newirth, J. (2003). Discussion of Eisold's "Profession of Psychoanalysis". *Contemporary Psychoanalysis*, *39*(4): 619–627.

Newman, K. M. (1996). Winnicott goes to the movies: the false self in ordinary people. *Psychoanalytic Quarterly*, *65*: 787–807.

Nicolopoulou, A., & Weintraub, J. (2009). Why operativity-in-context is not quite a sociocultural model. *Human Development, 52*(5): 320–328.

Oesterdiekhoff, G. W. (2007). The reciprocal causation of intelligence and culture: a commentary based on a Piagetian perspective. *European Journal of Personality, 21*(5): 742–743.

Ogden, T. H. (1989a). On the concept of an autistic-contiguous position. *International Journal of Psychoanalysis, 70*: 127–140.

Ogden, T. H. (1989b). *The Primitive Edge of Experience.* London: Jason Aronson.

Ogden, T. H. (1990). *On the Structure of Experience.* Northvale, NJ: Jason Aronson.

Ogden, T. H. (2002). A new reading of the origins of object-relations theory. *International Journal of Psychoanalysis, 83*(4): 767–782.

Ogden, T. H. (2004). On holding and containing, being and dreaming. *International Journal of Psychoanalysis, 85*(6): 1349–1364.

Ogden, T. H. (2007). *On Holding and Containing, Being and Dreaming.* London: Karnac.

Okada, G., Okamoto, Y., Kunisato, Y., Aoyama, S., Nishiyama, Y., Yoshimura, S., Onoda, K., Toki, S., Yamashita, H., & Yamawaki, S. (2011). The effect of negative and positive emotionality on associative memory: an fMRI study. *PLOS ONE, 6*(9). Online publication.

Orme, N. (2003). *Medieval Children.* London: Yale University Press.

Paley, J., & Alpert, J. (2003). Memory of infant trauma. *Psychoanalytic Psychology, 20*(2): 329–347.

Panhofer, H. (2011). Languaged and non-languaged ways of knowing in counselling and psychotherapy. *British Journal of Guidance & Counselling, 39*(5): 455–470.

Panzer, A. (2008). The neuroendocrinological sequelae of stress during brain development: the impact of child abuse and neglect. *African Journal of Psychiatry, 11*(1): 29–34.

Papousek, H. (1967a). *The Functions of Conditioning Stimulation in Human Neonates and Infants.* New York: Academic Press.

Papousek, H. (1967b). *Experimental Studies of Appetitional Behavior in Human Newborns and Infants.* New York: Wiley.

Papousek. H. (1969). *Stimulation in Early Infancy.* New York: Academic Press.

Papousek, H., Papousek, M., & Koester, L. S. (1986). Sharing emotionality and sharing knowledge: a microanalytic approach to parent–infant communication. In: C. Izard & P. Read (Eds.), *Measuring Emotions in Infants and Children* (Vol. 2, pp. 93–123). Cambridge: Cambridge University Press.

Pauli-Pott, U., & Beckmann, D. (2007). On the association of interparental conflict with developing behavioral inhibition and behavior problems in early childhood. *Journal of Family Psychology, 21*(3): 529–532.

Pauli-Pott, U., & Mertesacker, B. (2009). Affect expression in mother–infant interaction and subsequent attachment development. *Infant Behavior & Development, 32*(2): 208–215.

Pedersen, C. A. (2004). Biological aspects of social bonding and the roots of human violence. In: J. Devine (Ed.), *Youth Violence: Scientific Approaches to Prevention* (pp. 106–127). New York: New York Academy of Sciences.

Perez-Edgar, K., McDermott, J. N., Korelitz, K., Degnan, K. A., Curby, T. W., Pine, D. S., & Fox, N. A. (2010). Patterns of sustained attention in infancy shape the developmental trajectory of social behavior from toddlerhood through adolescence. *Developmental Psychology, 46*(6): 1723–1730.

Perris, E. E., Myers, N. A., & Clifton, R. K. (1990). Long-term memory for a single infancy experience. *Child Development, 61*: 1796–1807.

Persson-Blennow, I., & McNeil, T. F. (1988). Frequencies and stability of temperament types in childhood. *Journal of the American Academy of Child & Adolescent Psychiatry, 27*(5): 619–622.

Pfister, O. (1913). *Die Psycho-Analystische Methode*. Leipzig: Klinkhardt.

Phelps, E. A. (2006). Emotion and cognition: insights from studies of the human amygdala. *Annual Review of Psychology, 57*: 27–53.

Piaget, J. (1927). The child's first year. *British Journal of Psychology, 18*: 97–120.

Piaget, J. (1936). *The Origins of Intelligence in Children*. New York: W. W. Norton (1963).

Piaget, J. (1947). *The Psychology of Intelligence*. Oxford: Armand Colin.

Piaget, J. (1973). The affective unconscious and the cognitive unconscious. *Journal of the American Psychoanalytic Association, 21*(2): 249–261.

Piaget, J. (2003a). The language and thought of the child. In: M. P. Munger (Ed.), *The History of Psychology: Fundamental Questions* (pp. 368–388). New York: Oxford University Press.

Piaget, J. (2003b). Part I: Cognitive development in children: Piaget: Development and learning. *Journal of Research in Science Teaching, 40*(Suppl): S8–S18.

Piaget, J. (2008). Intellectual evolution from adolescence to adulthood. *Human Development, 51*(1): 40–47.

Piaget, J., & Cook, M. (1954a). The development of object concept. In: *The Construction of Reality in the Child* (pp. 3–96). New York: Basic Books.

Piaget, J., & Cook, M. (1954b). The temporal field. In: *The Construction of Reality in the Child* (pp. 320–349). New York: Basic Books.

Piaget, J., & Cook, M. (1954c). The spatial field and the elaboration of groups of displacements In: *The Construction of Reality in the Child* (pp. 97–218). New York: Basic Books.

Piaget, J., & Cook, M. (1954d). The development of causality. In: *The Construction of Reality in the Child* (pp. 219–319). New York: Basic Books.

Piaget, J., & Cook, M. (1954e). *The Construction of Reality in the Child*. New York: Basic Books.

Piaget, J., & Inhelder, B. (1969). *The Psychology of the Child*. London: Routledge and Kegan Paul.

Piaget, J., Lambercier, M., Boesch, E., & Albertini, B. (1942). Introduction to a study of perception in children, with an analysis of an illusion of visual perception of concentric circles, Delboeuf. *Archives de Psychologie*, 29(113): 111.

Pick, D. (2006). Memories of Melanie Klein. Part 1: Interviews with Hanna Segal. Accessed at: www.melanie-klein-trust.org.uk/segalinterview 2001.htm.

Pinquart, M., & Silbereisen, R. K. (2004). Transmission of values from adolescents to their parents: the role of value content and authoritative parenting. *Adolescence*, 39: 83–101.

Porder, M. S. (1987). Projective identification: an alternative hypothesis. *Psychoanalytic Quarterly*, 56: 431–451.

Quartz, S. R., & Sejnowski, T. J. (1997). The neural basis of cognitive development: a constructivist manifesto. *Behavioral and Brain Sciences*, 20: 537–556.

Quinodoz, J.-M. (2005). *Reading Freud: A Chronological Exploration of Freud's Writing*, D. Alcorn (Trans.). London: Routledge.

Rader, N. d. V. (1997). Change and variation in responses to perceptual information. In: *Evolving Explanations of Development: Ecological Approaches to Organism-Environment Systems* (pp. 129–157): Washington, DC: American Psychological Association.

Rahikainen, M. (2004). *Centuries of Child Labour: European Experiences from the Seventeenth to the Twentieth Century*. Farnham: Ashgate.

Rangell, L. (2006). An analysis of the course of psychoanalysis: the case for a unitary theory. *Psychoanalytic Psychology*, 23(2): 217–238.

Ravitz, P., Maunder, R., Hunter, J., Sthankiya, B., & Lancee, W. (2010). Adult attachment measures: a 25-year review. *Journal of Psychosomatic Research*, 69(4): 419–432.

Rayner, E. (1991). *The Independent Mind in British Psychoanalysis*. Northvale, NJ: Jason Aronson.

Reddy, V. (1993). Communication in infancy: mutual regulation of affect and attention. In: G. Bremmer, A. Slater, & G. Butterworth (Eds.), *Infant Development: Recent Advances* (pp. 247–268). Hove: Psychology Press.

Reddy, V., Williams, E., Costantini, C., & Lang, B. (2010). Engaging with the self: mirror behaviour in autism, Down syndrome and typical development. *Autism, 14*(5): 531–546.

Repacholi, B. M., Meltzoff, A. N., & Olsen, B. (2008). Infants' understanding of the link between visual perception and emotion: "If she can't see me doing it, she won't get angry". *Developmental Psychology, 44*(2): 561–574.

Richter, L. M. (2006). Studying adolescence. *Science, 312*(5782): 1902–1905.

Riddell, R. P., Campbell, L., Flora, D. B., Racine, N., Osmun, L. D., Garfield, H., & Greenberg, S. (2011). The relationship between caregiver sensitivity and infant pain behaviors across the first year of life. *Pain, 152*(12): 2819–2826.

Rieffe, C., Ketelaar, L., & Wiefferink, C. H. (2010). Assessing empathy in young children: construction and validation of an Empathy Questionnaire (EmQue). *Personality and Individual Differences, 49*(5): 362–367.

Rigato, S., Menon, E., Johnson, M. H., Faraguna, D., & Farroni, T. (2011). Direct gaze may modulate face recognition in newborns. *Infant and Child Development, 20*(1): 20–34.

Riviere, J. (1936). On the genesis of psychical conflict in earliest infancy. *International Journal of Psychoanalysis, 17*: 395–422.

Riviere, J. (1952). *General Introduction to Developments in Psycho-Analysis*. London: Hogarth Press.

Rizzolatti, G., & Craighero, L. (2004). The mirror-neuron system. *Annual Review of Neuroscience, 27*: 169–192.

Robertson, J. (1952). *A Two-Year-Old Goes to Hospital*. Scientific film. www.robertsonfilms.info/2_year_old.htm.

Robertson, L. (2010). Review of metacognition in young children. *Educational Psychology in Practice, 26*(4): 424–425.

Robson, S. (2010). Self-regulation and metacognition in young children's self-initiated play and reflective dialogue. *International Journal of Early Years Education, 18*(3): 227–241.

Rochat, P., Querido, J. G., & Striano, T. (1999). Emerging sensitivity to the timing and structure of protoconversation in early infancy. *Developmental Psychology, 35*(4): 950–957.

Rodriguez, M. L., Ayduk, O., Aber, J. L., Mischel, W., Sethi, A., & Shoda, Y. (2005). A contextual approach to the development of self-regulatory competencies: the role of maternal unresponsivity and toddlers' negative affect in stressful situations. *Social Development, 14*(1): 136–157.

Rohde-Dachser, C. (1992). Do we need a feminist psychoanalysis? *Psychoanalytic Contemporary Thought, 15*(2): 241–259.

Rosegrant, J. (2010). Three psychoanalytic realities. *Psychoanalytic Psychology, 27*(4): 492–512.

Rosen, H., & Zickler, E. (1996). Feminist psychoanalytic theory: American and French reactions to Freud. *Journal of the American Psychoanalytic Association, 44*(Suppl): 71–92.

Ross, J. M. (2007). Trauma and abuse in the case of Little Hans: a contemporary perspective. *Journal of the American Psychoanalytic Association, 55*(3): 779–797.

Roussillon, R. (2010). The deconstruction of primary narcissism. *International Journal of Psychoanalysis, 91*: 821–837.

Rovee-Collier, C. (1997). Dissociations in infant memory: rethinking the development of implicit and explicit memory. *Psychological Review, 104*: 467–498.

Rovee-Collier, C., & Cuevas, K. (2009a). Multiple memory systems are unnecessary to account for infant memory development: an ecological model. *Developmental Psychology, 45*(1): 160–174.

Rovee-Collier, C., & Cuevas, K. (2009b). The development of infant memory. In: M. L. Courage (Ed.), *The Development of Memory in Infancy and Childhood* (2nd edn, pp. 11–41). New York: Psychology Press.

Rovee-Collier, C., & Hayne, H. (1987). Reactivation of infant memory: implications for cognitive development. In: H. W. Reese (Ed.), *Advances in Child Development and Behaviour* (Vol. 20, pp. 85–255). New York: Academic Press.

Rubinstein, B. B. (1997). Person, organism, and self: their worlds and their psychoanalytically relevant relationships. *Psychological Issues, 62–63*: 415–445.

Ruppenthal, G. C., Arling, G. L., Harlow, H. F., Sackett, G. P., & Suomi, S. J. (1976). A 10-year perspective of motherless–mother monkey behavior. *Journal of Abnormal Psychology, 85*(4): 341–349.

Russ, S. W. (2006). Pretend play, affect, and creativity. In: P. Locher (Ed.), *New Directions in Aesthetics, Creativity and the Arts* (pp. 239–250). Amityville, NY: Baywood.

Rustin, J., & Sekaer, C. (2004). From the neuroscience of memory to psychoanalytic interaction: clinical implications. *Psychoanalytic Psychology, 21*(1): 70–82.

Sander, L. W. (1962). Issues in early mother–child interaction. *Journal of the American Academy of Child Psychiatry, 1*: 141–166.

Sander, L. W. (1988). The event-structure of regulation in the neonate-care-giver system as a biological background for early organization of psychic structure. *Progress in Self Psychology, 3*: 64–77.

Sandler, J. (1967). Trauma, strain and development. In: S. S. Furst (Ed.), *Psychic Trauma* (pp. 154–174). New York: Basic Books.

Sandler, J., & Freud, A. (1983). Discussions in the Hampstead Index on 'The ego and the mechanisms of defence': X. Identification with the aggressor. *Bulletin of the Anna Freud Centre, 6*(3): 247–275.

Sayers, J. (1989). Melanie Klein and mothering—a feminist perspective. *International Review of Psycho-Analysis, 16*: 363–376.

Scarr, S. (1992). Developmental theories for the 1990s: developmental and individual differences. *Child Development, 63*: 1–19.

Scarr, S. (1995). Psychology will be truly evolutionary when behavior genetics is included. *Psychological Inquiry, 6*(1): 68–71.

Scarr, S. (1996). How people make their own environments: implications for parents and policy makers. *Psychology, Public Policy, and Law, 2*(2): 204–228.

Scarr, S. (1997). Why child care has little impact on most children's development. *Current Directions in Psychological Science, 6*(5): 143–148.

Scarr, S. (1998). How do families affect intelligence? Social environmental and behavior genetic predictions. In: J. J. McArdle (Ed.), *Human Cognitive Abilities in Theory and Practice* (pp. 113–136). Mahwah, NJ: Lawrence Erlbaum.

Scarr, S., & Weinberg, R. A. (1990). The nature–nurture problem revisited: the Minnesota adoption studies. In: I. E. Sigel (Ed.), *Methods of Family Research: Biographies of Research Projects—Normal Families* (Vol. 1, pp. 121–151). Hillsdale, NJ: Lawrence Erlbaum.

Scher, A. (2002). Mother–infant relationship as a modulator of night waking. In: P. Salzarulo (Ed.), *Awakening and Sleep–wake Cycle across Development* (pp. 187–198). Amsterdam: John Benjamins.

Schleidt, M. (Ed.). (1991). *An Ethological Perspective on Infant Development.* Hillsdale, NJ: Lawrence Erlbaum.

Schore, A. N. (1994). *Affect Regulation and the Origins of the Self: The Neurobiology of Emotional Development.* Hillsdale, NJ: Lawrence Erlbaum.

Schore, A. N. (2003). *Affect Regulation and the Repair of the Self.* New York: Norton.

Schore, A. N. (2009). Relational trauma and the developing right brain: an interface of psychoanalytic self psychology and neuroscience. *Annals of the New York Academy of Sciences, 1159*: 189–203.

Schumann, C. M., & Nordahl, C. W. (2011). Bridging the gap between MRI and postmortem research in autism. *Brain Research, 1380*: 175–186.

Schwartz, P. D., Maynard, A. M., & Uzelac, S. M. (2008). Adolescent egocentrism: a contemporary view. *Adolescence, 43*(171): 441–448.

Segal, H. (1964). *Introduction to the Work of Melanie Klein*. London: Heinemann Medical Books.

Segal, H. (1979). *Melanie Klein*. New York: Viking Press.

Seginer, R., & Shoyer, S. (2012). Israel. In: J. J. Arnett (Ed.), *Adolescent Psychology Around the World* (pp. 29–45). New York: Psychology Press.

Seligman, S. (2008). Review of forms of intersubjectivity in infant research and adult treatment. *International Journal of Psychoanalysis, 89*(4): 885–889.

Seligman, S. (2009). Anchoring intersubjective models in recent advances in developmental psychology, cognitive neuroscience and parenting studies: introduction to papers by Trevarthen, Gallese, and Ammaniti & Trentini. *Psychoanalytic Dialogues, 19*(5): 503–506.

Seso-Simic, D., Sedmak, G., Hof, P., & Simic, G. (2010). Recent advances in the neurobiology of attachment behavior. *Translational Neuroscience, 1*(2): 148–159.

Shapiro, L. (2011). *Embodied Cognition*. New York: Routledge/Taylor & Francis.

Shedler, J., Mayman, M., & Manis, M. (1993). The illusion of mental health. *American Psychologist, 48*: 1117–1131.

Shevrin, H. (1996). *Conscious and Unconscious Processes: Psychodynamic, Cognitive, and Neurophysiological Convergences*. New York: Guilford Press.

Shevrin, H., & Dickman, S. (1980). The psychological unconscious: a necessary assumption for all psychological theory? *American Psychologist, 35*(5): 421–434.

Shields, P. J., & Rovee-Collier, C. K. (1992). Long-term memory for context-specific category information at 6 months. *Child Development, 63*: 175–214.

Siegler, R. S. (1994). Cognitive variability: a key to understanding cognitive development. *Current Directions, 3*(1): 1–5.

Siegler, R. S. (1996). *Emerging Minds: The Process of Change in Children's Thinking*. Oxford: Oxford University Press.

Siegler, R. S. (2005). Children's learning. *American Psychologist, 60*(8): 769–778.

Silk, K. R. (2005). Object relations and the nature of therapeutic interventions. *Journal of Psychotherapy Integration, 15*(1): 94–100.

Simcock, G., & Hayne, H. (2002). Breaking the barrier? Children fail to translate their preverbal memories into language. *Psychological Science, 13*(3): 225–231.

Simons, L. G., & Conger, R. D. (2007). Linking mother–father differences in parenting to a typology of family parenting styles and adolescent outcomes. *Journal of Family Issues, 28*(2): 212–241.

Skelton, R. M. (2006). *The Edinburgh International Encyclopedia of Psychoanalysis*. Edinburgh: Edinburgh University Press.

Skinner, B. F. (1938). *The Behavior of Organisms: An Experimental Analysis*. Oxford: Appleton-Century.

Skinner, B. F. (1953). *The Science of Human Behaviour*. New York: Free Press.

Skinner, J. (1957). James M. Barrie or the boy who wouldn't grow up. *American Imago, 14*(2): 111–141.

Slochower, J. (1996). *Holding and Psychoanalysis*. Hillsdale, NJ: Analytic Press.

Sobel, D. M., & Kirkham, N. Z. (2006). Blickets and babies: the development of causal reasoning in toddlers and infants. *Developmental Psychology, 42*(6): 1103–1115.

Sodian, B. (2011). Theory of mind in infancy. *Child Development Perspectives, 5*(1): 39–43.

Sokol, B., Müller, U., Carpendale, J., Young, A., & Iarocci, G. (Eds.). (2010). *Self and Social Regulation: Social Interaction and the Development of Social Understanding and Executive Functions*. Oxford: Oxford University Press.

Sommerville, J. A., & Woodward, A. L. (2005). Pulling out the intentional structure of action: the relation between action processing and action production in infancy. *Cognition and Emotion, 95*: 1–30.

Sorce, J. F., Emde, R. N., Campos, J., & Klinnert, M. D. (2000). Maternal emotional signaling: its effect on the visual cliff behavior of 1-year-olds. In: D. Muir & A. Slater (Eds.), *Infant Development: The Essential Readings* (pp. 282–292). New York: Wiley-Blackwell.

Spangler, G., & Grossmann, K. E. (1993). Biobehavioural organization in securely and insecurely attached infants. *Child Development, 64*: 1439–1450.

Spence, D. (1986). Narrative smoothing and clinical wisdom. In: T. R. Sarbin (Ed.), *Narrative Psychology: The Storied Nature of Human Conduct* (pp. 211–232). New York: Praeger.

Spezzano, C. (1993). *Affect in Psychoanalysis: A Clinical Synthesis*. Hillsdale, NJ: Analytic Press.

Spitz, R. A. (1945). Hospitalism: an inquiry into the genesis of psychiatric conditions in early childhood. *Psychoanalytic Study of the Child, 1*: 53–74).

Spitz, R. A. (1947). *Grief: A Peril in Infancy* (Script). New York: New York University Film Library.

Spitz, R. A. (1950a). Anxiety in infancy: a study of its manifestations in the first year of life. *International Journal of Psychoanalysis, 31*: 138–143.

Spitz, R. A. (1950b). Relevancy of direct infant observation. *Psychoanalytic Study of the Child, 5*: 66–73.

Spitz, R. A. (1951). The psychogenic diseases in infancy—an attempt at their etiologic classification. *Psychoanalytic Study of the Child, 6*: 255–275.

Spitz, R. A. (1965). *The First Year of Life: A Psychoanalytic Study of Normal and Deviant Development of Object Relations*. New York: International Universities Press.

Spivey, M. J., Tyler, M. J., Eberhard, K. M., & Tanenhaus, M. K. (2001). Linguistically mediated visual search. *Psychological Science, 12*(4): 282–286.

Squire, L. R., & Zola-Morgan, S. (1991). The medial temporal lobe memory system. *Science, 253*(5026): 1380–1386.

Sroufe, L. A., & Waters, E. (1977). Attachment as an organizational construct. *Child Development, 48*: 1184–1199.

Steinberg, L. D., Darling, N. E., & Fletcher, A. C. (1995). Authoritative parenting and adolescent development: an ecological journey. In: P. Moen, G. H. Elder, & K. Luscher (Eds.), *Examining Lives in Context* (pp. 423–466). Washington, DC: American Psychological Association.

Steinberg, M. (2011). The perversion of attunement: fundamentals gone awry in the service of an ideal. *International Journal of Psychoanalytic Self Psychology, 6*(3): 437–439.

Stern, D. N. (1985). *The Interpersonal World of the Infant: A View from Psychoanalysis and Developmental Psychology*. New York: Basic Books.

Stern, D. N. (1994). One way to build a clinically relevant baby. *Infant Mental Health Journal, 15*(1): 9–25.

Stern, D. N. (1995). *The Motherhood Constellation: A Unified View of Parent–Infant Psychotherapy*. New York: Basic Books.

Stern, D. N. (2010). Some implications of infant observations for psychoanalysis. In: A. M. Cooper (Ed.), *Contemporary Psychoanalysis in America* (pp. 641–666). Washington, DC: American Psychiatric Publishing.

Stern, J. (1998). Template or transference: some thoughts about Mark Gehrie's "Empathy in Broader Perspective". *Progress in Self Psychology, 14*: 63–70.

Stern, S. (1992). The opposing currents technique—for eating disorders and other false self problems. *Contemporary Psychoanalysis, 28*: 594–615.

Stern, W., & Barwell, A. (1924). The development of powers. In: *Psychology of Early Childhood: Up to the Sixth Year of Age* (3rd edn revised and enlarged, pp. 80–100): New York: Henry Holt.

Stolorow, R. D. (1992a). Subjectivity and self psychology: a personal odyssey. *Progress in Self Psychology, 8*: 241–250.

Stolorow, R. D. (1992b). Closing the gap between theory and practice with better psychoanalytic theory. *Psychotherapy: Theory, Research, Practice, Training, 29*(2): 159–166.

Stolorow, R. D. (2005). The contextuality of emotional experience. *Psychoanalytic Psychology, 22*(1): 101–106.

Stolorow, R. D. (2006). Heidegger's investigative method in *Being and Time. Psychoanalytic Psychology, 23*(3): 594–602.

Stolorow, R. D., & Atwood, G. E. (1978). A defensive–restitutive function of Freud's theory of psychosexual development. *Psychoanalytic Review, 65*(2): 217–238.

Stolorow, R. D., Brandchaft, B., & Atwood, G. (1987). *Psychoanalytic Treatment: An Intersubjective Approach.* Hillsdale, NJ: Analytic Press.

Strachey, J. (Ed.). (1966). *The Complete Letters of Sigmund Freud to Wilhelm Fleiss 1887–1904* (Vol. 1). London: Hogarth.

Strathearn, L. (2007). Exporing the neurobiology of attachment. In: L. Mayes, P. Fonagy, & M. Target (Eds.), *Developmental Science and Psychoanalysis: Integration and Innovation* (pp. 117–130). London: Karnac.

Street, E. R. (2007). Review of attachment from infancy to adulthood—the major longitudinal studies. *Journal of Family Therapy, 29*(1): 96–106.

Sugarman, A. (1992). A structural perspective on analytic activity. *Psychoanalytic Psychology, 9*(4): 433–446.

Sullivan, H. S. (1953). *The Interpersonal Theory of Psychiatry.* New York: Norton.

Sullivan, H. S. (1964). *The Fusion of Psychiatry and Social Science.* New York: Norton.

Swain, J. E., Lorberbaum, J. P., Kose, S., & Strathearn, L. (2007). Brain basis of early parent–infant interactions: psychology, physiology, and in vivo functional neuroimaging studies. *Journal of Child Psychology and Psychiatry, 48*(3–4): 262–287.

Sweatt, J. D. (2003). *Mechanisms of Memory.* San Diego, CA: Elsevier.

Taerk, G. (2002). Shattering the template: the effect of moments of meeting on enduring systems of pathological accommodation. *Progress in Self Psychology, 18*: 33–45.

Tagliacozzo, R. (1989). The rejected infant: false self, maintenance and breakdown: anxiety of the true self. Reflections on depersonalisation. *Rivista Psicoanalisis, 35*(4): 842–864.

Talberg, G., Cuoto, J. A., De Lourdes, M., & O'Donnell, S. (1988). Early affect development: empirical research. *International Journal of Psychoanalysis, 69*: 239–259.

Talvitie, V., & Ihanus, J. (2002). The repressed and implicit knowledge. *International Journal of Psychoanalysis, 83*(6): 1311–1323.

Tanenhaus, M. K., Spivey-Knowlton, M. J., Eberhard, K. M., & Sedivy, J. C. (1995). Integration of visual and linguistic information in spoken language comprehension. *Science, 268*: 1632–1634.

Tarullo, A. R., Mliner, S., & Gunnar, M. R. (2011). Inhibition and exuberance in preschool classrooms: associations with peer social experiences and changes in cortisol across the preschool year. *Developmental Psychology, 47*(5): 1374–1388.

Taylor, J. A. (1956). Drive theory and manifest anxiety. *Psychological Bulletin, 53*(4): 303–320.

Thomson, R., Bell, R., Holland, J., Henderson, S., McGrellis, S., & Sharpe, S. (2002). Critical moments: choice, chance and opportunity in young people's narratives of transition. *Sociology, 36*(2): 335–354.

Tinbergern, N. (1951). *The Study of Instinct*. Oxford: Oxford University Press.

Tisserand, D. J., van Boxtel, M. P. J., Pruessner, J. C., Hofman, P., Evans, A. C., & Jolles, J. (2004). A Voxel-based morphometric study to determine individual differences in gray matter density associated with age and cognitive change over time. *Cerebral Cortex, 14*(9): 966–973.

Tomkins, S. S. (1978). Script theory: differential magnification of affects. In: H. E. Howe & R. A. Dunstbier (Eds.), *Nebraska Symposium on Motivation* (pp. 201–236). Lincoln, NE: University of Nebraska Press.

Tomkins, S. S. (1991). *Affect, Imagery, Consciousness: The Negative Affects: Fear and Anger* (Vol. 3). New York: Springer.

Tops, M., & Boksem, M. A. (2011). Cortisol involvement in mechanisms of behavioral inhibition. *Psychophysiology, 48*(5): 723–732.

Tramo, M. J., Lense, M., Van Ness, C., Kagan, J., Doyle Settle, M., & Cronin, J. H. (2011). Effects of music on physiological and behavioral indices of acute pain and stress in premature infants: clinical trial and literature review. *Music and Medicine, 3*(2): 72–83.

Trauble, B., Marinovic, V., & Pauen, S. (2010). Early theory of mind competencies: do infants understand others' beliefs? *Infancy, 15*(4): 434–444.

Tronick, E. Z. (1989). Emotions and emotional communication in infants. *American Psychologist, 44*(2): 112–119.

Tronick, E. Z. (2002). A model of infant mood states and Sandarian affective waves. *Psychoanalytic Dialogues, 12*(1): 73–99.

Tronick, E. Z., & Beeghly, M. (2011). Infants' meaning-making and the development of mental health problems. *American Psychologist, 66*(2): 107.

Tuber, S. (2008). *Attachment, Play, and Authenticity: A Winnicott Primer*. Lanham, MD: Jason Aronson.

Tuckett, D., & Levinson, N. A. (2010). Development. *PEP Consolidated Psychoanalytic Glossary*.

Tulving, E. (1972). Episodic and semantic memory. In: E. Tulving & W. Donaldson (Eds.), *Organization of Memory* (pp. 381–403). New York: Academic Press.

Tulving, E. (1983). *Elements of Episodic Memory*. New York: Oxford University Press.

Tulving, E. (1985). How many memory systems are there? *American Psychologist, 40*: 385–398.

Tyson, P., & Tyson, R. L. (1999). *Development*. New Haven, CT: Yale University Press.

Van der Horst, F. C. (2011). *John Bowlby – From Psychoanalysis to Ethology. Unravelling the Roots of Attachment Theory*. Chichester: Wiley-Blackwell.

Van Haute, P., & Geyskens, T. (2007). *From Death Instinct to Attachment Theory: The Primacy of the Child in Freud, Klein, and Hermann*. New York: Other Press.

Van IJzendoorn, M. H., & Sagi, A. (1999). Cross-cultural patterns of attachment: universal and cultural dimensions. In: J. Cassidy & P. R. Shaver (Eds.), *Handbook of Attachment: Theory, Research, and Clinical Applications* (pp. 713–734). New York: Guilford Press.

Varga, S. (2011). Winnicott, symbolic play, and other minds. *Philosophical Psychology, 24*(5): 625–637.

Vasey, M. W., & Dadds, M. R. (Eds.). (2001). *The Developmental Psychopathology of Anxiety*. New York: Oxford University Press.

Vicedo, M. (2010). The evolution of Harry Harlow: from the nature to the nurture of love. *History of Psychiatry, 21*(2): 190–205.

Vivona, J. M. (2009). Leaping from brain to mind: a critique of mirror neuron explanations of countertransference. *Journal of the American Psychoanalytic Association, 57*(3): 525–550.

Von Hug-Hellmuth, H. (1920). Child psychology and education. *International Journal of Psychoanalysis, 1*: 316–318.

Von Hug-Hellmuth, H. (1921). On the technique of child-analysis. *International Journal of Psychoanalysis, 2*: 287–305.

Von Lupke, H. (2003). Obituary for W. Ernest Freud. Remaining in touch. *Zur Bedeutung der Kontinuität früher Beziehungserfahrungen*. In: *Zusammenarbeit mit dem Autor herausgegeben von Hans von Lüpke*. Frankfurt: Edition Déjà vu.

Vygotsky, L. (1997). *The Collected Works of L. S. Vygotsky* (Volume 4): *The History of the Development of Higher Mental Functions*, R. W. Rieber (Ed.), M. J. Hall (Trans.). New York: Plenum Press.

Vygotsky, L., Hanfmann, E., & Vakar, G. (1962). *Thought and Language*, E. Hanfmann & G. Vakar (Eds. & Trans.). Cambridge, MA: MIT Press.

Wakefield, J. C. (2007). Attachment and sibling rivalry in Little Hans: the fantasy of the two giraffes revisited. *Journal of the American Psychoanalytic Association, 55*(3): 821–849.

Wallin, D. J. (2007). *Attachment in Psychotherapy*. New York: Guilford Press.

Walum, H., Westberg, L., Henningsson, S., Neiderhiser, J. M., Reiss, D., Igl, W., Ganiban, J. M., Spotts, E. L., Pedersen, N. L., Eriksson, E., & Lichtenstein, P. (2008). Genetic variation in the vasopressin receptor 1a gene (AVPR1A) associates with pair-bonding behavior in humans. *PNAS Proceedings of the National Academy of Sciences of the United States of America, 105*(37): 14153–14156.

Watson, J. B. (1928). *The Ways of Behaviorism*. New York: Harper & Brothers.

Weaver, I. C. G., Cervoni, N., Champagne, F. A., D'Alessio, A. C., Sharma, S., Seckl, J. R., Dymov, S., Szyf, M., & Meaney, M. J. (2004). Epigenetic programming by maternal behavior. *Nature Neuroscience, 7*(8): 847–854.

Weinberg, E. (2006). Mentalization, affect regulation, and development of the self. *Journal of the American Psychoanalytic Association, 54*(1): 251–269.

Westen, D. (1998). Unconscious thought, feeling, and motivation: the end of a century-long debate. In: R. F. Bornstein (Ed.), *Empirical Perspectives on the Psychoanalytic Unconscious* (pp. 1–43). Washington, DC: American Psychological Association.

Westen, D. (1999). The scientific status of unconscious processes: is Freud really dead? *Journal of the American Psychoanalytic Association, 47*(4): 1061–1106.

Westermeyer, J. F. (2004). Predictors and characteristics of Erikson's life cycle model among men: a 32-year longitudinal study. *International Journal of Aging and Human Development, 58*(1): 29–48.

White, R. S. (2011). The nonverbal unconscious: collision and collusion of metaphor. *Psychoanalytic Inquiry, 31*(2): 147–158.

Whitehead, C. C. (2009). Mirror neurons, the self, and culture: an essay in neo-psychoanalysis. *Journal of the American Academy of Psychoanalysis & Dynamic Psychiatry, 37*(4): 701–711.

Whorf, B. L. (1956). *Language, Thought, and Reality: Selected Writings*. Oxford: Technology Press of MIT.

Wichert, A. (2011). The role of attention in the context of associative memory. *Cognitive Computation, 3*(1): 311–320.

Wicker, B., Keysers, C., Plailly, J., Royet, J.-P., Gallese, V., & Rizzolatti, G. (2003). Both of us disgusted in my insula: the common neural basis of seeing and feeling disgust. *Neuron 40*: 655–664.

Widlocher, D. (2001). *Primary Love and Infantile Sexuality: An Eternal Debate.* New York: Other Press.

Wilson, A. (1997). Psychoanalysis and infant research. *PsycCRITIQUES, 42*(4): 312–313. Accessed at: doi:Electronic Collection: 2004–17491–015.

Wilson, A., Fel, D., & Greenstein, M. (1992). The self-regulating child: converging evidence from psychoanalysis, infant research, and socio-linguistics. *Applied & Preventive Psychology, 1*(3): 165–175.

Wilson, T. D., Lindsey, S., & Schooler, T. Y. (2000). A model of dual attitudes. *Psychological Review, 107*: 101–126.

Winnicott, C. (1977). Winnicott en personne. *Revue l'Arc, 69*: 28–38.

Winnicott, D. W. (1941). The observation of infants in a set situation. *International Journal of Psychoanalysis, 22*: 229–249.

Winnicott, D. W. (1945). Primitive emotional development. *International Journal of Psychoanalysis, 26*: 137–143.

Winnicott, D. W. (1953). Transitional objects and transitional phenomenon—a study of the first not-me possession. *International Journal of Psychoanalysis, 34*: 89–97.

Winnicott, D. W. (1955). Metapsychological and clinical aspects of regression within the psycho-analytical set-up. *International Journal of Psychoanalysis, 36*: 16–26.

Winnicott, D. W. (1956). On transference. *International Journal of Psychoanalysis, 37*: 386–388.

Winnicott, D. W. (1958). The capacity to be alone. *International Journal of Psychoanalysis, 39*: 416–420.

Winnicott, D. W. (1960). The theory of the parent–infant relationship. *International Journal of Psychoanalysis, 41*: 585–595.

Winnicott, D.W. (1965a). *The Maturational Processes and the Facilitating Environment: Studies in the Theory of Emotional Development.* New York: International Universities Press.

Winnicott, D. W. (1965b). A clinical study of the effect of a failure of the average expectable environment on a child's mental functioning. *International Journal of Psychoanalysis, 46*: 81–87.

Winnicott, D. W. (1966). Becoming deprived as a fact: a psychotherapeutic consultation. *Journal of Child Psychotherapy, 1*: 5–12.

Winnicott, D. W. (1967). The location of cultural experience. *International Journal of Psychoanalysis, 48*: 368–372.

Winnicott, D. W. (1968). Playing: its theoretical status in the clinical situation. *International Journal of Psychoanalysis, 49*: 591–599.

Winnicott, D. W. (1969a). The use of an object. *International Journal of Psychoanalysis, 50*: 711–716.

Winnicott, D. W. (1969b). Foreword. In: Milner, M. *The Hands of the Living God: An Account of a Psycho-Analytic Treatment*. The International Psycho-Analytical Library, 76. London: Hogarth Press and the Institute of Psycho-Analysis.

Winnicott, D. W. (1971). *Playing and Reality*. London: Tavistock.

Winnicott, D. (1972). Basis for self in body. *International Journal of Child Psychotherapy, 1*(1): 7–16.

Winnicott, D. W. (1974). Fear of breakdown. In: D. Goldman (Ed.), *In One's Bones: The Genius of Winnicott* (pp. 39–47). Northvale, NJ: Jason Aronson.

Winnicott, D. W. (1986a). *The Theory of the Parent–Infant Relationship*. New York: New York University Press.

Winnicott, D. W. (1986b). *Holding and Interpretation*. International Psycho-Analytic Library, 115. London: Hogarth Press and the Institute of Psycho-Analysis.

Winnicott, D. W. (1989). The psychology of madness: a contribution from psychoanalysis. In: *Psychoanalytic Explorations* (pp. 119–129). Cambridge, MA: Harvard University Press.

Winnicott, D. W., & Khan, M. R. (1953). *Psychoanalytic Studies of the Personality: W. Ronald D. Fairbairn*. London: Tavistock.

Wise, R. A. (2004). Dopamine, learning and motivation. *Nature Reviews Neuroscience, 5*(6): 483–494.

Witter, S. (2004). Developing a framework for monitoring child poverty: results from a study in Uganda. *Children and Society, 18*(1): 3–15.

Wolfe, C. D., & Bell, M. A. (2007). The integration of cognition and emotion during infancy and early childhood: regulatory processes associated with the development of working memory. *Brain and Cognition, 65*(1): 3–13.

Wolff, P. H. (1966). The causes, controls, and organization of behavior in the neonate. *Psychological Issues, 5*: 17.

Wolff, P. H. (1969). The natural history of crying and other vocalizations in infancy. In: B. M. Foss (Ed.), *Determinants of Infant Behavior* (Vol. 4). London: Methuen.

Wolff, P. H. (1996). The irrelevance of infant observations for psychoanalysis. *Journal of the American Psychoanalytic Association, 44*(2): 369–392.

Wolpe, J., & Rachman, S. (1960). Psychoanalytic evidence: a critique based on Freud's case of Little Hans. *Journal of Nervous & Mental Disease, 131*: 135–148. Oxford: Pergamon.

Wu, P.-L., & Chiou, W.-B. (2008). Postformal thinking and creativity among late adolescents: a post-Piagetian approach. *Adolescence, 43*(170): 237–251.

Yerushalmi, H. (2001). Self-states and personal growth in analysis. *Contemporary Psychoanalysis, 37*(3): 471–488.

Yorke, C. (1971). Some suggestions for a critique of Kleinian psychology. *Psychoanalytic Study of the Child, 26*: 129–155.

Young, G. (2011). *Development and Causality: Neo-Piagetian Perspectives.* New York: Springer.

Young-Bruehl, E. (2004). Anna Freud and Dorothy Burlingham at Hampstead: the origins of psychoanalytic parent–infant observation. *The Annual of Psychoanalysis, 32*: 185–197.

Zeanah, C. H. (1996). Beyond insecurity: a reconceptualisation of attachment disorders of infancy. *Journal of Consulting and Clinical Psychology, 64* (1): 42–52.

Zeanah, C. H., & Fox, N. A. (2004). Temperament and attachment disorders. *Journal of Clinical Child & Adolescent Psychology, 33*(1): 32–41.

Zeanah, C. H., Anders, T. F., Seifer, R., & Stern, D. N. (1989). Implications of research on infant development for psychodynamic theory and practice. *Journal of the American Academy of Child & Adolescent Psychiatry, 28*(5): 657–668.

Zeddies, T. J. (2002). More than just words: a hermeneutic view of language in psychoanalysis. *Psychoanalytic Psychology, 19*(1): 3–23.

Zelazo, P. R., & Weiss, M. J. (2006). Infant swimming behaviors: cognitive control and the influence of experience. *Journal of Cognition and Development, 7*(1): 1–25.

Zelnick, L., & Buchholz, E. S. (1990). The concept of mental representations in light of recent infant research. *Psychoanalytic Psychology, 7*(1): 29–58.

INDEX